The Macmillan Handbook of English

Canadian Edition

The Macmillan Handbook of English

Canadian Edition

Robert F. Willson, Jr.
University of Missouri – Kansas City

John M. Kierzek
Late of Oregon State University

W. Walker Gibson
University of Massachusetts

Consulting Editors – Canadian Edition

John Orange
King's College, University of Western Ontario

David Silver
Seneca College

Collier Macmillan Canada, Inc.

Collier Macmillan Canada, Inc.
50 Gervais Drive
Don Mills, Ontario M3C 3K4

Canadian Cataloguing in Publication Data
Willson, Robert F. (Robert Frank), 1939–
    The Macmillan handbook of English

Includes indexes.
ISBN 0-02-997890-4

1. English language – Rhetoric. 2. English language –
Grammar – 1950–   I. Kierzek, John M., 1891–
II. Gibson, W. Walker.   III. Orange, John Charles.
IV. Silver, David.   V. Title.

PE1408.W54 1984   808'.042   C84-098054-X

Editor: Patrick Gallagher

Design: Michael van Elsen Design Inc.

Printed in Canada by John Deyell Company

1 2 3 4 5 6 7 8   88 87 86 85 84

PREFACE

The new Canadian edition of *The Macmillan Handbook of English* continues the tradition of its predecessors. It combines a discussion of the art of writing with a presentation of the mechanics of writing, to provide a practical and common-sense guide to effective and precise writing. In part one, "The Art of Writing," students progress from a study of words and phrases to sentences and paragraphs, and, finally, to the writing of the whole essay. In part two, "Writing and Revision," students are supplied with guides and principles for the preparation, presentation, and revision of their own writing. Each part supplements the other, however, and information and suggestions found in one can be approached and re-evaluated with fresh perspectives drawn from the other.

For this edition, difficult passages, such as the explanation of complex sentences, have been rewritten in order to make them clearer, and sections on usage practice have been revised to reflect recent changes. For example, the important (and still unresolved) question of gender and pronoun choice has been addressed anew.

One of the notable aspects of the book is its numerous examples. Discussions of important components of writing–intention, tone, parallel structure, euphony, beginnings and endings, imagery, point of view, and so on–are accompanied by illustrative selections chosen from over seventy-five different Canadian authors, including such writers as Margaret Laurence, Northrop Frye, Alice Munro, Robertson Davies, and Mordecai Richler. Two complete essays – one by Northrop Frye and one by Roderick Haig-Brown – are reprinted in their entirety and analysed and discussed so that students can see how professional writers of great skill are able to express their ideas. There are, as well, examples of student writing.

Good writing skills are needed not just by English students but by students of almost all subjects. *The Macmillan Handbook of English: Canadian Edition* is intended to be a useful reference manual for any student who needs, or wants, to write well.

CONTENTS

THE ART OF WRITING

Chapter 1
The Task of Writing

Chapter 2
Words and Phrases

Chapter 3
The Sentence

Chapter 4
The Paragraph

Chapter 5
Problems of Subject and Focus

Chapter 6
Problems of Composing

Chapter 7
Writing Essays About
Literature and Film

WRITING AND REVISION

Chapter 9
Grammar and Usage

Chapter 10
Mechanics

THE ART OF WRITING

1

THE TASK OF WRITING

Introduction

For most of us the direction to write about anything instills panic and incurable writer's cramp. Perhaps our fears are traceable to the belief that being creative through expressing ourselves on paper is beyond us and means putting our personalities on the line for others to criticize. But a moment's thought will persuade us that this fear is groundless; we are constantly creative whether we realize it or not. Earl Birney, a poet and writer, explains:

> "Creativity" is one of those words, or concepts, which seems plain enough, even simple, till you start fixing your eye on it. Then, like "innocence" or "internationalism" or "love," it begins to swell up like a cloud into something that fills the whole sky of meaning, and darkens it, and comes to signify everything or nothing. For it's almost impossible to think of a human being who isn't functioning creatively at all times, in order to stay alive. Even when we flake out into sleep, we're busy spinning fantasies, each unique and different, inventing situations for ourselves and solving them in totally original ways – in order that, when we wake, we can cope with conscious life. And con-

scious living is the process of apprehending the changing world of our senses at every moment, and reacting by instinct and by thinking to whatever the immediate situation is, in order to eat or plan or make love or walk to the corner store. It requires us constantly to invent, to fashion always new patterns of gestures, or words, or movements, out of whatever kind of a mind and a set of muscles each of us possesses. The outer world is never the same for any two people; and it never stays the same for anybody; we are all originals, and forced to be creative to exist.

– Earl Birney, *The Creative Writer*

Once we realize that we all function creatively at all times, then our fear of being on the line should be eased. We are *always* on the line; it is the normal human condition. Creativity is not something extraordinary that only exceptionally gifted people are favoured with; it is something in our nature. The problem then changes from, "Can I be creative?" to "How can I best express my creativity?" This book is intended to help you solve that problem.

In school and out, writing is a craft that can be invaluable. That craft will be explained so that you can use language for the purposes you wish. The first half of the book is designed as a rhetoric that will give you the basic tools for constructing expository writing, the kind of writing you will most often use.

Although the word *rhetoric* is often used to describe false or phony statements by political speakers, the term's original meaning – the art of spoken or written discourse – is the one stressed here. The rhetorical section of this book is designed to familiarize you with such terms as *style*, *tone*, *diction*, and *structure* and to show how these elements may be used in your own writing. Of special value are the excerpts from essays and books by professional writers like Earl Birney; these samples illustrate just how skilfully someone can apply the elements of rhetoric.

Professional essays and those written for English courses are composed in a form called the *expository essay*. *Expository* refers to the act of presenting or explaining facts and ideas.

Outlining the steps in changing a tire or criticizing the latest trend in movies requires the writer to use the techniques of exposition. The word *essay* comes from the Old French *essai*, which meant "an attempt or trying out," in the sense of a trial balloon. Knowing the derivation of this word will help you remember that your composition, report, or term paper will not be accepted as a work chiselled in stone but as a personal effort to convince your reader that your position is sound. Such writing is not creative in the same way that a poem, play, or piece of fiction is creative. Yet the expository essay can and should be creative within the bounds established by its main or controlling idea.

Good Expository Writing: Some Hints and a Sample

There are many opinions about what constitutes good expository writing. Business leaders are likely to value facts and brevity; their time for reading is limited and they look for the bottom line. Readers of book reviews may also value brevity, but they expect in addition some critical evaluation or comparison of the reviewed book with another like it. It is a sound idea to keep your audience in mind when you conduct an argument, select details, and adopt a particular tone. In most cases you will be writing for instructors who give their definition of good writing in the form of a grade. *That* particular audience is well worth knowing and understanding!

Some generally agreed-upon qualities of good expository writing can be listed here. These characteristics are not exclusive, however. Effective writing often seems to have about it an indefinable quality that emerges from the writer's ability to interest, entertain, or persuade. A successful essay will not automatically take shape, like French bread or chocolate cake, from a recipe. Following the recipe for good writing will help to develop readable essays, but it will not guarantee that you will become Mordecai Richler or Margaret Atwood after a few hours in the kitchen.

PRECISION AND CLARITY

Precision and clarity are inevitably linked because a precise description of something normally makes it clear to the reader. Much of writing, after all, involves describing an event, object, idea, or opinion to someone who has only your words and imagination to go on. Wherever possible, for instance, use *concrete* words that evoke vivid, specific images in your reader's mental eye. Concrete words appeal to the reader's five senses: taste, sound, touch, sight, and smell. Abstract words refer to intangible things such as love, freedom, and thought. Descriptive writing should use concrete instead of general or abstract words. In describing an event such as an accident, try to make the incident as vivid as possible: ''The green, late-model Cadillac rammed the right-rear fender of the yellow Toyota, crumpling the fender like a collapsed accordion.'' How much more picturesque that sentence is than the following one: ''This big car ran into a little one and wrecked it.'' The example is extreme but it illustrates the value of concrete details in achieving clarity and precision. The same approach should be used in essays that attempt to persuade, instruct, or entertain; often such essays require description to achieve their ends as well.

Lack of clarity may also result from errors in pronoun choice, misplaced modifiers, unparallel structure, and so forth. In order to ensure that you are making sense, it is probably a good idea to read your essay into a tape recorder and play it back several times. Words read aloud can be more readily visualized and assimilated; any weak links or confusing instructions should soon make themselves evident. Ideally you should enlist a friend as your sounding board. Ask for brutal truth: Is my argument clear? Have I used words in their correct senses? Is the whole essay coherent? If the answers are NO to any of these questions, take the required time to rewrite and rearrange. Precision and clarity are the primary requirements of effective writing, and weaknesses here are most vulnerable to criticism from casual readers and instructors.

HONESTY

One mistake beginning writers often make is to try to impress their readers by using big words they themselves do not fully understand or by adopting the third-person pronoun *one* in order to sound more impersonal and formal. The writer attempts to hide behind a mask of false authority rather than striving to find his or her own voice. Here is an example of such artificial language given by Geoffrey Durrant in his essay ''The New Barbarians'':

> Despite its appearance as a miscellaneous collection of quadrupeds, Dylan Thomas' flock is a closely united body of animals. Genetic unity customarily shows itself in the repetition and development of related features. Thomas' flock possesses such genetic coherence, and these features, furthermore, have as their subsuming source one ram.

A farmer would say that ''the flock came from a common stock.'' Unfortunately, as Durrant's article makes painfully clear, our language is being abused, even damaged, by writers and speakers who have forgotten the sound of the human voice. They seek instead to impress their audiences with professional jargon and legal- or governmentese. The evidence is convincing that proficient expository writers use precise, uninflated Anglo-Saxon – not multisyllabic – words in their essays. With these words, effective writers also create metaphors or pictures that allow the reader to visualize difficult concepts or emotional states. The goal of such word choices is honest and direct communication, the kind of writing that impresses the reader with the sincerity of the writer. Write as much as possible in your own voice or manner; sharp-eyed readers will quickly detect any attempt to inflate opinions with the hot air of artificial language.

INTENTION

Another essential quality of effective writing is the writer's awareness of intention or purpose. Rhetoric prescribes four widely accepted purposes or aims of the essay: *exposition, argumentation, narration,* and *description.* Most of the writing done for an English class will fall into the category of exposition. Essays that define political systems, outline the steps required to make a film, or compare the main characters in *Crime and Punishment* and *Great Expectations* have the specific purpose of informing and explaining. Writers who seek to convince or persuade their readers will enlist the aid of techniques used in argumentation. Such essays usually entail the testing out of a theory or thesis. Declarations that nuclear weapons should be banned or that laws against the use of marijuana must be rescinded call for support by persuasive arguments that depend more on logic and fact than on emotional appeals to like-minded people. Think of your audience as a jury instructed to decide only on the basis of the evidence presented. This will help you determine the course of your argumentative essay. Narrative essays represent action or events in chronological order and require the writer to entertain his or her audience. Short stories or novels take this form, as do essays in which the writer is asked to narrate a memorable trip or a stimulating moment. Many expository and argumentative essays use narrative effectively: a criticism of airport security, for example, can be buttressed by narrating a personal incident involving check-in or boarding procedures. Description may also be used in expository or argumentative essays to paint a detailed picture of some scene or person. Considerable meaning can be conveyed by juxtaposing (e.g., setting side by side) brushstrokes in a word picture. Hugh MacLennan, in his novel *Two Solitudes,* creates a vivid picture of Montreal by juxtaposing the bilingual images of the city:

> The traffic became steadily thicker as he neared the centre of town, newsboys on every corner selling copies of the *Star,* magazines from the States, crowds speaking French and English around him, signs and billboards repeating second-hand the slogans they had learned from the Americans, beckoning with Players, Sweet Caps, British Consuls, Black Horse Ale, Mother's Bread, the signs screaming bilingually in red, white, and yellow: BUVEZ COCA-COLA

—— THE PAUSE THAT REFRESHES —— LA BIERE DE VOTRE
GRANDPERE —— THE REMEDY YOUR UNCLE USED; street signs
telling him to keep to the right gardez votre droite no
parking here ne stationnez pas ici . . .

By deciding in advance what your primary purpose is (often
this decision is made for you by an instructor), you will know
the appropriate tools of rhetoric to select for the job. This knowledge will also help to balance concerns about your audience,
since a firm sense of objective can often overcome the reader's
biases about word choice, organization, and tone.

ORGANIZATION

Most of us must be prodded to arrange the clutter of impressions in our minds; the act of organization requires about the
same degree of energy as cleaning our rooms. Discarded clothes
and shoes seem to pile up, along with the dust, with a relentless
force we are hard pressed to control. Jumbled opinions, ideas,
beliefs, emotions – these, too, call for ordering if we are to write
with skill and precision.

No doubt you have experienced the sense of dismay with which
ideas tumble out of your head when someone mentions topics
like abortion, inflation, crime and punishment, or current
movies. Although it may not be necessary to outline statements
in a heated discussion with a friend, organizing arguments beforehand is of tremendous help when serious writing begins. If,
for example, your task is to convince the reader that a certain
new movie is worth seeing, decide what three or four main
reasons – the exciting plot, the inspired acting, the skilful direct-
ing – are most noteworthy. Then proceed to arrange these points,
adding examples or illustrations, in a sequence of increasing
importance that will build a sense of expectation into the essay.
Was the inspired direction the most arresting quality? Did the
acting save the film from an otherwise weak plot? Moving from
least significant to *most* significant quality is an almost sure-fire
method of giving your essay the climactic feel of a good play – or
a good movie. Whether you use this method of organization or

others that will be outlined later, selection and decision making are essential; if everything about a certain movie seems to you equally fascinating, it will be difficult to prove to your reader that you are a dependable guide. A key question to ask is: Why did this movie impress me *more* than others I have seen lately? The answer should spur the act of ordering that will result in a readable, effective essay.

TONE

We have all become familiar with clichéd lines that screenwriters turn to in certain dramatic situations. One favourite line is "I don't like the *tone* of your voice," or the standard variation, "Don't use that *tone* with me!" In this context *tone* means a certain inflection of voice by which anger, humour, irony, or disgust are expressed. Tone in writing has a somewhat more specialized meaning: the attitude of the writer, as expressed through the work, toward the subject or reader. A good writer consciously works to establish a tone that best suits the subject and purpose of the essay. In most writing situations, especially those involving exposition or analysis, the writer will strive for a neutral tone aimed at convincing the reader that the argument or analysis set forward is reasoned and objective. TV newscasters, for example, are supposed to acquire a neutral tone of voice for objectivity's sake.

Note the tone of reasonableness and erudition in the following excerpt:

> Everyone recognizes that a new world has emerged in Africa and Asia in our own time – the third world, as it is sometimes called, of newly-independent underdeveloped countries. This third world, neither communist nor capitalist, now comprises most of Africa and, except for China and the fragmentary states of North Korea and North Viet Nam, virtually all of South and East Asia. The peoples of this new world have achieved independence from colonial rule within the last ten or twenty years. Some got their independence only after a revolutionary struggle; others got theirs without an actual show of force. Either way, the

> change was so great that it may properly be called a
> revolution. These revolutions characteristically are made
> by an organized popular movement under leaders who are
> able to get mass support for their vision of the future. A
> part, if not the whole, of that vision has generally been a
> vision of democracy.
>
> – C.B. Macpherson, *The Real World of Democracy*

A moderate tone should probably be the one to strive for in your classroom writing, since for the beginning writer the temptation to shout opinions instead of reasoning them through with the reader is great indeed. (Read some letters to the editor of your daily newspaper for samples of strident tone.)

Sometimes a humorous tone can be used in an unexpected place. Here, for example, is an excerpt from an essay called "The Central Problem of Philosophy."

> I have never thought of myself as a philosopher. By
> "philosopher" here I mean one who displays the same
> professional competence in his subject that professors of
> other subjects do in theirs: one who, when you make any
> philosophical remark or ask any philosophical question,
> can tell you at once the sixteen things it may mean, the
> principal articles and books in which it is discussed, the
> positions taken up on it by the leading authorities both
> living and dead, which if any of those positions are aca-
> demically respectable – and, most important of all, whether
> what you have just said is fashionable. This competence I
> do not possess. When confronted with philosophical dis-
> course I am struck all of a heap. I cannot even give a clear
> and straightforward answer to such elementary questions
> as whether the will is free or what Plato's Theory of Ideas
> was; and this is not, as you probably think I am trying to
> imply, because my mind is too subtle, but because it is too
> confused. As the years go by I become more glib. But it is
> still true, as Augustine might have said, that if somebody
> asks me, I know; if nobody asks me, I don't know.
>
> – Francis Sparshott, "The Central Problem of Philosophy"

No matter what tone you adopt in any essay, try to maintain

it throughout. An occasional humorous or ironic comment in an otherwise serious essay will contribute variety, but the beginning writer should avoid abrupt changes in tone unless he or she is certain that the effect will be the one intended. If there are too many attempts at wit or informal joke-telling, the reader is likely to become impatient with the writer.

Speaking and Writing

As the discussion of tone illustrates, it is important to cite differences between speaking and writing. To many beginners the task of writing seems elementary because they assume they need only transfer their style of speaking to the page. They notice no distinction between their performance in conversation and their performance in composition – it is all a matter of "communication." Yet beginners soon learn, usually from the comments of their English instructors, that there are major differences between talking and writing, and that beginners had better discover quickly what those differences are. The root of the differences is that we get away with errors, inconsistencies, and assumptions in speech that are not tolerated in expository writing. They are not tolerated in writing because they hinder understanding.

Perhaps the primary distinction between speech and writing is that speech depends on sound, whereas writing depends on sight and on those processes of the mind that translate written symbols into sound and meaning. However, the reader's interpretation may be fundamentally different from the intended meaning of the writer. Speech benefits from the help of certain visual and aural aids writing does not have. In speech we add to and qualify our meaning by physical gestures: by movement of the hands, shrugs, and facial expressions such as smiles, frowns, or even the lifted eyebrow. Our resources of sound are many – intonation, the rise and fall of the voice, changes in pitch. We can vary the intensity or the volume of sound; we can, on occasion, whisper, shout, mumble, or even growl. All these add meaning; they are strengths that written language does not have.

On the other hand, spoken language has obvious weaknesses. That collection of fleeting, ephemeral noises we call human speech is gone a moment after it is uttered. Often it is gone even before it has been heard accurately. Perhaps our words linger for a while in someone's memory, especially if they are spoken lovingly or disparagingly, but the speech itself cannot be called back to life. It may be caught and preserved on tape or on a phonograph record, but most of what has been thus saved was first worked over and shaped and set down in writing before it was recited. It is only apparently spoken English; it is, for the most part, written English spoken aloud. Written English has a longer life, a greater permanence; it will exist, in Shakespeare's words, "So long as men can breathe or eyes can see." Writing is also the more accurate communication because it can be reread, examined, and studied; and because it is enduring and susceptible to critical review, it demands greater care in its composition. As a writer you assume a responsibility to build your sentences, to select and arrange your words, and to use or modify the rhetorical and stylistic devices that other writers have created and developed.

Standard English: Formal and Informal

In most communities people know and use at least two varieties of their national language. The most commonly heard variety is the local dialect, which is learned at home and in the neighbourhood. Co-existing with the local dialect is usually a "standard" dialect, which is used in education, business, government, and the professions. The local dialect of English that you speak (and we all speak at least one) is not inferior to standard English, it is merely different. Standard English is taught in the schools and all segments of society support, directly or indirectly, the use and promulgation of standard English. Two linguists explain:

Standardization is not simply a question of numbers, of being that variety spoken by the most populous segment of the community. Standardization is normally linked to some kind of institutional support, perhaps in the form of universal education, media, the growth and spread of government administration or of armies. Inherent in the process is the normalization and codification of the language. Normalization and codification may be performed by universities, academies, scientific and technical bodies, regulatory committees and so on. When, for example, a trade union stipulates that in all contracts and official documents specific functions will be designated in a given manner and that people performing those functions will be called by certain names, it is performing a standardizing function. This is particularly important where the trade union has national rather than just local influence. This same function is performed by individuals who write grammars and books on correct usage and who help to develop positive attitudes towards the norm.

–Michael Gregory and Susanne Carroll
Language and Situation

FORMAL VARIETIES

The variety of standard English that we call *formal* – for want of a term with less unfortunate connotations – is far from being by definition cold, reserved, or stodgy. It has warmth, strength, beauty, and an infinite range and variety. It is not confined to a few scientific and scholarly treatises. A great deal of our literature, from Shakespeare and Bacon down to the latest book on the international monetary crisis, is written in formal English. It is the language striven for by authors of most books of history, sociology, political science, botany, chemistry – many of the textbooks that you use. It is the language of the professions, such as law, medicine, teaching. It is the language of serious essays, of most novels and poems. Most business letters are written in formal English. As a matter of fact, a good share of the nation's private and public daily work is carried on with the help of formal English.

Formal English is very easy to recognize but difficult to master. When we write for public consumption we should, as Fowler so charmingly puts it, "tell our thoughts, like our children, to put on their hats and coats before they go out."

There are some generally agreed-on guidelines for formal writing that should be followed by anyone required to write, for example, a business letter, letter of application, graduate thesis, or formal speech.

1. Slang or colloquial diction should not be used. Expressions such as "spaced out" or "turned on" imply a forced familiarity with the reader that cannot exist in formal writing.

2. An objective tone characterizes formal writing because the writer is usually striving for a mood of rationality or straightforwardness.

3. Third-person pronouns (especially the neutral pronoun *one*), rather than the informal *you*, are found in formal essays and books. The pronoun *I* is also generally not found in formal essays, although many writers today do not follow the rule closely.

4. Contractions are not found in formal writing: "Drivers *should not* drink" instead of "Drivers *shouldn't* drink."

The following two passages are written according to the rules of formal English. The writers distance themselves from their audiences but do not assume a condescending pose.

> The soundscape of the world is changing. Modern man is beginning to inhabit a world with an acoustic environment radically different from any he has hitherto known. These new sounds, which differ in quality and intensity from those of the past, have alerted many researchers to the dangers of an indiscriminate and imperialistic spread of more and larger sounds into every corner of man's life. Noise pollution is now a world problem. It would seem that the world soundscape has reached an apex of vulgarity in our time, and many experts have predicted universal deaf-

ness as the ultimate consequence unless the problem can be brought quickly under control.

–R. Murray Schafer, The Tuning of the World

(The seriousness of formal writing is especially effective when the subject is one of some magnitude, such as Schafer's discussion on the effects of indiscriminate sounds on human life.)

If there is a single word which more accurately than any other sums up all the factors that have shaped the complex civilization known as Western Christendom, that word is *charity* – even if, symptomatically, we are not completely certain what this word means. But if there is a single word which performs the like function for the Hellenic world, that word is *Fate*. The most fundamental concept at work in Greco-Roman culture was the idea that whatever happens, happens necessarily. The course of events is essentially inexorable; the problem of man is how to cope with a world of reality, and with a human situation, the outcome of which is (at least in principle) set beforehand. Despite a seemingly innate human inclination to endeavour and to strive, all human efforts appear, upon reflection, utterly vain.

– Leslie Dewart, The Foundations of Belief

(Dewart uses the word *we* in the formal sense of a community of educated scholars or readers who are familiar with the subject of the discussion. Note also the fairly long sentences and the use of dashes, parentheses, and semi-colons.)

Many stylists who otherwise observe the guidelines of formal prose will sometimes use the personal pronoun *I* instead of *one*. The important thing to remember, however, is that formal English essays are marked by appropriate diction, orderly structure, and a neutral tone. The expression and communication of ideas are part of a planned process, not a spontaneous outpouring. Ideas are grouped and arranged in some logical sequence. There is a serious attempt to show the interrelationship between ideas. As a consequence, paragraphs tend to be more fully developed than in the informal varieties of English; the complexity of a sentence is usually proportionate to the maturity of its thought.

INFORMAL VARIETIES

A professional essayist does not stop writing formal English and begin writing informal English as if stepping through a door from one room to another. In most informal writing, the actual extent of the informality consists in no more than the attitude of the writer to the material and to the reader. (Remember the definition of *tone*.) You may find in such essays the same discriminating taste in choice of words, the same respect for current standards of grammatical correctness and usage, and the same mature structure of the best formal writing. The only difference is that the writers frankly and freely interpret their subjects through their own personalities or through their own preferences and prejudices. The personal pronoun *I* regularly appears in informal essays, contractions are allowed, and colloquial words or idioms often surprise by their appropriateness.

The following selections show the range of styles that can be found in informal writing. Note the strong substructure of organization beneath the apparently relaxed, conversational manner.

> Since the financial rewards of painting are so few, it might well be asked why anyone should devote his life to art. The answer is simple; the true artist cannot help himself.
>
> Artists would continue to paint even if they had no sales at all; a creative urge impels them. Lismer used to boast that he possessed the largest collection of Lismers in the country, and Emily Carr's work piled up with only occasional sales at ridiculously low prices. There were times when she could not afford canvas, and painted on wrapping paper. In spite of such impressive evidence of the lack of public interest in their work, both continued to paint, undaunted by it and by the knowledge that in Canada only the poets rank lower than the painters in the financial scale. Someone once remarked that wealthy Canadians would as soon keep a boa constrictor as support a poet.
>
> – A.Y. Jackson, *A Painter's Country*

(Jackson's prose is informal, but not colloquial. A close reading will turn up some of the hallmarks of serious writing: long sentences; words such as *impels*, *undaunted*, which are a cut above the language of everyday discourse; an adherence to the rules of grammar that is the conscious product of a careful writer. The passage progresses logically, a question is asked and answered, and examples are given to substantiate Jackson's assertion that "the true artist cannot help himself." The passage ends with a wryly humorous comment that refers back to the original statement about the poverty of artists.)

> I made new acquaintances among English people as well as Somalis. I was asked to help out with a group of Somali girls who were learning to make crocheted table-mats and lace edging with the idea that this skill could develop into some sort of cottage industry. I did not know a crochet hook from a knitting needle, but I agreed to help sort out the girls' work and iron the finished mats. When the first of these sessions was over, I began to talk with the English-woman who was in charge of the class. To my surprise, I found that she too, was a writer and, like myself, she was extremely interested in the translation of African poetry and folk-tales and had done this kind of work herself some years ago when she was living in Kenya. I had long ago given up the hope of ever talking to anyone here about writing in general, and even the Europeans who were interested in Somali literature were exceedingly few and far between. I was delighted to have discovered one other person who shared my interests, and when we had been talking enthusiastically for an hour or so, I was about to suggest that she drop over to my bungalow the following day for a beer and a continuation of the discussion. I recalled in time, however, that this was not possible. One does not ask the Governor's wife to drop over for a beer. This kind of formality, which prevents people from talking with one another, seemed idiotic to me then, and it still does.
>
> – Margaret Laurence, *The Prophet's Camel Bell*

(The conversational tone that Laurence uses is well suited to the informal narrative of her travel book. She uses common, ordinary words and the personal pronoun *I* appears in every sentence save the last two. The paragraph is, however, too carefully structured to be mistaken for a report of a casual conversation. The author devotes the majority of the sentences to establishing the background and skilfully leads the reader to a surprise ending, a "twist." The paragraph ends with its topic sentence rather than beginning with it. The reader, having been carefully prepared by the preceding discussion, accepts the premise that formality that prevents people from talking with one another is idiotic.)

A more intimate kind of informal writing echoes the style of everyday conversation. Many "how-to" or "do-it-yourself" books and manuals are written in this manner, because the writer wants to achieve a friendly relationship with the reader. The following example is taken from a book on the pleasures of photography.

> Some photographers seem to think that selecting a film is like choosing a husband or wife. In fact, some photographers seem far more committed to a particular film than they are to their spouse. However, no film is perfect. All colour and all black-and-white films have certain characteristics which make them excellent choices for some circumstances, and not so good for others. You can learn a lot about films by reading test reports in popular photographic magazines and trade publications, but you'll never know a film well until you have used it with your own lenses in a variety of situations. No matter how much you read, you can't tell whether you'll like a new model of car until you drive it.

– Freeman Patterson, *Photography for the Joy of It.*

FORMAL OR INFORMAL? – THE STUDENT'S CHOICE

A logical question at this point would be, "What level of usage should I adopt in my classroom writing assignments?" That decision – and many others – may in fact be made by your instructor. Follow his or her directions. An informal style is obviously appropriate for essays describing personal reminiscences or trips; in other words, it works best for the writer who is asked to recount personal experiences. Argumentative essays, on the other hand, call for a more formal approach in which analysis is conducted in an objective manner. The third-person pronoun may not be necessary in such essays, but formal diction and organization are. Remember that a formal stylist does not automatically employ big or bookish words and a cold, distant tone. Too much intimacy is likewise out of place. Aim for consistency whatever your – or your instructor's – choice of style.

Gender and Pronoun Choice

During the last few years everyone has become aware of the controversy over the use of the generic *man* to represent both male and female members of the human race. Whatever one's political leanings, it must be agreed that words such as *workman*, *spokesman*, and *chairman* imply that only men hold these positions. Clearly, traditional usage is in conflict with the reality of the modern, industrialized society in which all occupations are equally likely to be performed by males or females.

Suggested modifications have sometimes proven successful, even inspired: *worker*, *drafter*, and the like, make clear that most jobs do not need a gender suffix. Other changes – *chairperson*, *spokesperson*, *anchorperson* – seem artificial and contrived, but are now widely used and accepted. Many titles – *president*, *doctor*, *professor*, *judge*, *counsellor* – need no change since the positions to which they refer have for many years included men and women. Since there will be many situations in which the gender question will arise, especially in the use of pronouns, it is important to be aware of the accepted alternatives to the use of the generic *man* and the masculine pronoun.

Traditionally, one of the masculine pronouns, *he*, *his*, *him*, has been written to refer to nouns that give no indication of gender.

It is now widely recognized as correct to acknowledge both genders in the pronoun.

Every doctor must follow *her* or *his* conscience in this matter. The member who forgets this lesson may lose *his* or *her* seat in the election.

This alternative may at first sound awkward, but this is because of its unfamiliarity and the ingrained expectation of the familiar *he* in such constructions. (By the way, never use the shorthand device *he/she* for *he or she*. It has no equivalent in speech and is sure to alienate readers concerned with precision.) It sometimes proves cumbersome to repeat the *he or she* formula in long sentences: "The typical consumer buys ten cars in *his or her* lifetime; *he or she* eats six tons of food; seven hundred suits or dresses grace *his or her* body. . . ." Plural constructions are often the best way out of this maze: "Typical consumers buy ten cars in a lifetime; they eat six tons of food; seven hundred suits or dresses grace their bodies. . . ." Using the plural pronoun also helps to break the habit of beginning sentences with dictatorial-sounding generalizations: "Every pilot should thoroughly check *his or her* plane before take-off." Note how the following plurals help to create a somewhat more relaxed tone.

Pilots should thoroughly check *their* planes before take-off.
If instructors expect good work, *they* need to give clear instructions.

Generally it is advisable to avoid using masculine pronouns unless referring specifically to a man. Even when the task is undeniably a formal document, the writer can consult with superiors or colleagues about the prevailing policy, or, if in an academic environment, seek direction from his or her instructor.

The Essay

To write essays you should read essays. Read them on a variety of subjects. Magazines, such as *Saturday Night* and *The Canadian Forum*, regularly feature articles on subjects ranging from cancer to culture shock written in a manner designed both to inform and to provoke the reader's thoughts. These essays are addressed to a literate and informed audience; many of the allusions found in them are to the works of literature and art commonly introduced in undergraduate survey courses. Yet the writers of these essays assume no specialized knowledge in their readers, and their work is, as a result, a useful model for students who want to instruct and entertain a wide audience. Although the styles of magazine essays are sometimes marred by excessive wit and sarcasm, their arguments are generally tightly constructed, with a clear sense of purpose and an easy movement from the statement of a thesis to its proof. You can also find good essays in books of collected essays. Reading essays like the following with an eye to the logic of the argument, the use of proof, and the form of the conclusion will help you understand the scope – and limitation – of the papers you will probably be called on to write.

The Writer
and the University

Northrop Frye

Universities in a democracy must remain universities, and that means academic freedom, the unrestricted pursuit of undiscovered truth, and not the repeating of the truths that the different pressure groups in society think they already have. All pressure groups in society are anti-educational, no matter what they are pressing for. In Wilkie Collins' detective story *The Moonstone* there's an unpleasant nosy female who speaks of "the blessed prospect of interfering," and there are people like that in every country. But the more remote and diverse the financial support of a university is, the less easy it is for them to get inspired by that prospect.

Now, with the Canada Council Act, federal aid for universities is linked with federal aid for culture. The principles involved for culture are precisely the same. Federal

aid cannot be the sole or even the main financial support
of Canadian culture, but having it establishes the same
double recognition of its necessity and its freedom: it has
to be there, and it has to be left alone. It is logical to link
the university and culture: in fact it could almost be said
that the university today is to culture what the church
is to religion: the social institution that makes it possible.
It teaches the culture of the past, and it tries to build up
an educated public for the culture of the present.

In the Soviet Union, as I understand it, culture is
regarded as a function of the state, and hence all culture
comes directly under political criticism. I dare say a great
deal of lively discussion results, which may often be quite
free in its own context, or even help the artist from a
Marxist point of view. Still, the principle involved strikes
us here in the democracies as pernicious. Yet it seems to me
that a good deal of public thinking about culture here is still
stuck in the laissez-faire economics of a century ago. For us
the writer is still a small retailer, who has to be subsidized
to compete with the mass media. This makes the writer an
economic absurdity. A few novelists, most of them bad
ones, may eke out a small living by writing, or even hit a
best-seller jackpot; but a poet would have to be spectacularly bad before he could live on his poetry. The writer,
unlike the painter, has nothing to sell that becomes the
exclusive property of the buyer. Speaking of literature,
which is the aspect of culture I know most about, I should
say that the writer as such really has no economic position
at all, and depends for his living on various official and
semi-official devices.

One obvious place for the writer to work in is the
university, and most serious writers are now university
employees, at least in the summer. Of course there is no
reason why a university should employ writers who are not
scholars or teachers, and not all good writers are. Still, if
it does employ a good writer, it also recognizes his social
importance, and it covers his freedom with its own academic
freedom.

A writer who does not feel that he is developing as well as
reflecting public taste will lose his self-respect very quickly.

In the mass media of radio and television, as everywhere else, the democratic way is a middle way between rigid control and the anarchy of laissez-faire. This applies also to the grants for writers through wealthy foundations which help them to devote a certain amount of free time to writing. Such assistance only goes so far, but here is still another way of recognizing the importance of the writer without trying to control what he says. Sometimes it may be a very moderate talent that is being encouraged, but you never know: if such a grant had been made to Keats in the summer of 1819 the whole sensibility of the modern world might have been very different. In all these fields democracy has to follow its own trial-and-error, inductive, illogical and well-meaning way. It will not solve large problems by this method, but it will do a great deal of piecemeal good. And as with the Canada Council Act we enter a new era in the recognition of culture by society, we may keep in mind the shrewd advice of William Blake:

> He who would do good to another must do it in Minute Particulars; General Good is the plea of the scoundrel, hypocrite and flatterer.

Children in Canadian schools study Canadian geography, not because it is better than the geography of other nations, but because it is theirs: and similarly with Canadian history and politics. Canadian writing, too, has a value for Canadians independent of its international value. It tells us how Canadian imaginations have reacted to their environment, and therefore it tells us something about Canada that nothing else can tell us. Even if it were not very good in itself, still a Canadian who did not know something of his own literature would be as handicapped as if he had heard of Paris and Rome but never of Ottawa. The study of Canadian literature is not a painful patriotic duty like voting, but a simple necessity of getting one's bearings.

It is reasonable to assume that most Canadian literature would be roughly Canadian in subject-matter, not because it ought to be, but because a serious writer finds it easier to write if he knows what he is talking about. It is often assumed that there is something unique, or at least distinctive, about the Canadian environment or character, and that it is the duty of our writers to interpret those distinctive qualities. Well, this is, of course, the most hackneyed problem in Canadian culture: all our intellectuals are thoroughly tired of it, and very suspicious of attempts to revive it. But they would not feel tired or suspicious if it were or ever had been a genuine problem. The question is put the wrong way round. Writers don't interpret national characters; they create them. But what they create is a series of individual things, characters in novels, images in poems, landscapes in pictures. Types and distinctive qualities are second-hand conventions. If you see what you think is a typical Englishman, it's a hundred to one that you've got your notion of a typical Englishman from your second-hand reading. It is only in satire that types are properly used: a typical Englishman can exist only in such figures as Low's Colonel Blimp. If you look at A.Y. Jackson's paintings, you will see a most impressive pictorial survey of Canada: pictures of Georgian Bay and Lake Superior, pictures of the Quebec Laurentians, pictures of Great Bear Lake and the Mackenzie river. What you will not see is a typically Canadian landscape: no such place exists. In fiction too, there is nothing typically Canadian, and Canada would not be a very interesting place to live in if there were. Only the outsider to a country finds characters or patterns of behavior that are seriously typical. *Maria Chapdelaine* has something of this typifying quality, but then *Maria Chapdelaine* is a tourist's novel.

I insist on this point because it's a special case of widespread misunderstanding about literature. It is often believed that a new environment is a creative influence: that because we have a lot of new things and experiences in Canada, we ought to have a new literature too. So we ought, except that novelty relates to content, not to form or technique. Form and technique don't exist outside literature, and a writer's technical power will depend, not on new experience or new feelings, but only on how well he can absorb what he reads. A hundred years ago Canada was a much newer experience than it is now, and critics were predicting that new Iliads and heroic sagas would emerge from the virgin forests. But what the poets produced was faint echoes of Tom Moore and a few bits of Byron and Wordsworth, because that was what they had absorbed from their reading. That is why the ultimate standards of Canadian literature have to be international ones. The forms in which Canadian writers must write are established in the literary world as a whole, chiefly in Great Britain and the United States for writers in English. The independent value of Canadian culture for Canadians that I just spoke of doesn't excuse the Canadian writer from being judged by world standards. So a good deal of serious Canadian writing is likely to seem like second-hand echoes of American and British writers, who are not only remote from the Canadian scene but often seem to be unreasonably difficult in themselves. Many people in that case would be apt to feel that if the Canada Council encourages the sort of culture that only a small minority can understand, or if it only helps Canadians to imitate writers who have nothing to do with Canada, it can only widen the gap between the Canadian writer and his public. I am not speaking of the yahoos who sound off about feeding arty bums at the public trough and so forth; I am speaking of what a responsible citizen might reasonably feel.

This raises the question of how far a serious Canadian literature can also be popular, in the sense of being a genuine possession of its people. There are several kinds of popular literature. One kind is the commercial or bestseller type of popular book, usually fiction; its popularity depends on its news value, and when that dies the book dies too. Or it depends on sexual stimulation, which is equally short-lived, as most of you have already discovered. Then there is the kind of book that appeals to the eternal bourgeois in the heart of man, the book that tells him how to get ahead in life and supplies him with inspiring slogans and proverbial philosophy. Books on the power of positive thinking and on winning friends and influencing people have been popular since the days of ancient Egypt: an eighteenth-century example was called "The Way to be Rich and Respectable," which is as good a title as any. Devotees of these books attach an exaggerated

importance to such poems as Kipling's *If* or Longfellow's
Psalm of Life, which represent the same kind of thing in
poetry. There seems to be an inner law that prevents this
proverbial philosophy from getting beyond a certain point
of literary merit. I once heard a speaker recommending
Shakespeare as a poet who said profound things about life,
but this was the kind of poetry he liked, and I couldn't help
noticing that all his quotations were from Polonius and
Iago.

But there is another kind of popular literature which is
more important. This comes into the reading and listening
of the child, in the songs and the stories, the history and the
wisdom, which are central in our cultural tradition. Whatever literature we learn early, from pre-school nursery
rhymes to high-school Shakespeare and beyond, provides
us with the keys to nearly all the imaginative experience
that it is possible for us to have in life. The central part
of this training consists of the Bible, the Classics, and
the great heritage of our mother tongue. Such education
includes genuinely popular literature: that is, literature
which provides a simple and direct form of imaginative
experience. In America this would include Rip van Winkle
and Huckleberry Finn, the songs of Foster, the tall tales of
the West and the comic strips that develop similar folklore
cycles in the Tennessee hills and the Florida swamps. We
have very little of it in Canada independent of its North
American context. The popular in this sense is the contemporary primitive, what in previous ages was folk song
and folk tale. Much of it is rubbish, and it includes the
cheap fiction and comic books that the enormous maw and
the ostrich digestion of a ten-year-old reader assimilates
after school hours.

What is popular, in the sense of being permanently and
genuinely well loved, is a by-product of education, and as
one's education improves, the quality of what one likes
improves too, until we reach the fully mature level at which
the Bible and Shakespeare and the other staples of culture
are popular. A good deal of the worry over the ten-year-
old's comic books would be far better expended on making
sure that the central educational structure is a sound

one. I recently heard of a grade-eight teacher in an expensive regressive school in New York, welcoming a boy who had been away with some joke about the prodigal's return, and gradually realizing that no one in her class had heard the story of the prodigal son. Now a grade-eight student who does not know that story has not simply missed out on a piece of information that can be supplied at any time. He has been deprived of one of the keys to the whole imagination and thought of western culture, no less than if he had been deprived of the multiplication table. An educational theory which does not recognize this is not just a mistaken theory: it is criminally negligent.

If his elementary education is sound, no student will find contemporary literature remote from him. On the contrary, he will realize that T.S. Eliot and William Faulkner and Dylan Thomas have far more in common with popular literature, as I have defined it, than any positive thinker could ever have. But by this time he is beginning to feel something of the weight and power of the forces at work in society that are trying to prevent him from getting educated. Contemporary culture is very obviously about us, and it talks to us in a fully mature way. Society consists largely of adolescents and arrested adolescents, and departments of education who have to arrange high-school curricula are well aware of the fact. As a rule a student has to get to university before he can make much contact with the culture of his own time.

This suggests that much of what is now central in our cultural tradition was in its day equally disturbing in its impact, and still can be. The earliest of the prophets of Israel, we are told, was Amos, and the Book of Amos includes a few of the agonized squeals of his contemporaries: "the land is not able to bear all his words," they said. That has been the history of great culture ever since. When Wordsworth said:

> We must be free or die, who speak the tongue
> That Shakespeare spake; the faith and morals hold
> That Milton held.

he meant what he said and he was telling the truth. But

school texts of Shakespeare continue to be expurgated, for this fair land is still unable to bear all Shakespeare's words; the faith and morals of Milton are as violently resented today as they ever were. If we subsidize our culture properly, we are certain to encourage a good deal that will be described by a good many people as everything from longhair to filthy. If you think that society has outgrown such narrow-mindedness, I would call your attention to the fact that Canada, like all other countries, has laws of book censorship that no serious student of literature can possibly have the slightest respect for.

Being dissatisfied with society is the price we pay for being free men and women. And that should help us to understand the Canadian writer better, because he's so often forced to say most loudly what his audience least wants to hear. If people are morally smug, they will think their writers blasphemous; if they are sodden with integration and adjustment, they will think their writers neurotic; if they accept a way of life, they will think their writers subversive. Sometimes, of course, they will be right, but their rightness is not important, and poems which are immoral or hopelessly obscure today may be babbled happily from infant lips tomorrow. Whatever people do, most of their best writers will be doing the opposite. And if the worst of all came upon us, if we had to fight to the last ditch for our freedom, with our brothers killed and our cities in smoking ruins, our poets would still stand over against us, and break out in hymns to the glory of God and in praise of his beautiful world.

DISCUSSION AND EVALUATION

Northrop Frye's essay is an attempt to locate the importance of writers in our own culture; in other words, an attempt at exposition. In order to persuade us of the crucial role of our writers, Frye has to weave together a number of culturally related topics that include economics, politics, and the nature of art itself. His argument, or thesis, is that in order for Canadian culture to grow and to thrive, we must subsidize our artists, yet at the same time we must leave them free to develop as they will. The essay is persuasive because it builds from the practical concerns of economics to much wider concerns of cultural survival, sound education, and human freedom. By the time we come to the end we are convinced that it is not only a good idea to support our writers, but that it is *mandatory* for our own well-being. The tone of the essay is both authoritative and personal. Note, for example, the humble qualifying "as I understand it," "I dare say," "it seems to me" in the beginning sentences of paragraph three, and compare that tone of voice to the one in "but a poet would have to be spectacularly bad before he could live on his poetry," later in the same paragraph. The writer's authority is also enhanced by his references to literature, painting, history, and the Bible. Quotations from the writings of Blake, Wordsworth, and the Book of Amos are used to concentrate an idea into a few well-chosen words for startling effect while at the same time putting the writer in league with other great writers.

Citing historical authorities is not the only device Frye uses in his argument. The essay ranges throughout the various levels of usage. The diction or word selection, especially as illustrated by such words as *pernicious* (paragraph three) or *eternal bourgeois* and *inspiring slogans and proverbial philosophy* (paragraph nine) is typical of formal essays; many sentences exhibit classical *balance*, employing the semi-colon or colon to join two or more independent clauses as in the fourth sentence of paragraph two, or the seventh sentence of the third paragraph. Frye sometimes uses devices to offset his serious tone so that he avoids monotony or scaring away his readers. One such device, for example, is the use of a witty turn of phrase such as the last sentence in paragraph eight or many of the phrases in paragraph nine. At that point (about half-way) in the essay Frye also includes a few colloquial words and an anecdote ("I once heard a speaker . . .") as a way of encouraging the reader to press on to the even more important points in the second part of the essay. The mixture of formal diction and an informal style from time to time makes the essay livelier, more personal and readable, and consequently more convincing, without in the least endangering the writer's credibility. This is a delicate balancing act, which is performed only after a great deal of practice.

The strength of the essay rests on the wide-ranging intelligence displayed in it. Frye considers the Soviet system and laissez-faire economics, the importance of national literature as well as international standards of evaluation, the conventional definition of "popular" art versus his own definition of what is genuinely popular, censorship and freedom, genuine education as opposed to social complacency. In all these concerns he draws examples from English and American poetry, comic books, Canadian painting, French-Canadian fiction, classical literature, and the Bible. By the time he makes his point about "adolescents and arrested adolescents" in paragraph twelve the reader has already tacitly agreed that authentic culture is valuable, as personified by the author of this very essay.

Although it is difficult to reach the professional heights represented by Frye's essay, it is possible to write successfully by incorporating many of its characteristics into your own style. That accomplishment should help to make the adventure worthwhile, even if it also requires attention to detail and the hard work of reading and research. Writing is one of those skills, like mountain climbing, that improves with practice.

The next chapters, on words, sentences, and paragraphs, will familiarize you with the basic tools and techniques of composing. Once you have mastered these, you will be ready to begin the process of planning and writing effective essays.

EXERCISES

EXERCISE 1, CLARITY AND PRECISION. *Translate these unclear and garbled sentences into clear, concise informal English.*

1. Owing to the failure to finalize the meeting, we were required to relocate in a different time frame.
2. Emilia arrives after Desdemona has received fatal abuse at the hands of Othello.

3. The whole poem evolves only about him.
4. Once the chairperson has prioritized this year's goals, the entire committee can begin to interface.
5. Seeking input about educational philosophy is essential to viable interaction between experiencing parents and teachers.
6. We must access the TV program at the optimum time.
7. As the motorized vehicle continued along its prescribed route it impacted the two-wheeled vehicle at an intersection.
8. After our last telephonic communication I was of the opinion that we had reached a mutual commitment on the program.
9. The bullies were told to cease and desist from their assault and battery against my friend and companion Eric.
10. The two leaders dialogued about the meaningful role each would play in the evolution of a peaceful world order.

EXERCISE 2, FORMAL, INFORMAL, AND COLLOQUIAL USAGE. *Identify the level of usage in each of the following sentences. Indicate the words or phrases that prove your claim. Change any colloquial or formal sentences to informal sentences by making the appropriate changes in diction, punctuation, and so forth.*

1. We cannot fail to comprehend the significance of the context.
2. I bombed out on the exam today.
3. We shouldn't have tried to jump that electrified fence.
4. One feels apprehensive about the future military growth in our democratic society.
5. Got wheels, man?
6. Their claim of superiority is exaggerated; our team will vanquish them handily.
7. I was nervous about the upcoming talk with the dean.
8. Even though I hit the sheets before the witching hour, I felt wasted the next day.
9. We shall nominate a candidate with exceptional intelligence, proven experience, and the will to prevail.
10. She's positive that Mike is wired pretty good today.

EXERCISE 3, GENDER. *Rewrite the following sentences, eliminating references to gender or using pronouns that acknowledge both genders.*

1. A student needs to be sure of his objectives in order to succeed.
2. Man will halt his aggression when he finds the path to peace.
3. Jane is the spokesman for the local sportswriters.
4. A chairman should listen closely to the complaints of his faculty.
5. Anyone who knows his math can solve that problem easily.
6. She is one of the best lady lawyers in the country.
7. The ticket-buyer should mail in his money and form as soon as possible.
8. If the jaguar is frightened he will attack with blinding speed.
9. A witness must be careful to record his impressions before the deadline.
10. Salesmen are rarely courteous to customers returning merchandise.

EXERCISE 4, TONE. *Describe the dominant tone in each of the following excerpts. Determine as well the level of usage – formal, informal, colloquial – in each sentence.*

1. Unless everything in a man's memory of childhood is misleading, there is a time somewhere between the ages of five and twelve which corresponds to the phase ethologists have isolated in the development of birds, when an impression lasting only a few seconds may be imprinted on the young bird for life. This is the way a bird emerging from the darkness of the egg knows itself, the mechanism of its relating to the world. Expose a just-hatched duckling to an alarm clock, or a wooden decoy on rollers, or a man, or any other object that moves and makes a noise, and it will react for life as if that object were its mother. Expose a child to a particular environment at his susceptible time and he will perceive in the shapes of that environment until he dies. The perceptive habits that are like imprintings or like conditioned responses carry their habitual and remembered emotions. Wolf willow is a sample, but things

other than smells will do it. I can sing an old Pres-
byterian Sunday School hymn, "The Fight Is On, Oh
Christian Soldiers," and instantly I am seven or eight
years old, it is a June day on the homestead, the coulee
is full of buttercups, and a flickertail's close-eared
head is emerging in jerks from a burrow, the unblinking
almond eye watching to see if I move. Only because I
must have sung it to myself in that spot, a few bars of
that tune can immerse me in the old sun and space,
return me to the big geometry of the prairie and the
tension of the prairie wind.

– Wallace Stegner, *Wolf Willow*

2.   Anti-Semitism is incompatible with Christianity. It
is, first of all, contrary to the universality of redemp-
tion, as is any form of racism. The hatred of any ethnic
group or human family cannot go hand in hand with
faith in Christ. The catholicity of love is the touch-
stone of Christianity. "If anyone says 'I love God'
and hates his brother, he is a liar" (1 John 4:20). Hatred
for the Jewish people, however, has an added vice in it,
for if a man detests all Jews he will also detest the Jew
Jesus Christ, or at least regret that the eternal God has
become man as a son of the Jewish people.

– Gregory Baum, *Progress and Perspectives*

3.   It was somewhere in the dying weeks of December,
1946, that Old Rawhide was born and rose, more like a
Quasimodo than a Phoenix, from the ashes of the old
year. As the newest addition to the announce staff of CBC
Halifax, I took my turn at all the various assignments in
the normal program day – newscaster, host of record
shows, farm broadcast announcer, wet nurse to women
commentators and, of course, surf and gull man on
Harmony Harbour. At the end of my second week, I
reported for duty on a Saturday morning, checked my
schedule of duties and found to my horror that they
included a half hour of cowboy records called *After
Breakfast Breakdown*. With the exception of a very few
legitimate songs which were actually sung by cowboys

and have come down to us from the old frontier days of the American west, I loathe the entire field of Tin Pan Alley hokum loosely termed "cowboy music." Moreover, at twenty-one I was a good bit more impressionable than I am now and being a fully fledged CBC announcer was to me, at least in those days, only a rank or two below beatification. I had already blabbed all over Halifax to any who would listen the long list of vital and indispensable duties with which I had been entrusted by the CBC. What on earth would these people think now if they should hear me feigning an enthusiastic introduction to some guitar-twanging drugstore cowboy singing, "I Rapped On the Hearse Window, Granny, But You Did Not Look Out," or something of similar inspiration.

– Max Ferguson, *And Now Here's Max*

4. Though women were an essential part of the Canadian working class, their status both at home and at work was that of a group separate and unequal. In the first sixty years of this century only a handful of women wage-earners were organized, and still fewer held union office. Indeed the woman worker was widely regarded as marginal, temporary, and lacking in militancy. That this could be a misleading assumption is shown not only by the occasional strike early in the 1900s – textile workers, garment workers, and telephone operators participated in hard and partly successful battles – but by the choices that thousands of women over several generations made by moving from one occupation to another. In this respect they, like the vast majority of unorganized males, were "voting with their feet." It was virtually the only choice they had. At home and at work women faced incredibly long hours, sweated and often dirty conditions, and starvation wages; above all, they had virtually no control over their own lives.

– Irving Abella and David Millar
The Canadian Worker in the Twentieth Century

5. A little before noon she lit the lamp. Demented wind fled keening past the house: a wail through the eaves that died every minute or two. Three days now without respite it had held. The dust was thickening to an impenetrable fog.

She lit the lamp, then for a long time stood at the window motionless. In dim, fitful outline the stable and oat granary still were visible; beyond, obscuring fields and landmarks, the lower of dust clouds made the farmyard seem an isolated acre, poised aloft above a sombre void. At each blast of wind it shook, as if to topple and spin hurtling with the dust-reel into space.

From the window she went to the door, opening it a little, and peering toward the stable again. He was not coming yet. As she watched there was a sudden rift overhead, and for a moment through the tattered clouds the sun raced like a wizened orange. It shed a soft, diffused light, dim and yellow as if it were the light from the lamp reaching out through the open door.

– Sinclair Ross, *The Lamp at Noon*

EXERCISE 5, WRITING EFFECTIVE PARAGRAPHS. *Compose a paragraph of about 75–80 words in which you attack the present state of popular music. Adopt an angry tone as you address an audience of classmates. Then rewrite the paragraph in a more objective or neutral tone for an older audience. Remember to adopt the level of usage that best suits the subject and audience.*

SUGGESTED FURTHER READING

The following books dealing with some of the matters discussed in this chapter – the levels and varieties of English usage, the sources of its vocabulary, the relation of spoken to written English – will be found in almost every college library.

ADAMS, J. DONALD. *The Magic and Mystery of Words.* New York: Holt, Rinehart and Winston, 1963.

BLOOMFIELD, MORTON W., and LEONARD NEWMARK. *A

Linguistic Introduction to the History of English. New York: Alfred A. Knopf, 1963. Reprinted 1979.

BRYANT, MARGARET M. *Modern English and Its Heritage.* 2nd ed. New York: Macmillan Publishing Co., Inc., 1962.

BRYANT, MARGARET M. (ed.) *Current American Usage: How Americans Say It and Write It.* New York: Funk and Wagnall's, 1965.

CARROLL, JOHN B. *The Study of Language.* Cambridge: Harvard University Press, 1958.

COPPERUD, ROY H. *American Usage: The Consensus.* New York: Van Nostrand Reinhold, 1970.

COPPERUD, ROY H. *American Usage and Style: The Consensus.* New York: Van Nostrand Reinhold, 1979.

DEAN, LEONARD F., WALKER GIBSON, and KENNETH G. WILSON. *The Play of Language.* New York: Oxford University Press, 1971.

FOLLETT, WILSON. *Modern American Usage.* New York: Warner Books, 1974.

FOLLETT, WILSON. *Modern American Usage: A Guide.* New York: Hill and Wang, 1966.

FOWLER, H. W. *A Dictionary of Modern English Usage.* 2nd ed. Oxford: Clarendon Press, 1965

GIBSON, WALKER, Editor. *The Limits of Language.* New York: Hill and Wang, 1962.

JESPERSEN, OTTO. *Growth and Structure of the English Language,* 9th ed. New York: Doubleday and Co., 1955.

NEWMAN, EDWIN. *Strictly Speaking: Will America Be the Death of English?* Indianapolis: Bobbs-Merrill, 1974. Reprinted 1975.

PYLES, THOMAS. *Words and Ways of American English.* New York: Random House, 1952.

PYLES, THOMAS. *Origins and Development of the English Language.* 3rd ed. New York: Harcourt Brace Jovanovich, 1982.

ROBERTSON, STUART. *The Development of Modern English.* New York: Random House, 1952.

2

WORDS
AND PHRASES

English Words and Our Language's History

Although it is not crucial to good writing to know the detailed history of our language, some knowledge of that history can help any writer develop an enriched sense of the range and variety of words in English. Unabridged dictionaries generally list about 200 000 words, an inventory so large that it qualifies English as the General Motors of languages. None of us will ever learn the meanings of all these words, let alone their origins. The purpose of this section is simply to describe the three main periods of English and to discuss various changes that have occurred during those periods.

OLD ENGLISH (OE) OR ANGLO-SAXON (AS) – 449–1066 A.D.

The English language belongs to a family of languages called Indo-European. This large group of languages is supposed to have originated in Central East Europe in about 3500 B.C. Although no one has ever heard or read an Indo-European word, historians of language have long recognized evidence that such a language did exist. Armenian, Hellenic (Greek), and Italic (Latin) are members of the Indo-European family; one branch, Germanic, is the direct parent of Anglo-Saxon or Old English. There were inhabitants of Britain before the Angles and Saxons invaded the country, and their language too was a part of the Indo-European family. Britain had also been conquered and ruled by Romans from 55 B.C. on, but the early Briton tongue has left no significant trace on our present-day language.

Sailing from the mainland of Europe in 449 A.D., the Angles, Saxons, and Jutes helped the Britons defeat northern enemies, the Picts and Irish, who had invaded their country. The European allies helped King Vortigern to victory, but they overstayed their welcome, essentially controlling the country until 1066 A.D., when William of Normandy defeated Saxon King Harold at the Battle of Hastings. During this 600-year period, England became increasingly civilized and largely Christianized. The political map divided the country into four kingdoms – Northumbria, Mercia, Wessex, and Kent – and each of these cultures exerted its influence on the country at various times. Nearly sixty thousand words made up the language during this period, including an influx of Danish words resulting from sporadic invasions and conquests by the Vikings. Like Anglo-Saxon, Danish borrowings were simple and descriptive of family life and daily work: *give*, *hit*, *sister*, *low*.

Anglo-Saxon was an *inflected language*; that is, words changed form, usually by the addition of prefixes or suffixes, to express grammatical or syntactical relations. The OE verb *gefrūon* means "have heard," with the *ge-* prefix signalling the past tense. (German is a modern inflected language.) Modern English, however, is an *uninflected language*; that is, the position of the word in the sentence determines meaning, function, and so forth. We know *sail* is the verb in the following sentence because it comes after the subject and before the object: "They sailed to Sicily." The movement away from an inflected to an uninflected form was a gradual one and no doubt allowed for a greater influx of words from other languages. During the Anglo-Saxon period, however, the language spoken and written in England looked more like modern German than modern English.

MIDDLE ENGLISH – 1066–1500 A.D.

When William the Conqueror defeated King Harold at Hastings, he began almost immediately to establish the language and culture of Norman France in the English court. The people of Britain, however, still spoke Anglo-Saxon in their daily commerce and the Catholic Church continued to use Latin as its official language. By the middle of the fourteenth century, English was the accepted language of the ruling classes, the legal system, and the Church. In fact, the dominant dialect became the East Midland dialect of London, which has persisted to this day. Geoffrey Chaucer, the famous English poet, wrote his *Canterbury Tales* in the East Midland dialect.

Although Norman French did not take over from Anglo-Saxon the position of universal language in England, it did contribute many social, political, and economic words to our language. *Parliament, crown, sovereign, jury, plaintiff, castle, grocer,* and *chamber* are all Norman words. But Norman words did not automatically replace Anglo-Saxon ones. In many instances pairs of words, one from each language, have survived and may be used synonymously: *work* (OE) and *labour* (OF), *cow* (OE) and *beef* (OF), *deer* (OE) and *venison* (OF), *room* (OE) and *chamber* (OF). Note that in most instances the Norman word sounds more formal than the Old English one.

Norman words made their steady way into English not only because they were used by court, legal, and literary figures, but also because Norman French was uninflected. The English that was evolving from Anglo-Saxon in the fourteenth century was also becoming less inflected. This change meant that English was able to grow, adding new words from European cultures and societies. The result was Middle English, the language perfected by such writers as William Langland and Geoffrey Chaucer.

By the end of the fourteenth century, Middle English had acquired a distinctly modern look and sound. Except for the somewhat strange spellings, the following passage from the Bible, translated by John Wycliffe in 1380 A.D., should be easily comprehended after one careful reading.

> **And eft Jhesus bigan to teche at the see; and myche puple was gaderid to him, so that he wente into a boot, and sat in the see, and al the puple was aboute the see on the loond. And he taughte hem in parablis many thingis.**

In this excerpt you can see that Middle English writing, like Anglo-Saxon, functions largely through co-ordinate clauses; that is, independent clauses joined by *and*. Modern English, on the other hand, has developed the subordinate clause as a means of indicating relations and shades of meaning. Note also that the ME plural pronoun was *hem* instead of *them*.

MODERN ENGLISH – 1500–PRESENT

Two significant events ushered in the Modern English period: William Caxton's establishment of a printing press in 1476 A.D., and the continental Renaissance contribution of many Greek and Latin words. By printing a large number of books in London English, Caxton helped to set the dialect of that region as the national standard. His translations in particular regulated usage since he selected words that could be understood by the largest body of readers. During the early sixteenth century many Latin and Greek words appeared in literature and government documents as humanist scholars like William Lyly and John Colet fostered an interest in works from the classical world. Although there was a reaction against such Latinate words as *laureate*, *impediment*, and *prolixity*, the Elizabethan age (1558–1603) marked a stage of rapid growth in English vocabulary. With the performing and publishing of Shakespeare's plays and the appearance of the King James Bible (1611 A.D.), Modern English became one of the richest and most diverse languages. The King James Bible was particularly important in preventing the language from becoming too heavily Latinate and pedantic. Translators, many of whom were in fact scholars, sought to use language that was simple and dignified.

Our Changing Language

Three major influences on the course of the English language since 1500 are worth noting. First, dictionaries, grammars, and printing houses, the earliest of which appeared in the eighteenth century, instituted standards of correctness in spelling, pronunciation, and meaning that had not until then existed. (Shakespeare, like most of his contemporaries, spelled his last name in several different ways.) Second, the introduction of universal education has contributed to the growth of awareness about standards of usage in writing, reading, and speaking. Third, the speech heard on television, on radio, and in the movies has strongly influenced usage throughout England and North America, all but obliterating regional differences. Although the changes that have resulted from these influences may at times perplex us (every TV anchorperson now seems to say *hopefully* instead of *it is hoped*), we cannot forget that weeds as well as flowers are bound to grow in the garden of a living language. Trying to impose strict laws on usage and on the importing of foreign words, as has in fact been tried in France, would lead to a stultified, probably pedantic language – if such lawmaking could work. It is reassuring to note as well that although certain nonwords like *input* and *prioritize* do from time to time spring up in the garden, other growths like "Far out!" and *rehab* die from neglect.

Although the spoken language is subject to fads and rages, written English requires us to compose in a language that will be understood by the widest possible audience. One of the reasons we have such a rich vocabulary is that writers have kept alive words and images that might otherwise fade from conversation. By following the practice of these writers you will be helping to enrich a language that has already proved indispensable to people throughout the world. By studying the history of our language, in particular the original meanings of words and phrases, your own writing will begin to reflect the versatility and simplicity that are the strengths of standard written English.

Using the Dictionary

If a word always stood for only one thing or only one idea, communication would be simple indeed. But words have a way of acquiring many meanings through their use by different people at different times under different conditions. The review of the history of the English language shows just how fluid and adaptable a living language can be. Some of the most common words, such as *get*, *give*, *hard*, *take*, *run*, *read*, *stand*, *shoot*, have dozens of meanings. As an illustration of the complexity and multiplicity of meanings that a word can acquire, consider the first word in the list – *get*.

He got a reward. I'll get home early. Did you get him on the phone? Can you get *Hockey Night in Canada* on your TV set? Go get your coat. Can you get him to eat? Get going. Get the supplies to them. He got six months for that. He's got the habit. Drugs will get him. Did you get the wig she was wearing? You'll get caught in the storm. Get it?

Language users know the difference between the *denotation*, or the exact, literal meaning of a word, and of the *connotation*, or associated meaning of a word. But literal meanings and associated meanings blend and merge, change with time and circumstance, and to some extent differ with every different person using these words. Consider a very common noun – *dog*. How did so many opposite associated meanings attach themselves to this poor animal?

Faithful as a dog. The bill collector dogged him. They showed dogged courage. She's a lucky dog. He's going to the dogs. It's a dog's life. It's dog eat dog with him.

Many words – and very important ones too – seem to live perpetually in a fog, because there is nothing tangible or visible for which they stand: nothing at which you can point your finger and say, "This is it. This is what I mean." When you say *dog* or *chair* or *book*, you can, if it is important enough, find some dog or chair or book to point to and say, "This is it." But when words stand for ideas, such as *temperance* or *democracy* or *security*, the problem is much harder. All you can do is qualify and define, or point to a person who is temperate, a state that is democratic, a social system that provides security. Such vagueness is not a very satisfactory condition for speakers and writers, but it is the best we have. When we do not choose our words carefully, when we do not define, or point to examples, we may be talking about one thing and our listeners or readers may be thinking about another. And that is worse than vagueness.

To make the art of exact communication by words even more difficult, some people use words in devious ways. Words have always been used by some people to conceal meaning, not to reveal it. Think of the way some politicians or their spokesmen distort meaning by using euphemisms: *sovereignty association* used by politicians in place of *separation* during Quebec elections in the nineteen seventies. With other people, abstract words have only one real meaning – the meaning *they* have assigned. A difference of opinion over what a word means, however, does not always imply dishonesty or evil intent. Profoundly honest people may differ in their understanding of words, depending on differences in their background, their training, and their temperament. The meaning of a word can also change under the stress of emotion, or even under the strain of political campaigns and elections. Such words as *socialism*, *capitalism*, *extremism*, *recession*, and *bureaucracy* mean one thing to members of a political party when they are in office and another thing when they are out of office.

A dictionary lists the words of a language in alphabetical order, and gives information about their meaning, their spelling, their use, their pronunciation, and their history; the degree of completeness of this information depends on the size and purpose of the dictionary. The information found in a dictionary is based on an extensive study of the language in action; for every word listed, a great mass of information has been collected, classified, filed, and studied by a trained staff and, where necessary, by consultants from special fields in which the word is used. All information in a reliable dictionary is based on a study of usage. *A dictionary reflects usage; it does not prescribe it.* It is an authority only insofar as it accurately reflects usage.

The various dictionaries of the English language fall into the following classes:

1. The monumentally complete ones, in which a word gets full historical treatment, with quotations illustrating its use from the time of its birth to the date of completion of the dictionary:

> *The New English Dictionary*, in 10 vols. and a supplement, 1888–1928, reissued in corrected edition as *Oxford English Dictionary*, 12 vols., 1933 (also known as *N.E.D.*, *O.E.D.*, the *Oxford*, and *Murray's*). *The Compact Edition*, 2 vols. 1971. In the *N.E.D.* there are 1 827 306 quotations of usage.

2. The one-volume unabridged dictionaries, which you find in schoolrooms and libraries for reference use. They are usually kept up to date by spot revisions and by "New Word" sections.

> *Webster's Third New International Dictionary*. Springfield, Mass.: G.&C. Merriam Company, 1971, 1976, 1981.

> *Funk and Wagnall's Standard Desk Dictionary*. rev. ed. T.Y. Crowell, 1980.

> *Gage Canadian Dictionary*. Toronto: Gage Publishing Ltd., 1983.

> *The Random House Dictionary of the English Language*. New York: Random House, 1966, 1976, 1973, 1981.

3. The one-volume, desk-size dictionaries, one of which almost all college students buy as a part of their working equipment. Each one listed here is well worth the cost; the choice is usually governed by the recommendation of the English instructor.

> *Webster's New World Dictionary*, 2nd College Edition. Cleveland and New York: The World Publishing Company, 1976, 1980.

> *Webster's New Collegiate Dictionary*. Springfield, Mass.: G.&C. Merriam Company, 1975, 1977, 8th ed. 1981.

The American College Dictionary. New York: Random House, 1973.

The American Heritage Dictionary of the English Language. New College Edition, 1980. New York and Boston: American Heritage and Houghton Mifflin.

The Concise Oxford Dictionary. New York: Oxford University Press, 7th ed. 1982.

The Random House College Dictionary, New York: Random House, 1982.

Funk and Wagnall's Standard Desk Dictionary. rev. ed. New York: Funk and Wagnall's, 1980.

The following kinds of information may be secured from a desk dictionary:

1. The Meaning of a Word. As you can see by examining the various dictionary excerpts that are reprinted here, a dictionary uses several methods of clarifying the meaning of a word. First, it uses *phrases of definition*, and it often follows the definition with illustrative examples. Second, it uses *synonyms*, either immediately after the defining phrase or in a group where the synonyms are compared and contrasted. Then, at times, it may present a special list of *idiomatic phrases* using the word. The dictionary also classifies the different meanings a word may have, numbers them, and, if a word has special technical uses, labels these uses and explains them. Some dictionaries list the oldest meanings first; others begin with the most commonly used meanings. It is important to know which method your dictionary uses. You should read *all* the definitions of a word before deciding to use the word in a certain sentence.

In the selection from *The Canadian Dictionary for Schools*[1], note that the most recent, the most commonly used sense of the word is given first. The eight different uses of *pull* as a transi-

---

[1]From *The Canadian Dictionary for Schools*. Copyright 1981 Collier Macmillan Canada, Inc.

tive verb (*v.t.*) are given in order, numbered, and, where necessary labelled, as: **6.** *Informal.*

> **pull** (pool) *v.t.* **1.** to use force on (something) so as to cause
> it to move toward the force: *Two horses pulled the wagon.*
> *She pulled the closet door open.* **2.** to tug at; yank: *She
> pulled his sleeve to get his attention.* **3.** to tear away or
> remove: *to pull a tooth, to pull a branch from a tree.*
> **4.** to rip or tear: *The puppy pulled the blanket to pieces.*
> **5.** to injure or weaken by too much stretching; strain: *The
> baseball player pulled a muscle in his shoulder.* **6.** *Infor-
> mal.* to carry out; bring about; do: *He was suspected of
> pulling the robbery.* **7.** *Informal.* to draw or attract: *That
> new motion picture is pulling crowds.* **8.** *Informal.* to draw
> out so as to use: *The bandit pulled a gun.* —*v.i.* **1.** to draw
> or tug: *The jockey pulled on the reins to slow up the horse.*
> **2.** to go, move, or proceed: *The car pulled into the driveway.*
> **3.** to row: *They pulled toward the bank of the river.*
> —*n.* **1.** the act of pulling. **2.** the effort used in pulling: *It
> was a long, hard pull for them to reach the top of the hill.*
> **3.** anything used for pulling, such as a handle, knob, or
> rope. **4.** a drawing or attracting force: *the pull of a magnet.*
> **5.** *Informal.* influence or advantage: *He got his job through
> pull, because he knew the boss.* **6.** *Informal.* the ability to
> attract or appeal: *That star has great pull at the box office.*
> —**pull′er,** *n.*
> > **to pull for.** *Informal.* to hope for the success of: *We are
> > all pulling for our home baseball team.*
> > **to pull off.** *Informal.* to accomplish in spite of difficulties.
> > **to pull oneself together.** to regain one's self-control.
> > **to pull through.** to get through a serious or difficult situa-
> > tion successfully.
> > **to pull up.** to halt; stop: *The car pulled up at the curb.*

2. The Spelling of a Word. If your instructor has marked *rythem*
as misspelled, you may have trouble finding the correct spelling,
rhythm, in the dictionary. The difficulty, however, is rare; ignorance of the first letter or two in a word is much less common
than vagueness about those at about the middle or at the end.
In by far the greater number of instances, the dictionary is the
quickest and surest check for the spelling of a word. Some words
have variant spellings. Where these are indicated, you will be
safe in using the first one listed. In Canadian dictionaries the
Canadian version of variant spelling is usually given first.

3. The Pronunciation of a Word. The pronunciation of a word is usually indicated by respelling it with diacritical marks and symbols or respelling it in some form of a phonetic alphabet. The method used is explained in detail at the front of every dictionary. A study of these explanations is worthwhile. A brief summary of the symbols used is given at the foot of every page or every two pages facing each other in the dictionary proper. Where two or more pronunciations are current, the dictionary will give both. Check the respelling, the variant accent, the pronunciation symbols, and the stress or accent points in the following from *The Canadian Dictionary for Schools.*

> **scep·tre** (sep′tər) *also,* **scep·ter.** *n.* **1.** a rod or staff carried by a king or queen and serving as a symbol of royal office or power. **2.** royal office or power.
> **sched·ule** (skej′ool, shej′ool) *n.* **1.** a list of the times when certain events are to take place: *a television schedule, a train schedule.* **2.** a plan or group of things to do, or of events to occur at or during a particular time: *Kathy has a busy social schedule.* **3.** the time planned upon or shown, as in a schedule: *The train was running behind schedule because of an accident.* **4.** a written or printed table or list, as of rates or prices: *a schedule of postal rates.* —*v.t.,*

Pronunciation symbols and the indication of accents may vary between dictionaries. Observe these symbols carefully in the dictionary you use.

4. Labels: Subject, Geographical, Usage. Every dictionary uses geographical and subject labels to show that a word in the sense indicated is characteristic of a region or language or that it has a special meaning in connection with a certain subject. To understand this more clearly, you might check the labels used with the following words: *pone, jollity, Erse, tot, trauma, suture,* *kirk, syne, cannikin.* You will find some of these words with a subject label in one dictionary and no label in another. A similar lack of agreement exists in connection with usage labels. *The Canadian Dictionary for Schools* uses the following where in the judgement of its editors these labels are called for: *slang, archaic, informal, trademark, Canadian, Scottish, French, Norse Mythology, Greek Mythology, Music, Hockey, Biology.* Labels you might find in other dictionaries include: *obsolete, dialect, poetic, colloquial, rare.* Note the various usage labels in the following excerpt from *The Canadian Dictionary for Schools*:

> **cool** (kool) *adj.* **1.** lacking warmth but not very cold: *a cool breeze.* **2.** giving protection or relief from heat: *a cool summer dress.* **3.** not excited; calm; composed: *He remained cool in the face of danger.* **4.** lacking enthusiasm or warmth; not cordial: *The movie got a cool reception from the critics.* **5.** *Slang.* excellent; great. **6.** *Informal.* without exaggeration; actual: *a cool million dollars.* —*n.* **1.** something cool, as a time or place: *He took a walk in the cool of the morning.* **2.** *Slang.* calmness: *She cautioned him to keep his cool.* —*v.t.* to make cool: *to cool soup.* —*v.i.* to become cool: *The air cooled over night. Her anger over the incident cooled as time passed.* —**cool′ly,** *adv.* —**cool′- ness,** *n.*

5. Derivation of a Word. As you know, English words have come from many languages, and some have undergone many changes in form and meaning. A daisy, for instance, was a "day's eye," a nasturtium was a "nose twister," our common dandelion was once a "lion's tooth." And would you believe that our word *emerald* had an ancestor that in Latin was once *smaragdus* and in Greek *smaragdos*? The Roman Emperor Nero once used a polished *smaragdus* as a lens in front of his near-sighted eye. So you see that the derivations of words are interesting in themselves, and they might enrich your understanding of words.

The following words have unusually interesting origins: *bedlam, boycott, broker, calico, curfew, dollar, exhume, lunacy, panic, sandwich, sinister, saxophone, tawdry, thug, vandal.*

6. Grammatical Information. A desk-sized dictionary gives adequate information about plurals of nouns and the principal parts of verbs. Inflectional forms are usually given only when they are irregular or when they present difficulties of spelling or pronunciation. For example, no plurals are given for *book*, *chair*, *handkerchief* because it is assumed that these nouns, and all others like them, form their plurals in the regular way. But after *index* you find two plurals: *indexes*, *indices*; after *deer* you find the information that the plural is also *deer* (occasionally *deers*); after *ox* you find the plural is *oxen* (rarely *ox*). Similarly, no principal parts are given after regular verbs, especially when no special problems are involved: see *talk*, *walk*. But note that *study* is followed by *studied*, *studying* to show what happens to the ending in the formation of the past tense and the present participle and gerund. Then look up the verb *lie*, which has two main meanings, and note that the principal parts are necessary to distinguish between the two meanings: *lie* [recline], *lay*, *lain*, *lying*; *lie* [prevaricate], *lied*, *lying*. The last example also illustrates that when the past tense and the past participle have the same form, it is given only once:

> **lie:** He *lied*. I had *lied* about it. [lie, lied, lying]
> **bring:** He *brought* it. I had *brought* it with me. [bring, brought, bringing]
> **ring:** He *rang* the bell. I had *rung* it a minute earlier. [ring, rang, rung, ringing]

7. Idiomatic Phrases. Many of the simple, everyday verbs of the language, through many years of various uses and associations, have acquired special meanings in phrases that we call *idioms*. The quotation from *The Canadian Dictionary for Schools* on page 62 clearly shows what is meant by an idiom: *to pull for* [to hope for the success of], *to pull off* [to accomplish in spite of difficulties], *to pull oneself together* [to regain one's self-control], *to pull through* [to get through a serious or difficult situation successfully], *to pull up* [to halt]. Anyone can see that these are not literal meanings of the verb. Here are a few more examples of idioms, from various dictionaries: *give ground*, *take stock*, *take the floor*, *have it in for*, *have it out*, *run out of*, *do away with*, *do* *for, put one down, shoot the breeze.* See § 23 for a fuller discussion of idiomatic speech.[2]

8. Synonyms and Antonyms. Pairs of words that have exactly the same meaning – literal and associated – are not too common in the English language, but pairs of words may have approximately the same meaning, or approximately the same meaning in certain uses. Note that synonyms are used in illustrative phrases and then sometimes in a separate list where they are compared and contrasted. Antonyms are listed less commonly than synonyms.

EXERCISES

EXERCISE 1, DEFINITIONS. *Look up the meanings of each of the following words. List at least two very different meanings for each.*

intern	aggravate	irony	criticize
propaganda	fellow	nice	curious

EXERCISE 2, SPELLING. *Look up each of the following words. Decide whether both spellings are used in your locality or whether one is more common than the other.*

adviser, advisor	night, nite
although, altho	sulfur, sulphur
glamorize, glamourize	theatre, theater

EXERCISE 3, PRONUNCIATION. *Look up the pronunciation of the following words. Note where the accent is placed in each word. Where more than one pronunciation is listed try pronouncing the word in each way. Which form do you use in your own conversation?*

acumen	data	Don Quixote	inquiry
adult	decade	exquisite	irreparable
aspirant	decadence	finance	lamentable
combatant	despicable	formidable	perseverance
culinary	Don Juan	gondola	superfluous

[2]The symbol § refers to numbered sections in the second part of the book.

EXERCISE 4, STATUS OR USAGE LABELS. *What usage or status label – if any – follows each of the following words?*

alarum	coulee	heap	loser
belike	enthuse	hokum	petrol
bozo	goober	joker	scam

EXERCISE 5, DERIVATION. *From what language did each of the following words come?*

banjo	lava	prairie	anorak
chinook	mosquito	rebus	sapphire
ersatz	pongee	riata	soprano

EXERCISE 6, IDIOMATIC PREPOSITIONS. *Supply the idiomatic prepositions as required in the following sentences.*

1. Since I was so concerned (   ) my business at that time, she was concerned (   ) my health.
2. At that period we differed (   ) almost everything.
3. She especially differed (   ) me about money matters.
4. Finally we separated (   ) one another.
5. Neither of us, however, proved to be capable (   ) living alone.

Concreteness

In general, a concrete word with a clear image has more effect than an abstract one, a specific word evokes more response than a general one, and a homely word makes more friends than a bookish or pretentious one.

A concrete noun, such as *bridge, wall, needle, cloud, smoke, shoe,* or *apple,* names something that can be perceived through the senses. In other words, it names something you can touch, see, hear, taste, smell, or feel. Abstract words name ideas, or qualities, such as *beauty, cleverness, elitism, truth, loyalty,* or *doubt.*

Of course you can seldom give a concrete equivalent of an abstract word, but you can – and should – spell out your concept of the abstraction you use. To say "My father is both stubborn and easygoing" is not enough if you want to present him dramatically; bring him out on the stage for us to see, and show him in the middle of an argument.

General words name classes or groups; specific words name the individual objects, actions, or qualities that compose the group. The terms are to some extent relative: *furniture* is a class of things; *chair* is more specific than *furniture*, more general than *armchair* or *rocking chair*.

Weapon is a general noun. When, for example, you write, "Mrs. Hanks assaulted her husband with a deadly weapon," what control do you have over what goes on in your reader's mind? What picture do your words call up? Did she stab him with a steak knife, club him with a baseball bat, slash him with a safety razor blade that she had slipped out of the medicine chest, or shoot him with a .22 calibre pistol? You say the police found an ornament that she had dropped in the scuffle. It was probably a piece of jewellery – which is more specific than *ornament* – but it would be more specific and more effective to say "a jade green earring."

The verb *move* is general; *stride*, *amble*, *creep*, *glide*, *jog* are all more specific ways of moving. The adjective *large* is general; when you try to make it more specific, you discover that different varieties of largeness are associated with different nouns. For instance, *bulky*, *towering*, *brawny*, *fat*, *spacious*, *hulking* are applicable to which of these – a building, a man, a room, a tree?

Homely words are those associated with the objects and activities of everyday living; bookish or pretentious words are those associated with excessive literary formality.

The following pairs of words and expressions will help to make the distinctions clearer:

Abstract Words
the faithfulness of an animal; the harmony of music; a misfortune of battle; extreme intoxication.

Concrete Words
She served him like a dog; my mother hummed a ballad; a shell fragment ripped open his right arm; he was lit up like a Christmas tree.

General Words
Furniture, clothing, cutlery, kitchen utensil, a crime, an industrial worker, a flower, an animal.

Specific Words
Sofa, raincoat, a carving knife, a frying pan, burglary, a welder, a rose, a lion.

Bookish or Pretentious Words
Frigidity, inebriated, suspend, incarcerated, the matutinal meal, to delve, intestinal fortitude.

Homely Words
Coldness, drunk, hang, jailed, breakfast, to dig, courage.

These are by no means scientific classifications applicable to all words in the language. They are merely samples and you are simply being told, "Look at these. This type of word seems to do something more to your imagination and comprehension than that one." Abstract and general words are not bad words; they are necessary for the expression of abstract qualities and general ideas. Bookish words are natural in certain scholarly, formal contexts. But in the writing of the average student, abstract and general words are used too often where concrete and specific words would do a better job. Remember, disagreement over the meaning of an abstract term is frequent.

The following examples should help to make the idea clearer. You may assume that the "General and Ineffective" examples are not topic, or thesis, sentences.

General and Ineffective Writing
Minn went downstairs to crush some ice for a daiquiri. After she had finished, she went to tidy the living room.

Concrete and Specific Writing

Minn went down the long steep staircase, caressing the sticky bannister, to the back kitchen to crush the ice for Jane-Regina's daiquiri. She put the ice in the freezer (once again moving the snowball she had put away in a plastic bag for Louisa) and went to tidy the living room, which belonged to their early, over-decorated period, when she had been clever with curtains and remnants and fringe, had had time to go to the sales and reconstruct the Victorian room: furniture collected annually from home, odd chairs and tables from the Salvation Army, half a dozen wicker plantstands containing dying aspidistras and ferns in the bay window; on the walls, articles associated with the lovers' game 'our past': a case of surgical instruments which had originally (gleaming in a midnight store window on the Boulevard St Germain) prompted them to go to bed, a row of covetable, childish wooden spoons, a bad map of Paris and a good one of Alexandria, a Majolica plate, a Portobello photograph: nonsense, all, but pleasing. The upholstery would have been more impressive in velvet rather than corduroy, and the staples were showing badly.

– Marian Engel, *The Honeyman Festival*

General and Ineffective Writing

The first session of Parliament commenced on November 7, 1867.

Concrete and Specific Writing

On Thursday afternoon, November 7, 1867, Macdonald, along with the other members of the Commons, stood waiting expectantly and somewhat nervously in the Senate chamber of the Parliament Buildings at Ottawa. The Governor-General, Lord Monck, was reading the speech from the throne to the first federal Parliament of Canada. The legislative history of the new Dominion was about to commence. Outside, though the season was far advanced in

autumn, the day was fine. Most of the shops in town were
shut. A great crowd had pressed behind the rows of regulars
and militia which lined the carriage drive up to the great
central door of the building; and inside, in the Senate
chamber, the galleries were crowded with people. Behind
the rows of Senators, nearly a hundred ladies, the wives
and daughters of the members, gay in crinoline toilettes,
watched the ceremony: and out in front, close to the
Governor-General's chair, a little group of seats had been
specially reserved for Lady Monck and the wives of the
Cabinet ministers.

–Donald Creighton,
John A. Macdonald: The Old Chieftain

General and Ineffective Writing

In the early years of the twentieth century, immigrants to Canada found recreation, and sometimes economic opportunity, in the sports of boxing, basketball, and, above all, baseball.

Concrete and Specific Writing

Three sports drew parent and child together; prize
fighting was a downtown, often immigrant, game and the
chance to make one's way in America with one's fists
tempted many young men. Basketball, because it was a
game of settlement houses, small schoolyards, and YMCA's
had some appeal. The equipment was cheap and, as with
boxing, there were immigrant stars to emulate. Without
doubt, though, the game that was quintessentially North
American was baseball. The immigrant parents and children
shared big league heroes; the schools organized baseball teams
from the earliest grades on. The game offered skills without
violence and a cheap way to idle away summer twilights. At
least one immigrant's son from the sandlots of Toronto made
the Big League, playing for the Brooklyn Dodgers.

–Robert Harney and Harold Troper,
Immigrants: A Portrait of the Urban Experience

EXERCISES

EXERCISE 1, GENERAL AND SPECIFIC WORDS. *Find several specific words for each of the following general words.*

jewellery	car	grass
flower	to move	bird
entertainment	to speak	to laugh
animal	to sing	to dance
ship	road	to hit

EXERCISE 2, ABSTRACT AND CONCRETE WORDS. *Construct sentences in which you give concrete examples of each of the following abstract terms.*

unselfishness	ignorance	fear
efficiency	stubbornness	laziness

EXERCISE 3, REVISING WITH SPECIFIC AND CONCRETE WORDS. *Rewrite the following sentences, making them more specific and concrete.*

1. On the porch a row of elderly women sat and rocked and watched the new guests come in.
2. An irritated and impatient police officer was trying to give directions to a driver.
3. The sounds at midnight are interesting to hear.
4. A little boy was happily playing in the alley.
5. The man leaned against the wall and fell asleep.

Diction

Selecting the right word for the right situation is an important key to good writing. Words that work together are like parts of a jigsaw puzzle snapped snugly into place to form a beautiful picture. Forcing parts to fit when they refuse will create a distorted picture; words that do not fit will only confuse your reader.

The art of choosing and arranging words in writing is called *diction*. (Further suggestions for improving word choice can be found in § 21–25.)

INFORMAL AND COLLOQUIAL WORDS

Words labelled "Informal" or "Colloquial" in the dictionary should not be used in formal essay writing. They may be used in dialogue or when quoting someone, but they do not belong in the body of your papers. Words that are not labelled in the dictionary represent general English usage and can be used in your essays and examinations. Remember not to use contractions; write out all contracted forms.

Colloquial or Informal Writing

The prof didn't hand back our exams today. We lived it up the whole night, but by six I was wiped out.

General Writing

The professor did not hand back our examinations today. We had an exciting time for part of the night, but by six A.M. I was ready for bed.

SLANG

As a general rule, it is best not to use slang in the essays you write for your English class. Attitudes are changing toward the labelling and use of slang words; some articles written for magazines such as *Saturday Night* and *Maclean's* do reveal instances of slang from time to time. Words like *chump, yahoo, schlemiel,* and *creep* have a vivid, descriptive quality that cannot be denied. Words like *cool, lousy,* and *scummy,* however, do not have the same pictorial impact and are not generally found in published writing, except in dialogue.

EXERCISE. *Try to find more descriptive words or phrases for those in italics. You may rewrite the sentences in any way that you believe makes them better.*

1. Brian Mulroney is a *boss dude* who gives off *good vibes*.

2. Little Ronnie's behaviour has been *yucky*.
3. The music at last night's concert was *far out*.
4. The way he answered the phone showed that he was a *total jerk*.
5. When are you going to stop wearing such *scummy-looking threads*?

REGIONALISMS

Many words or phrases are native to a particular region of the country. They are natural and handy when inhabitants of that region are talking to one another. In writing anything other than personal letters, however, you should avoid these localisms, mainly because there is a possibility your reader will not understand them. You can probably find a reasonable substitution in the dictionary.

Regionalisms
Remember to pay *the Bell*.
The two farmers chatted amiably as they drove down the *grid road*.
She gave me a *dandelion look* as I opened the door.
He's so *stomachy* it's no wonder they fought.

General Words
Remember to pay the telephone bill.
The two farmers chatted amiably as they drove down the rural road.
She gave me a hard stare as I opened the door.
He's so irritable it's no wonder they fought.

TECHNICAL, SCIENTIFIC WORDS

Your reader is not likely to be familiar with technical or scientific terms for everyday objects. Use general words wherever possible, except in an essay that is intended for an audience of specialists. Do not try to impress your readers with specialized jargon; unless you explain that *heliotrope* refers to any plant that turns toward the sun, do not use it.

Technical
His sentences exhibit the notable *taint of periphrasis*. John had a

pericardial episode. From time to time it is healthful to pause and encounter the *flora and fauna* of the region.

General
His sentences say things in a roundabout way. John had a heart attack. Stop and smell the roses.

ORNATE AND ARCHAIC WORDS
In the movie *My Little Chickadee*, W.C. Fields tells Mae West that her name (Floribel) is "a euphonious appellation." Fields had a penchant for such florid expressions, most of which only served to puff up otherwise mundane statements. ("Euphonious appellation" translates as "pleasant-sounding name.") Avoid such overwriting in your essays. Remember that the strength of our language lies in the many concrete, one-syllable words that gracefully convey sound and sense when joined together.

Archaic or out-of-date words may also often be found in over-written passages. Your dictionary labels such words to help you in making decisions about their use. Remember that age does not automatically lend character to words and phrases.

Florid and Archaic Writing
We found that all the company was *forspent* after its long *sojourn*. The *puerile pleasures* of youth must inevitably give way to the *privations* of one's *majority*.

General Writing
Everyone was *tired* after the long *trip*. *Childhood pleasures* must eventually give way to *adult hardships*.

More examples of current usage can be found in the "Guide to Usage," pp. 532–556. If you are doubtful about the appropriateness of any word or phrase, consult your dictionary.

EXERCISE, DICTION. *Following is a selection of letters to the editor about a variety of subjects. Read them carefully, keeping an eye on word choice: colloquialisms, slang, regionalisms, ornateness, general vs. concrete words, and so forth. Make corrections as you see fit, giving reasons for your decision. How does your correction improve the sentence?*

I was glad to learn that the Massasauga Rattler is now classified as rare. In my view, the sooner it is classified as extinct, the better.

Who needs the rattlesnake? There are many non-poisonous snakes that do not enjoy the benefits and attention provided by our National Park at Beausoleil Island. It seems an unusual place for a refuge for a poisonous species as the summer brings many campers, accompanied by small children.

I have lived on the Georgian Bay all my life and, while the average length of the snake may be only two feet, I have seen larger ones. Even the smallest are deadly. It is the only snake I have known in the area that will challenge a human. One bite can be fatal and one death is too many.

In these days of strict government economy, I cannot understand why funds would be allocated for the implantation of transmitters in snakes.

While the above comments may offend reptile lovers, they must be a minority group. The place for the Massasauga Rattler is in the zoo, in a glass case.

– Doris J. Corbeau

Unable to swim. Isn't it strange. Almost 100 years ago, during the industrial revolution, the first environmental scientist, Ellen Swallow, warned governments and society of the danger of polluted waters. She pointedly emphasized, with her introduction of The Normal Chlorine Map, that a choice would need to be made between ruthless progress and "environmental sanctity based on scientific fact."

So, now, we who have remained ignorant, or have been kept ignorant, of the whys and hows of our contaminated environment, feel personally affronted by the sign at the water's edge: Swim at your own risk. Well, well, well. Did we really think that we could go on so unaware, so uncaring and still enjoy our natural surroundings "forever."

Hear ye, hear ye! This is not simply affecting our

beaches, our city, our province, our world; this is our planet, the planet we named "earth." Open your eyes. Recognize the process. Take positive action; so that we might breathe more easily, if it's not too late.

– Maja Bannerman

Apropos the butchering of the English language (letter – Aug. 28). I suggest that of more importance than "Herizons" and the like is the vogue for turning a noun into a verb by the suffix "ize" and turning it back into a noun again by the further addition of "ation." This has caused pain and grief to me for some time.

Evening foodization being completed, I therefore strategized the situation and then went through priorization procedures – after which I decided to chairize myself and letterize you on the subject. Almost any noun can be nounized and nounizationed, but what are we doing to the language? When the butcherization is finished, it will probably read and sound something like this letter.

– Colin L.J. Proudman

The police have announced recently that they will be tightening enforcement of seat belt legislation.

In view of this, and of the fact that some people may still resent the legislation, I thought that the following information might be of interest:

Accident surgeons of the Edinburgh Royal Infirmary, in the Aug. 6 issue of "The Lancet" have contributed a letter entitled "Effect of seat belt legislation" (seat belt wearing became compulsory in the United Kingdom on Jan. 31, 1983).

From a study of two comparative two month periods in 1982 and 1983, and of 234 traffic accidents during that time, it was found that in 1982 there were 93 head and facial injuries treated. In 1983, after seat belt legislation, the numbers had dropped to 32 for the same period.

There were 43 (severe) head injuries in 1982; only 12 in 1983.

Among accident victims in 1983 who were not wearing

seat belts in spite of the legislation, the injury figures were almost the same as those of 1982 before legislation was introduced, which means that observance of the law more or less halved the number of severe injuries.

Eighteen years ago, long before seat belt wearing was made compulsory in Ontario, I was firmly convinced of the importance of this safety measure because of surgical experience in treating traffic accidents, and I was able to convince my teenage daughters of this.

One summer afternoon while my wife and I were out of town, my daughter drove her sister for a short distance from Sarnia to the old Dual Highway. They did not apply their seat belts on this occasion because they were wearing swim suits, and the pressure of seat belts against bare skin is uncomfortable.

Their car was involved in a head-on collision through no fault of their own and they were both thrown out onto the road.

The driver was seriously injured, having extensive skull fractures and brain damage. Fortunately they both recovered and have never driven in a car since without buckling their seat belts.

Recently a police officer was reported as saying that ''he had never yet had to unbuckle a dead body.''

I hope that the public will realize that the police are not attempting to enforce an irksome regulation, or to interfere with individual freedom, but are acting in the public's best interest.

                                                    – A.J. Abraham, MD

3

THE SENTENCE

What is Grammar?

Grammar is the systematic description of a language as it is, or was, spoken. The editors of *The Canadian Dictionary for Schools* provide five definitions of grammar, two of which are, "a system of rules describing how the users of a language form sentences to communicate with each other," and, "the use of words according to accepted or standard principles; usage."

The subject of this book is the grammar of contemporary Canadian English; and a genuinely scientific or linguistic approach would develop a *descriptive grammar*, a grammar in which there were no rules handed down, but, instead, generalizations derived from observing how people actually speak and write Canadian English.

DISTINCTION BETWEEN GRAMMAR AND USAGE

Unfortunately, a strictly descriptive approach to language poses a problem. The scientific grammarian recognizes no such thing as good grammar or bad grammar, for the way each individual speaks and writes is *a* valid grammar, following patterns acquired or established during a lifetime. To acknowledge only that everyone has a grammar, however, is to ignore the practical consideration that a grammar must be reasonably understandable to at least two people if language is to serve its function, which is to let Ferdinand tell Isabella that he is unexpectedly called to a business meeting in Antigonish, that he has lost the car keys, or that the laundromat is closed. To concede, however, that grammar is not only a unique and variable phenomenon but a desirable common medium of communication, opens the door to the *prescriptive* grammarian, the grammarian ready to say, "The grammar I choose shall be the common one." Oppressive as that declaration sounds, two facts support it: it has a practical foundation and a well-established reputation. Many people do think there is a right and a wrong way to put words together. As long as that belief survives – and it shows little sign of going away – there is reason for learning what people think is correct. As you can see from the definition quoted on page 79, the problem is that the term *grammar* can cover both the scientific analysis of language as it comes spontaneously off a multitude of speakers' tongues and the concept of proper and improper speech. Only the second meaning involves the speaker's judgement, the conscious selection of one phrasing over another in response to some external measure of propriety, such as occasion, subject, audience, argument, or simply the opinion of society. The linguist dealing with issues of grammatical judgement uses the term *usage* to avoid confusing the imposed conventions of language with the grammar of daily speech. For the purposes of this book, however, the distinction is unnecessary. Correct usage, like any other form of functioning language, has its grammar too. A handbook having as its objective the improvement of its readers' use of language must make judgements, make comparisons, and point out appropriate and effective language patterns in terms of the standards of the day. In this book, *grammar* means a descriptive grammar of usage as defined by the speech and, especially, by the writings of men and women whose sensitivity to the precise, effective use of language has earned them faithful audiences and enduring respect. They at once follow and lead the conventions of correct usage.

It is important to remember that correct usage can be modified. No grammar known has proved unchangeable, like the law of gravity, and good grammar is constantly in the process of alteration. That is why even its cultivated landscape is mapped descriptively – in terms of what is actually happening.

IS KNOWLEDGE OF GRAMMAR HELPFUL?

Many students, at some time or other, question the value of a knowledge of grammar as an aid to better writing. What part of grammar is useful? What part is useless? The answer must be different for every person. Many people write well and speak well without knowing much about grammar, but for those who admit their capacity for self-improvement, grammar is both a convenient set of tools and a practical code of communication. Like a set of tools it enables the student to build effective sentences and to repair faulty ones. It is a code or a technical vocabulary, understood by both teacher and learner, and necessary for learning and teaching.

How, for instance, can students correct the eccentricities of such a sentence as, "This is strictly between she and I," if they know nothing about pronouns, about prepositions, or about the conventional uses of the objective case? How can a teacher explain the punctuation of phrases and clauses in a series if students do not know what phrases and clauses are? When a person says, "I done pretty good in the test today," that student expresses a thought with absolute clearness – but clearness is not enough. How can this speaker learn to make the statement in a more generally acceptable form, and how can a teacher help, if the speaker does not have some understanding of verb forms in current usage or of the accepted use of adjectives and adverbs? A knowledge of grammatical terms will at least provide a common ground of explanation between students and instructor, and a mutual understanding of the technical vocabulary involved is the first requirement in the explanation of any procedure.

The Parts of Speech or Word Classes

Words are classified according to their *function* or *use in the sentence* into what are called parts of speech. Notice that in this system of classification it is the word's use in the sentence that determines which part of speech it is. Many words, especially those that have been in the language for a long time, have acquired several uses, just as they have acquired many meanings. In your dictionary, look up a few simple, everyday words that occur to you as you glance about the room: *glass, floor, wall.* You can immediately think of such uses as *the glass in the window, you live in a glass house, we glassed in our porch,* and you have used the word *glass* as a noun, as an adjective, and as a verb. Now make the same test for *floor* and *wall.*

The parts of speech are *nouns, pronouns, verbs, adverbs, adjectives, prepositions, conjunctions,* and *interjections.*

THE NOUN

A *noun,* also called a *substantive,* is a word that names something. It may name a person, a thing, a place, an animal, a plant, an idea, a quality, a substance, a state, an action. Use each of the following properly in sentences and try to determine under which classification each noun falls: *man, lion, city, oak, book, liquids, beauty, affection, flight, stupor, relativity.* When a noun names a person, a place, or an object, it is called a *concrete noun;* when it names a quality, an idea, or a mental concept, it is called an *abstract noun.* Concrete nouns name physical, visible, tangible objects; abstract nouns name things that do not have a physical substance. For the practical value of this information, see §§ 21, 24, 26. A proper noun is the name of some individual person, place, or object; a common noun names any one of a class or kind. In English, proper nouns are capitalized; common nouns are not. See § 8.

Nouns

I was looking for a four-letter *word* for "narrow *path*,"
when I heard high *heels* on the *stairs*. High *heels* usually
means *business* for me rather than for *Dr. Bushmill*, the
chiropodist. With *men* on the *stairs*, it was only guessing. I
put away the *newspaper* in time to see a fuzzy *silhouette*
through the frosted *glass* of the *door* hesitate for a *moment*
before knocking. I called "Come in already!" and she did.

She was the sort of *woman* that made you wish you'd
stayed in the *shower* for an extra *minute* or taken another
three *minutes* shaving. I felt a little underdressed in my own
office. She had what you could call a tailored *look*.
Everything was so understated it screamed. I could hear
the *echo* bouncing off the *bank* across the *street*.

– Howard Engel, *The Suicide Murders*

THE VERB

A *verb* is a word (or group of words) that expresses action,
occurrence, being, or mode of being. See § 3 and § 6.

Verbs

The bells *jingled* louder, and a thin reedy voice *drifted*
through the doors. "Ho-ooooo, ho-ooooo, ho-ooooo!"

This asthmatic wheeze, sounding like a forlorn cry for
help, *was* my first communication from Santa Claus. There
was something in it that *made* me shiver, but the excitement
swelled as the older kids *slipped* off their chairs and *stood*
peering toward the door. The handle *rattled* and the door
swung open. There *was* a general surge and cheer. I *climbed*
on the seat, the better *to see* the happy old saint, clutching
his bottle of Coca-Cola. I *had* a moment of delirious vision
in which everything I ever *needed* and *wanted flashed* into
view at once. This ecstasy *passed*; my eyes *cleared*.

A skinny little dwarf *stood* in the doorway. I *thought* it
was one of the elves *scouting* the hall, until I *saw* the lumpy
potato sack he *was lugging* behind him. It *was* Santa Claus,
but he *had been beaten* and *starved*. His red suit *was tattered*

and full of moth holes. His stomach *didn't shake* like a bowl
of jelly at all, but *hung* like a wet dishrag. His boots, the
big, polished, black leather boots, *had become* scuffy old
rubbers which barely *came* up to his ankles. His pants
bagged everywhere.

But the worst *was* not the costume. For some crazy
reason, he *had covered* his beaming face with a
putrid-looking mask the colour of stale bologna. Maybe,
I *thought*, he *was suffering* from frostbite.

> – Ken Mitchell, ''You Better Not Pout''

THE PRONOUN

A *pronoun* is usually defined as a word that takes the place of a
noun. And, like a noun, it can be called a *substantive*. This brief
definition, useful enough as a practical shortcut, must be modified by pointing out that certain pronouns, such as *none*, *nobody*,
anything, and the impersonal *it*, do not take the place of any
noun but are words more or less arbitrarily classified by gram-
marians and lexicographers as pronouns. Pronouns are further
classified as personal, demonstrative, relative, interrogative, and
indefinite. See §4. The following table indicates how certain
words usually function in these classes. It must be understood,
however, that some of these words may also be used as other
parts of speech.

Personal
I, you, he, she, it, they, we, thee, thou

Demonstrative
this, that, these, those

Relative
who, which, what, that, whoever, whatever, whichever

Interrogative
who, which, what

Indefinite
one, none, some, any, anyone, anybody, someone, each,
somebody, nobody, everyone, everybody, either, neither, both

THE ADJECTIVE

An *adjective* is a word that modifies (describes or limits) a noun or pronoun. It may denote quality, quantity, number, or extent. The articles *a*, *an*, *the*, and the possessive forms of nouns and pronouns, when used to modify nouns, are here considered as adjectives. Pronouns have two forms of the possessive: the first form (*my*, *our*, *your*, *her*, *his*, *its*, *their*), when placed before a noun, functions as an adjective; the second form (*mine*, *ours*, *yours*, *his*, *hers*, *theirs*) functions as a pronoun.

Adjectives

On *first* arrival the city has so awed him that even the most *elementary* precautions are avoided; the *immense* crowds praying outside the mosques, which are themselves jammed at the *prayer* hours with the *earlier* and the more *powerful* faithful; the river in its *wide*, *brown November* confluence; the *paved* and *sloping* banks stacked up with *grenabia* pots and slabs of *mined* salt from Taoudenni which resemble marble; the women who have freed *their upper* bodies from *their* cloths as they wash *their* family or *their master*'s clothing in the *thin* and now *sudsfoamed* space between the *paving* stones of the *slanting* bank and the *river* pirogues or the *large cargo* boats, powered by *old automobile* engines and roofed with *raffia* mats.

– David Godfrey, *The New Ancestors*

Pronoun

That horse of *mine* is a problem. May I borrow one of *yours* to get me back to the ranch?

THE ADVERB

An *adverb* is a word that modifies a verb, an adjective, or another adverb. Less commonly, an adverb modifies a preposition, a phrase, a clause, or a whole sentence. Adverbs express the following relations in a sentence: time, place, manner, degree, frequency, affirmation, or negation. See also § 5.

Time

It will rain *tomorrow.* The guests will *soon* be here. They are *now* arriving.

Place

Come *in.* Leave your umbrellas *outside.* Place them *here,* please.

Manner

She expresses herself *clearly.* Her sister sings *beautifully.* She learns *quickly.*

Degree

You are *very* kind. This is *too* good. It is *entirely too* expensive.

Frequency

She is *always* pleasant. She called *twice.* It rains *often.* It *never* snows.

Affirmation or Negation

Do *not* go there. *Certainly,* he will return. *Yes,* he was there. *No,* you can *not* see him. *Perhaps* he will call you. *Undoubtedly* he is busy.

THE PREPOSITION

A *preposition* is a word that links a noun or pronoun, called the object of the preposition, and some other part of the sentence. Many prepositions are single, short words:

at the game, *by* the house, *in* the room, *for* payment, *from* home, *off* duty, *on* land, *above* the clouds, *after* the concert, *around* her neck, *before* dawn, *behind* his back, *between* dances, *below* the covering, *over* the top, *through* the skin, *until* daybreak

There are also a number of so-called group prepositions, the use of which you can readily see:

by means of, in front of, on account of, in place of, with respect to, according to, because of, in addition to, in spite of.

See page 97 for a discussion of prepositions and phrases.

THE CONJUNCTION

A *conjunction* is a word that connects words, phrases, or clauses. Conjunctions are either co-ordinating or subordinating. Adverbs used as connectives, either co-ordinating or subordinating, are called *conjunctive adverbs.*

The words commonly used as co-ordinating conjunctions are *and, but, for, or, nor, yet, both – and, not only – but also, either – or, neither – nor.* In contemporary usage, *so* is used as a co-ordinating conjunction in loose, informal writing and in speech, but its use should be avoided in serious writing.

Some of the words used as subordinating conjunctions are *if, although, though, that, because, since, so that, in order that, as, unless, before, than, where, when.*

Correlative conjunctions (conjunctions used in pairs) are *both – and, not only – but also, either – or, neither – nor.*

Some words commonly functioning as adverbs may be used as conjunctions: *how, why, where, before, after.* Such connectives as *however, therefore, nevertheless, hence,* and *accordingly* are often classified as conjunctive adverbs. In modern prose they are commonly used as transitional expressions. There is no profit in worrying about whether they are transitional or conjunctive adverbs; the only important fact is that in modern writing these expressions, with the exception of *hence, thus,* and *still,* are usually not placed at the beginnings of clauses in compound sentences. They function more accurately when they are set within the clauses. See § 14 for a discussion of the punctuation that should be used with these transitional expressions.

THE INTERJECTION

An *interjection* is a word or group of words used to express sudden or strong feeling. Note that an exclamation point is not the inevitable punctuation of an interjection. For most interjections, especially the mild ones, a comma or a period is sufficient. Examples are *Ah, Oh, How . . . .*

The Verbals

The *verbals* – gerunds, participles, and infinitives – are mutations derived from verbs. They have some of the forms and functions of verbs, but they serve primarily as other parts of speech. Like verbs, they may have tense forms, they may take complements, and they may be modified by adverbs. Their primary function, however, is to serve as nouns, adjectives, and adverbs.

THE GERUND
A *gerund* is a verbal used as a noun.

> The man began *shouting* incoherently. [Note that *shouting* is the object of the verb *began*. It is modified by the adverb *incoherently*.]

> *Writing* a poem is not easy. [*Writing* is the subject of the verb *is*, and has *poem* as its object.]

> His eligibility for office was established by his *having been* so successful as union representative. [Note the form of the gerund. Note also that it takes the adjective *successful* as its complement.]

THE PARTICIPLE
A *participle* is a verbal used as an adjective. It is, of course, also used as a part of a verb phrase, as in "He *was reading* a book." It may appear in an adverbial sense, as in "They came *bringing* gifts" or "The boys ran off, *shouting* protests." The main concern here, however, is with the adjective use of the participle: "*driving* rhythm; *framed* picture." Note also such sentences as "He *was asking* you a question" and "Teasing her was *asking* for trouble," in which *asking* is part of the verb phrase in the first combination and a gerund in the second.

> The *overworked* men again faced the *howling* wind. *Gripping* the rope, they slowly pulled the *mired* truck past the *waiting* soldiers. They noted a staff car *turning* in their direction. *Having saved* the truck, they relaxed for a moment. [Note the tense forms and the positions of the participles.]

THE INFINITIVE

An *infinitive* is a verbal that may be used as a noun, an adjective, or an adverb. The infinitive may be recognized by its sign *to*. Occasionally the sign is omitted.

Mary did not want *to drive* her car. [Used as a noun object of the verb *did want*. Note that it takes an object.]

Mary hoped *to be taken* home. [Note the passive form.]

We did not dare *refuse* her request. [Note the omission of the sign *to*.]

She had no car *to drive*. [Used as an adjective to modify *car*]

She was happy *to come* with us. [Used in an adverbial sense to modify *happy*]

To *watch* her happiness was a pleasure. [Used in a noun sense, as subject of verb *was*]

In this last instance the infinitive can replace or be replaced by its participle, as in "*Watching* her happiness was a pleasure." Note, however, that the meaning changes slightly.

EXERCISES

EXERCISE 1, PARTS OF SPEECH AND VERBALS. *Identify the parts of speech and the verbals in the following selections:*

Public sentiment was unsettled and often confused – unsettled over the prospect of foreigners coming to Canada and confused by endless and tiresome debates over refugees, displaced persons, immigration policy, manpower needs and ethnic selectivity. In all, questions outnumbered answers, and a May 1946 editorial in the *London Free Press* posed yet another: "Have We a Policy?" – the paper was not sure, and time, it warned, was working against any fruitful debate. "We must," the *Free Press* demanded, "make up our minds what course we are to

follow, and we must do it soon. Are we, as Prime Minister
King suggested, not to consider any new immigration policy
until all Canadians are employed? Can we agree on what
constitutes full employment? Is there employment if there
are jobs available, but at wages which are not acceptable?
Must we agree on this before admitting immigrants?''

— Irving Abella and Harold Troper, *None is Too Many*

One of my first discoveries in Cape Breton was that we
lived on earth. Before that I certainly knew we had earth.
Earth was something you put things on or, conversely, it
was something that had things on it. Generally you put
pavement on top of earth – street pavement, schoolground
pavement, sidewalk pavement, driveway pavement,
parking lot pavement. Earth was black and dirty. There
was lots of it.

The first intimations I had that we actually lived on
earth occurred during the drive with my Uncle Phil from
Sydney Airport to the village – that unnerving sense of
space as we drove towards the northern end of the island; of
the earth curving under the sky. It's a sensation that can't
be felt in the city. There's too much clutter, too many
objects.

Earth isn't an easy feeling to get used to. At the
beginning I was dogged by the feeling that Grandfather
should have surrounded the house with trees and hedges;
that there should be something to disguise the earth. It was
unsettling. Earth should be like it is in the city, covered
and placed delicately out of sight, to be glimpsed at
occasionally while gardening. Yet, as the summer passed,
I gradually outgrew my fear of living on earth. I'm not sure
how it happened, only that it happened slowly. It had
something to do with learning to expect distances in front
of your eyes, to expect to be able to let your line of vision
sweep along the coastline for miles and miles, or to look
across fields up to the summer pastures and from there to
the green mountains before your eyes met the blueness of
the sky. It had something to do with lying in the grass on
Sunday afternoon and swearing you could feel the earth
slowly revolving beneath your back. It had something to do

with hummocky pasture grass. It had something to do with
the picked over barnyard and the green fields of timothy.
Earth.

– Clive Doucet, *My Grandfather's Cape Breton*

EXERCISE 2, VERBALS. *Identify the verbals in the following
sentences. The verbals are gerunds, participles, and infinitives.*

1. Attending a boat christening is fun; I usually like to go.
2. Being a devoted bowler, John has his average to consider.
3. Lorna, a tired and harried stockbroker, tries to avoid being
   involved in charity telethons.
4. Arriving late, still absorbed in his chess game, Carl tries to be
   courteous to a roomful of relatives without revealing that he is
   unable to recall a single name.
5. Having finished milking the cow, Larry retreats to his cabin.
6. One day Jean took my protesting brother to church to watch
   two strangers being married.
7. The night being hot and muggy, we sat there sweltering as we
   listened to the concert.
8. Wishing to avoid an argument, the officer pretended to be
   enjoying himself as Tommy kicked his shins.
9. Sitting in the next row were two old and respected friends
   dressed in gorilla suits.
10. Having bowed politely, the butler began to study the expressions
    on the faces of the assembled guests.

The Elements
of the Simple Sentence

A sentence may be thought of as a unit of related words that
begins with a capital letter and ends with a period, question
mark, or exclamation mark.

I like ice cream.

Defined grammatically, a *sentence* is a basic unit of language that has at its core a subject and a predicate. It nearly always provides two pieces of information that users of language expect to learn: who or what is doing something (subject), and what he, she, or it is doing (predicate).

She laughed.

On the basis of the types of clauses (co-ordinate or subordinate) that form their structure, sentences are classified as *simple*, *complex*, or *compound*.

The following sentence diagrams are included to help you identify the main parts of a sentence. In a simple sentence the parts are referred to as *subject* and *verb*, and the diagram divides them in the following way.

S | V

A sentence containing a *direct object* looks like this in diagram form:

S | V | O

Addition of an *indirect object* is signified in the following way:

S | V | O
\ IO

Subjective and *objective complements* (see pages 95–96) are identified by slanted lines:

S | V \ SC

S | V / OC

Articles, adjectives, prepositions, and other *modifiers* are indicated by slanted lines below the main line:

Whenever a *phrase* is *subject* or *object* in the sentence, it is represented by the following symbol:

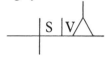

THE INDEPENDENT CLAUSE

The independent clause is another basic unit of grammar that should be understood now to avoid confusion later. An *independent clause* is a group of words that contains a subject and a verb, and whose meaning, like that of the average sentence, is complete. In fact, the independent clause constitutes the basic form of the sentence, and is often found as a sentence in its own right. The *simple sentence* may be defined as a single independent clause. The following examples are both sentences and independent clauses.

$$\text{S} \qquad \text{V}$$
People are working.

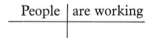

$$\text{S} \qquad \text{S} \quad \text{V}$$
Boys and girls play.

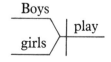

```
 S      S    V      V
```
Boys and girls laugh and shout.

COMPLEMENTS

Some verbs express a general action, and the sentences they help to form have a sense of completeness. Other verbs, however, require a third element – in addition to a subject and a verb – to form a complete thought. That element is called a *complement* (because it completes). There are three main types of complements: *direct objects*, *indirect objects*, and *subjective complements*. Less common are the *objective complement* and the *retained object*.

The Direct Object. The *direct object* of a verb denotes that which is immediately acted upon or receives the direct action of the verb.

```
   S      V      O
```
Mary bought a record.

```
   V      O
```
Read this book.

The Indirect Object. The *indirect object* names, without the use of a preposition, the one to whom or for whom the action involving a direct object is done.

Marilyn told *me* a story.

$$\begin{array}{c|c|c}
\text{Marilyn} & \text{told} & \text{story} \\
\hline
& \diagdown\text{me}
\end{array}$$

He taught *us* a lesson.
I gave the *dog* a bath.

Note that when *to* or *for* is expressed, the substantive following becomes the object of a preposition, as in "Marilyn told a story to me," "Dr. Jones taught mathematics to us," "She gave a dollar to the man."

The Subjective Complement. The *subjective complement* refers to the subject and describes or limits it. It is often called a *predicate substantive* if it is a noun or pronoun, and a *predicate adjective* if it is an adjective. See also § 5.

Tom is a *major* now. [Predicate substantive]

$$\begin{array}{c|c}
\text{Tom} & \text{is} \diagdown \text{major}
\end{array}$$

It looks *good* to me. [Predicate adjective]

$$\begin{array}{c|c}
\text{It} & \text{looks} \diagdown \text{good}
\end{array}$$

A common error committed by beginning writers is the misuse of adverbs for subjective complements. In the sentence above, "It looks *well* to me" would be incorrect – and sound pretentious as well. Verbs such as *seem, become, go, remain,* and *prove* often invite the misuse of an adverb complement. Verbs of the senses – *feel*, *look*, *smell*, *sound*, *taste* – also require adjective subjective complements.

>He felt *bad* about it. [not *badly*]

>It tastes *sour* to me. [not *sourly*]

>The air smells *foul* tonight. [not *foully*]

The Objective Complement. The *objective complement*, used with verbs such as *elect*, *choose*, *make*, *call*, *appoint*, and the like, refers to the direct object.

>They made her their *chairperson*.

$$\text{They} \mid \text{made} \diagup \text{chairperson} \mid \text{her}$$

>They called him *crazy*.

The Retained Object. The *retained object* is used with a verb in the passive voice.

>They were given *food*.

$$\text{They} \mid \text{were given} \mid \text{food}$$

>He was taught a good *lesson*.

A simple sentence may have adjectives, adverbs, and phrases as modifiers. Do not be confused by the number of these modifiers. Diagramming the sentence will help you to show it is still a simple sentence.

>The little boy gave his mother a red rose.

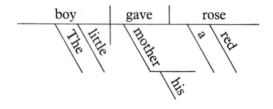

PHRASES

In a general, loose sense, a *phrase* is any group of words. Thus we say that a man "phrases his thoughts" when he puts them into words, or that a woman expresses her ideas in "well-balanced phrases" when her sentences are well built and rhythmical. The word *phrase* in this general sense has its legitimate place in the language. In the study of grammar, however, the word refers to a group of related words that is missing a subject or predicate. There are three kinds of phrases: the verb phrase, the prepositional phrase, and the verbal phrase.

The verb phrase, which is not discussed in this chapter, is actually a verb consisting of more than one word, such as *have been persuaded, has loved, will be honoured.*

The Prepositional Phrase. A *prepositional phrase* consists of a preposition, its object, and modifiers of the phrase or any of its parts.

A prepositional phrase may be used as an adjective.

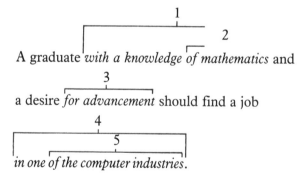

(Note that the first phrase modifies *graduate*, the second modifies *knowledge*, the third modifies *desire*, the fourth modifies *job*, and the fifth modifies *one*. Note also that the second phrase is a part of the first and the fifth is a part of the fourth.)

He must have studied several subjects *of no particular value.*
[The phrase, a modifier of *subjects*, has within it two modifiers. *Must have studied* is an example of a verb phrase.]

The father *of the child* [adjective] watched *from the window* [adverb].

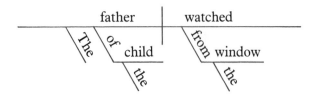

A prepositional phrase may be used as an adverb.

Slowly he walked *toward the door.* [The phrase functions as an adverb of place or direction, modifying the verb *walked.*]

She sat *on a stool* and selected a cherry *from the basket.*

If you are angry *at your best friend*, you must be careful *with your speech.* [Here the phrases function as adverbs modifying adjectives.]

Under the bridge two hikers had built a fire.

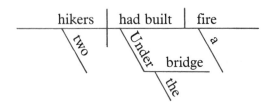

The Verbal Phrase. A *verbal phrase* consists of a participle, a gerund, or an infinitive and any complements and modifiers.

The Participial Phrase. A participial phrase consists of a participle, its complement, if it has one, and any modifiers of the phrase or any of its parts. It is generally used as an adjective. A thorough understanding of the uses of participial phrases is of practical value to any writer because their misuse results in a stylistic fault known as the *dangling modifier.* For a discussion of dangling modifiers, see §28.

The car *now turning the corner* belongs to my father. [The phrase modifies *car*. The participle *turning* is modified by the adverb *now*, and it has for its object the noun *corner*.]

The letter, *stamped and sealed*, lay on the table. *Distracted by the sudden noise*, the speaker hesitated and then stopped in mid-sentence. [Note the possible positions of the participle in relation to the word it modifies.]

Having given him the required amount, I left the store. [Notice that within the participial phrase there is another participle, *required*, modifying *amount*.]

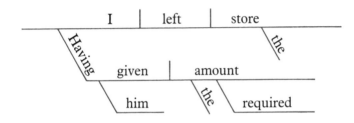

The Absolute Phrase. The absolute phrase is made up of a noun or pronoun (a substantive) followed by a participle. The substantive has no grammatical relation to any word in the sentence outside the phrase; it stands as an independent element. An absolute phrase cannot become a dangler. Note the following examples carefully.

Our assignment having been finished, we asked for our pay. [*Having been finished* modifies *assignment*.]

If the same thought is expressed as a participial phrase, "*Having finished our assignment*, we asked for our pay," it is no longer grammatically independent of the rest of the sentence. The assignment must have been finished *by* somebody or something that the remainder of the sentence is required to furnish, whereas in the absolute phrase it is simply given as finished by a person or persons unknown.

The class having been dismissed, the instructor wearily picked up his books. We walked toward the north, *each taking one side of the ridge*. [The substantive is *each*.]

The Gerund Phrase. A gerund phrase consists of a gerund, its complement, if it has one, and any modifiers of the phrase or any of its parts. A gerund phrase is always used as a noun; it may therefore function as the subject of a verb, as a complement, or as the object of a preposition.

Arguing with him does little good. *Piloting a speed boat* requires great skill. [In both sentences the gerund phrase is used as a subject. By this time you should be able to identify the modifiers and the complements.]

Willard enjoyed *watching television*. [Direct object]

You can get the address by *stopping at our house*. [Object of preposition]

I would call that *violating the spirit of our agreement*. [The phrase is used as an objective complement referring to *that*.]

Hearing that song brings back sad memories to me. [Subject of verb]

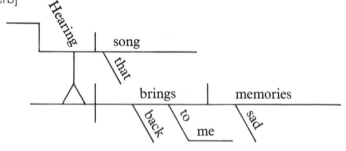

Mary objected to *my telling the story*. [Object of preposition]

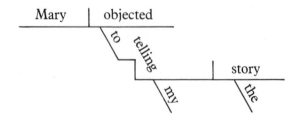

The Infinitive Phrase. An infinitive phrase, like other verbal phrases, may have a complement and modifiers. In addition it may have what is called the *assumed subject* of the infinitive. The assumed subject of an infinitive is in the objective case (see page 350). An infinitive phrase may be used as an adverb, an adjective, or a noun.

We stood up *to see better.* [Modifies the verb]

We are happy *to have you back with us.* [Modifies an adjective]

Whether to believe him or to call Taylor was a real problem for me. [A noun, used as the subject of the sentence]

We knew him *to be the worst troublemaker in school.* [Notice that the infinitive *to be* has *him* as its assumed subject. "We knew him; he was the worst troublemaker in school" puts an actual subject in place of the assumed one, and, incidentally, takes the sentence out of the *simple* class.]

My orders were *to deliver the guns.* [Noun used as subjective complement]

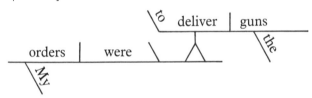

I am happy *to see you again.*

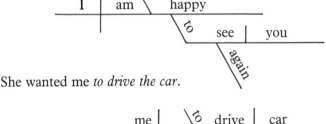

She wanted me *to drive the car.*

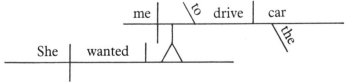

EXERCISES

EXERCISE 1, PARTICIPLES. *Pick out the participles in the following sentences and tell what word each participle modifies.*

1. The doctor's Porsche is a complicated machine.
2. Compressed to a minimum, my study is the size of a telephone booth.
3. In spite of its reduced area, it contains thousands of socks that don't match.
4. In it are over seven miles of extension cord winding back and forth.
5. Only a genius could design this amazing mess.
6. The designer was faced with several puzzling limitations, like walls and doors.
7. Every bit of needed clothing had to be identified with colour-coding.
8. Having succeeded in solving one problem, he soon faced another.
9. The completed arrangement of furniture meant finding room for a bed.
10. In addition this seemingly snarled and confused location had to allow for the presence of the designer.

EXERCISE 2, PARTICIPLES AND GERUNDS. *Pick out each gerund and participle in the following sentences and tell how each is used.*

1. Most students entering college enjoy being welcomed to a new experience.
2. Having been duly warned and advised, they return to their normal routines.
3. Some students, impressed and perhaps disturbed by the advice, resolve to become devoted scholars.
4. Urged on by curiosity, some begin exploring their new and exciting surroundings.
5. Finding old friends and making new contacts are in themselves rewarding experiences.

6. There are always a few lost, unhappy souls who, unable to make new friends, amuse themselves sadly by browsing in the library.

7. Some even think of writing home to surprised and pleased parents, thereby revealing their homesickness without actually admitting it.

8. The happiest are the extroverts, adjusted to life anywhere, taking life day by day as it comes and not worrying much about it.

9. Classes soon start, and then loneliness is forgotten in the excitement of meeting new professors, buying books, and getting a routine of studying established.

10. College life becomes a challenging adventure, demanding much from each student and giving much in return.

EXERCISE 3, PHRASES. *In the following sentences pick out each phrase and tell whether it is a prepositional, participial, gerund, or infinitive phrase.*

1. My sister urged me not to miss the concert.
2. I telephoned Pat early in the afternoon.
3. Thanking me warmly, Pat agreed to come with me.
4. Getting two tickets was the problem of the moment.
5. Knowing the condition of my bank account, I decided to get help from my friends.
6. A friend in need seems to be the only kind of friend that I have.
7. I found everyone in great need of financial help.
8. In despair I decided to test my sister's family loyalty.
9. She had a long sermon to give me, but in the end she agreed to help me.
10. Looking very relaxed, Pat added greatly to an evening of exciting music.

The Elements of
the Compound Sentence

A *compound sentence*, as the name indicates, is made by compounding or joining two or more simple sentences. The parts are of equal or *co-ordinate* grammatical weight. Each has its own subject and verb. Such joining may involve the use of conjunctions and proper punctuation. See §§ 13 and 14. The examples used here are shorter than typical compound sentences.

She should not take risks; she has three small children.
I warned her, but she was persistent.

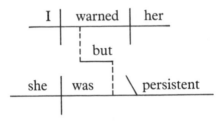

The walk was slippery, and she fell and hurt herself badly.

Note that the parts of a compound sentence must relate to each other. Do not make two independent sentences into a compound one. Your writing, however, will be smoother if two related thoughts are compounded rather than written as two separate sentences.

The Elements of
the Complex Sentence

A simple sentence is made up of one independent clause. A compound sentence is made up of two or more independent clauses. A complex sentence is made up of at least one independent clause and one or more dependent clauses. As you might guess from its name, a dependent clause depends on an independent clause for meaning.

"After I read the manuscript, I decided to take a holiday."

The independent clause, "I decided to take a holiday," is the main idea of the sentence (and if left on its own would be a simple sentence). "After I read the manuscript" is a secondary, or subordinate, idea and is therefore a dependent clause. It only has meaning because of its relation to the independent clause. Dependent clauses are commonly known as subordinate clauses. They may function as nouns, adjectives, or, as in this example, as adverbs. Because of their ability to express many differences in relationships between ideas, complex sentences, such as the one you are now reading, are very important for communicating complicated and precise thoughts.

In a complex sentence, the dependent clause is often joined to the main clause by a relative pronoun – *who, which,* or *that* – or by one of the numerous subordinating conjunctions – *after, although, because, as, before, if, since, unless, when, where, why.* Sometimes, however, these conjunctions are omitted, as in the following examples.

The progress [that] *they made in school* depended on the friends [whom] *they had found.*

I realized [that] *he had not understood the error* [that] *I had pointed out to him.*

The boy [whom] *he referred to* was the one who had begged, "Say [that] *it isn't so, mister!*"

The Noun Clause. A dependent clause may be used as a noun.

As Subject of a Verb
What he says means little to me.

As Object of a Verb
She thought *that she would go to Paris.*

As Subjective Complement
Her explanation was *that she was bored with life.*

As Object of a Verbal
Be sure to accept *whatever she offers you.*

As Object of a Preposition
It depends upon *how many can play Saturday.*

As an Appositive
His first argument, *that women are inferior to men,* was easily proved false.

Examples
What he told the officers was never revealed. [Noun clause used as subject]

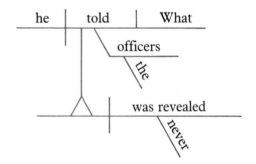

The teacher said *that the answer was correct.* [Noun clause used as direct object]

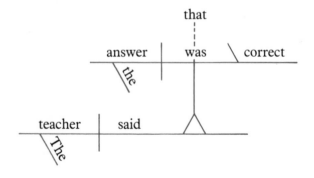

Give it to *whoever calls for it.* [Noun clause used as object of a preposition]

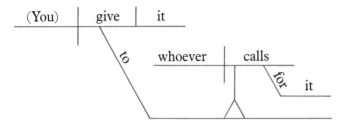

The Adjective Clause. A dependent clause may be used as an adjective. Adjective clauses are either restrictive or non-restrictive. An important thing to remember in this connection is that restrictive clauses are *not* set off by commas. See § 13.

Restrictive

We needed a car *that was rugged and light.*

Do you know anyone *who has two tickets to sell?*

A teacher *who speaks poor English* is badly handicapped.

Try to remember the exact time *when you saw the accident.*

Isn't this the shop *where you found your bargains?*

Non-restrictive

I have been reading *The Voice of Emma Sachs, which was written by D.M. Fraser.*

We camped that night near Peterborough, *where we saw some Indian drawings on stone.*

My father, *who is a lapidary,* was delighted with the find.

I am rooming with Joan Cooper, *who is now a producer.*

A restrictive clause helps to identify the word it modifies by pointing it out. The restrictive clause says, ''That particular person or thing and no other.'' In the group of sentences that use non-restrictive clauses, no identification is added. The person or thing is already identified, sometimes by name, sometimes by other means.

Note that if you are looking for structural signals to recognize clauses, the words *where*, *when*, and *why* may introduce adjective clauses. Think of them in terms of "place where," "time when," and "reason why," and you will not be confused. These three words, however, have other uses too. See the following examples.

Adjective Clauses

We found no reason *why he should be held.*

He was seen near the place *where the crime had been committed.*

It was the hour *when thieves and tired students prowl.*

This is the boy *who brought the papers.* [Adjective clause modifying boy]

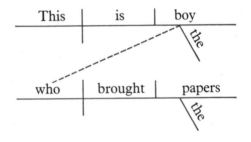

In the following examples, the words introduce clauses that are not adjectival.

Adverbial Clauses

You will begin writing *when I give the signal.* [Modifies will begin writing]

Put it back *where you found it.* [Modifies put]

Noun Clauses

We never did know *where he found it.* [Object of did know]

Why he went home is a mystery to me. [Subject of is]

The Adverbial Clause. The dependent clause may be used as an adverb to show time, place, cause, condition, concession, comparison, manner, purpose, or result.

Time

You must sit still *while the orchestra plays.*

Parents may come in *before the main doors are opened.*

He played professional lacrosse *until he was injured.*

After you finish your test, hand in your papers.

Place

I will go *where they send me.*

He hid *where no one thought to look.*

Cause

He grows roses *because he loves flowers.*

Since no one volunteered, Jane finished the work herself.

I can't go with you, *as that would be breaking my promise.*

Condition

If I were he I should invest in tax-exempt bonds.

Children will not be admitted *unless they are accompanied by their parents.*

In case you have no parents, any adult will do.

Concession

I agreed to go with her *although I was very tired.*

No matter what he says, I will not be angry.

Comparison

She is as dependable *as the rising sun.*

Jack is older *than I am.*

Manner

Marion looks *as if she were ready for bed.*

He speaks *as a tactful man should speak*.

Purpose

They came to the New World *in order that they might find religious freedom*.

Result

The night was so stormy *that we could not see the highway*.

Additional Examples

Carol is happier *than I am*. [An adverbial clause of comparison]

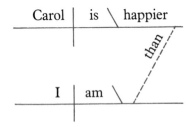

The whistle blew *before the ball was fumbled*. [An adverbial clause of time, modifying the verb *blew*]

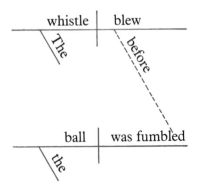

We found no reason why he should be held *until he is arraigned.*
[An adverbial clause modifying an adjective clause]

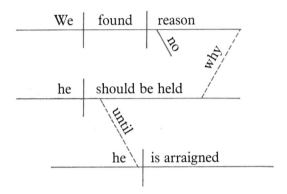

EXERCISES

EXERCISE 1, NOUN CLAUSES. *In the following sentences pick out each noun clause and tell whether it is used as the subject of a verb, as the complement of a verb or verbal, or as the object of a preposition.*

1. At noon they told me that I was selected to be the first to jump.
2. Why they handled the selection in such a way puzzled me at the time.
3. I forgot to tell them what my target was.
4. My assistant and I joked about what we had planned to do that night.
5. Then I remembered that my husband must be informed.
6. The starter wanted to show me what I should do with the timing watch.
7. Of course I realized that he was joking.
8. I had expected severe anxiety after the final count and the start.
9. That there was little nausea came as a pleasant surprise.
10. I announced that everything was going according to schedule.

EXERCISE 2, ADJECTIVE CLAUSES. *Pick out the adjective clauses in the following sentences and tell what word each clause modifies. Be able to tell which clauses are restrictive and which are non-restrictive.*

1. I have been reading books that tell about human rights.
2. One writer asserts there is no such thing as a natural right.
3. His contention, which I agree with, is that all rights are made by human beings.
4. I asked him where we got the rights that are mentioned in the Charter of Rights.
5. The author I speak of is a man whom my father knew at the University of Alberta.
6. He rubbed his chin with a gesture that indicated he was thinking deeply.
7. I understood the reason why he was careful about his choice of words.
8. "The rights you mention," he said, "are rights that people had to fight for."
9. We talked about the reasons why the Prime Minister called them inalienable.
10. It is a pleasure to know people with whom you can discuss ideas.

EXERCISE 3, ADVERBIAL CLAUSES. *Pick out the adverbial clause in the following sentences.*

1. The rain that had been threatening us all day came before we had finished our work.
2. We were working where the rocks had to be blasted out.
3. Because the traffic was heavy, we kept one lane of the road open.
4. Before each blast was set off, two workers waved the traffic to a halt.
5. Ashley, who was more experienced than I, told me what to do.
6. Although we had never had an accident, we worked under constant tension.
7. When the highway was clear, I pressed the handle down, and a long strip of roadway shuddered as if it were writhing in agony.

8. While the traffic waited, the bulldozers quickly shoved loose rocks off the open lane so that the cars and trucks could proceed again.
9. I think that some of the drivers were as relieved as we were.
10. While we were clearing off the rocks, the downpour came; soon the cut was so muddy that we had to stop work for the day.

The Problem of Sentence Effectiveness

Effective use of language does not always mean "correct" use of language. The explanation of a famous Confederate American general – "I git thar fustest with the mostest men" – is a famous formula for winning battles. It is not correct according to the standards of the educated speaker, the experienced, careful worker with words; but it is more effective, in the right place, than "I arrive on the scene first with the greater number of troops." Indeed, one might suspect the leader who used this alternative of being a desk-bound campaigner.

Is effectiveness, then, independent of correctness? Absolutely not. Those few happy accidents in which ignorance has stumbled upon a successful phrasing are too rare to count on as a principle to follow. Correctness comes first. Only when correctness is thoroughly understood can it be misused for the sake of effectiveness. Even then it will always risk looking just sloppy.

Correctness is important because it is universally functional. A misspelled word in a business letter or a misused verb in an interview can brand an otherwise able executive or professional person as careless and perhaps unreliable in his or her own field. Bad spelling and bad grammar show; educated people notice them immediately. Crudity in vocabulary or usage makes many people wince. In your own courses, many an otherwise excellent answer, test paper, or report may get a lower grade because of slips in spelling or grammar. Outside school, in industry, in business, in the professions, these mistakes can be even more damaging. It is no mystery, then, why correctness in language studies is emphasized.

To be realistic about effectiveness, as distinguished from correctness, it should be acknowledged that for most routine occasions "correct" writing is good enough. The concern of this section is with students who are not satisfied with merely "correct" writing, students who are disturbed that although they write correctly and honestly, they are nevertheless ineffective communicators.

Remember that diction is important. The words a writer uses should be exact, fresh, alive. Picture-making words are better than vague, general words. A fresh perspective can flavour a style. Humour can lighten and liven it. Even such devices as spacing on the page and the use of properly opaque paper are important.

Effective writing also depends on the grouping or arrangement of words in sentences – not exclusively, of course, because no skilful juggling of poorly chosen words can make effective sentences. The first thing to examine is sentence unity.

Sentence Unity

The completeness or unity of a sentence is based on its content and on its structure. Because the sentence is a grammatical unit of great variety and flexibility, there is no sure-fire rule to follow for sentence unity. Rather, the problem of sentence unity, which is primarily one of "not enough" or "too much," can be solved only by the good sense of the writer, who can be the only judge of when "not enough" becomes "complete," and when "complete" becomes "too much."

NOT ENOUGH IN THE SENTENCE

Often there is "not enough" in a sentence when the writer fails to describe, narrate, or explain exactly what is happening. In such weak sentences there are either too few details or the wrong ones. Like a jury trying to make a decision about an accused, readers need to have enough evidence about the crime. Here is the opening paragraph of a student essay about a first accident:

> Not being careful can lead to a lot of trouble, especially in driving a car. One of the most terrifying experiences in driving a car is having an accident. This happened to me last summer.

The first sentence may be sound advice, but its tone could easily turn readers away, since it is the kind of advice – "Be careful when crossing the street" – that people tend to tune out. The second sentence is a better opening for the essay, yet it is unconvincing without some feel for the experience itself. Consider this alternative: "The sound of screeching brakes, the odour of leaking antifreeze, the jolt of a straining seat belt – these are the frightening sensations of an automobile accident." Although we may not want to be at the scene, the writer has placed us there by means of skilful description. It may then be right to go on to say something about how the victim thought such an experience could only happen to someone else. Isn't this a feeling that could be shared by most readers? The third sentence might then begin: "Last summer I discovered not only that such a frightening thing could happen, but also that I could do little to prevent it." In the present state of the first paragraph, the writer does not really tell much about the accident. More details about the surprise and disorientation involved in the experience would transform these "not enough" sentences into "complete" ones.

Obviously, a sentence is "not enough" when it is not grammatically complete; that is, when it does not have an expressed or implied subject and verb or a required object. For a discussion of sentence fragments see §1.

TOO MUCH IN THE SENTENCE

A sentence may have "too much" in several ways. First, two unrelated ideas of the same weight and importance may be thrown together to make a compound sentence. The proper cure for this sort of fault is subordination. Second, a sentence may appear bulging and baggy from having too many related minor details thrown into it. Finally, a sentence may lack unity because the writer tossed into it some unrelated minor detail.

Unrelated Details
The library, old and dusty and well lit with bright new fixtures, was a melancholy place to work. ["Melancholy" seems related to "old and dusty" but not to the new lighting.]

Unified
The library, though well lit with new fixtures, was old and dusty and a melancholy place to work.

Unrelated Details
After the Liberals won power, foreign takeovers, which had been common in Europe for many years, were carefully scrutinized. [If the sentence is about Canada, the reference to the situation in Europe is merely thrown in. If it is part of a contrast between Canada and Europe, it might be acceptable.]

Unified
After the Liberals won power, foreign takeovers were carefully scrutinized.

Unrelated Details
The good sense of the director, who is a corpulent individual, is respected by all who know him. [His good sense has nothing to do with his shape.]

Unified
The good sense of the director is respected by all who know him.

Overloading a sentence with details can obscure its meaning and destroy its clearness and order. If the details are important, they should be told in separate sentences where they can be given proper value. If they are unimportant, they may be omitted.

Confused
Military training teaches people to stand up straight and walk with their heads up; this helps in future life because it becomes a habit and so many people have the bad habit of walk-

ing stooped and this leads to poor health and poor appearance.

Military science teaches also common courtesies, not only to your superior officers but to everyone to whom courtesy is due; for instance when you enter offices, or the courtesies you should use when you are using firearms while hunting or shooting in the presence of another person.

The remedy for sentences like these is a return to the first principles of communication: say one thing at a time; say it as simply and clearly as possible; say it so that it cannot be misunderstood.

What does the reconstruction suggest the writer meant to say in these sentences?

Revised

Military training teaches people to stand erect and to walk with their heads up. [That is enough for one sentence.] Good posture [Is that what the writer meant by "this" and "it"?] becomes habitual. It leads directly to better health and better appearance.

Military science also teaches common courtesy, not only to officers superior in rank but to everyone. [Are there some persons to whom "courtesy is not due"?] For instance, it teaches one how to enter an office, or how to handle firearms with safety to others. [These two examples are so badly chosen that no sentence can make them apt or congruous.]

Uses of Subordination: Sentence Combining

The phrase "sentence combining" is now popular among teachers and theorists of composition. Its popularity can be traced to the ease with which the phrase is used to illustrate the more traditional concepts of co-ordination and subordination. By means of artful combining, the beginning writer can achieve greater sentence variety, placing main ideas in main clauses and subordinating ideas in dependent clauses and phrases.

Many student writers find subordination difficult because from their earliest days of speaking they have fallen into the habit of co-ordinating ideas by using the conjunction *and*. Think of how many times you have heard reports like this one: "We drove to the river and brought out the cooler and it started to rain and we played volleyball. . . ." In that fast-moving convoy of facts there is no distinction among the various details; all of the events appear to have happened consecutively and to have had the same impact on the speaker. But because rain fell, the picnic and the volleyball game had to be postponed, unless the picnickers ate and played in the rain. They may have done just that, but the reader cannot tell from the account. The order and significance of events may be clarified by the artful use of subordination: "After we arrived at the river and unloaded the cooler, the rains came, delaying lunch and the volleyball game for about an hour." Now we have a clear picture of the episode, with the rain falling where it ought to fall.

Excessive use of co-ordination or of short declarative sentences can also cause problems of emphasis. Unclear or shifted emphasis in a sentence will make your reader wonder whether you are a trustworthy guide for the journey. Practice will help you find your way along the trail. Let us try arranging the details in the following sentences to illustrate the importance of proper emphasis.

My car is light blue.

My car is an '82 Ford.

My car has an automatic transmission.

My car was in an accident last Thursday.

A standard rewriting might read: "My car, a light blue, '82 Ford with an automatic transmission, was in an accident last Thursday." The main idea is that the car was in an accident. Although no one would write the improbable sentence that follows, it demonstrates how important the decision about the main idea is: "My car, a light blue '82 Ford involved in an accident last Thursday, has an automatic transmission." Unless this writer is trying to be satiric, he or she has subordinated the main piece of information and given independence to a trivial detail. Most readers would want out of this essay at the first stop sign.

It is possible to emphasize equally important details through subordination. You may write "My car, an '82 Ford, is sleek and fast" or "My car, sleek and fast, is an '82 Ford." The decision is yours and depends on the sentence's purpose in context. Either of these alternatives would be better than separate declarative sentences or a co-ordinate sentence (i.e., two independent clauses joined by *and*).

EXERCISES

EXERCISE, SENTENCE COMBINING. *The following sets of sentences can be rewritten as one sentence by using the techniques of subordination. In each rewrite you should compose a complex sentence with a major clause and subordinate clauses or phrases.*

1. The little boy was lost in the woods.
   He wandered away from home on Friday.
   He slept on the cold ground all night.
   He was found early Saturday morning.
   He was dirty and shivering but alive.
2. Tony has a powerful serve.
   I usually can't return it.
   My only hope of beating him is to tire him out.
   I hit many drop shots and lobs.
3. His cigarette was lighted.
   It dropped behind the cushions.
   The sofa burst into flames.
   No one escaped alive.
4. She knows what is required to be a good doctor.
   Physicians have to be intelligent.
   They must work long hours.
   They have to be humane and sensitive.

5. The movie was a flop.
   It was too long.
   The dialogue was stilted and unrealistic.
   There was no action to speak of.

ACCURACY AND VARIETY

Combining sentences is important for developing style in your writing. For this reason you should also be aware of the ways in which clauses and phrases can be arranged to arrive at greater accuracy and variety. Here are some examples of sentence elements that will help you in becoming a successful sentence combiner.

The Dependent Clause. By this time you should be familiar with the various types of dependent clauses and with the structural signals that show their dependence. In the following examples, does the revision improve the accuracy of expression, give unity to sentences, or relieve the monotony of too many clauses on the same level?

A. I well remember a strange conversation I had with a man once. This man was a friend of mine. He and I had served together in the army.
B. I well remember a strange conversation I once had with a friend of mine, with whom I had served in the army.

A. Do not be in too much of a hurry to join an organization. Study its membership before you join.
B. Before you join an organization, investigate its membership.

A. Diving suits are personalized garments. You must make many alterations on one of them. Otherwise it will not fit properly. In this respect it is like a bridal gown.
B. Because diving suits are personalized garments, you need to make more alterations on one of them to make it fit properly than you do on a bridal gown.

The Useful Participial Phrase. The substance of a co-ordinate clause may often be better expressed in a *participial phrase*.

Co-ordinate
My decision to enter college came suddenly, and I soon faced several obstacles.

Participial
Having made a sudden decision to enter college, I soon faced several obstacles.

But the participial phrase, useful as it is, contains several built-in dangers: it can become a dangler (see § 28); its overuse can produce a stiff, awkward style; and, if the wrong detail is subordinated, it can distort rather than clarify meaning. With these warnings in mind, study and analyse the following examples:

A. A law school or a medical school can be an essential part of a great university. Each school must be properly staffed and directed.

B. A law school or a medical school, if properly staffed and directed, can be an essential part of a great university. [Past participles]

A. I could not overcome my difficulty. I could not understand it.

B. Unable to understand my difficulty, I could not overcome it. [*Being* is understood before *Unable*.]

A. There was one problem not solved by the Ministry. This was how to widen the highway without moving the historic church.

B. The problem left unsolved by the Ministry was how to widen the highway without moving the historic church.

Gerund and Infinitive Phrases. Gerund and infinitive phrases may be used on occasion to gain economy and compactness in writing.

A. For three days she punished me. She refused to eat my desserts.

B. For three days she punished me by refusing to eat my desserts.

A. Their working hours were shortened. This resulted in more spare time for recreation and enjoyment.

B. Shortening their hours of work resulted in more time available for recreation and enjoyment. [Note how the vague *this* has been avoided.]

A. The housewife has children whom she must clothe. She must take care of them and worry about them. The married working woman often has all these duties and, in addition, must face the sometimes harsh demands of her job.

B. The housewife has children to clothe, to care for, to worry about; the married working woman often has all these duties and, in addition, must face the sometimes harsh demands of her job.

Conciseness: The Prepositional Phrase. A prepositional phrase may be used to express a detail more accurately and more concisely than a clause or a sentence.

A. We wrote our exams at separate tables. There was a proctor in front of us. Another one stood behind us.

B. We wrote our exams at separate tables, with one proctor in front of us and another behind us.

A. The professor repeated his instructions. It was to help those who came late.

B. For the benefit of the latecomers, the professor repeated his instructions.

A. The examination was over. Then the students got together and compared their answers.

B. After the examination the students got together to compare answers.

A. I turned in my exam. I did not stop to go over my answers.

B. I turned in my exam without a second glance at my answers.

Notice that in A of the preceding examples traits of informal conversation – shortened sentences, unsubordinated thoughts – stand out.

Compactness and Economy: The Single Word. A minor detail worth only a single word instead of a whole sentence or a clause is better expressed in a single word.

  A. There were two new girls, and they both wore green double-knit dresses that had short sleeves.
  B. The two new girls both wore short-sleeved green double-knit dresses.

  A. The house was old. The lawn around it was enclosed by yew hedges. These hedges were neatly clipped.
  B. The lawn around the old house was shut in by neatly clipped yew hedges.

Uses of the Appositive. Like clauses, phrases, and verbals, the appositive (i.e., a word or phrase that restates another word or phrase in terms that expand or define it) may be used to express details the writer wishes to subordinate. Consider this piece of autobiographical writing:

  A. I was born in Maple, Ontario. It's a small town. Most of the people in it are farmers. They raise cows for milk and a lot of apples. Still, it's the administrative centre of Vaughan Township.

Obviously this is a wordy passage that can be improved by the use of appositives:

  B. I was born in Maple, Ontario, a small dairy and apple-farming community and the administrative centre of Vaughan Township.

The following groups of sentences will further illustrate the resources of the appositive:

  A. Lutetium was discovered in 1905. It is a chemical element. It is one of the rare-earth elements. The name comes from *Lutetia*. In ancient days Paris was called that.

B. Lutetium, a chemical element, member of the rare-earth group, was discovered in 1905; its name was derived from *Lutetia*, the ancient name of Paris.

A. The custom of kissing under the mistletoe was once an old Druid religious ceremony. It is now a pleasant part of our Christmas.

B. The custom of kissing under the mistletoe, once an old Druid religious ceremony, is now a pleasant part of our Christmas.

A. Tony is a friendly sort of person, and he hasn't made an enemy in his life.

B. Tony, a friendly sort of person, has not made an enemy in his life.

To sum up the subject of subordination, two parallel versions of a paragraph are provided. The sentences in the second version use dependent clauses or phrases to give a more effective allocation of meaning and emphasis. As a result, the writing in the second paragraph should seem more mature, more sophisticated, more accurate in conveying different shades of meaning, and more pleasing in style.

Version A

The older generation of writers in Canada must have thought Mordecai Richler to be rather wild. He seemed wild in much the same way as Irving Layton had earlier and Leonard Cohen was promising to be. Richler's writing seemed brash. It was too proletarian. It made the more considered styles of Hugh MacLennan and Morley Callahan seem almost elegiac. But time plays funny tricks. Our speeded-up world doesn't wait around very long before playing them. The newer generation of writers think differently. To them, it's doubtless Richler's prose that seems elegiac. It invites comparison to the modes which they have all but abandoned. The new writers write in much more open, freely improvisational modes. This attitude does not stem from enmity. There is no new wave of artists who would like to see Richler's ship sink. Surely, no serious writer or reader can fail to appreciate the magnitude of his attempt to create a symphonic novel. Richler's novel contains the four movements and the many themes that weave congruently through the entire work. All must admire the animated writing with which he attempts to achieve a comic triumph of spirit over some grim modern realities. They respect the attempt. But it will doubtless be precisely the imposed superstructure from which a good many younger artists will flinch. They will find it an unnecessary burden to carry on their bent and straining backs. *Heavy, heavy* does hang over Mordecai Richler's typewriter.

Version B

For an older generation of writers in Canada, young Mordecai Richler must have seemed rather markedly a wild one in much the same way as the older Irving Layton and younger Leonard Cohen seemed also wild – then. And so he was – then. His brash, wrong-side-of-the-tracks writing rushes make the more considered styles of Hugh MacLennan and Morley Callahan seem almost elegiac. But time plays funny tricks, and in our speeded-up world doesn't wait around very long before playing them. To a newer generation of writers it's doubtless Richler's prose that seems elegiac, inviting comparison, not forward to the much more open, freely improvisational modes in which they work, but back to modes they have all but abandoned. This isn't enmity, a new wave of artists who would like to see Richler's ship sink. Surely, no serious writer or reader can fail to appreciate the magnitude of his attempt to create a symphonic novel, the four movements, the many themes that weave congruently through the entire work, the animated writing with which he attempts to achieve a comic triumph of spirit over some modern realities. But respect it as they may, it will doubtless be precisely the imposed superstructure from which a good many younger artists will flinch as being an unnecessary burden for any writer to carry on his bent and straining back. *Heavy, heavy* often does hang over his typewriter.

– Warren Tallman, "Need for Laughter"

Long and Short Sentences

Has the length of sentences much to do with effectiveness, as it has with style? Turn back to the last two selections, which you have just studied for subordination. Version A contains twenty short sentences; version B has only eight sentences, most of them fairly long. Both selections say essentially the same thing – but the first seems aimless, undeveloped, and at times is misplaced in emphasis.

Before you arrive at any hasty decision that a paragraph of long, complex sentences is more effective than a paragraph of short, simple ones, you should compare the ways in which two good writers choose to report similar moods of nostalgia and regret. The first writer composes her piece in short sentences.

> But for me it is different. Now the wind in the casuarina trees is only a wind. The drums at night are only men pounding on skins stretched over wood. The Drummer of all the world is gone. He no longer drums himself, for me. A spider is only an insect, and not the child of Ananse. A deserted hut on the shore is only a heap of mud and dried palm leaves. Death no longer keeps such a simple establishment.
>
> I shall be leaving soon. Leaving the surf that stretches up long white fingers to clutch the brown land. The fetid village enclosed and darkened by a green sky of over-hanging palm trees. The giant heartbeat of the night drums. The flame tree whose beauty is suddenly splendid – and shortlived – like the beauty of African women. The little girl dancing with her shadow in the stifling streets. The child sleeping, unmindful, while flies caress his eyes and mouth with the small bright wings of decay. The squalor, the exultation, the pain. I shall be leaving it all.
>
> But – oh Kwabena, do you think I will ever forget?
>
> – Margaret Laurence, "The Drummer of All the World"

Notice how differently another writer says almost the same thing, ''This is the place and the people that I loved. I shall miss them and remember them always.''

> When I look at it with its fading areas of colour and its too-perfect lettering I remember Dr. Galill and Miss Menzies, the way they were that last day when they waved goodbye to us from the wooden railroad platform at Gimli.
>
> It was just turning dusk, a warm, late summer dusk. We had boarded the train, found seats, and my mother had settled us around her. Just outside the window Miss Menzies and Dr. Galill stood waving to us. As the train began to heave and creak out of the station, the smell of lake water and sand came to me through the glass like something alive. We were losing it, losing it!
>
> Without knowing why, I felt frantic. I wanted to lean out of the window and to shout that I was sorry to Dr. Galill, sorry that I didn't think he was handsome. And to Miss Menzies I wanted to cry out that I didn't mean to ask her about George, really, I never meant to ask! But the train was moving and wouldn't stop, and the weak light of the sun hit Miss Menzies' hair and made it glow for the last time, blue-green like peacock feathers.
>
> – Miriam Waddington, ''Summer At Lonely Beach ''

Notice that out of the seventeen sentences in the Laurence selection, eight contain ten or fewer words and three others contain twelve or fewer. Some of them are incomplete sentences since Laurence is obviously trying to give the effect of many memories and impressions going through the mind of her character, who at the end of a long stay in a foreign country regrets leaving it. In the Waddington selection, most of the sentences are longer than thirteen words; the longest is forty words long. The occasional use of a short sentence breaks up the pattern – and does so with dramatic effect. There is a complex mood here, as the image of the adults on the platform waving goodbye is contrasted with the urgency of the child-narrator's feeling. Both writers, however, successfully convey a feeling of loss and regret.

Variations in Order

Sentences should fit the thoughts they contain, or, as in the preceding examples, the mood they are creating. Most sentences, without any conscious effort on the writer's part, fall into a regular pattern: subject – verb – complement. This pattern is not sacred; it can be changed to make a statement more exact or more attractive by inverting the elements or shifting any modifiers, but it should be left alone unless there is something to be gained by tampering with it. The following pairs of sentences illustrate changes of emphasis created by varying the word order.

A. They elected him their president. [Now change the basic S – V – C order.]
B. Him they elected their president. [What word is emphasized here?]
A. All six hundred rode into the valley of death. [Normal order]
B. All into the valley of death rode the six hundred. [Note the change of emphasis because of the inversion.]

It is relatively easy to throw modifiers around *(the cry was loud – loud was the cry)* or to shift from the active to passive voice *(Susan hit me – I was hit by Susan)*, but an alternative order should not hinder the linking of one sentence to another. The following paragraph shows how well variety and coherence can be achieved when the writer keeps clearly in mind the central idea of the paragraph.

> At the same time the authors of the charter have pointedly exempted such things as the family and property rights from protection. The minute property rights are conspicuously overlooked, the most fundamental plank in the structure of individual liberty is removed. The enjoyment of property provides the only tangible basis for an individual to arrange his life independently of the whims of the state. This is true for rich and poor alike. Property rights are probably least important for the intellectuals, professionals, and civil-servant classes who

may own a lot of "property" in terms of technical skills. Property rights are most important for those who, lacking great accomplishments of skill or education, can only rely on the house, land, restaurant or little work-shop they may have acquired through hard work and prudence to guarantee the independence of their existence.

– Barbara Amiel, "Danger in the Chains of Freedom"

Loose and Periodic Sentences

A *periodic sentence* is a complex sentence in which the main clause comes at the end, such as "Just as the technicians were locking the hatch in place, one of the bolts broke." A *loose sentence* is a complex sentence in which the main clause comes first, followed by dependent clauses and other modifying elements, such as "I realized that I had discussed the wrong topic only after I had handed in my paper." Short sentences are often periodic; long sentences tend to be loose. Since the mind grasps the thought of a short sentence, or even of a moderately long one, quickly, it is only in long sentences that periodic structure has any noticeable psychological effect.

The periodic sentence builds suspense. It tends to hold up the meaning until the end, to force the reader to consider first the various details on which the main thought is based. It makes him or her wait. Overused periodic structure is a little like someone at a party cornering you and telling you every detail of a European holiday.

Notice in the following paragraph how a skilful writer combines the two types of complex sentences. In writing, the occasional conscious change from a loose to a periodic sentence, like tightening the belt, helps keep things from dragging.

In a culture like ours, long accustomed to splitting and dividing all things as a means of control, it is sometimes a bit of a shock to be reminded that, in operational and practical fact, the medium is the message. [Periodic] This is merely to say that the personal and social consequences of any medium – that is, of any extension of ourselves – result from the new scale that is introduced into our affairs by each extension of ourselves, or by any new technology. [Loose] Thus, with automation, for example, the new patterns of human association tend to eliminate jobs, it is true. [Simple: periodic effect] That is the negative result. [Simple] Positively, automation creates roles for people, which is to say depth of involvement in their work and human association that our preceding mechanical technology had destroyed. [Loose] Many people would be disposed to say that it was not the machine, but what one did with the machine, that was its meaning or message. [Loose] In terms of the ways in which the machine altered our relations to one another and to ourselves, it mattered not in the least whether it turned out cornflakes or Cadillacs. [Periodic] The restructuring of human work and association was shaped by the technique of fragmentation that is the essence of machine technology. [Loose] The essence of automation technology is the opposite. [Simple: periodic effect] It is integral and decentralist in depth, just as the machine was fragmentary, centralist, and superficial in its patterning of human relationships. [Loose]

> – Marshall McLuhan,
> *Understanding Media: The Extensions of Man*

Parallel Structure and Balance

One of the rhetorical devices available to writers is known as the balanced or parallel construction. At its elementary level, the device is a thoroughly practical means of writing a graceful sentence by making a noun parallel with another noun, a gerund with another gerund, a phrase with another phrase, a clause with another clause.

Scattered
Choose a house that is spacious, with a good exposure to the

sun and that people like to look at. [An adjective, a phrase, a clause]

Parallel
Choose a house that is spacious, sunny, and attractive. [Three adjectives]

Scattered
I was glad to be there for the lecture and seeing how the models work. [A noun and a phrase]

Parallel
I was glad to be there for the lecture and the demonstration of models. [Two nouns]

Scattered
I have only one suggestion to make: cultivate friends who are loyal, have a cheerful disposition, and who are ambitious. [An adjective, a verb, and an adjective]

Parallel
I have only one suggestion to make: cultivate friends who are loyal, cheerful, and ambitious. [Three adjectives]

For a discussion of the "false parallel," see § 31.

Forced into service when it is not required to give wandering sentences focus, parallel structure becomes a conspicuous art. Carried too far it becomes a mannerism. Used judiciously, however, to fit thought and occasion, it will seldom reach the point of affectation. In his essay on studies, Francis Bacon deftly balances phrase with phrase without excess.

Reading maketh a full man;
conference a ready man; and
writing an exact man.

And therefore

if a man write little	he had need to have great memory;
if he confer little	he had need to have a present wit; and
if he read little	he had need to have much cunning,

to seem to know what he doth not.

Since Bacon's contemporaries not only tolerated, but admired rhetorical mannerisms, it is, perhaps, his restraint rather than his elaboration that is remarkable. You can find other examples of skilful parallelism in the work of present-day writers. Here is an example of balance in a passage by a well-known satirist:

> Tax Reform and the Family Income Security Plan would force the greedy to help the needy. The rich would pay their capital gains tax and so would the family farmer and the small businessman. The rich would not get their family allowance cheques and neither would the big city breadwinner making $10 500 a year. The Department of Regional Economic Expansion would persuade American business to open branchplants in the Maritimes and Quebec to replace the ones they'd just shut down in Ontario. Pensioners, widows, orphans and exports would be protected by the War Against Inflation. The dangers of radioactive economic fallout would be contained by the umbrella of a new unemployment insurance scheme.
>
> Should that not suffice, then labour-intensive manufacturing and processing industries would have their taxes cut and their new equipment and machinery given a speedy tax write-off. Should this result in the introduction of automated techniques and less jobs, there were always the joys of the Leisure Society which, like Prosperity, was just around the corner.
>
> – Larry Zolf, *The Dance of the Dialectic*

ANTITHESIS

Antithesis is another effective way of achieving balance in sentences. The device is a favourite of political speakers like Churchill: "This is not the end. It is not even the beginning of the end. But it is, perhaps, the end of the beginning"; "Never in the field of human conflict was so much owed by so many to so few." The second example vividly demonstrates balance by opposing "many" to "few." As with parallel structure, antithesis can be carried too far by the beginning writer striving to sound like a great orator. Remember that both devices tend to be more appropriate to speech-making than to the essays you are likely to write.

In the following selection, notice the varied and pleasing rhythm of loose and periodic sentences throughout, the frequent use of balance, and here and there the effective development of climax. Notice too how the argument, like the style in which it is presented, is both compelling and balanced.

The most obvious tension in the Canadian literary situation is in the use of language. Here, first of all, a traditional standard English collides with the need for a North American vocabulary and phrasing. . . . As long as the North American speaker feels that he belongs in a minority, the European speech will impose a standard of correctness. This is to a considerable extent still true of French in Canada, with its campaigns against "joual" and the like. But as Americans began to outnumber the British, Canada tended in practice to fall in with the American developments, though a good deal of Canadian theory is still Anglophile. A much more complicated cultural tension arises from the impact of the sophisticated on the primitive, and vice versa. The most dramatic example, and one I have given elsewhere, is that of Duncan Campbell Scott, working in the Department of Indian Affairs in Ottawa. He writes of a starving squaw baiting a fish-hook with her own flesh, and he writes of the music of Debussy and the poetry of Henry Vaughan. In English literature we have to go back to Anglo-Saxon times to encounter so incongruous a collision of cultures.

Cultural history, we said, has its own rhythms. It is possible that one of these rhythms is very like an organic rhythm: that there must be a period, of a certain magnitude, as Aristotle would say, in which a social imagination can take root and establish a tradition. American literature had this period, in the northeastern part of the country, between the Revolution and the Civil War. Canada has never had it. English Canada was first a part of the wilderness, then a part of North America and the British Empire, then a part of the world. But it has gone through these revolutions too quickly for a tradition of

writing to be founded on any one of them. Canadian
writers are, even now, still trying to assimilate a Canadian
environment at a time when new techniques of communication, many of which, like television, constitute a
verbal market, are annihilating the boundaries of that
environment. This foreshortening of Canadian history, if it
really does have any relevance to Canadian culture, would
account for many features of it: its fixation on its own past,
its penchant for old-fashioned literary techniques, its
preoccupation with the theme of strangled articulateness. It
seems to me that Canadian sensibility has been profoundly
disturbed, not so much by our famous problem of identity,
important as that is, as by a series of paradoxes in what
confronts that identity. It is less perplexed by the question
"Who am I?" than by some such riddle as "Where is here?"

> – Northrop Frye,
> "Conclusion" from *Literary History of Canada*

Repetition, Sound, and Rhythm

Balance, parallel structure, and opposition are, in a sense, forms
of repetition – repetitions primarily of phrasing or structure rather
than of words, although within balanced phrases words may be
repeated. Note this repetition in the quotation from Bacon on
page 131.

a full man	write little	he had need to have great memory
a ready man	confer little	he had need to have a present wit
an exact man	read little	he had need to have much cunning

Single words may be repeated for emphasis or for a smoother
rhythmic flow of sounds, quite apart from a balance of structural units, as you will notice in the following:

Ontario, *a place* to stand, *a place* to grow.
Everything in *nature* contains all the powers of *nature*.

Single words may also be used in contrasting pairs, achieving a flow of symmetrical phrases that gives the sentence a smooth rhythm and a structural balance:

Hope and despondency, joy and sorrow, pleasure and pain diversify life with their sudden contrasts.
I am Alpha and Omega, the beginning and the end, the first and the last.

EUPHONY

Good prose should be easy to read aloud. Pleasing audible effects depend partly on an avoidance of harsh sounds or combinations of letters difficult to pronounce and partly on combinations of sounds, stresses, and variations in pitch that appeal to our sense of hearing. *Cacophony* is the name for jarring and harsh sounds. Many tongue twisters are familiar examples of cacophony.

She sells sea shells . . .
The Leith police dismisseth us.

Euphony is the word that describes pleasing sounds. Some of the pleasure we get from good prose comes from various patterns of stresses called *rhythm*. Occasionally – and largely by accident – prose rhythms approach the regular metric forms of verse, but any conscious effort to arrange prose accents in poetic forms is usually out of place. The rhythms of prose are irregular – and yet one feels that in rhythmic prose there is an appropriate music. Read the following passage aloud, always remembering that the syllables stressed may be stressed in many different degrees:

The most eéry, the most inspiríng, the most Céltic of treés is the fórest píne, the whíte píne, as we fínd it on the nórthern wáste, perhaps the ténant of some lófty ledge, reáching fár into heáven, slénder, leáning, with a few cloúd-like flákes of fóliage that seém to have drífted óff from its stém and to lié afloát upon the inaccéssible air. We heár it múrmuring fár abóve us in the quiét wínd of mórning, and its voíce is like the dístant soúnd of mány lóng wáves upon a sándy shóre. At súnset it stánds against

the bright and silent west, unchanging, delicate, dark, and
with a stillness, as we dream, like the stillness of eternity.
The pine is the priest of the forest, leading heavenward the
thoughts of men and the flights of birds.

– Archibald Lampman, *At the Mermaid Inn*

The final selection in this chapter was written a decade ago,
but it has lost none of its freshness and power. It is part of a
speech given to the Analytical Psychology Society of Ontario
by one of Canada's foremost writers, Robertson Davies. The
prose rhythms in it cannot be felt through silent reading. It
should be read aloud.

In that same autumn, however, I saw *A Midsummer
Night's Dream* for the first time. The company had little
money, but they had a good deal of talent and they acted
the play in a setting which was simply curtains. The
magical flower which figures in the action was obviously a
paper flower, and when Bottom appeared in the ass's head
it was plain that it was a head made of *papier mâché*. This
was the very opposite of Realism. But it was a great dream,
and nobody in the audience cared a damn about realism
after the first ten minutes. I have seen that play, I suppose,
at least a dozen times since, sometimes sparely set on the
stage, and sometimes very lavishly and beautifully
mounted. Every time I respond in the same way: I am the
Duke, I am both the male lovers, I am all the clowns, I am
Bottom the Weaver making a glorious ass of himself in the
enchanted wood. Because, you see, this is one of the very
greatest dreams of the tribe, and whenever I see it I feel
both immeasurably enriched in myself and also very much
more a member of the tribe. Here, in the present, the past
has spoken to me, as I know that it will speak to the future
when I am no more. And this is not Realism which is an
imitation of surfaces; it is the vast, complex panorama of
life itself, of which I am a part, and which the great dream
permits me to experience, for the duration of the play, at
the very centre.

– Robertson Davies, ''Jung and the Theatre''

Techniques for Sentence Building

The ten samples that follow were taken from a variety of sources: books, articles, student essays, radio and TV programs, speeches. They represent a somewhat limited range of errors or lapses, but the comments on improving them describe strategies that could be followed in other sentence-correcting exercises.

1. "Anyone who watches evening TV receives a heavy diet of violence."

The writer has tried to strengthen this sentence with a metaphor. Although the idea of comparing consumption of TV to food intake is not a novel one, the appropriateness of the metaphor should be obvious. We nibble on sitcoms while munching potato chips; both are certainly mindless activities. The section to be strengthened here concerns the verb *receives.* Note that this verb is too vague: One can receive a package and a blow to the head – both very different receptions. It could be argued that the passive voice also has legitimacy because the TV audience for any program would hardly be called active. Still, to give the metaphor greater weight and logic, would not the verb *consumes* be better? If the passive is more desirable, why not *is fed* in place of *receive?*

Work to achieve complete consistency in the use of metaphors. Make verbs and nouns work for you.

2. "The pilot apparently died of a heart attack."

In this example the writer has not seen the inadvertently humorous situation created by the misplacement of the modifier *apparently.* The sentence should be rewritten, "The pilot died of an apparent heart attack." This blooper was delivered on the evening news, a good occasion to hear such mistakes, since the writers of news stories are often required to read them as well.

Place modifiers next to the words they modify. Whenever you use adjectives or adverbs, take a look at the words that come before and after them.

3. "A campaign was started in 1972 by the Union of Canadian Writers and other supportive members to receive aid from the government."

You can see the disadvantages of using the passive voice to describe some event. The reader must wait until after the verb phrase *was started* in order to find out who began the campaign. A revision that answers this question and gives directness would read: "In 1972 the UCW and other supportive members [Who are these: Does the writer really mean to say *supporters*?] started a campaign to receive aid from the government." Notice that the passive nature of the sentence is reinforced by the verb *receive*; campaigns are designed to "win" something, not "receive" it.

Give your readers as much specific detail as possible. The following questions are left unanswered in this example. Who are the supporters? What agency in the government grants such aid? How much money was sought?

4. "To someone with no ability to scrutinize what he or she does in terms of greater goals, early ratification can be, and usually is, stultifying."

Although public speakers sometimes can be forgiven excesses or confused phrasing in a moment of inspiration, this speaker seems not to have thought carefully about meaning. *Someone* is too general a pronoun; the speech is about acting, so *an actor* would be better. And what does "scrutinize what he or she does in terms of greater goals" really mean? It is likely that the speaker really means to warn the beginning actor against believing favourable reviews and to urge the value of long-range planning: "In terms of" qualifies as the culprit phrase: it is too indefinite. Another trouble spot is "early ratification can be, and usually is, stultifying." If something usually is true, it is better simply to say so, without unduly interrupting the flow of the sentence. A suggested revision reads: "To an actor incapable of self-evaluation and unsure of career goals, early approval is stultifying."

5. "He is and always has been, an aggressive-type hitter."

Too many writers these days tack on *type* to adjectives that should stand alone. "It is a fast-type car," a student said the other day. The "and always has been" interrupter functions to underscore the longstanding aggressiveness of the hitter. But is it necessary? Doesn't the sentence, like the batter's swing, gain power from simplicity and directness? "He's an aggressive hitter" has the sharpness of a line-drive double to the wall.

Don't try to build sentences by adding the flab of superfluous or redundant words.

6. "It is interesting to note the fact that many men find no satisfaction in their careers."

The fact that sentences are good examples of verbal cluttering. Unless you refer to specific facts in a report or analysis – "There are several facts that support this conclusion" – it is best to avoid using the construction. Here the problem is compounded by the introductory pronoun subject and verb *It is*. The pronoun refers to no clearly distinguishable noun; it simply signals the arrival of the subject *many men*. Depending on the context (let us say this sentence is part of an analysis of a report on male career planning), the sentence can be cleaned up to read, "Many men find no satisfaction in their careers."

7. "The defensive players began digging themselves into a hole when they made some mental errors in the first half, and they were buried later in the game when the backs failed to cover receivers going for long passes."

The sentence attempts an analysis of reasons for losing a football game. There is nothing wrong with the diction or the punctuation; the writer even succeeds in developing a metaphor to describe the team's collapse. To achieve greater impact, however, the writer should have taken advantage of punctuation designed to provide variety and economy. By substituting a semicolon for the comma and conjunction, the sentence also becomes better balanced. Many sentences that follow the pattern of two independent clauses joined by *and* could be made more direct and economical by this method.

You must, however, be sure that the second half of the sentence is in fact an independent clause. If it is a dependent clause or participial phrase, a comma must be used.

> 8. "They come from all sides of the political spectrum, they're as honest as the day is long, and most work as hard as dogs."

This writer attempts a heartfelt description of municipal colleagues. Although the sincerity of the statement cannot be doubted, the speaker's knowledge of physics can be questioned. A colour spectrum or band is divided by shades of colour; to say that a spectrum has sides is to distort the metaphor. The writer's colleagues may "range from one end to the other" of the spectrum, but they probably will not be found on its sides. More important, the expression *political spectrum* has become a cliché, and although it may not be as worn out as *honest as the day is long* or *work as hard as dogs*, it should be avoided in serious writing. Although it is not always easy to know when you are using a cliché, test yourself by asking whether or not the comparison (clichés often emerge in comparisons: *smooth as silk*, *slimy as a snake*, and so on) is yours or one you have heard spoken frequently. The answer should give some idea about the originality of your statement.

> 9. "My decision to buy a car came suddenly, and I ran into many problems with financing."

One of the most difficult things for beginning writers to do is to subordinate their ideas in sentences. Often it is simply easier to write two sentences: "I ran into Paul at the game. We decided to eat together afterward." But the events are really connected in the writer's mind and in time. "After Paul and I met at the game, we went out to eat." In the opening example the writer has tried to make the two clauses co-ordinate, joining them with a comma and *and*. A participle would help to subordinate one part of the sentence to the other: "Having decided suddenly to buy a car, I ran into many problems with financing." This arrangement focusses your reader's attention on a process with stages rather than on two separate events.

Whenever you find yourself overusing a co-ordinate conjunction to join two independent clauses, see whether or not you can use a participle to indicate subordination.

10. "At least an hour was spent examining the evidence, and the police finally concluded that the accident was my fault."

At first glance this sentence appears to require subordination: ". . . examining the evidence, the police finally concluded that. . . ." In fact, the sentence suffers from a lack of detail, thereby sounding more like a report filled out on a form than a vivid representation of what actually happened. What evidence was examined? How many and what kind of police (i.e., constables, detectives) were involved? Did the police interview the other driver? What was the weather like during this period? What was the *writer* feeling during this ordeal? Not that all of these questions can – or should – be answered in one sentence. But the impact of the sentence on the reader can be heightened by a skilful selection of concrete details.

Read some of your favourite fiction with an eye to how the novelist sets certain scenes.

4

THE PARAGRAPH

What is a Paragraph?

One beauty of our native tongue is that English can always borrow from another language when it is at a loss for words. *Paragraph*, for example, is derived from two Greek words, *para*, "beside," and *graphein*, "to write." It was at one time a mark, usually ¶, written in the margin of a manuscript beside the place where a unit or subdivision of the text was to begin. The conventional signal now used to indicate a new paragraph is, of course, indention–that is, beginning a line a little to the right of the margin. (In some situations paragraphing is indicated instead by a skipped line and a new sentence beginning at the left-hand margin.) However it is marked, paragraphing can be considered a form of punctuation. It suggests that readers are to make a major pause in their progress – as much as several seconds if they are reading aloud – and that they are to prepare for a new unit of discourse that follows, in some reasonable order, the one they have just finished.

The function of this punctuated, or paragraphed, unit varies with different kinds of prose. In dialogue, the paragraph often marks off a single speech of a character. In description it may divide the details of a scene or object being presented. Paragraphs may be organized into a simple sequence of time, as when one writes instructions on the operation of a machine. They may mark off units into which a subject has been divided, a familiar textbook formula (three causes of a war, four classes of a society) In discussions of facts and ideas – usually spoken of as exposition – a common paragraph unit comprises a step in a logical argument. Since it is exposition or persuasion that most concerns students, attention will be given primarily to such paragraphs. To speak of a paragraph of exposition as a related group of sentences calculated to advance an argument, with or without a summarizing or topic sentence, probably comes close to describing the actual practice of writers.

Writers who begin a sentence with a dependent clause – for instance, "When I saw him on the street yesterday . . ." – have a pretty good idea what their main clause is going to say. "When I saw him on the street yesterday, he looked perfectly well." Similarly, experienced writers, composing an introductory sentence in a paragraph, have a fair idea of how that sentence is going to relate to the major point of the paragraph – a point they may be preparing to state in what is called a *topic sentence* later on. In terms of larger structures yet, practiced writers are aware of what a particular paragraph is going to contribute to the whole point of an article, or even a book. Writers should constantly be ready to change schemes, for they learn as they compose. But writers can save a lot of energy if they remain aware of the various relationships between a particular unit being written and all the other units of which it is to become a working part.

For beginning writers, simultaneous co-ordination of all these relationships comes hard, and planning paragraphs by outline, in the same way entire essays are planned, is advisable, at least in the early attempts. The topic sentence of a paragraph is that sentence that states the subject of the paragraph, suggests the attitude taken toward the subject of the paragraph, and, usually, anticipates the paragraph's conclusion. Experimental drafting of a few topic sentences can be helpful, even when the writer knows that the topic sentence may have to be rewritten and that it need not be the opening sentence. Any procedure, in fact, that helps students recognize a number of possible relations between the component sentences of the paragraph is useful.

The most familiar diagnosis of poor paragraphs in exposition is that they lack organization. By this is meant:

1. *Lack of coherence* – that is, unrelated statements are made; relations between statements are not clearly shown.
2. *Lack of unity* – that is, digressions from the main thought or the topical idea are made; irrelevant details are included.

It is fruitless to consider paragraphs in isolation from the larger units of which they are a part. Perhaps the fairest way to approach the paragraph as a single piece is to concentrate on introductions, the first paragraphs in expository essays. You can study an introductory paragraph without the sense that you have missed what went before it, for the simple reason that nothing, except the title, does go before it. In the next few sections of this chapter, several introductory paragraphs of the sort found in essay collections will be considered in detail. In each case, the writer is *introducing* the reader to the exposition that is to follow. This work on the paragraph can be related to the section "Beginnings and Endings" in chapter 6, where larger problems of organization are considered.

Kinds of Introductory Paragraphs

COHERENCE IN PARAGRAPHS

Since introductions can be made in many different ways, it is not very helpful to say, without elaboration, that writers in their first paragraphs are introducing the reader to their exposition. There are at least three common and useful ways a paragraph can introduce a piece of expository prose.

First, the paragraph can contain a statement of a thesis to be argued. This is an obvious and sensible mode of beginning. You are saying, in effect, "Here is what I am going to show you."

Often such a paragraph will include a reference to general opinion on the subject and how the writer's treatment will differ.

Second, the paragraph may tell a story, or begin to tell one, even though it will be clear that the whole essay is not fiction at all. The story will then be used as an example or as a piece of evidence to support a thesis being argued.

Third, the paragraph may concentrate on a single key term to be defined, as a way of launching the demonstration to come.

In addition to setting the stage for what is to follow, an introductory paragraph also introduces something of immense importance to the whole essay: the writer. Or, to be more exact, the introductory paragraph introduces that particular self the writer wishes to put forward for the particular circumstances and purposes of that piece of writing. The way sentences in a paragraph relate to each other to introduce an argument, then, must be appreciated not only as a strategy in logic but as the image of a personality that assumes a definite relation (or *tone*) toward us. While writers are presenting *arguments*, they are dramatizing through language a *person* speaking formally, informally, intimately, or distantly, as the case may be. The composition of a well-organized paragraph requires paying as much attention to tone as to the logical arrangement of ideas. In the good writer, the argument and the voice presenting it are fused.

THE PARAGRAPH AS A STATEMENT OF A THESIS TO BE ARGUED

In expository writing it is of course common practice to state at the outset the thesis or argument that the writer proposes to advance in the essay. For one thing, this is simple politeness to the reader. Often the statement is preceded or immediately followed by a reference to prevailing opinion on the subject, or to a condition that needs correcting, or to past treatments of the subject by other writers. The reader is to assume that prevailing opinion and past treatments are to be qualified, or perhaps demolished utterly, by the new treatment the author is putting forward. If some condition needs correcting, the author may begin by suggesting that action is needed now. This approach can, however, come dangerously close to a formula, and students should take note of the various ways in which professional writers modify the formula.

Here is a passage from an address given at an American college in 1929 by Canada's then ambassador to the United States, Vincent Massey. This passage illustrates the development of a theme. Massey begins by stating a concern of modern society about the standardization of life and "almost art itself." The theme of the paragraph is not introduced until the second sentence. It does, however, follow naturally from the opening sentence. Read the passage carefully and observe how the theme is developed logically throughout the paragraph.

[1] **We live, as we know – and often say – in a mechanical age when most of life, including almost art itself, seems standardized.**[2] **But in our attitude toward art, in other words in the sphere of taste, we should be able to find one happy means of escape from this all-pervading mechanization of life.**[3] **No two minds, if they function honestly, will reveal quite the same reaction to a given stimulus.**[4] **If we are true to ourselves each of us will follow, as far as we are permitted, his own or her own law in this matter of taste.**[5] **A character in a novel of Mr. E.V. Lucas asked that his only epitaph should be the two words, "He discriminated."**[6] **Perhaps it sounds a bit snobbish, at first blush, this boast of having distinguished between the right things and the wrong things – almost as if one was proud to have chosen the right people as**

[1] Opening with an observation on life and art, Massey deftly secures his audience's agreement by the use of such phrases as "as we know – and often say."

[2] Following the venerable formula of *yes-but*, Massey, having acknowledged that life has become standardized, states his thesis that we can find a "happy means of escape" through "the sphere of taste."

[3] Here Massey begins to support his thesis: each mind is distinct and responds to stimuli in a different way.

[4] If each individual is different, the argument continues, it follows that we can detach ourselves from the herd and follow our own path in matters of "taste."

[5–6] Massey is using the traditional rhetorical technique of *procatalepsis* (anticipating an argument and preventing it). Discrimination, even in 1929, had negative connotations and Massey is raising the spectre of elitism in order to lay it to rest.

[6] The implied charge of snobbism is discredited, if not quite

companions rather than the wrong ones.[7] **But that is an unfair construction.[8] After all, there should not be anything improper or unusual about such an attitude.[9] It is surely the duty of educated men and women to exercise their critical faculty wisely and courageously.[10] One of the major tasks performed by the college is surely to give its spiritual off-spring first the desire, and secondly the capacity to know the difference between the genuine and the meretricious in what they see about them; to distinguish real feeling from sentimentality, the noble from the merely florid, the tragic from the sordid, the dramatic from the theatrical.**

– Vincent Massey, ''Taste''

refuted, by the use of *analogy*. Distinguishing (discriminating) between right and wrong things is as bad, Massey says ironically, as being proud of choosing good companions over bad.

[7–8] The thesis is further supported by the view that if it is acceptable to associate with certain *people* and not others, it is acceptable to like some *things* and not others.

[9] What was an *opportunity* in the second sentence becomes a *duty*.

[10] Massey ends with a rhetorical flourish, using the technique of *antithesis* (the juxtaposition of contrasting ideas, often in parallel structure) to assert that it is the aim of the college to equip its students with the ability to discriminate.

The next passage is by Stephen Leacock.

[1] **Old age is the ''Front Line'' of life, moving into No Man's Land.[2] No Man's Land is covered with mist.[3] Beyond it is Eternity.[4] As we have moved forward, the tumult that now lies behind us has died down.[5] The sounds grow less and less.[6] It is almost silence.[7] There is an increasing feeling of**

[1] The first sentence establishes the metaphor of old age as a battlefield. The ''soldiers'' move across the empty space between the opposing armies [No Man's Land], into the annihilating machine gun fire of the enemy.

[2] Most attacks are launched at daybreak, hence the mist, also suggesting diminished eyesight. Note the writer's use of the same phrase *No Man's Land* to close the first sentence and to begin the second, providing a bridge between the two.

[3] The soldier is advancing to certain death.

[4] This evokes Kipling's famous line ''the tumult and the shouting dies; the Captains

isolation, of being alone.[8]
We seem so far apart.[9]
Here and there one falls,
silently, and lies a little
bundle on the ground that
the rolling mist is
burying.[10] Can we not
keep nearer?[11] It's hard
to see one another.[12] Can
you hear me?[13] Call to
me.[14] I am alone.[15]
This must be near the
end.

–Stephen Leacock,
  ''Three Score and Ten''

and the Kings depart.'' The *tumult* of life has been left behind with friends and comrades as the metaphor of *No Man's Land* is extended.

[5] This line, and the next three, expresses Leacock's sadness at seeing the ranks of the survivors thinned.

[9] The battlefield metaphor is continued; the remnants of the advancing line are struck down by an unseen hand and lie on the ground ''buried'' by the rolling mist. The next five lines are cries of apprehension and fear as the writer calls to other survivors to close ranks and maintain contact.

[15] The last line closes the metaphor by echoing the implications of the first – none of the soldiers of the *Front Line* survives *No Man's Land.*

As you can see, Leacock has taken pains to connect his sentences to one another by using images that support the central metaphor. The descriptive words that he chooses all support and link the theme of death and battle: silence, isolation, alone, apart, silently. As the paragraph proceeds, the sentences become shorter, culminating in a series of sharp, anguished appeals to his comrades, who cannot answer.

The difference in tone between the two paragraphs, which should be obvious even on a first quick reading, may be explained by a number of differences in their rhetoric, at least some of which can be mentioned here. For one thing, note the length of the sentences. Whereas Stephen Leacock, in a paragraph of just over one hundred and ten words, writes fifteen sentences, Vincent Massey, in a considerably longer paragraph, writes only ten. Massey expects a good deal of his audience. He addresses them formally, and does not make things any easier by using a metaphor. The relations between Massey's sentences are logical, not structural. The thesis is carried forward, each part of the argument dependent upon the preceding parts. We can partially account for the difference in rhetoric and tone by noting that the two writers are addressing different audiences. Massey is speaking to university students and faculty while Leacock is addressing the general reader. Moreover, the speaking personality each writer has chosen to adopt is also quite different. Leacock speaks of serious matters in an informal way and Massey speaks of serious matters in a formal way.

You have now examined two expository paragraphs employing variations of the thesis-to-be-argued formula. Each paragraph is constructed of sentences knit together with rhetorical devices, some more obvious than others, but all expertly handled. The tone of each selection is different, but note that the second writer's tone is suited to his subject matter and his controlling metaphor while the first's is appropriate to oratory.

THE PARAGRAPH OF ANECDOTE AS EVIDENCE FOR A THESIS

This section begins with a selection that takes a stand on the axiom, "nice guys finish last." See how the argument is begun with a seemingly ingenuous remark by Conn Smythe.

[1] I don't remember the first time I said it, but the most misunderstood remark I ever made was, "If you can't beat 'em in the alley, you can't beat 'em on ice."[2] Even as wise a man as J.V. McAree, the *Globe and Mail*'s editorial page columnist of the time and the best they ever had, got all outraged about it, so you can imagine how the real career do-gooders reacted.[3] They claimed I was telling my players to go out and bully the opposition.[4] The exact opposite is true: I was telling them to refuse to be bullied.[5] If you back up when challenged, somebody is

[1] A candid, frank topic sentence: note how the author establishes the reader's expectations by saying that his statement was misunderstood.

[2] If even a wise man misunderstood, and was outraged, what can one expect of a "real career do-gooder"?

[3] "They" refers back to the "do-gooders" of the previous sentence.

[4] The "truth" leads to no more misunderstanding.

[5] This is the consequence of not heeding the truth.

always going to be making you
back up.[6] It can be in an alley,
across a boardroom table, across
your boss's desk, or in an NHL
rink.[7] Of course, it is a great line
for the stimulation of self-
righteousness among people who
would have trouble staring down
a bunny rabbit, but I never
found any trouble explaining the
idea to people whose aim in life is
to be a winner.

— Conn Smythe and Scott Young,
   If You Can't Beat 'Em in the Alley

[6] Referring back to the "alley" of the topic sentence, the concept is extended to include workers, management, and hockey players.

[7] Closing off the thesis: "the great line" is deliberately misunderstood by those timid souls "who would have trouble staring down a bunny rabbit," although winners, of course, understand instinctively what was intended.

This technique is a form of what is called the *inductive approach*, starting with a specific occasion or instance and moving to a generalization. (See chapter 6, "Problems of Composing.") One advantage to using a personal observation as evidence is that the reader is drawn to the viewpoint of the writer. Hockey is a tough game, Smythe is saying, and only the tough win. Life is also a tough game and those that are easily intimidated end up on the bench. If a generalization, such as "only the tough get ahead in life" begins the discussion there is every likelihood the reader will stop to say "I can think of exceptions." And if the writer immediately provokes the reader's antagonism, the rest of the argument will have an uphill fight. In a personal narration such as this one, however, the speaker's relation to his reader is easy and relaxed; he is speaking directly to us on a topic that is soon expanded to include us.

In another example of a personal anecdote as an introductory device, we encounter a speaker who is indignant at a common belief about the legitimacy of teaching Canadian literature in Canadian schools. Notice how dramatically the tone shifts mid-point in the passage from informal conversation to impassioned oratory.

[1] There are still those in our country who talk about the uselessness of teaching CanLit because "there is no such thing," or "it doesn't accord with international standards," by which they mean that Canadian writing isn't the same as British or American.[2] No, it isn't.[3] Rudy Wiebe once told me that someone had asked him, "But, if you don't constantly apply international standards, how can you develop any standards at all?" (For "international" here, read "British.")[4] Rudy replied, "I think we just make them up as we go along." Exactly.[5] How else did Chaucer write?[6] How else the writers of any culture?[7] They simply wrote what they were compelled to write, as best they could, and those of their writings that struck deep chords among their own people and sometimes beyond their own people, endured.[8] This is not to say that we remain untouched by literature elsewhere, or that we reject the great writings of the past, from whichever culture they have come.[9] Anyone who writes in the English language is in some way an inheritor of Shakespeare and Milton, of Fielding and Jane Austen, of Dickens and Thackeray.[10] Our task is not to reject the past but to assimilate it, to take the language and make it truly ours, to write out of our

[1] Note the direct, almost belligerent way the topic is broached.

[2] This is the rhetorical device of *paramologia*, the conceding of a point in order to strengthen one's own argument.

[3&4] The common argument against CanLit is recounted by means of an exchange between "someone" and Rudy Wiebe, one of Canada's most respected novelists.

[5, 6, 7] Laurence uses the argumentative device of *anthypophora*, the asking and the answering of questions.

[8] The criticisms having been laid to rest, the tone changes to a calmer one in which the author points out the universality of literature.

[9] The rich heritage of English literature is acknowledged.

[10] A classic *peroration*, an impassioned summary that neatly explains how Canadian literature is to develop from its English roots into a unique and Canadian art form.

own familiar idiom and out of
our deepest observations of our
people and our place of belonging
on this planet.

– Margaret Laurence,
  "Ivory Tower or Grassroots:
  The Novelist as Socio-Political
  Being"

In her use of classical argumentative techniques of rhetoric,
Laurence reveals her intimacy with the great writers of the
past. This passage is as carefully structured and the argument
as carefully presented as any by Pope or Swift.

THE PARAGRAPH AS A DEFINITION OF A TERM

The point of a piece of exposition often depends on one or two
significant words. Many of the significant words have been so
overworked that they have lost the precision and clarity that
they once possessed. Hence, such words as *communism*, *censorship*, *tolerance*, tend to have different meanings for readers with
preconceived ideas of these concepts. Anyone writing an essay
that makes important use of such terms must anticipate a reader's
very proper question: What do you mean by that? In the following paragraphs, a definition of terms is the central problem each
paragraph must solve, or at least face.

The following excerpt is from an essay entitled "Reflections
on Quebec's Cultural Nationalism." Although the opening is
divided into two paragraphs, they may be treated as one.

[1] It has always seemed easier for an observer who is detached from all manifestations of cultural nationalism to study its cause, its consequences, and its effects on a society, an ethnic group, a country.[2] But, first, it is	[1] Opening introductory sentence. [2] A statement of the problem.

most important to define the
words culture and nationalism
before attempting to legitimate
their raison d'être in French
Canada and in Quebec.

[3] Culture is nothing else than
"la mémoire du peuple" – a
people's memory, and an
anticipation of its future.[4] It is
the very essence of that part of
man which is not material, which
is a longing for God.[5]
Nationalism is a feeling of
belonging to a group of people.[6]
It has many other connotations,
many other emotions – even
passions – attached to it.

[3] A direct statement of what the
author means by *culture*.

[4] An elaboration of the meaning
given in the previous sentence.

[5] A definition of the second term,
nationalism.

[6] The author recognizes that there
are other possible definitions of
this term.

–Solange Chaput Rolland,
 "Reflections on Quebec's
 Cultural Nationalism"

The writer is now ready to proceed with her discussion of cultural nationalism in Quebec. She has set up a working definition of *cultural nationalism*, however personal it may be. Readers may agree or disagree with this definition, but they are now able to follow the writer's argument with a clear understanding of its foundations.

Now look at another problem with a term, the term *modern*. This is the opening of a lecture on art and literature.

[1] Let us begin by looking at
some of the characteristics that
we generally associate with the
word "modern," especially in
the arts.[2] "Modern," in itself,
means simply recent: in
Shakespeare's day it meant

[1] The speaker immediately addresses the problem of defining
the key term. Note how the reader
is drawn into the analytical process
by the introductory phrase "let us."

[2] *Modern* is repeated; its historical usage and present-day connotations are explained.

mediocre, and it still sometimes carries that meaning as an emotional overtone.[3] In its ordinary colloquial sense it implies an advanced state of technology and the social attitudes of a highly urbanized life.[4] In some Western Canadian towns, for example, houses with outdoor privies are advertised as "unmodern."[5] But "modern" has also become a historical term like "Romantic," "Baroque," or "Renaissance."[6] It would be convenient if, like "Romantic," the colloquial uses of the word were spelled in lower case and the cultural term with a capital, but this is not established.[7] Like "Romantic" again, "modern" as a cultural term refers partly to a historical period, roughly the last century, but it is also partly a descriptive term, not a purely historical term like "mediaeval."[8] Just as we feel that Keats or Byron are Romantic and that some of their contemporaries, Jane Austen for example, are either not Romantic at all or are less Romantic, so we feel that "modern" is in part a style or attitude in recent culture, and that some of the artists and writers of the last century have been "more modern" than others.

– Northrop Frye,
  The Modern Century

[3] *Its* refers to *modern*. The "ordinary" usage obscures the technical use of the term in criticism.

[4] A humorous aside illustrates the different uses of the term.

[5] The word *term* refers to *modern*.

[6] A proposed solution to the problem. *Word* is once again used as a substitute for *modern*.

[7] The discussion continues and *modern* is repeated, linking this sentence with the preceding ones.

[8] The definition of the term is justified and summarized. The term *modern* is repeated twice.

Frye's tone is a good deal lighter than Solange Chaput Rolland's, partly because of his clever inclusion of the reader in the discussion. Although technical terms abound and the passage is clearly that of a scholar, the language is not arcane nor the effect didactic.

The definition of *modern* given in the final sentence becomes the linchpin for the rest of the lecture. The paragraph of definition, in this instance, deals with a term, the agreement upon whose meaning is essential before any meaningful discussion of the topic can take place.

Frye uses here the third technique described in this chapter, the definition of a key term. In practice, however, the writer does not ask beforehand, "Now which of three, or six, or fifteen techniques should I use in this paragraph?" The practical question the writer does ask is much harder: "How can I organize this paragraph so that the reader will respond exactly as I want?" Knowing the techniques of critical analysis will not, alone, solve all paragraphing problems – you can discover plenty of excellent introductory paragraphs that seem to fit none of the categories – but it will help the inexperienced writer who must sometimes choose an opening self-consciously and deliberately; for example, when answering an examination question.

It does not follow that because a topic is supposed to be serious, you must necessarily speak of it seriously. Consistency in the way you write is another matter; "the departed" at the beginning should not turn up as "the stiff" near the end, unless the best you can do is cheap humour. The quality of tone is the writer's own decision and, as the following passage shows, the decision can be surprising. Here is a professor of English introducing a serious topic, literacy.

[1] When I let it slip among ordinary company that I'm a professor of English, you can guess what the reaction is: "Oh-oh," they say with nervous smiles, "I'd better watch my

[1] The speaker, with his breezy informality, obliquely introduces his subject, language.

language.''[2] No use explaining that I don't teach composition.[3] If English professors hit the front page, or confront public awareness at all, it's not when they have had profound or brilliant ideas about literature, but when they are testily muttering that their latest crop of freshmen can neither read nor write.[4] And the truth is, of course, that we are – we must be – concerned with language.[5] It is the medium both of the works we study, and of our attempts to teach it.[6] If language should decay far enough, the study of literature becomes difficult or impossible.[7] I won't play for headlines by pretending this is the condition we have reached; but such a condition is at least imaginable, as things are going.[8] So I worry a good deal about language, myself.[9] And I think the most useful way to put my worries before you is to pursue that automatic reaction: ''Oh-oh, I'd better watch my language.''

– Michael Hornyansky,
  ''Is Your English Destroying
  Your Image?''

[2] The presence of a professor of English in a group has the same effect as the presence of a clergyman; it makes everyone self-conscious about the language they use.

[3] A tongue-in-cheek comment. Note the phrase ''read nor write,'' which links the sentence to its predecessors and reinforces the topic.

[4] The *truth* refers to the topic.

[5] The *medium* refers back to *language*.

[6] The consequences if present trends continue. *Language* is repeated.

[7] Highly informal, but a vividly effective expression of concern about the future of the language.

[8] The writer, an eminent authority, worries about language, as does the reader by this point in the discussion.

[9] The quotation that opened the paragraph is used to close it effectively. It has taken on additional meaning and significance from the sentences between.

Adequate Paragraph Development

Rarely do college students write paragraphs that are too long; the chief difficulty is finding enough to say so that their paragraphs will not resemble a series of slightly expanded sentences.

If three or four paragraphs appear on every page of an essay, the paragraphs are probably too short. A five-hundred-word essay split into ten or twelve paragraphs contains paragraphs that are too short. The paragraphs of a newspaper story are short, it is true; so are the paragraphs of a business letter. But expository writing does not refer to those special types of writing. In expository writing it is customary to develop ideas more fully or to group ideas into larger units than in news stories or in business letters. In expository writing a series of very short paragraphs is an indication of malnutrition; paragraphs need to be fed details to make them effective.

Undeveloped Paragraph

Advertisements in magazines and on television these days are a lot better than they are given credit for. Some of them are quite funny. I think advertising is more interesting than a lot of other things going on nowadays. [This is vague, repetitious, undeveloped. Note especially some of the undefined words and phrases: *a lot better* (how are they better?), *more interesting* (in what way?), *a lot of other things* (what sort of things?).]

Rewritten Paragraph

The growth of humour in the writing of advertisements is a pleasant phenomenon of recent years. Many writers of ads for magazines and television have been exploiting a sense of the absurd, almost as if they were making fun of themselves. A well-known Canadian wine company has produced commercials featuring a glamorous young couple vaguely reminiscent of Fred Astaire and Ginger Rogers. Their engaging clumsiness in delivering a sophisticated song and dance routine makes you laugh while your attention is riveted to the screen and the name of the wine is fixed in your memory. In a somewhat different approach one beer company has modified the traditional beer commercial that depicts beautiful young people pursuing glamorous and exotic sports to a background of pulsating music. This company shows young people in social settings, but uses verbal exchanges consisting of puns, corny one-liners, and hackneyed jokes to amuse and capture the viewer. This kind of fun-making is a healthy development in a profession that often appears to take salesmanship all too solemnly.

Undeveloped Paragraph

I like to travel all right, but it is the people you meet rather than the things you see that I appreciate. When I visit a new place I am really happy to find some new faces and names that I can make friends with. [This paragraph has reduced informality to not much more than chattering. Again it is vague and unconvincing. Note how, in the revision, the writer has exploited the unintended rhyme – new places, new faces – to enliven the first sentence. The writer then provides some concrete, memorable examples.]

Rewritten Paragraph

When I go travelling, it is new faces, not new places, that I go to see. The Rocky Mountains are certainly an awesome sight, but what I remember most vividly from my visit there is the figure of a priest I met in a hotel lobby. Lean, ascetic, with flashing black eyes, he spoke to me of his order and its commitment to teaching. And at Lake Louise where I was duly impressed with the grandeur of the scenery, an elderly woman with bright silver hair and the manner of an actress took one look and sniffed. "Another dull show in the provinces," she concluded scornfully. Sightseeing is all very well, but I suspect our own human depths may be more mysterious and fascinating than mountains or lakes.

Some sketchy paragraphs are the result of a failure to think in larger units. The writer fails to decide on the central idea, and then does not see that those miniature paragraphs are really only parts of the topic idea.

Sketchy Paragraphs

Dad and Mother marvelled at the way my sister Lois and I got along; they still do in fact. They are proud of the family unity we show.

When Lois married, I was as thrilled and happy as she, I am sure. I think I knew better than anyone else what a wonderful wife she would be. Her marriage is an example to me.

Although my sister never attended college, she has encouraged me greatly. I am working to live up to the high standards she set for me, and I am constantly hoping that some day I can in some way repay her.

[Try combining these short paragraphs under a topic sentence like this: *My sister Lois has been a companion and an example to me.*]

The buzzard usually glides over wooded areas in search of food because a domestic animal is more likely to meet a mishap in the forest than out in a plain pasture. Also one will find buzzards around the sloughs in the summer because the water is drying up and the buzzard will feed on the dead fish.

The buzzard lives in a nest on top of high cliffs and in tree tops.

It is against the law to shoot buzzards because they scavenge the animals that have died in the woods through accident.

[Try combining these three paragraphs under a topic sentence that makes a statement about the feeding and nesting habits of buzzards.]

I suppose any mother is happy and proud when her children surprise her by cooking a meal. I know that my mother always is. This is one way in which we like to make her happy.

Mother always remembers kindness, whether it be in thoughts or actions, and always forgets the unkindness of others. She appreciates having us cook for her.

[Try constructing a topic sentence about Mother's appreciation of a kind act.]

The tendency of beginners is to write in generalizations and abstractions: "The closing hour at the cafe is always a scene of great confusion." What actually is going on? Why not make us see – hear and smell, too – the various details of that confusion? Just what did you see that justified your conclusion that the closing hour at the cafe is a scene of confusion? In criticism, the statement "I like this poem" is practically meaningless. Why do you like it? Because it irritates you? or because it soothes you? "My father is an honest man." How is he honest? What does he do that shows honesty? Introduce him to us and let us watch him being honest. "Dormitory rules are more liberal, and thus more demanding, than parental rules." Give us examples, many of them. Let us see college men and women in situations that require choice; let us see how they behave and what they think in relation to questions of social morality. Give us action and proof. Give us the evidence that you have observed.

Here are some examples to show how details can be used.

Before

Holding a little boy by the hand, a fat old woman waddled slowly up the staircase.

After

Her carpet slippers flapping against the stone steps, the huge woman made her way laboriously up the staircase. Her dark shapelessness almost hid the little boy beside her, his thin white arm stretched taut as she pulled him along.

Before

The closing hour at the cafe where I work is always a scene of great confusion. The jukebox is playing, the customers are shouting their orders, everyone is impatient and in a hurry.

After

The raucous blast of a rock group from the jukebox and the bellowing of customers impatient for their final orders of hamburgers and french fries turn closing hour at the cafe where I work into a fair approximation of the last moments aboard the *Titanic*.

Notice that the writer's "scene of great confusion" has now become more vivid for the reader through the addition of a few concrete details. Remember that concrete writing does not call for overwhelming the reader with descriptive minutiae. It ought to be the art of making each statement specific and unmistakably pertinent.

Problems of Internal Organization

You have seen that most paragraphs, wherever they may appear, are built around a *central theme* or *idea,* which is often expressed in a single *topic sentence;* and that most paragraphs are made up of sentences connected by transitional devices that can be identified. There are other techniques for organizing, or unifying, or holding together expository paragraphs.

In the following paragraph, notice how all the details have been chosen to relate to the initial topic sentence. This is a simple approach that consists of seeing to it that all the items of a list belong in that list. It is not as easy as it looks.

> In no characteristic is existing society in the west so sharply distinguished from the earlier societies, whether of Europe or the East, than in its conception of time. To the ancient Chinese or Greek, to the Arab herdsman or Mexican peon of today, time is represented by the cyclic processes of nature, the alternation of day and night, the passage from season to season. The nomads and farmers measured and still measure their day from sunrise to sunset, and their year in terms of seedtime and harvest, of the falling leaf and the ice thawing on the lakes and rivers. The farmer worked according to the elements, the craftsman for as long as he felt it necessary to perfect his product. Time was seen as a process of natural change, and men were not concerned in its exact measurement. For this reason civilizations highly developed in other respects had the most primitive means of measuring time: the hour glass with its trickling sand or dripping water, the sun dial,

useless on a dull day, and the candle or lamp whose unburnt remnant of oil or wax indicated the hours. All these devices were approximate and inexact, and were often rendered unreliable by the weather or the personal laziness of the tender. Nowhere in the ancient or mediaeval world were more than a tiny minority of men concerned with time in the terms of mathematical exactitude.

– George Woodcock, "The Tyranny of the Clock"

Still another technique of unifying a paragraph is to build all or most of the sentences around a comparison or a contrast. Comparison requires finding similarities in two things. Usually the more familiar thing or idea is used to explain the less familiar one: to explain the game of squash show how it is similar to the more familiar game of tennis. In what ways is piloting a plane like driving a car? How are Canadians like their continental neighbours in the United States? Contrast, on the other hand, is telling what a thing is not like. How does the Western way of living differ from the Eastern way? How does capitalism differ from communism? How does propaganda differ from news? These are typical subjects that invite treatment by contrast, not in paragraphs alone but also in entire essays or articles.

Who that knows the North can ever deny its lure? Wherever you be, it will call and call to you. In the sluggish South you will hear it, will long for the keen tingle of its silver days, the vaster glory of its star-strewn nights. In the city's heart it will come to you till you hunger for its big, clean spaces, its racing rivers, its purple tundras. In the homes of the rich its voice will seek you out, and you will ache for your lonely camp-fire, a sunset splendouring to golden death, the night where the silence clutches and the heavens vomit forth white fire. Yes, you will hear it, and hear it, till a madness comes over you, till you leave the crawling men of the sticky pavements to seek it out once more, the sapphire of its lustrous lakes, the white yearning of its peaks to the myriad stars. Then, as a child comes home, will you come home.

– Robert Service, *The Trail of '98: A Northland Romance*

The following, with its touches of sardonic humour that readers have come to associate with the author, discusses the contrast between exaggerated claims and reality.

> In recent years, it is fair to say that films have become less juvenile, more intelligent. An increasing number of good, satisfying films have come from Europe. There have been two or three that are arguably great. But, by and large, I am convinced that the new films are not nearly so good as they are cracked up to be, their seriousness is often spurious and half-educated, and they are being critically oversold. A major trouble is we are so grateful for even a modicum of originality on the screen, we are so flattered to be addressed directly, we seldom realize that the so-called serious film is, for the most part, shamelessly derivative, taking up a position abandoned by novelists years ago.
>
> Meanwhile, film reviewers continue to gush. Unmissable! Electrifying! Breath-taking! Beautiful! Once-in-a-lifetime! One of those rare. . . . ! Raw with genius! To open up a London or New York newspaper at the cinema pages is to discover masterpieces held over for the third month everywhere. Film masterpieces are minted at least twice a month. No other art form, as they say, can make that claim. However, it is equally true that the masterpieces in no other art form are so relentlessly up-to-date. Or date so quickly.
>
> – Mordecai Richler, ''Writing for the Movies''

Specific transitional words and phrases in the preceding paragraphs help relate the component sentences to each other. Such terms as *echo*, *refer*, and *link* have been used to signify these relations. These connecting expressions can be summarized as follows:

1. *Conjunctions and transitional adverbs*, which include words and phrases such as *and*, *but*, *yet*, *however*, *therefore*, *consequently*, *moreover*, *accordingly*, *at the same time*, *as a result*, *for example*, *on the other hand*, *finally*.
2. *Pronouns*, such as *this*, *that*, *these*, *those*, *his*, *her*, and *its*, which refer to an antecedent in a previous sentence. It is extremely

important that writers make sure references of pronouns are clear. See § 26.

3. *Repetition of key words*, of which examples, particularly clear in paragraphs of definition, appear in earlier pages of this chapter.

4. *Parallel structure*, through which the reader is led back to sentences phrased in similar forms.

For a close study of connectives, transitions, and internal organization, follow the themes and variations, almost like musical motifs, in the following passage:

[1] **In Vancouver, the** *Sons of the Orient Aid Society* **took** *them* **in charge.** [2] **For** *each* **one** *it* **tried to discover, in the breadth and length of this almost unpeopled country, the spot that might be most suitable.** [3] *They* **were made to take a course of several weeks in English to at least learn its rudiments.** [4] *Each* **immigrant also received a loan to get him started.** [5] **Paid back,** *little by little*, **the money would be lent again to some new** *son of the Orient* **arriving, so to speak, on the heels of his predecessor.** [6] *Thus* **there would be no drying-up of the** *thin flow* **of money or the** *thin trickle*, **tightly controlled, of Chinese immigration.**

[7] **In fact the** *Aid Society* **had very few jobs to offer the little yellow men arriving from Canton, Peking, or Manchuria.** [8] *They* **almost all,** *therefore*, **ended up in the same odd occupation.** [9] **In the distances of** *the endless plains*, **flat and without contours,** *mini-*

[1] Introduces key words. Pronoun *them* refers to previous sentence.

[2] *Each* and *it* refer to *them* and *society* in previous sentence.

[3] *They* refers to *them* from sentence one.

[4] Repeats *each*.

[5] Introduces another key word *little*; repeats *son of the Orient* from first sentence.

[6] Transition *thus*; repetition of *thin* repeats notion of *little by little*.

[7] Repeats *Aid Society*.

[8] Pronoun *they*. Transition *therefore*.

[9] Repeats notions of space and size and introduces *villages*.

scule villages had sprung up ten or fifteen years before.[10] If *they* were big enough to contain one Chinaman they put him in a restaurant.[11] If a *village* were even more flourishing and could afford a second Chinaman, the latter of necessity opened a laundry.[12] That's how it went in these poor *villages*, almost deprived of all tradition except that of always putting their newcomers from Asia into the same occupations.[13] The astonishing thing was that the Chinese laundrymen soon acquired the reputation of being the best in the world.[14] As for the restaurants, it is less certain that *they* were the first in their field.[15] *Yet* who but a Chinese with nothing to lose would have opened a café in one of these scrawny *little towns* where catching a single customer was a major feat!

[10] Pronoun *they*.

[11, 12] Repeats *village* from 9.

[14] Pronoun *they*.

[15] Transition word *yet*; repeats *village* as *little towns*.

 –Gabrielle Roy,
   ''Where Will You Go,
   Sam Lee Wong?''

Organizing Paragraphs In Sequences

To understand how paragraphs are related to one another is to begin to see how a whole essay is organized. A paragraph that lists a series of items to be considered is one obvious illustration. Note that in the following essay, which is on the responsibility of newspapers, the author has listed his reasons for his position on the issue of Quebec separatism in separate paragraphs, and he has developed each one at some length.

[1] It should give all viewpoints a reasonable opportunity for expression in the news columns. But it would betray its mission if it avoided choice.

[1] Summary of preceding paragraph.

[2] We choose the Canadian hypothesis for three principal reasons.[3] The first reason relates to the very tradition of *Le Devoir*.[4] The newspaper under its first three directors was a great Canadian newspaper.[5] Henri Bourassa never wanted to limit his horizons to the province of Quebec. He considered that the whole of Canada was his country, that he ought to be at home everywhere in this country.[6] Georges Pelletier also attached a great importance to Canadian realities. He liked to approach the most complex problems, for example those of transport, with an objectivity and rigour that would have prevented him from closing them within a narrow compass.[7] The third director, Gérard Filion, was of rural origin, but he had learned early at the school of the Catholic Union of Farmers the need for co-operation with the rest of the country. He was often severe toward Ottawa centralizers, but never negative or closed with regard to Canada itself.

[2] Topic sentence for the whole section to follow.

[3] Topic sentence of the paragraph.

[4] Transition to the following three examples.

[5] First example.

[6] Second example.

[7] Third example.

[8] The second reason lies in the

[8] Topic sentence of the paragraph.

economic order. It is sufficient to glance at a map of the country in order to establish that Quebec and Canada are tied together in many ways.[9] **Quebec's economy presents two important characteristics.**[10] **It needs external markets for the dispersal of its products.**[11] **It needs capital from outside for the development of its resources.**[12] **Why should we say no to Canada today if that must only mean saying yes to others tomorrow? One does not deny his history for the simple pleasure of hypothetically changing partners.**

[9] Topic sentence of the second half of the paragraph.

[10] First characteristic.

[11] Second characteristic.

[12] Answer to previous question and transition to next paragraph.

[13] **Our most important motives lie in the political order.**[14] **On the condition that Quebec enjoys all the autonomy which it needs to develop its own life and institutions, we believe that the preservation of the Canadian tie offers precious advantages.**[15] **The first of these advantages is surely the possibility of maintaining and developing the French way of life in the rest of the country.** *Le Devoir* has always maintained an attitude of solidarity with the French minorities in other parts of the country. Whatever could have been said on this subject for some time, the present direction of *Le Devoir* holds that we must continue to support our compatriots in the other provinces. We refuse to join the

[13] Third and best reason saved until the last provides the topic sentence of the paragraph.

[14] Develops topic sentence and prepares the ground for the next part of the paragraph.

[15] Principal advantage.

prophets of doom who affirm,
without ever having worked
assiduously with these groups,
that the French minorities of the
other provinces are doomed to
extinction.

  –Claude Ryan,
    "The Canadian Solution,"
    Le Devoir

The next example is from a 1968 article in which René Lévesque predicts the separation of Quebec from the rest of Canada. His major device for linking paragraphs is the repetition of the word *dream*. What other ways of making transitions can you identify?

It's an old dream. A very powerful and no less normal dream, but so long repressed that it's often relegated deep down in the recesses of the French-Canadian mind. Some of us have given up on it. Others are scared of the changes it would require: so they hide it and caress it secretly, when nobody is looking, and since for them it's like an illicit love affair, they'll be the last to admit it.

But they will eventually. For the first time in a couple of hundred years, the dream is now clearly feasible. That was all it needed. As this becomes more evident, the latent majority that was always there will reveal itself and grow and pretty soon fulfil the dream.

In the Quebec election of June 1966, the "dreamers" got the equivalent of 10 percent of the votes. Right now it would be at least 15 percent. A year from now it could be as much as 25 percent. In the next two to five years, I'm convinced it will become a solid majority.

  –René Lévesque,
    "To Be Masters in Our Own House,"
    Toronto Star

In reading the essays of professionals, as well as those written by classmates, it is helpful to develop a sensitivity to various techniques of transition from paragraph to paragraph. "How has the writer connected these parts?'' can be your repeated question – and sometimes you will find that both professional and amateur have not connected them as well as they might. Similarly, when writing your own compositions, you can develop a critical awareness of paragraph sequence by giving regular attention to the endings and beginnings of paragraphs. Fairly early in the development of reading skill, and eventually in the development of proficiency in writing, this awareness of how paragraphs can be linked together becomes almost automatic – and an impressive feature of a mature style.

By now you should feel more at home with the elements – words, sentences, paragraphs – that make up whole essays. It is time to try your hand at composing something more ambitious than a nicely turned paragraph. In the next chapter you will find some suggestions for workable subjects, then a full-scale discussion of the various ways these subjects might be treated.

EXERCISES

EXERCISE 1, INTRODUCTORY PARAGRAPHS. *Look through an anthology of modern essays, noting the introductory paragraphs. Find a paragraph stating a thesis to be argued, one telling an anecdote, and one offering a definition. Find one using a combination of these methods. Find one that fits none of these categories. Can you invent a useful fourth category to contain it?*

EXERCISE 2, WRITING INTRODUCTORY PARAGRAPHS. *Write three possible opening paragraphs for an essay, "The Roles of the Sexes in Society Today." Use each of the three approaches outlined in the first part of this chapter.*

EXERCISE 3, TONE. *Rewrite your three paragraphs, drastically changing the tone (e.g., from serious to humorous, distant to familiar) in each case.*

EXERCISE 4, PARAGRAPH VARIETY. *Locate examples of the following:*

1. A paragraph with a topic sentence at the end.
2. A paragraph used as a transition between two topics of an essay.
3. A paragraph with a light tone on a heavy subject.
4. A paragraph within which the tone shifts.
5. A paragraph summarizing a section of an essay or chapter.

EXERCISE 5, REVISING A PARAGRAPH. *In the following passage, revise and combine the sentences, inserting transitions where necessary, in order to produce a logical and readable paragraph:*

Students of the English language have divided its historical growth into three main periods; the Old English Period, from 450 to 1100, was the first one. The Middle English Period lasted from 1100 until 1500. The Modern English Period began in 1500 and lasted up to the present time. The people of England did not stop speaking one kind of language and begin speaking another in any one year. The change was gradual. There were definite historical events occurring at the times mentioned which caused a more rapid change in the language of the people of England. The Angles, Saxons, and Jutes invaded England in 449. The Norman Conquest occurred in 1066. The English Renaissance began about 1500.

5

PROBLEMS OF SUBJECT AND FOCUS

Selecting a Subject

One of the questions on a history examination reads: "What were the chief social and political arguments against Pierre Trudeau proclaiming the War Measures Act in 1970?" A proper answer will take at least a paragraph or two of discussion, a characteristic that designates the question as an *essay question*. Like any essay, the answer requires some thought and organization, but one problem is solved by the question itself: there is no doubt what is to be written about. Now, by way of contrast, observe the devious mind of the English instructor: "Write a five-hundred-word essay on the subject of humour." That is not a question but an order; it has no correct answer. Humour is in addition a broad topic that must be narrowed and focussed if it is to be covered at all in five hundred words. Deciding where to begin is the preliminary step in any piece of writing, but it is a crucial step when no specific information has been requested.

PRELIMINARY PLANNING

If the length of a paper is established in advance, it will automatically affect the paper's subject. An eight-hundred-word essay on some new fad, a recent development in science, the author Timothy Findley, or any other subject is, before all other considerations, an eight-hundred-word essay. The student faced with such an essay and the professional writer paid to supply a six-thousand-word article on the commercial uses of nuclear energy have a common obligation to interest the reader. When filling space receives more attention than interesting the reader, the temptation is to think of large subjects that promise to take up room with little effort. Subjects like "Humour," "Games People Play," "Street Crime," "Politics," or "Vacations" are not suitable subjects for short papers; they are warehouses full of random facts, opinions, and impressions.

Replace the problem of filling a blank space with that of engaging a reader's interest, however, and the task changes from a matter of *discovering* what to talk about to one of *selecting* what is most important to say.

An effective piece of writing forces the reader to notice aspects of the subject he or she has not already considered. The more general the treatment of the subject, the greater the probability is that the reader will have heard it or thought it before. When writing about something, therefore, you must be prepared to describe it in detail. Everyone can visualize a forest, but the writer describes the kinds of trees composing it, the colours and shapes of the leaves, the depth of the shade, the thickness of the undergrowth, the positions of the trunks, and the texture of the barks until it is no longer *a* forest but *the* forest. An immense subject, such as the Canadian economy, requires proportionately elaborate detail, which means more exposition. A six-thousand-word subject will not fit into an eight-hundred-word essay.

LIMITING THE SUBJECT: "PREWRITING"

How does one know when a subject is the right size? One way is by thinking about it carefully before beginning to write. Let us

say an eight-hundred-word essay is assigned with no more prescriptive reference to subject than that it should be based on an
interest or hobby. A quick review of your interests produces
the subject of folk music. Since the assignment requires that
you inform your readers about something, the techniques of
exposition are called for. These techniques will allow you to approach the subject in a variety of ways: Your essay might define
folk music, compare or contrast it with other kinds of music,
identify some of the typical instruments, such as acoustic guitar
or fiddle, classify such styles as voyageur songs or patriotic
ballads, or explain how folk music is created. Although in the
act of writing the essay you may narrate the events, let us say, at
a folk concert, or describe the dress or customs of folk artists,
or argue for the need to preserve the songs of native singers,
your main purpose will be expository, that is, to inform your
readers about some aspect of a subject they may have heard about
but do not fully appreciate or understand.

Now ask what you can tell your readers about folk music that
lies within your experience and is neither trite nor general. In
response to that tough question, you may decide to focus the
essay on a single idea, the relationship between folk and country music. Note that this idea, though still broad, yields the
advantage of referring to a kind of music that is probably better
known to many people than folk music. The next step is to state
the main idea in the form of a summarizing sentence. A more
conventional term for such a statement is *thesis sentence*, which
indicates that the main idea is being presented as something to
be proved or demonstrated to the reader. While the essay on
folk music may not require an impassioned argument or plea,
its thesis should be convincingly enough developed so that the
reader believes in the authority of the writer's assertions. Stating a thesis will also help you get away from the simple listing
approach – "Another point to mention is . . ." – that too often
characterizes weak expository essays. Pursuing a thesis means
giving your readers an expanding knowledge of the subject, not
a shopping list of details arranged in no apparent order.

Let us say that your general purpose in writing the essay on folk music is to illustrate how folk lyrics are more simple and genuine than the lyrics of present-day country songs. Jotting down this purpose will give you the first component of a rough outline that should prove helpful in the actual writing stage. The next step is to devise a sentence that expresses your main idea in specific language: "While folk and country song lyrics touch on similar themes of unrequited love and extramarital affairs, folk lyrics tend to be more genuine and sincere." Now you have a target to shoot at, a rough plan of operations, and some idea of the ammunition you are going to use. Comparison and contrast will play an important role in this project. In fact, you can clearly see that a good way to begin such an essay is by pointing out a major difference between folk and country music: lyrics in folk music were not written down but transmitted orally through the songs. Another contrast can be traced to this same oral tradition, by which many folk songs were brought to this country from Britain and France. Modern country music is strongly influenced by the writing style of popular music, which tends to be more urban and sophisticated than folk sources. By listing these contrasting points, you will soon be engaged in the process of giving concreteness to your essay. The unavoidable task, given the thesis statement, is to compare two specific songs, one folk, the other country, which present a similar theme. Such a comparison will represent the centre of your essay, the proof that clinches your original claim about folk lyrics. Remember that although other matters – acoustic versus electrified instruments, natural versus slick production values – may interest you, they are not a direct part of the main idea and should be kept out of the body of the essay. Such observations may be inserted by way of parenthetical remarks or footnotes, but only if they illustrate some aspect of the thesis.

Deciding on a good title for the paper is the third step in the planning or prewriting stage. Good titles attract readers and help to keep writers on the track. They reveal the writer's thoroughness in exploring the subject by telling the reader that an interesting conclusion has been reached. "Folk Music" would not stand as an effective title for this essay; it is too broad and uninteresting. The following title, however, is almost sure to catch a reader's eye: "Folk Versus Country Lyrics: A Loss of Innocence." This title yields information not just about the subject but about the thesis as well.

The practice, then, of limiting the subject calls for three steps:

1. State your objective or goal as a main idea.
2. Write out a summarizing or thesis sentence.
3. Devise a suitable title.

You will probably change your plan as you proceed, but every writer must do that. It may prove difficult, for example, to find a folk song and a country song that tell a similar story or deal with a similar theme. So long as you keep your main idea and your first general plan, change will improve the final product.

NATURE OF THE PLAN OR OUTLINE

Every paper needs a plan, although some plans spend their life cycles in the heads of the writers without ever emerging on paper in the form of outlines. Some plans take the form of a series of notes on the back of an old envelope. The experienced writer may plan almost subconsciously. Some writers say that they do all their outlining mentally, whereas others say that they write out elaborate outlines on paper. But inexperienced writers have everything to gain by using paper and pencil to record and clarify the planning that goes on in their heads. Even when inspiration is powerful enough and spontaneous enough to leap onto a page without intermediate steps, an outline of the finished work is an excellent check of organization and logic. If there are flaws in the product of inspiration, an outline may reveal them.

The Informal Outline. A short paper should have a short outline. A few notes on a piece of scrap paper may suffice. Suppose the urge comes to write a thoughtful little essay on childhood memories. Seize your scrap paper at that moment and begin a list of things you recall from early childhood. Some recollections will be vivid, some won't. Perhaps the difficulty of remembering them at all strikes you. Jot that thought down too.

Now sit back and consider what you have, a list of things that must once have impressed you and the thought that they are a good deal less impressive today. Think how the two might fit together. One solution is to begin with the result, the difficulty of remembering. Start your actual paper with a short paragraph developing that subject, lead in your list of memories, and then pause. What you need is a conclusion, although you may have already glimpsed one from reviewing your notes. A speculative paragraph on why these particular recollections should surface while a million other experiences lie undisturbed in the subconscious is one acceptable choice for rounding off the topic, but there are others. An appealing short essay can be written in this way and perhaps always should be. Its spontaneity would more than likely be dampened by the imposed order of a full-blown formal outline.

The Process of Synthesis. Making an outline is often spoken of as a process of dividing a subject. It is assumed that the thought exists in its entirety in the writer's mind, and in preparing it for the market the writer methodically slices it up into pieces called topics and subtopics. That may be true for some. For most, however, outlining is a process of synthesis, not division. We usually begin with a problem and the necessity of doing something about it. Our first suggestion may be an ill-favoured and disreputable little idea. We pull it out and look it over. It seems promising – possibly. But then we look around again – by thinking, by reading, by observing – and pull out other ideas to add to it. We jot down these ideas on paper. Some writers use file cards, which they can later organize in coherent order. Before long, if we are fortunate, we have enough, or perhaps more than enough, for our purpose. Then and only then can we begin to select and arrange and divide.

Some people have minds that require formal approaches to any activity, in particular, writing. For that reason, specific information on the steps in putting together a formal outline is provided.

Conventions of the Formal Outline

There are a number of conventions governing the formal outline:

1. The parts of the outline, heads and subheads, should be labelled by alternating figures and letters as follows: I, II, III, and so on; A, B, C, and so on; 1, 2, 3, and so on; a, b, c, and so on. Periods, not dashes, should be placed after these figures and letters.

2. No punctuation is needed after the topics in a topic outline. In a sentence outline, each sentence should be punctuated in the conventional manner.

3. The heads in any series should be of equal importance. That is, the heads numbered I, II, III, IV, and so on, should actually be divisions of the whole paper; heads numbered with capital letters should be co-ordinate divisions of heads numbered with Roman numerals; and so on.

4. Co-ordinate heads should be expressed in parallel form – that is, in a given series, nouns should be made parallel with nouns, adjectives with adjectives, and so on. But although parallel structure is desirable and logical, clarity and directness should never be sacrificed to gain strict parallelism. There are times when nouns and gerunds can live side by side in a formal outline.

5. In a topic outline, all heads and subheads must be topics. In a sentence outline, all heads and subheads must be sentences. Sentences should not run over from one head to another.

6. Each head and subhead should be as specific as it is possible to make it in an outline. Vague topics and sentences are bad because they tend to hide flaws in the logic or organization of the outline.

7. Using such headings as "I. Introduction," "II. Body," "III. Conclusion" is unnecessary and undesirable. Such divisions do not indicate correctly the structure of most essays or articles. Many papers written by students are too short for a formal introduction or conclusion. In most long papers the

conclusion is simply the main topic that the writer wants the reader to hear about last. Separate introductions are used more often than separate conclusions in essays of six thousand words or more, but in the outline it is better to use a topic that tells what is said in the introduction than to use the vague "Introduction" itself.

8. Since an outline represents a grouping of parallel parts, it is illogical to have a single subhead under any head. A single subhead can usually be combined with its head with benefit to the logic and organization of the outline.

Here are two kinds of conventional outline examining the subject of choosing a college and career.

Topic Outline

Choices – In College and After

Thesis: The decisions I have to make in choosing college courses depend on larger questions I am beginning to ask about myself and my life work.

I. Two decisions described
   A. Art history or chemistry?
      1. Professional considerations
      2. Personal considerations
   B. A second year of French?
      1. Practical advantages of knowing a foreign language
      2. Intellectual advantages
      3. The issue of necessity

II. Definition of the problem
   A. Decisions about occupation
   B. Decisions about a kind of life to lead

III. Temporary resolution of the problem
   A. To hold open a professional possibility: chemistry
   B. To take advantage of cultural gains already made: French

A sentence outline is similar in organization to a topic outline. It differs from a topic outline in that every topic and subtopic is translated into a complete sentence, stating the central idea of the particular topic. The sentence outline has two advantages over the topic outline: (1) It forces the writer to study the material carefully in order to say something specific for each head and subhead; and (2), much more effectively than the topic outline, it conveys information in logical sequence to the reader. The topic outline merely states a series of subjects, rather like titles, that the writer intends to say something about. The sentence outline actually summarizes what will be said.

Here is an example of a sentence outline based on the previous topic outline.

Sentence Outline

Choices – In College and After

Thesis: The decisions I have to make in choosing college courses depend on larger questions I am beginning to ask about myself and my life work.

I. I have two decisions to make with respect to choosing college courses in the immediate future.

   A. One decision is whether to take a course in art history or in chemistry.

      1. Since at one time I planned to be a chemical engineer and still have this career much in mind, professional considerations would indicate the choice of chemistry.

      2. On the other hand I enjoy art and plan to travel to see more of it; I need training in art history if I am going to be more than just another ignorant museum-goer.

   B. The second decision is whether to continue for a second year of French.

      1. French might be practically useful to me, both in business (including engineering) and in the travel I hope to undertake.

      2. Furthermore I am eager to put to actual use, in the

      reading of good books, the elementary French I have already mastered.

    3. But how necessary are these considerations in the light of other courses I might take instead?

  II. My problem can be put in the form of a dilemma involving larger questions about my whole future.

    A. On the one hand I want to hold a highly trained position in a lucrative profession.

    B. On the other hand I want to lead a certain kind of life, with capacities for values not connected with the making of money.

  III. I will have to make a decision balancing the conflicting desires I have described.

    A. I will hold open the professional possibilities by taking chemistry.

    B. I will improve and solidify what cultural proficiency in another language I have already gained, by taking French.

A solid outline will help you see exactly where your essay is headed. Equipped with this road map, you may now wish to consider the range of destinations or subjects available to you.

Some Types of Subject

To write about certain subjects – the War of 1812, the making of solar panels – you need to consult encyclopaedias and other reference books in the library. For the moment, however, the essay based on personal experience, or, at most, on sources of information more readily available than those in the library, is an excellent field for experiment. The various kinds of writing discussed in the following passages should reveal a bit of the raw material most writers have immediately at hand.

AUTOBIOGRAPHICAL NARRATIVES
"The Story of My Life" or "How I Spent My Summer Vacation" are favourite topics of instructors in beginning composition

courses. The resulting essays prove to be useful in getting to know the students. But there are dangers for the writer. Beware of writing a narrative account of your life, listing in chronological order such items as when and where you were born, who your parents are, where you went to school, and so on. Instead, try telling about the development of your interest in music, your social life, or your attitude toward a career. Alternatively, isolate one aspect of your character: intelligence, sense of humour, pride, aggression. Remember that it is not you but your reader who must be interested in your portrait and do not announce, "Compassion is the dominant trait of my character" and expect the world to hang on your lips waiting for the next pearl. Recount instead an incident, as does the author of the following example, to show some aspect of your character at work.

> The eyes of the dying woman were glassy and half closed.
> I knelt beside her and put my hand over her cold bony one.
> My blouse touched her and she opened her eyes wide.
> Turning her hand, she feebly clutched the silk of my sleeve.
> "Is there something you want, Mary?"
> "Good," she whispered, still clutching the sleeve.
> I thought that she was dead, holding my sleeve in a death grip. One of the women came in and tried to free me.
> Mary's eyes opened and she spoke in Indian.
> "Mary wants your blouse," said the stooping woman to me.
> "Wants my blouse?"
> "Uh huh – wants for grave."
> "To be buried in?"
> "No, for grave-house."
> I understood. Mary had not many things now but she had been important once. They would build a little wooden room with a show window in it over her grave. Here they would display her few poor possessions, the few hoarded trifles of her strong days. My blouse would be an addition.
> The dying woman's eyes were on my face.
> I scrambled out of the blouse and into my jacket. I laid the blouse across Mary. She died with her hands upon it.
>
> – Emily Carr, *Klee Wyck*

A single memorable incident is often a better choice than a number of sketchily treated events in your life. And be wary of the obvious incidents everyone has talked about: the camping trip, the auto accident, the big fire downtown (unless, of course, you are asked to write about these). Much more effective is some apparently minor incident, so developed with concrete detail that it acquires importance in the telling.

> Interest in girls started early. Just after pollywog nests had become an old story. But the first step was not to carry her books home from school. The first step was to shout some mild gibe at her. If she brought the books down on your head you knew she liked you too.
>
> The courage for such advances could only be found, of course, if you were in a group. If one boy found himself alone with one girl this swagger wilted at once. ("Your father rowed up his garden yet?" "I don't know. I imagine. Yours?" "I don't know. I imagine.")
>
> Later on, the byplay was standard. After a dance you sidled up to her while she was putting on her rubbers and mumbled, "Please may I see you home tonight?" Or if you were too nervous about the plunge to get that many words out, "Comp'ny?" would do. She either "gave you a look" or giggled.
>
> If she gave you a look, you had got what was known as "the mitten." And it was talked about for days. ("Did you know that Bonnie gave Ed the mitten Friday night? And Saturday night he bids on her pie just the same. I'd *see* myself.")
>
> On the other hand, if she giggled and let you take her arm, that was not lost on anyone either. You were "teased" about her from that day on.
>
> Though certainly nothing romantic took place on the way to her door. One merry grandmother used to tell about the first time *she* was seen home. Not a word was said until they reached her gate. Right then a bubble of gas made its long thunderous round of her escort's lower intestine. He turned to her in the pearly moonlight and made his one remark of the night: "Did you hear my guts a-rollin!"
>
> – Ernest Buckler, *Ox Bells and Fireflies*

Have you ever found yourself in a situation where you are the victim of an act of terror? Consider the difficulties involved in trying to recall and to narrate such an incident. Note how this writer vivifies her account through the use of concrete detail, realistic dialogue, and the present tense.

> Another day I am in the garage, behind the huge pile of sawdust. I have arranged a bed for my dolls out of baby blankets. I have many many dolls, and stuffed animals. Baby dolls with breakable hard heads and straw-filled bodies, children dolls, grown-up dolls, a rabbit, a bear, a furry mouse. I have tea sets and doll shoes and socks and dresses.
>
> Mr. Gower is standing beside me and looking down. I cannot play because he is watching. I wait for him to go away. He squats down. I wish to go to my mother. His hand holds my skirt as I get up to go. The soft elastic around the waist pulls at the straps criss-crossing over my shoulders. I cannot move. I cannot look at his face. It is unthinkable to be held by force.
>
> He lifts me up saying that my knee has a scratch on it and he will fix it for me. I know this is a lie. The scratch is hardly visible and does not hurt. Is it the lie that first introduces me to the darkness?
>
> The room is dark, the blind drawn almost to the bottom. I am unfamiliar with such darkness. The bed is strange and pristine, deathly in its untouched splendour. I have never seen his wife. Does she not live here? Is this where they sleep?
>
> "Don't be afraid," he says. "I know another little girl just like you and she isn't afraid."
>
> He tells me her name is Veronica and she talks to him. She is also four years old. I cannot imagine Veronica actually talking to Old Man Gower. If I speak, I will split open and spill out. To be whole and safe I must hide in the foliage, odourless as a newborn fawn. But already the lie grows like a horn, an unfurled fiddlehead fist, through the soft fontanelle of my four-year-old mind.
>
> He stands me on the bathroom toilet and opens the medicine cabinet. He begins to undress me. I do not resist.

One does not resist adults. But I know this is unnecessary for my knee. He is only pretending to fix my scratch.

From outside the bathroom window I can hear Stephen calling for me, his high voice singing the two-tone chant "O-mi."

"Sh," Mr. Gower says. One finger is on his lips and the other hand on my mouth.

Mr. Gower closes the bathroom door, locking me in.

I hear him calling Stephen from the kitchen door. "She's hurt her knee," he says, "I'm fixing it."

He is giving Stephen a penny to go and buy some candy. My mother never does this. I know he only wants to send Stephen away so we will be safe. I want Stephen to rescue me from this strange room. But I do not wish him to see me half undressed. I am not permitted to move, to dress, or to cry out. I am ashamed. If Stephen comes he will see my shame. He will know what I feel and the knowing will flood the landscape. There will be nowhere to hide.

"Run away little girl. Hide. Hide," he says, putting me down in the bathroom. I am Snow White in the forest, unable to run. He is the forest full of eyes and arms. He is the tree root that trips Snow White. He is the lightning flashing through the dark sky.

– Joy Kogawa, *Obasan*

Narrating any event calls for the use of chronological organization. Each stage of action will be marked by the passage of time (note the beginning of the first paragraph in Kogawa's account), which means that the writer has a handy way to break his or her story into paragraphs. In recounting a Sunday softball game, for instance, you need simply divide the action into paragraphs about the early, middle, and late innings. There is little chance that you will misplace events or that you will give in to the temptation to wander. Remember that although the score of the game is of interest to your readers, they are more likely to be caught up in the detailing of a spectacular hit, catch, or error. Careful selection of details – the way players are dressed, the taunts thrown at umpires or coaches – gives readers the same feeling they experience in reading good fiction. The point of the story should come through the narration rather than be imposed on it. If a narrated incident is part of a larger expository or argumentative essay, let it serve as an example whose application to the essay's main idea is clear without being overstated.

Don't forget that the one danger in narration is that you are likely to digress from the main elements of the story. Exploring the marital problems of the softball players is likely to change the focus of the account unless the game is being played by recently divorced couples. To avoid digression, keep the purpose or objective of the story firmly in mind; let that purpose guide you in the selection of details.

DESCRIPTIONS

Description, telling what is to be seen, heard, tasted, touched, smelled, and possibly surmised, seems so clearcut a task that its chief pitfall sometimes escapes notice until it is too late. That problem is unity, the importance of each element relating coherently to the others. A verbal picture may be unified by a summarizing statement that ties the components together or by a dominant and consistent attitude toward the images described. A visual scene assembled on the page as through a fish-eye lens with every detail simultaneously and indiscriminately distinct is usually confusing. What is more, it is impersonal; there is nothing in it to connect writer and reader, and only a very confident, or very rash, writer throws away the bond of understanding with the reader. That bond may be preserved in a consistent point of view. Remember that the reader is seeing through Someone Else's eyes, and, if Someone Else is admiring the blaze in the third-floor kitchen and, at the same time, noting how the fire truck takes the corner at Broad and Victoria, the reader is going to have a headache. Do not give readers headaches! A shift in point of view is permissible if the reader is given warning that a shift is coming or occurring, but the shift should be for a purpose, to contribute to a conclusion, not just because a lot of facts or impressions present themselves with the price of admission.

Like lovely Barbara in Honey Harbour, Ontario fills out her dress with opulence and almost unimaginable variety. We learn from geographical and demographical studies that the hunting tracts of the Eskimos of central North America do not extend far below the 55th parallel; yet this is part of Ontario. From Fort Albany at the mouth of the Albany River on James Bay west and north to the mouth of the Severn and beyond to the Manitoba border, we are in the country of "the people."

And yet . . . and yet . . . driving along Highway 8 from Hamilton to Niagara Falls, you pass through Winona, Grimsby, Beamsville and Vineland, eventually coming to a town called Jordan. It seems very natural that Vineland and Jordan should be found so close together in the wine-growing country of the Ontario southwest. If Jordan is a sacred river in a holy place, then wine – the most humane of drinks – is rightly produced there. Vineland: the Norse name for North America. Wine-growing country strikes every myth-maker as warm, lovely, sunny, rich, and in fact the Niagara peninsula *is* all these things. Ontario has warm feet and a cool head, exactly the reverse of what I had, courting the girl in Honey Harbour. Paradoxes, Eskimos and wine: there's something Hegelian about this province.

– Hugh Hood, *The Governor's Bridge is Closed*

The art of description is comparable to painting or photography. A successful artist has an "eye" for a compelling scene, recognizing how to represent an arrangement of flowers or people in a dramatic, eye-catching way. After a close look at paintings like Alex Colville's *Refrigerator* or Van Gogh's *Sunflowers* you suddenly realize that the impact of such works can be traced to the selection and arrangement of details.

Like narrated incidents, descriptions too provide their own ready-made form of organization. Living rooms can be described from top to bottom, or bottom to top, street scenes from foreground to background. Profiles of personalities may follow a pattern that guides the eye from least significant details (physical features) to most significant facts (typical expressions or actions). These organizational guides keep the writer from transforming a descriptive sketch into a jumble of impressions guaranteed to strain the reader's eyes and attention.

Two approaches may be used in the art of describing: the objective and the impressionistic. An objective piece of description details a scene or subject as a camera might, with all the features in place. Such an approach characterizes much scientific writing, since the findings of investigators must be presented to others for verification. We also want a precise, realistic account of events from journalists, who in a sense are taking our place at major events like political speeches or catastrophes. As we shall see later, the objective method is of special value in outlining any process involving steps or stages; when changing a washer on a leaky faucet, the amateur plumber is likely to want a simple, clear description of the unfamiliar objects required for the job.

The following passage is a good example of the scientific approach to description.

> There is a plant in our woods, known by the names of man-drake, may-apple, and duck-foot: the botanical name of the plant is *Podophyllum*; it belongs to the class and order *Polyandria monogynia*. The blossom is yellowish white, the corolla consisting of six petals; the fruit is oblong; when ripe, of a greenish yellow; in size that of a plum; when fully ripe it has the flavour of preserved tamarind, a pleasant brisk acid; it increases rapidly in rich moist woodlands. The leaves come up singly, are palmated and shade the ground very much when a number of them grow near each other; the stalk supports the leaf from the centre: when they first appear above the ground, they resemble a folded umbrella or parasol, all the edges of the leaves bending downward, by degrees expanding into a slightly convex canopy. The fruit would make a delicate preserve with sugar.
>
> – Catharine Parr Traill, *The Backwoods of Canada*

Impressionistic or subjective description is interpretive in nature. The writer makes us aware of a certain impression the object or scene has made on him or her. An emotional response is sought from the reader of such descriptive passages. In creating this mood the writer of subjective description will also tend to use more figurative language than the objective writer. For example, metaphors and similes help to set a scene by comparing what is observed to something else the reader may be better aware of. A simile is a comparison in which the writer uses *like* or *as*, emphasizing a particular trait in the thing or person described: *He had a temper like a wildcat: Her forehand was as fast as a whiplash*. Metaphors draw parallels by suggesting analogies or likenesses between one object and another: *He had a volcanic temper; Her serve boomed out of a cannon*. Metaphors and similes are indispensable in both kinds of description, and both kinds may also be found together in essays containing some form of description.

In the following selection the writer describes a ride home in a horse-drawn sleigh after a fierce snowstorm. Is the description primarily objective or impressionistic? How can you tell?

> I came to places where the wind had had its moments of frolicsome humour, where it had made grim fun of its own massive and cumbersome and yet so pliable and elastic majesty. It had turned around and around, running with breathless speed, with its tongue lolling out, as it were, and probably yapping and snapping in mocking mimicry of a pup trying to catch its tail; and it had scooped out a spiral trough with overhanging rim. I felt sorry that I had not been there to watch it, because after all, what I saw was only the dead record of something that had been very much alive and vociferatingly noisy. And in another place it had reared and raised its head like a boa constrictor, ready to strike at its prey; up to the flashing, forked tongue it was there. But one spot I remember, where it looked exactly as if quite consciously it had attempted the outright ludicrous: it had thrown up the snow into the semblance of some formidable animal – more like a gorilla than anything else it looked, a gorilla that stands on its four hands and raises every hair on its back and snarls in order to frighten that which it is afraid of itself – a leopard maybe.

> – Frederick Philip Grove, *Over Prairie Trails*

PROFILES

A favourite assignment for teachers of writing is to ask students to create a profile or portrait of an "unforgettable" character. Depending heavily on the techniques of description, a profile is a short biographical sketch that relies for its effect on a few well-chosen, vivid facts and details. When you draw on autobiographical material for a subject, the aim is to isolate a single circumstance worth discussing. In a profile a very different process is followed; you portray the whole person in terms of several selected traits or acts. The subject of a successful portrait need not be famous – or notorious; as a matter of fact, the writer of a profile often takes some totally obscure person and tries to convince the reader that he or she is worth knowing.

The following selection reveals how a professional writer solves the problem of introducing a personality into his narrative and to the reader who will be asked to trace his path through the rest of the study. In one paragraph we have an unmistakable impression of the figure's physical appearance, personality, and behaviour.

> Pierre Elliott Trudeau often seems more like the hero of a novel about the occult than a Canadian prime minister. He looks distant, pagan, ageless, like the photographs of Nijinsky: the aquiline nose and high Slavic cheekbones, the taut, sculptured face, the ambiguous grace. His countenance, chilly and cerebral, flared nostrils hinting at a sneer, gives him a natural, aristocratic quality of dominion over others. Above all, there are the pale and predatory eyes, that tell at once of skepticism, inquiry, ferocity. "Eyes very blue, very bright," as a Sudanese child once said of General Gordon of Khartoum, "and I frighted when I see eyes." Not to mention the voice: languid and sing-song, like a monk chanting the responses to a Latin mass, yet encompassing within its cadences the bullhorn of a parade square. A man smaller than you expect, and slighter, but with the presence and bearing of a pro-consul.
>
> – Richard Gwyn, *The Northern Magus*

While you may not want to attempt a portrait of an important political figure like Pierre Trudeau, another possible project is to write a profile of a distinguished citizen or personality in your community, one whom you have known fairly well. Select one you have liked and admired. A trip to the library may help you find background facts. Then organize your profile on the basis of a number of the following divisions:

I. An interview, in which you introduce your subject and give a quick picture of his or her appearance
II. A glimpse of the subject at work
III. A transition to the facts about this person's career, education and so on
IV. The subject's dominant traits
V. A typical professional performance (a major article or speech)
VI. What others say about the subject

You need not use all of these divisions, but if you want to compress, remember that I, III, and V are essential.

If you want to do a more ambitious biographical piece, one that will take you to some of the reference books in the library, try writing a biographical sketch of (1) the author of a book you are reading; (2) a community leader; (3) the man or woman who represents you in parliament; (4) a well-known scientist who is connected with your college or university. You will find more detailed assistance for writing such papers in chapter 6. Be careful to give all your borrowed information in your own words! To lift commentary verbatim without acknowledging the author is to commit plagiarism, the name for passing stolen ideas, and the penalties are usually severe.

Robertson Davies has always admired the humorist Stephen Leacock. In his monograph on Leacock he includes a short profile of the man, which attempts to capture his complexity in a very few words. Note how Davies uses a combination of analogy, paradox, quotation, and personal impression to make this a persuasive piece of writing in this genre.

> Do you know the characteristic wine of Madeira? Some of it is dry and not unlike a heavy sherry; some of it is sweet and rivals port as a fine dessert wine. But all of it has a

curious aftertaste, much appreciated by connoisseurs, which is like brimstone and is caused by the volcanic soil of the island. I do not know whether Leacock ever drank Madeira himself – he was very much a Scotch-whisky man – but I enjoy Madeira greatly, and I never drink it without thinking of Leacock, who was sometimes dry, sometimes sweet, but who always leaves upon the tongue a hint of brimstone. His amiability was great, but those who knew him have stories of his sudden flashes of hot temper, of impatience and irascibility. He wrote of his friend, Sir Andrew Macphail:

> I am certain that he never quite knew what he believed and what he didn't; but underneath it was a deep-seated feeling that the real virtue of a nation is bred in the country, that the city is an unnatural product. From this point of view Andrew, though frequenting the rich in his daily walk of life, was never quite satisfied of their right to be. Towards plutocrats, bankers, manufacturers, and such, he felt a little bit as a rough country dog feels towards a city cat. He didn't quite accept them. Andrew would have made a fine radical if he hadn't hated radicalism.

> In this description he might have been writing of himself. Leacock was a life-long professed Tory; he valued money and was pleased by the big income his writings brought him. But he never really seems to have liked rich people or aristocrats and he never misses a chance to take a dig at them. Yet he, like Bernard Shaw, came of a privileged class and, again like Shaw, of a family that was down on its luck. Despite their best efforts, neither of them ever really got over having been born a gentleman. Leacock too would have made a fine radical, but the hooligan element that attaches itself to radicalism repelled him.

– Robertson Davies, Stephen Leacock

BOOK OR FILM REVIEW

In recent years, the tempo of book publication has increased to the point where no one can expect to read all the new books, even those restricted to a particular field of interest. Readers, therefore, must depend on the reports of others to select the particular books they may want to buy and read. The same is true of movies. To meet this demand for quick and ready information, there has developed in newspapers and magazines a special kind of review: a very short, informal description of a book (film), with some brief information about the author (director), and at least an implied evaluation of his or her work. You will find such brief reports in the *Globe and Mail*, in *Quill & Quire*, and in several other magazines and newspapers that are likely to reach moviegoers and serious readers of books.

Sometimes such an informal review can be accomplished – or at least attempted – in a single paragraph. In the examples below you will note the almost breezy tone adopted by the reviewers. But beneath the informality there is much serious purpose, and much important information is presented in short and palatable form. Note the style of these two reviews, one of a film, the other of a book.

Le Vrai Nature de Bernadette, dir. Gilles Carle.

Bernadette is a pretty young wife and mother who leaves her city home and family to find freedom and purity in the fresh clean air of country life. Taking over an old farm, she also provides sexual gratification for a variety of men, young and aged, crippled and robust. She persuades a mute, abandoned child to speak, and finds a horde of handicapped villagers at her door begging for a miracle cure. Meanwhile, two of her visitors turn on her household with guns, a young boy is shot, and farmers dump their produce on the highway in a revolt never really explained. This summary indicates perhaps, that while Gilles Carle's vitality as a film-maker never seems to flag, he doesn't give himself enough time to work out or properly motivate his screenplays, resulting in slap-dash ideas and incidents, superficiality, melodrama and ultimately confusion. Fortunately, he has injected a good deal of comedy into the proceedings, and is helped considerably – by the appealing performance of Micheline Lanctot – in getting away with subject matter which only Bunuel has treated successfully.

FEEDING YOUR CHILD: From Infancy to Six Years Old (Rev. ed.), Louise Lambert-Legacé, General Publishing,

$8.95 paper ISBN 0 7736 1120 7, 233 pp., index, biblio., 1982

Louise Lambert-Legacé, author of one of the most informative and down-to-earth guides on child nutrition, has completely revised and updated her 1975 version of *Feeding Your Child*.

Lambert-Legacé, nutrition editor for the French edition of *Chatelaine* and nutrition consultant for *Le Devoir*, has rewritten the 10 chapters dealing with pregnancy, breast-feeding, and the first 18 months of life. These chapters are jam-packed with information compiled from the latest government recommended dietary guides as well as menus complete with caloric and nutritive values for the pregnant or nursing mother. She also includes several interviews with eminent and qualified medical consultants. Weight gain in pregnancy is dealt with in some depth. Naturally the importance of good eating habits and healthful foods is stressed.

The book continues with helpful advice on feeding children up to the age of six. It deals with feeding problems, provides menus for each age group, including the vegetarian child, and provides many simple but precise recipes.

Any parent or health care professional should consider purchasing this new edition; it does not talk down to the reader and is written in a straightforward, commonsense way. The book is consistently professional and extremely practical.

In attempting such a brief review yourself, you should keep in mind at least three purposes. First, you should indicate something of the author's or director's reputation or qualifications. Second, you should summarize the contents of the book or film in a brief survey of the chief points of its argument or plot. Third, let your reader know whether you think the work good or bad. The modest reviewer also provides some reason for his or her judgement.

DIRECTIONS AND PROCESSES

The "how to do it" and "how it was done" literature of North America is impressive in extent, and some of it, at least, is of impressive literary quality. The ability to give accurate directions is extremely important and should be cultivated just as strictly as the more creative kinds of writing. Here are a few exercises that you may find useful:

1. Take two points that lie far apart in your locality, such as your home and a distant shopping centre. Draw up a short set of directions by which a total stranger might arrive at your home starting from the centre. *Do not* use any of the points of the compass – North, South, East, or West – in your instructions. Depend entirely on an accurate description of landmarks and distances.
2. Explain to an unmechanical friend how to start and operate a power mower. Do not use a single technical term without explaining it in clear, untechnical language.
3. Tell one of your younger friends what to do to register in college. Go from one building to another, and explain every step of the procedure in words that cannot fail to be understood.

Setting out directions is a useful exercise not only in clarity but in establishing order. All instructions have a clear beginning and a virtually unalterable sequence in which they must be given if they are to work. It is no good explaining how to change an ordinary household fuse without first telling where the fusebox is.

An explanation of a process is not necessarily a set of directions to be followed by someone. Thousands of such explanations are written merely because there are people who like to know how things work. If you try one of the following subjects, you might try making it an interesting explanation as well as a set of directions to be followed:

1. Measuring wind velocity
2. Photographing children
3. Coming about in a sailboat
4. How to change a tire
5. Making Christmas cards
6. Format in the school paper

7. How to model clothes
8. Operating a motorcycle
9. Transplanting wild flowers
10. Making a banana split

As you move from step to step in the process, be sure that each term is explained fully. Let us say you have chosen to explain how to change a tire. *Lug nut* may well be an unfamiliar term to novice tire changers; a short description of this vital part is in order. Any unfamiliar act, such as reversing the direction of the jack handle, must also be explained in detail. If a switch or lever must be thrown to change the direction of the jack, it is necessary to indicate precisely where it is located. For any step in the process, an explanation of the reason behind it can build the reader's confidence. Placing the jack under the front or rear bumper instead of next to the wheel opening is necessary for safety's sake, so the car will not slip off the jack in mid-change. Such explanations, delivered at times with deft touches of humour ("After jacking up the car, stand back and give it a moment to decide whether or not it wants to drop on your foot"), help the harried victim relax and glimpse the overall project more clearly. Finally, make sure your readers are aware not only of what to do but of what *not* to do. It would be wise, for example, to warn against loosening the nuts holding the tire until the whole wheel is off the ground. Doing so beforehand could lead to the tire falling suddenly and unexpectedly on the head of the poor tire changer.

One world of activity in which "how to do it" writing plays an important role is sports. The following example describes in precise, simple language the method a goaltender should use to poke the puck away from an opponent.

When you reach out to poke the puck away from an opponent crossing in front of you, wait until he is almost even with the net before making your move, and play the puck with the bottom of your blade. If you hook the puck with the top of your blade, there is a chance that the puck will follow the handle and slide toward you for a goal.

Do not hold your stick back for fear of tripping the puck carrier. If you do, he will often have enough room to pull back and beat you.

Make sure the stick faces centre ice, not the side boards, when you reach out after the puck. If you do not, a clever opponent will often have enough time to pull away from you or stop to score on the short side.

When you reach out on this play, always drop your back knee to the ice to protect yourself against a possible shot on the short side or between your legs.

To poke the puck away from a player cutting in front of the goal, throw your stick forward in a very aggressive move, holding the handle at the very end and holding your stretched-out position.

But first, you must have absolute confidence in your ability to force your opponent to cut in front of the net, rather than go to the short side. To succeed, slide your hand about four inches above the stick shoulders, in position to attack. This attack must be like a snake striking, not allowing the enemy time to react.

This move is best done when the goaltender throws himself on his knees as he sends his stick toward the centre of the ice. The leg on the short side of the post remains straight out behind you, to protect the short side.

If one of your knees stays up as you play the puck, it hits your stomach and shortens your reach by about two feet . . . enough room for the puck carrier to deke you. You should be able to stretch your stick as far as two small lines painted between the face-off circles.

All these moves will be useless if you cannot put your stick flat on the ice. To succeed move the back of your glove out of the way and turn your fingers, so they do not touch the ice.

Remember: (1) keep the heel of your stick facing the puck; (2) slide the hand from the shoulders to the end of the handle; (3) move forward while dropping your front knee to the ice; (4) don't try to poke the puck away from an opponent coming straight at you.

-Jacques Plante, *Goaltending*

A good test of a "how to do it" article is to put the process into operation yourself. "Can you do it?" is generally appropriate in the case of an unfamiliar process. Here, for example, is a nineteenth century settler's account of how to make "coffee" from dandelion roots. She included her instructions in her account of living in the bush so that other settlers would know how to survive.

The first year we came to this country, I met with an account of dandelion coffee, published in the *New York Albion*, given by a Dr Harrison, of Edinburgh, who earnestly recommended it as an article of general use.

"It possesses," he says, "all the fine flavour and exhilarating properties of coffee, without any of its deleterious effects. The plant being of a soporific nature, the coffee made from it when drunk at night produces a tendency to sleep, instead of exciting wakefulness, and may be safely used as a cheap and wholesome substitute for the Arabian berry, being equal in substance and flavour to the best Mocha coffee."

I was much struck with this paragraph at the time, and for several years felt a great inclination to try the Doctor's coffee; but something or other always came in the way, and it was put off till another opportunity. During the fall of '35, I was assisting my husband in taking up a crop of potatoes in the field, and observing a vast number of fine dandelion roots among the potatoes, it brought the dandelion coffee back to my memory, and I determined to try some for our supper. Without saying anything to my husband, I threw aside some of the roots, and when we left work, collecting a sufficient quantity for the experiment, I carefully washed the roots quite clean, without depriving them of the fine brown skin which covers them, and which contains the aromatic flavour which so nearly resembles coffee that it is difficult to distinguish it from it while roasting.

I cut my roots into small pieces, the size of a kidney-bean, and roasted them on an iron baking-pan in the stove-oven, until they were as brown and crisp as coffee. I then ground and transferred a small cupful of the powder to the coffee-pot, pouring upon it scalding water, and boiling it

for a few minutes briskly over the fire. The result was
beyond my expectations. The coffee proved excellent –
far superior to the common coffee we procured at the stores.

– Susanna Moodie, *Roughing it in the Bush*

As has been said, a complex operation can be described with
the purpose of putting the reader into a position to perform it.
That is the implication in Moodie's recollection. (It is also the
implication in this book.)

DEFINITION

One of the best ways to convince readers of your authority and
knowledge is to define a word or term for them. This act saves
them a trip to the dictionary and gives you a premise from which
to argue or pursue some larger question.

There is a great temptation among beginning writers simply
to quote dictionary definitions of words or terms at the opening
of their essays. But such a step is not always the best one to
take. Consider a word like *justice*. Most readers have a vague
idea of its meaning, so to quote from the dictionary will only
invite boredom, especially if you do not plan to disagree with or
challenge the meaning. Instead of taking the easy way, an inventive writer will begin by recounting an incident in which justice
– or injustice – was done. Rather than focussing on questions of
etymology, this approach gives the reader a working or contex-
tual definition from which may be extracted a variety of applications. Granted, a particular denotation can sometimes surprise:
assassin, for example, derives from the word *hashhashin*, used
to identify drug-crazed killers in Turkey. If a writer were trying
to prove that assassins are often fanatics, such a detail would
help. Here, as in all other forms of composition, a clear sense of
purpose will guide the selection of approach. On the whole, the
writer who finds many applications of a word or term is most
likely to hold the interest of readers while building a successful
essay.

One good way to define a word or term is to narrate an incident in which the meaning of the word or term is exemplified.

Friendship, for instance, may be generally understood by your readers. However, if you tell them how your friend Jack or Joan lent you bus fare to go home for your sister's wedding, drove you to the bus station, and on the way helped you pick out a fitting gift, your tale reveals the many dimensions of friendship in action. An essay that mixes personal anecdotes with more famous accounts – Mercutio's willingness to fight and die for his friend Romeo – would not only define the word but entertain and instruct readers.

Pierre Berton, in an attempt to explain the Canadian character, recounts an anecdote about the gold rush to show the Canadian predilection for honesty. Rather than simply stating his thesis in abstract terms, he illustrates it with a tale.

> The richest man in the Klondike was Big Alex McDonald, a huge, awkward prospector from Antigonish, Nova Scotia. He was so wealthy that he kept a bowl of nuggets on a shelf in his cabin to give away to visitors. His string of mules, each loaded with a hundred-pound sack of gold, was a familiar sight, moving in single file from his claim on Eldorado creek to the bank in Dawson City. One day, one of these mules broke away from the string, strayed into the hills and didn't turn up in Dawson for a fortnight.
>
> This errant animal, stumbling about through the birches and aspens, brushing past trappers' cabins and prospectors' tents, stands for me as a symbol of Canadian probity. For it must have been seen and recognized by scores of men who had come to the north hoping to find a fortune. On its back, for the taking, was a treasure worth twenty thousand dollars. Yet nobody touched it: Big Alex got his mule back with the gold intact.
>
> – Pierre Berton, *Why We Act Like Canadians*

A useful way to begin an essay of definition is to cite the need to define a term before the essay can proceed. Note the authoritative "I know what I am talking about" tone in the following sentence: "Although most of us have a general understanding of socialism, the term needs to be defined specifically before tracing its application to Polish society." In concluding the essay you might remind the reader that a concept like socialism, when understood in practice, differs considerably from the dictionary definition of the word. If you have traced the evolution in meaning of a certain word your conclusion might show how the word has evolved into a meaning that is not only different from the original meaning but quite opposite to it. Whatever approach you choose, avoid simply restating your introduction.

Humorous definitions – one-liners – can often arrest attention and help guide your reader to a fuller understanding of an essay's main idea. Stephen Leacock loved such concise, satirical definitions:

> An education, when it is all written out on foolscap, covers nearly ten sheets.

> The landlady of a boarding-house is a parallelogram – that is, an oblong angular figure, which cannot be described, but which is equal to anything.

> The meaning of the [Ph.D.] degree is that the recipient of instruction is examined for the last time in his life, and is pronounced completely full. After this, no new ideas can be imparted to him.

COMPARISON AND CONTRAST

Most of us follow the habit of making comparisons on a daily basis. Think of how you have compared last night's dinner at the Punjabi Garden with last month's feast there. How did *Staying Alive* hold up against *Saturday Night Fever*? Was last summer's vacation in Muskoka as much fun as this year's trip to the Calgary Stampede? In making such comparisons we are looking for similarities – good service, spicy curries – and differences – a smaller crowd last month, greater variety in the menu this time. To put it another way, comparison is a form of analysis or evaluation that requires the writer to identify similarities and differences in the person, thing, or event being observed.

There are at least three good reasons for writing comparison essays:

1. To demonstrate that one thing or event is *better* than another. There must be significant points of similarity – two movies

starring John Travolta – in order to draw a comparison of this kind. However, brought off well, such a comparison will find you defending the reasons behind your choice of films or Indian dinners with specific examples.

2. To point out how two similar persons, things, or events are *in fact different*. You might be comparing two totalitarian regimes, such as those in Guatemala and Czechoslovakia. In this situation the aim is not to show that one is better than the other, but to discuss how the differences influence the behaviour of the two countries.

3. To uncover *surprising similarities* in two apparently different persons, things, or events. The advantage of this act of comparison is that your readers are led to consider something from a new perspective. You might try comparing human and animal behaviour, reading and television viewing, driving a car and managing a household. Reflection on specific details will start the engine of your mind and get the essay rolling.

As we have said, reviews of movies or books often involve comparison between the reviewed work and another by the same author or director. Keep the preceding purposes in mind as you consider writing reviews or critiques.

Organizing Comparison Essays. The effectiveness of a comparison paper is directly related to careful organization. There are some accepted guides to organizing such essays, and these guides might well be copied out and kept handy.

1. Separate Comparison. If you plan to compare the leader of a NATO country with the leader of a Warsaw Pact nation, your essay may function best by discussing each leader separately, letting your readers make the comparison or selecting important points to discuss in your conclusion. You should compare each leader in the same areas: First, assess the prime minister's stance on the world situation, on defence, on peace; then examine the Soviet leader on the same points. The same order of areas should be followed for each analysis, keeping in mind that your readers will be better able to follow you if you do so.

2. Similarities/Differences Comparison. If you choose to write about two events – an early Beatles concert and a recent Rush concert – the best method may be to consider all the similarities between the two, then all the differences. This method works best with persons, things, and events that are not on the surface strikingly different. Rock concerts belong to the same class of events, and often appear very similar. You might begin this type of essay by noting that the age of the audiences, the level of sound, and the general attitude toward rock music were the same at the two concerts but that the nature of the instruments, lyrics, and performance styles has changed considerably over the years. Just remember that your categories are *Similarities* and *Differences*, not *The Beatles Concert* and *The Rush Concert*.

3. Alternating Comparison. Certain comparisons work best when the writer breaks down the essay into topics and compares the persons, things, and events on this basis. For the essay on political leaders, you may keep the same topics – attitudes toward the world situation, defence , and peace – but you discuss the similarities and differences between the two leaders under the general topics. Sentences in this type of comparison essay tend to be constructed in the following way: "Whereas the prime minister sees the countries in NATO as a buffer against Soviet aggression, the Soviet leader tends to regard them as menacing enemies armed with American-made weapons." In order to pursue the alternating method, you will have to decide on general topics with some care: Is there, for instance, enough information about the prime minister's stance on defence? But once the topics are chosen, the essay almost writes itself.

No matter what method you choose you should begin by writing down the names of the two persons, things, or events to be compared, then proceed to list details about each under the headings. This technique will build up the substance of the paper and start you thinking about the subject in a comparative way. Comparison methods can be adopted in both essays of exposition and argumentation; they work especially well in persuading readers that one particular book, movie, or political system is better than another.

6

PROBLEMS OF COMPOSING

The methods or approaches outlined in chapter 5 give you some notion of how to go about organizing your thoughts into an effective pattern. In this chapter you will find more practical advice on how to begin filling the blank space of the page with words that will win your reader's attention. Through an analysis of an essay written by an expert, you will see the steps involved in conducting an argument. Finally, the chapter will offer some suggestions for revising and proofreading the final draft.

Beginnings and Endings

Every writer faced with the task of setting his or her ideas down on paper is conscious of the overwhelming importance of an effective beginning. It seems as important as first impressions in the first interview with your employer, or the introduction to your future parents-in-law. There is something terrifying about it because its success, or lack thereof, is bound to colour everything that follows.

"The best way to begin is to begin. Do not write introductions. Just plunge in." All this is sound advice, but not very helpful to the beginner. You might as well be told to learn to dance by plunging in – some persons do dance that way, after all. You need to know what to do after plunging in. Another piece of advice, possibly more helpful, goes this way: "Just write down anything about your subject. Keep going until you get well into your first main topic. Then, in revision, cross out the first two paragraphs." This advice rings true, but it may result in lopping off a good idea or two. A cleansing and healing of the afflicted part may prove as effective as amputation and will certainly hurt less. Learn to diagnose ailments before prescribing surgery.

There are, however, a number of specific devices that writers may use to introduce their subject appropriately and interestingly, just as there are similar devices for the easier task of appropriately ending their paper. Anyone glancing over a recent file of a serious magazine in which various kinds of articles appear – *Maclean's* for instance – is sure to find repeated examples of particular techniques for beginning as well as for ending. As the following selections will show, there is usually a close logical and rhetorical relation between the two. To connect your beginning and ending is one obvious way to give your paper organization.

Eight possible ways to begin (among many) are illustrated below. In each case the author's ending is also quoted. Their relation is worth study. As always, your choice of any particular technique depends not only on personal taste but on the kind of article you are writing and the kind of reader you are addressing. In studying these illustrations, note how the various beginnings and endings are, in part, responses to the subject and tone that the author has chosen.

The Dramatized Example or Incident. A familiar opening is a dramatized example or incident from which a larger generalization is to emerge. Here is such an introduction in the first few sentences of an essay on the work ethic.

> On my seventeenth birthday, which fell on July 12, 1937, one of the worst years of the Depression, I went to work for pay and there was jubilation among my friends and relatives. In an era when jobs were scarce I had a job; and having a job was the goal of everyone in those days. Having a job in

the Thirties was a bit like having a swimming pool in the
Sixties; it conferred status. It didn't really matter what the
job was. It could be unrewarding, mindless, foolish, unpro-
ductive, even degrading – no matter: it set you apart as a
paying member of a society whose creed was that everyone
must work at something, and the harder the better, too.

The author proceeds to argue that back-breaking work, which
is usually believed to be ennobling, is often degrading, destruc-
tive, and useless. His point is ironically restated in his concluding paragraph.

The one valuable asset that I recovered from my mining
camp experience was status. It allows me to use a line in my
official biography which I notice is seized upon joyfully by
those who have to introduce me when I make after-dinner-
speeches: ''During the Thirties, he worked in Yukon mining camps to help put himself through university.'' When
that line is uttered the audience is prepared to forgive me
almost anything: outlandishly radical opinions, dangerous
views on matters sexual, alarming attitudes toward religion.
I am pronounced worthy because, in that one sentence, is
summed up the great Canadian myth: that work – *any* work
– is the most important thing in life, and that anybody who
is willing to work hard enough can by his own initiative get
as far as he wants.

> – Pierre Berton, ''The Religion of Work
> and the Dirtiest Job in the World,'' *The Smug Minority*

The Anecdote. A related technique is to begin with an anecdote,
true or fictitious, but told in the manner of the storyteller.

Last May about 200 people, including the premier of
New Brunswick, Richard Hatfield, gathered at Mathieu
Martin High School in Moncton (quite literally a far cry
from Rideau Hall) to watch the Governor General present
his annual literary awards. I envy the judges, said His
Excellency Edward Schreyer to the assembled writers,
politicians, academics, and miscellany, their opportunity
to examine the collective soul of the nation.

The author contrasts the dignified and thoughtful words of the Governor General with the angry controversies that often arise from the decision of the judges. She continues by providing a brief history of the Governor General's awards as well as criticisms of some winning choices and the judging methods used in making the choices. Nevertheless, the author concludes, the Governor General's awards are important to Canadian writing.

> Macmillan publisher Doug Gibson once remarked that if the GGs didn't exist something like them would have to be invented. So watch for them again this spring. The GGs. The awards you love to hate.
>
> – Eleanor Wachtel, "Prize and Prejudice"

The Autobiographical Incident. A similar opening technique is the illustrative incident taken from a moment in the writer's own life. Here the writer mixes autobiographical fact and reflection to start his essay on the nature of estuaries.

> I remember thinking, as a very small boy, that one of the supreme sights of the world must be the mouth of a river. I could not satisfactorily imagine this meeting of the river's flow and the sea's surge and I knew it would be a waste of time to ask anyone to describe it to me. Just what I expected I am not at all sure, but I suppose some sudden and violent outpouring of fresh water into salt, plainly visible, dramatic, and splendid. I knew little or nothing of tides and even less of the fearful things men do to river mouths in the process of civilization. So the first few estuaries I did finally see were disappointing and unconvincing.

Gradually, through experience, the writer begins to appreciate different landscapes, kinds of fish, tides, and challenges offered by various estuaries. He closes with an assertion about his changed perceptions.

> These, then, are my estuaries, little places, often unconsidered, highly uncertain, pleasantly demanding of the skills a fisherman delights in. They are special places, ever changing with the tide's movements, full of the special life of the

sea's meeting with the land. One grows to know them gradually, in rain and fog and sunshine, in wind and calm, at
dawn and dusk; and as knowledge builds to intimacy the
dramatic values are plain at last, richer and stronger than
the simple splendour the child's mind hoped to discover.

> – Roderick Haig-Brown,
> "The Nature of Estuaries," *Fisherman's Fall*

The Stereotype Refuted. A common device for opening an essay is to summarize stereotyped beliefs about a given subject,
then proceed to refute them. Effectively done this opening can
impress your audience with your learning and audacity. Here is
an example from an essay in which Pierre Trudeau addresses
his fellow French Canadians.

> We have expended a great deal of time and energy
> proclaiming the rights due our nationality, invoking our
> divine mission, trumpeting our virtues, bewailing our
> misfortunes, denouncing our enemies, and avowing our
> independence; and for all that not one of our workmen is
> the more skilled, nor a civil servant the more efficient, a
> financier the richer, a doctor the more advanced, a bishop
> the more learned, nor a single solitary politician the less
> ignorant. Now, except for a few stubborn eccentrics, there
> is probably not one French-Canadian intellectual who has
> not spent at least four hours a week over the last year
> discussing separatism. That makes how many thousand
> times two hundred hours spent just flapping our arms?

The author then asserts that Quebec nationalists are self-deluded
political reactionaries whose policies can only lead to the collapse of French-Canadian society. He concludes by listing what
the actual consequences of separation will be.

> It is a serious thing to ask French Canadians to embark
> on several decades of privation and sacrifice, just so that
> they can indulge themselves in the luxury of choosing
> "freely" a destiny more or less identical to the one they
> have rejected. But the ultimate tragedy would be in not
> realizing that French Canada is too culturally anaemic,

too economically destitute, too intellectually retarded,
too spiritually paralysed, to be able to survive more than
a couple of decades of stagnation, emptying herself of all
her vitality into nothing but a cesspit, the mirror of her
nationalistic vanity and "dignity."

> – Pierre Trudeau, "The Sorry Tale of French-Canadian
> Nationalism," *Federalism and the French Canadians*

The Surprise Opening (Serious). A variation on the use of the
stereotype is to begin an essay with a surprising or even shocking statement, one that is distinctly *not* a stereotype. Sometimes
such a beginning may take the form of a series of ironic statements calculated to create a mild shock in the reader.

> Perhaps we should rejoice in the disappearance of Canada.
> We leave the narrow provincialism and our backwoods
> culture; we enter the excitement of the United States where
> all the great things are being done. Who would compare
> the science, the art, the politics, the entertainment of our
> petty world to the overflowing achievements of New York,
> Washington, Chicago, and San Francisco? Think of William
> Faulkner and then think of Morley Callaghan. Think of the
> Kennedys and the Rockefellers and then think of Pearson
> and E.P. Taylor. This is the profoundest argument for the
> Liberals. They governed so as to break down our
> parochialism and lead us into the future.

The author then proceeds to demonstrate how Liberal philosophy, based on the ideas of necessity and progress, has led to
notions of world government in general and continentalism in
particular. These notions can result in larger tyrannies and global
war. He concludes by saying that if we cannot predict the future,
at least we can rely on our traditions.

> My lament is not based on philosophy but on tradition.
> If one cannot be sure about the answer to the most important
> questions, then tradition is the best basis for the practical
> life. Those who loved the older traditions of Canada may be
> allowed to lament what has been lost, even though they do
> not know whether or not that loss will lead to some greater

political good. But lamentation falls easily into the vice of self-pity. To live with courage is a virtue, whatever one may think of the dominant assumptions of one's age. Multitudes of human beings through the course of history have had to live when their only political allegiance was irretrievably lost. What was lost was often something far nobler than what Canadians have lost. Beyond courage, it is also possible to live in the ancient faith, which asserts that changes in the world, even if they be recognized more as a loss than a gain, take place within an eternal order that is not affected by their taking place. Whatever the difficulty of philosophy, the religious man has been told that process is not all. "*Tendebantque manus ripae ulterioris amore.*"[5]

> – George Grant, "The Disappearance
> of Canada," *Lament for a Nation*

The Surprise Opening (Humorous). Another kind of shock opening, far less aggressive in tone, can be achieved by putting forward an argument that is absurd on the face of it. Can the writer *mean* it? we ask. The writer in the following example begins his essay with a ludicrous political observation.

> There is something strange about Canada. It is the home of The Bachelor Party. It enjoys being run by lonely, selfish men – that being one definition of a bachelor. Does this mean our leaders (Ottawa? the country?) don't like sex? Or does it mean that our leaders (Ottawa? the country?) are promiscuous? A discussion follows.

After listing some prominent past and present bachelor leaders in the Liberal party, Fotheringham asserts that these grim, abstemious men epitomize the personality of Ottawa and the country. He concludes:

> Mackenzie King tried to commune with his dead mother and talked to his beloved dog. MacEachen talks to his broken calculator, and Coutts talks to Davey who talks only to Goldfarb. Trudeau (the famous nonnewspaper reader) revealed during the 1981 CBC technicians' strike that it wasn't important because he never listened to radio or

[5]Virgil *Aeneid*, bk. 6: "They were holding their arms outstretched in love toward the further shore."

watched TV. It is natural. The voters of this country like monks, inward-turning men who are obsessed with self.

It is not an accident that Liberal leaders are bachelors and bachelors are Liberals. It goes with the territory.

> – Allan Fotheringham, "Second Digression:
> The Bachelor Party," *Malice in Blunderland*

Questions to Be Answered. The rhetorical question, the question with only one possible answer, is often used as an ending technique. It is also familiar as a beginning. But even more familiar, and clearly appropriate for many kinds of serious argumentation essays, is the technique of asking questions that do not have easy answers. The effort to provide answers, then, becomes the central concern of the essay. Here is an example in which a writer questions the nature of heroism in the modern age.

> Where are the genuine heroes, those large souls bigger than life, big enough for bronze gesticulation among traffic lights? Big enough to sustain our songs of triumphs in bed and battle, of beauty, bravery, money, fame, loves!

Part of the appeal of this essay is that the author cannot find adequate answers to these questions. He argues that heroes who fight the machinery of the post-national state only create similar new horrors of their own. Sports and movie heroes are part of commercial illusions, like the state. Thus, he concludes, the real heroes battle the creators of those illusions.

> This is the ground for intellectual heroism. The intellectual hero is one who pricks the bubble of illusion, who sees through the goblins. Despite all attempts to turn him into a goblin himself, he fights ruthlessly on. Marshall McLuhan is such a hero. Northrop Frye is another. They are both Canadians and they are both engaged in a universal conflict, champions of reality in a world of illusion.
>
> – Kildare Dobbs, "Canadian Heroes?"

The Appeal of Importance. In all the beginnings we have discussed, the author has been responsible for convincing his or her reader that the article will be worth the reading, that it is important or significant or amusing. Sometimes, instead of asking questions or telling stories to arouse interest, an author may simply *tell* the reader of the subject's urgency.

> The rise of Marxism during the past century and its adoption by the Soviet Union as a state ideology have confronted Western nations with an external challenge. At the same time, communism has confronted the Western nations with an internal challenge that is, in some ways, more testing than the overt threat represented by Soviet military strength and influence in the world. In Canada, this internal challenge does not lie in the possibility that communists may acquire actual power and influence; the challenge is to our attitudes, to our institutions, and to our ideas about the limits of dissent.

In the rest of the essay the author describes the way Canadian governments and institutions have harassed and vilified communists and often deprived them of their democratic rights as citizens. He concludes by stating that we must tolerate dissent and insist upon freedom of speech for all Canadians.

> In the contest between the Western democracies and the communist nations, we must be careful not to cede the very things that will make the outcome of this contest significant to all people. It is not a struggle between capitalism and communism, the eighteenth and nineteenth-century offspring of the Industrial Revolution. Rather, the question is whether or not the regime of tolerance will prevail among men and women and among the nations. This regime represents the proudest achievement of the West, our claim to the verdict of history: it is an insistence upon the right of the individual to think as he will, to believe what he chooses, and to speak his own truth.
>
> > – Thomas Berger, ''The Communist Party and the Limits of Dissent,'' *Fragile Freedoms*

Persuasion: the Whole Essay

The persuasion or argumentation essay is both the most diffi-cult and most rewarding essay to compose. That is why this section outlines its features in detail, taking you from start to finish. Such essays are difficult to do because they demand that the writer take a position, state a thesis to be argued, then argue that thesis according to the dictates of reason and logic. They are rewarding because they allow the writer to express strongly held beliefs in a forum that is free of the distractions that attend spoken debates. Learning the techniques of argumentation will be of special value when you are asked to take a stand on ques-tions like the mandatory use of seat belts or drinking for nineteen-year-olds. Research papers are also often assigned as questions calling for a thesis to be argued by the writer.

Organizing a Persuasion Paper

The first step in organizing a persuasion paper is to state the thesis as a question to be argued. *Convince* or *persuade* are words that ought to appear in the sentence as you state it in the pre-writing stage. This thesis should be specific enough to give your readers an idea of where the essay is headed, but broad enough to allow for flexibility in the actual conduct of the argument. The following statement of purpose is probably close to the one Roderick Haig-Brown had in mind when he wrote the essay used in this chapter as an example of persuasive writing.

Purpose: To convince the reader that although security is desired, for good reasons, by everyone, a growing nation has more need of people who are willing to sacrifice security for higher, less tangible values.

Title: Choice for Canadians: Security or Freedom

Central Idea: There are many advantages to, and historical reasons for, our search for security and the consequent development of the welfare state. However, a growing nation must project and foster some absolute standards if it is to avoid stagnation, and in order to achieve its goals it must encourage risk-takers and non-conformists.

The next step is to decide how *to present your case* to readers on the lookout for hard evidence. How you will order your material depends on what you have to say and on the sort of reader you are addressing. Two standard methods, outlined in the paragraphs that follow, are widely recognized by theorists of composition.

INDUCTIVE ORDER (ORDER OF EASY ACCEPTANCE)

Often readers are best led toward an unconventional idea by starting with a presentation of numerous facts, instances, or observations that build up support for that main idea. For instance, if you are advocating the institution of student government in school, you may get a more favourable response from your readers if you convince them first that a system of strict, paternalistic government has resulted in inattention to grading policies, student placement, and non-academic activities. If you are urging the establishment of teenage night clubs, begin by picturing the present undesirable conditions in the neighbourhood: students on the streets late at night, involved in vandalism and other misdeeds. Following the inductive order means stating your generalization *after* citing individual instances that illustrate the main idea.

DEDUCTIVE ORDER ("FROM THE GENERAL TO THE PARTICULAR")

It is frequently possible to win over your reader with a well-worded generalization or premise, the truth of which is substantiated in the body of the essay by a series of specific examples. In logic the syllogism is a form of argument based on deduction. It consists of a major premise – "All people love peace" – a minor premise – "Lester Pearson was a person" – and a conclusion – "Lester Pearson loved peace." As you can see, this method of

argument has certain advantages. If you accept the major premise, the other two propositions must also be accepted; the force
of logic serves to drive the point home. Many readers also equate
eloquent generalizations like "All people love peace" with truth,
even though such assertions may not hold up under scrutiny.
(How can the claim be verified, especially in light of the many
wars in human history?) In order to use this method successfully
the writer must be sure that the generalization or major premise is
workable and defensible. This means that the process of deduction should be tested before you write the essay; you cannot
depend solely on the authority of your own voice to carry it
through. A handy rule is to make sure your generalization ("All
people love peace") has been carefully qualified ("*Most* people
love peace") so that readers will not be able to point to obvious
exceptions before you have had a chance to persuade them.

LOGIC

As the preceding paragraph hints, some knowledge of the conventions of logic is of considerable value in conducting the argument in a persuasion essay.

Most of us, however, are put off by the word *logic*. It connotes a cold, unfeeling approach to life. Yet in writing for an
audience that you are trying to sway, impress, cajole, or move
in some way, logic can be a useful tool. It may even serve as the
machete that you can wield to cut your way through a jungle of
ideas or impressions in your own mind. One thing is sure: if
you make too many errors in logic, your reader will soon begin
to suspect the authority of your statements. Once lost, that reader
is difficult to win back to your point of view with emotional
appeals alone.

Below are a few of the more common errors in logic or reasoning. Try out your understanding of them by testing them
against the arguments that appear in the editorial sections of
newspapers or magazines.

False Analogy. Analogy is a means of arguing by comparing
something to something else. Recently we have heard of a "war

on inflation" conducted by the federal government; and the argument in support of urgent measures for economic health has depended on the analogy. We are made to feel that we must conquer inflation before it conquers us.

False analogies result when the comparison does not rest on any basic similarities or when the analogy is substituted for a proof in an argument. To justify certain actions in governmental organizations by comparing the organization to a "team" that is out "to win" is an example of substituting an analogy for a proof. Government is not a game.

False Cause. False cause has several variations, but the most common one confuses cause with effect. Because North American society is so impressed with statistics, we are often susceptible to false cause arguments that employ them. For instance, an irate speaker recently used the following statistics to "prove" that rock music is evil: "Of 1000 girls who became pregnant out of wedlock, 994 committed fornication while rock music was being played." One wonders what the other six were doing!

The *post hoc, ergo propter hoc* fallacy is another example of false cause argument. Translated the phrase means "after this, therefore because of this," and it describes a statement asserting that two events are related because the first preceded the second. Those who claim there is a direct relationship between the election of the Conservative governments in 1930, 1957, and 1979, and the economic depressions that followed are using the *post hoc* argument. The assertion that the election of Liberal governments brought back prosperity only compounds the error.

Begging the Question. Any argument that assumes the truth of the very point to be proved begs the question. One of the symptoms of this fallacy is circular reasoning, in which the conclusion of the argument simply restates the assumption. Those who claim that the country's moral fibre has been weakened by too much television watching and that we will grow strong again if we destroy television sets have assumed too much. They must first prove that the nation's morality has indeed become corrupted in the period since the invention of television.

Argumentum ad Hominem. An "argument against the person" might simply be called avoiding the question, since it draws attention to the character of the individual and not his or her assertion. We immediately think of abuse or invective as examples of *ad hominem* arguments: "He has never done an honest day's work in his life, so how can he dare to introduce a bill improving the rights of the average worker?" But a speaker who uses emotional generalities to win our approval is also ignoring the question: "Many long years of loyal service to and love for this company qualify me to speak about what is best for its employees."

Non Sequitur ("it does not follow"). When the premises of an argument do not establish a firm basis for the conclusion, then the conclusion is called a *non sequitur*. Often the cause is a failure to provide a step in the argument: "I bought one of those cars and it turned out to be a lemon. The company later went out of business." More often the conclusion is based on irrelevant evidence: "Wayne Gretzky eats that chocolate bar so it must be good." Notice how many companies attempt to "prove" the quality or popularity of their products by getting endorsements from famous people.

No doubt the most obvious error in argumentation is overgeneralization. It is not specifically an error in logic, though many people might claim that a failure to qualify any statements about events or people violates their sense of the real world. More important, hasty generalizations give the reader the impression that you have not taken the time to look closely at the evidence. They are the basis as well for prejudice and bias. "*All* Italians belong to the Mafia"; "The Irish are fighting with each other *all the time.*" We are especially susceptible to overgeneralization when our emotions are aroused. It was not until some time after World War II that many Americans chose to recognize that the Japanese had planned to inform them about the attack on Pearl Harbor *before* it took place, but their Washington ambassador was delayed because of problems in decoding the message from Tokyo.

When you find yourself using such words as *always*, *never*, *all*, *only*, and *every*, it is time to examine your statement in detail. Don't claim that *only* truck drivers sit in front of their television sets, beer cans in hand and watching football, until you have checked around. If you claim that *most* women want a home and husband, make sure that at least two-thirds in fact do or you will be open not only to a charge of overgeneralization but also to a charge of sexism. To avoid such serious predicaments, and to improve your writing, take advantage of the numerous qualifying terms available to you. Select the ones that accurately describe the facts in your argument: "*Some* men feel pressured by the company's affirmative action policy in hiring"; "She *often* wants me to do the shopping so that she can have more time to write." Remember that the reader will heed statements based on a realistic assessment of the facts more readily than loose generalizations of the kind he or she hears frequently in informal and uninformed conversation.

FACT, BELIEF, OPINION DISTINCTIONS

Facts may be verified by referring to our senses. We can see that a table is not a chair; we can taste the difference between sugar and salt. Factual statements may be substantiated by some arbiter – an encyclopaedia, a dictionary, a ruler. Not all facts are physical, that is, involve measuring or weighing or counting. Some facts are historical in nature; they may be verified by artifacts or signs of the event. If we claim that one third of London's population died during the plague years of 1601–1605, we can produce the plague bills or death lists as proof. In some cases we may not possess these pieces of evidence. There is no birth certificate to prove, for example, that Shakespeare was born on April 23, 1564. But the important point is that this date is widely accepted by scholars because they have his record of baptism, which traditionally took place three days after birth. Such verification is at least a prerequisite of good writing; proof convinces readers of the writer's authority on the subject.

Beliefs may be strongly held (e.g., "I believe in UFO's"), but they are not verifiable in any recognized way. Religious belief may be stated in certain contexts, but the mere statement of it should not be mistaken for proof. Qualifying beliefs helps, yet if you find yourself in an area – creation of the world, for instance – where belief must be stated in place of argument, it is best to delete such avowals.

Opinions may well be verified but not under the guise of opinions. *Theory* might well be used as a synonym for *opinion*: Einstein's theory of relativity has been supported by mathematical calculations and other means. "Pigs are smarter than horses" stands as Johnny Carson's opinion about animal intelligence. He has had a running feud with announcer Ed McMahon over the issue, but the evidence – pigs playing chess, horses talking – can never be conclusive. Commonly held opinion may support one or the other opinion, but it would be impossible to survey a sufficient sample of pigs and horses to settle the matter.

"CHOICE FOR CANADIANS": STEPS IN THE ARGUMENT

In his essay, Haig-Brown uses the deductive approach to outline why security should not be the ultimate goal of a nation or of an individual. This means that he must provide evidence for his claims. He must show why security is disadvantageous and why risk-taking is valuable.

An important step in the process is to challenge the opposing opinions by selecting the central points of contention and refuting them. In your essays, this is where a knowledge of logic will come in handy. On the question of seat belts, opponents might argue that there has been no significant reduction in fatalities since the seat belt law has been in effect. This sort of contention can easily be refuted by citing statistics kept by relevant government agencies; in provinces where seat belts must be worn, there have been fewer deaths in traffic accidents. Claims that seat belts cause deaths or that individuals' rights are being taken away can be dismissed on the grounds of faulty logic. More people have been saved than endangered by wearing seat belts, and other rights besides those of individual choice are involved. A satiric or biting tone is not required to puncture such balloons of bad thinking, however. Readers are more likely to respond favourably to a reasoned, analytical tone that simply lets out the hot air without damaging the balloon.

One major claim against the thesis in ''Choice for Canadians: Security or Freedom'' is that the security offered to its citizens by the welfare state frees them from poverty and ignorance and allows them the time to reflect and discuss concerns essential to a democracy. Another is that history has taught us the necessity of a welfare-state economy. Haig-Brown contends with these claims by admitting the benefits of economic security while at the same time listing some of its negative effects. Complacency, the illusion of well-being, mediocrity, and a stifling of the human spirit can result when citizens are too well taken care of.

When you refute opposing claims in your own essays, be sure as well to recognize their validity when the facts support them. Haig-Brown, for example, acknowledges that the security offered by the industrial welfare state makes life much more tolerable than it was in a class-dominated society. Specialization in jobs, too, has had some very positive effects. His aim is to establish a balance between security and freedom and to argue in favour of dimensions in living that material security alone cannot give. Generally, by conceding some of the opposing points, you not only provide a context from which to conduct your argument, but you show your readers how fair-minded you are. Notice how successfully Roderick Haig-Brown has established a balanced context for his argument.

Proving your thesis – the activity that constitutes the body of your paper – calls for care in arranging your arguments and opinions in an order that is likely to be persuasive. Do not begin with your most significant or telling point. By moving from the least to the most important argument, you prepare the reader's attention for the clincher. State your ideas in a straightforward, soundly qualified way; avoid being excessively clever or witty. As much as possible, educate your readers about the subject while informing them of the background for the controversy or question your essay attempts to settle. In his essay Roderick

Haig-Brown outlines the argument from history that the industrial welfare state is a reaction to the abuses of various tyrannies and that undoubtedly many people are better off than their ancestors. However, he maintains that every country, if it is to become truly civilized, must establish for itself standards that include more than a comfortable life. The author constructs his essay so that it rises in tone and vision to attributes such as self-sacrifice, ambition, self-reliance, generosity, devotion, and idealism; and he advises a broad education for Canadians if our young nation is to become a strong nation.

The final step in a persuasion essay is *to recapitulate your main points*, especially if the paper is long (7–10 typewritten pages). Rather than listing all your points, it may be more effective to select two or three main points that your readers are likely to remember. Haig-Brown creates a strong conclusion by summarizing his whole thesis in the last two paragraphs of his essay, and by making his argument relevant to our own national interests.

Outline

Choice for Canadians: Security or Freedom

Thesis: Although material security is a worthwhile goal, we must be careful that in the creation of a welfare state we do not lose sight of more important values and standards for the building of our country. Otherwise we can become stagnant and mediocre.

I. Canadians must choose between security and freedom.
   A. Material security offers many benefits.
   B. Material security also has many negative effects on individuals and on society.
   C. The industrial welfare state has improved living conditions.
   D. These advantages are not enough for a nation to survive.
II. The historical data provides important information.
   A. Socio-political changes have generally exchanged one advantaged group for another.

    B. Victorians and their children, especially those who suffered through the Depression, have been concerned mostly with steady jobs and the security they can bring. Society trains people for specialized work earlier and earlier.

    C. Industry and efficiency are not the most important concerns in building a nation.

III. Arguments for an alternative can be made.

    A. Specialized education limits minds and fosters conformity and mediocrity in the long run.

    B. We need people who seek more than secure comfort. There is no formula for producing such people, but they are always available and should be encouraged.

    C. They can be recognized by their actions.

    D. Examples of this kind of person can be given.

IV. There are good reasons for fostering the free spirit of growth and inquiry.

    A. It is important to learn a broad range of things.

    B. There are absolute standards of values and we need to know them in order to make sound judgements.

    C. If we want to be first-rate then we need citizens who are free to question and able to judge the answers they get.

Choice for Canadians
Security or Freedom

Roderick Haig-Brown

Material security is a fine thing. It can make for stable families, well-adjusted children, reasonable contentment, and the sort of cushioned lives that most people feel they need. A good measure of it, through family allowances, old age pensions, veterans' pensions, government and private pension schemes of many kinds, unemployment insurance, and ready social assistance, is undoubtedly needed to maintain the modern industrial economy of produce and use and throw away.

Certain other merits are claimed for it, notably that it makes men free to think and talk and develop into the positive individuals that a democracy needs. Of these claims I am much more doubtful. Security, like anything else, has its price, and the price is not payable in taxes alone. Security is a stifling and deadly thing for many people. The idea of it grips their minds in the schoolroom, limits them in choice of university training, grooves and patterns their working lives, gently eases them into the second-rate satisfactions of shiny mass production, and eventually plants them in well-kept graves after a lifelong illusion of life. So far from having lived as free and constructive citizens they will have paid unceasing tribute to all the second-rate satisfactions dreamed up for them – superficial knowledge, bad taste in art and entertainment, false standards in personal conduct, and a narrow, distorted view of the world they have passed through.

When all this is said, the moderate security of the industrial welfare state remains infinitely preferable to the poverty, exploitation, squalor, and ignorance of most civilizations that have preceded it. No doubt virtuous simplicity and rugged honour existed under these conditions, as they do today; but they were wrapped in physical miseries that can have done little to increase the stature of mankind, and in hereditary distinctions between man and man that were false and founded in meanness of spirit. At least the industrial state has living seeds of growth and freedom in it, and it can place within physical reach of man, any man, the things his soul should seek. If it obscures them from him with the glossy froth of its own waste, it still offers more than its predecessors.

But without rebels and sports, such a state is bound to die. Canada could die very easily, before she is fairly born, under the sheer weight of short-lived automobiles, the welter of shoddy entertainment, and the burden of a time-serving, pension-conscious citizenry.

Fortunately, human social organizations don't work that way. In seeking to favour one group, however large or small, they invariably foster a new group that reaps the real advantage. The age of chivalry made things easy for the merchant prince. The French Revolution built an elegant bourgeois state. The Russian experiment in a classless society . . . has raised a supreme tyrant, supported by an oligarchy of ruthless lieutenants, who are served in turn by a petty aristocracy of bureaucrats. The welfare state, or at least that version of it current in North America, offers most to those bold citizens who disregard security at every turning point of their lives – and it stands to gain most from them.

The pattern of security is not really new. Every respectable Victorian parent urged his child into a ''nice, steady job, with prospects,'' and seems to have been disregarded as often as not, at least by those who left a mark. The famous Depression of the thirties made the big change. Those of us old enough to start our working lives in the bright world just before it, have usually held to our old, improvident ways, sure that having survived once we shall survive again. But somehow, probably by dramatizing our early difficulties, we bred a race of children with wary eyes for the economic weather. And we quickly hedged them round with all the temptations and limitations of the incipient welfare state.

We declared it an age of specialization, a time when most jobs are so complicated that learning must start early and life must be grooved into them. Industry was ready to go along with that, so was labour, so was the state. And so were the children. You named it in high school and began preparing there, selected an appropriate university course, went from that to the job and presumably followed safely on through nicely graduated promotions to an early pension. It is a useful pattern for an industrialized, urban civilization, which is exactly why it has been allowed to develop. But it doesn't make for first-rate satisfactions or first-rate people.

This may or may not be all right for finding new oil wells, building new factories and running everything more or less efficiently. But there is an enormous amount of work to be done and service to be given in a new nation – or an old one, for that matter – which has little to do with material production. The children in school and university

today, and probably their children after them, are going to
have a great deal to do with setting the ways of Canada,
building her national life, creating her art and literature
and music, forming her laws, establishing the quality of
service she will give her own people and the rest of the
world.

These things cannot be well done, and some of them
cannot be done at all, by minds limited by specialized
education for specialized jobs, for whom security and
conformity are guiding principles. They will be done, as
always, by people who sense in themselves a capacity to
reach for the infinite and the undefined, by people who
know, if they bother to think about it at all, that their only
security is in their own worth and that every compromise
they make for security reduces their worth.

There is no formula for producing such people. They come
from farms and factories and the woods, from city streets
and highly-priced residential areas and forgotten fishing
villages. But the times can encourage them and educators
can watch for them and parents can bear with them –
perhaps even suffer a little for them. For they are the people
who do unlikely and unpredictable things, the people who
give body and life and meaning to a nation.

It is absurdly difficult to point to the sort of people I am
thinking of, except by saying they are people who not only
fill, but overflow whatever jobs they do, people who bring
to their lives as well as their jobs a breadth and generosity
and devotion that doesn't shut off with an eight-hour day
and is never ready to go to pension. One may be a railroad
conductor who is known to everyone in the length of his
run and somehow makes it mean much more than that.
Another may be a teacher who has watched forty years of
changing faces without a slackening of interest. Still
another may be a painter who has kept his vision clear and
bright through five or fifty years of poverty. It doesn't
matter very much who they are or where they are; their
quality is what they do and give.

Performance that rejects security is everywhere, but
when I search for examples I think of the young lawyer who

takes his learning and inexperience out to a small town, to
practise criminal law, draw up contracts and wills, listen
to people's troubles, give you advice and whatever else
he is asked for, instead of settling to a profitable lifetime
of divorce court practice in the city. I think of the young
doctor or priest who goes out to a mining settlement in the
sincere conviction he is needed there. I think of the boy
who has just left high school and works with a survey crew
instead of where the pay is better "because there's a chance
to learn something."

But the same thing can happen in a million other ways
and a million other lives. It's no use trying to call it, but it
is important not to stifle it, because it can mean an urgency
of life and happiness that no amount of security can ever
give. To my own children I say: "By all means learn to do
something useful but take the broadest education you can
find, fit everything you know into it, and everything else
you learn into the total. And don't stop learning."

The reason I tell them this is because I believe there are
absolute standards of value, at least within the framework
of the civilization we are trying to build, and that there
is enough stored-up human wisdom by which to learn
to judge them. There is a clearly detectable difference
between the first-rate and the second-rate in everything
that is of the slightest importance – in the arts and in
literature, in politics and in law, in religious teaching and
secular teaching, in human lives and human performance.

It is important for Canada that she should have an abundance of citizens who will constantly question everything
about her – government, industry, art, education, the
church, the judiciary, public services, their own lives and
their own jobs – by first-rate standards. Ultimately these
same citizens are going to have to ask themselves the most
difficult and important question of all: "How can Canada
behave humanely and wisely and safely in her dealings
with the rest of mankind?" If they don't find the right
answer to that, by first-rate standards, the security of the
welfare state and the shiny yield of the industrial state will
have little meaning for anyone.

PREPARING THE FINAL DRAFT: REVISING, PROOFREADING

Every essay can stand one more look: for weaknesses in organization, transition, support; for errors in spelling, word choice,
punctuation. Of all writing performances, revising is probably
the most difficult to master. It is, however, one of the most crucial to a successful essay. Here are some suggestions for shaping
your work of words into a finished product.

Try to complete a draft of a paper at least a day or two before
it is due. This means giving up the bad habit of composing *and*
typing the essay the night before handing it in. Then take from
the remaining time an hour or two when you are at your most
alert, when you are feeling efficient and sensitive. Pick up your
manuscript and begin to read. As you do so, try to pretend it
was written by somebody else. In your role as just another reader
of this composition, make quick notes in the margin of everything that makes you hesitate, for any reason. Ask yourself, How
can I tell that this essay was written by an amateur, not a professional? Here are some of the kinds of evidence you may notice:
weak transitions between sentences and paragraphs, loose logical connections between ideas, inexact use of certain words, a
vague pronoun or two (*it* and *this* are regular offenders), a run-on
sentence, a series of very short sentences, a failure to organize
the whole essay around a single theme.

After you have made notes of this sort, take steps to correct
all these weaknesses, using your dictionary, thesaurus, and this
book as you need them. Then try reading your paper again, but
this time read it aloud, and listen to yourself. A tape recorder
can be very handy for this purpose, and for the general task of
remembering certain details about your subject. If you do not
have a recorder, ask a friend to act as an audience for your
pronouncements. Sometimes the person you choose will question points of your argument or style you have failed to notice.
In the process you should be able to recognize more revisable
items: harsh sound effects, awkward repetition of words, clauses
and phrases that seem to have no connection with the main

thoughts of sentences. When this analysis is completed, you are ready to begin shaping your final draft.

Attempts to make substantial changes while typing or writing this final copy are inadvisable, although you may notice one or two additional details for improvement. If you have carried out the rereading and revising process thoroughly, drastic changes during the copying will do more harm than good. But your final act of proofreading is absolutely essential. Now you are on the lookout, not for the logic and phrasing of your argument, but for those mechanical errors that so irritate and distract a reader. This is the time to make final corrections of punctuation and spelling. To many students such things seem trivial, and in a way they are, but, unfortunately, to ignore them is foolish. The plain fact is that no matter how clever your words may be, if you spell them badly your reader will assume that you are ignorant and illiterate. You would assume the same thing about someone else's sloppy manuscript.

Finally, it is a fine thing to be proud of what you do. To hand in a clean, solid composition should be no less satisfying than to score a clean, solid winner on the tennis court or to execute successfully a difficult piano piece. A performance is a performance. Never be content with less than the best you can do.

THE WHOLE ESSAY: A CHECKLIST

The following are selected questions about the essay as a whole. They are worth raising *before* you hand in the finished work, as they are certain to occur to an experienced reader like your instructor. As with the questions raised about grammar and mechanics these possible problem areas must be attended to carefully if the impact of your writing is to be strong and persuasive.

1. If you follow the deductive approach (see, for example, page 213), have you included your thesis statement in the opening paragraph? Is the rest of the essay organized and documented most effectively to prove the thesis?
2. If you follow the inductive approach (see page 213), have you at least hinted at your thesis in the introduction? How

long must the reader wait to know where you stand? (A reader other than you should be asked about this matter.)

3. Does the concluding paragraph merely repeat the introductory one? (See "Beginnings and Endings," pages 203–211.) Have you given your reader a sense that the argument has moved toward a conclusion? Does the essay just stop, or does it have an ending?

4. Are your paragraphs arranged so that the reader has the impression of moving from *least* to *most* important points? At any stage does a paragraph seem to digress unnecessarily from the mainstream of your argument? (See page 144.)

5. Have you achieved smooth transition from paragraph to paragraph? Ask yourself, or your reader, whether or not the essay seems disjointed or choppy because the reader is forced to leap from topic to topic in successive paragraphs.

6. If you argue by means of comparison and contrast (see pages 200–202), are the similarities and differences adequately explained? If the whole essay is a comparison and contrast of the Canadian and American forms of government, for example, have you presented a balanced picture and reached some definite conclusion? To conclude by stating that both forms of government feature advantages and disadvantages is to leave the reader hanging.

7. Is the tone of your essay consistent? If you intend a light-hearted examination of laws against drug use, don't suddenly turn preachy or crusading at the close of your paper. Be sure you understand how you feel about the subject before presenting an opinion to the reader.

8. Have you used active verbs throughout? Check the number of passive constructions and if they represent more than a third of the verbs and verb phrases in your paper, revise the affected sentences. (See page 506.)

9. Does your essay stand as a reasoned process, or does it consist of a series of unsupported assertions or opinions? Watch for clues in the openings of your sentences. "I believe . . . ," "I think . . ." are signs that the statements cannot stand alone and need your presence to convince the reader. (See pages 217–218.)

10. Have you sufficiently defined and narrowed the topic? If in looking over the paper you find it studded with grand generalizations, you have probably taken on a topic that is too big. Be sure to consult your instructor before beginning to be sure the subject can be covered adequately in the time and space allotted. (See "Problems of Subject and Focus," pages 171–202.)

EXERCISES

EXERCISE 1, FOCUS. *Write out summarizing sentences and titles for the following statements of purpose. For the sake of the exercise, suppose that you have been asked to write 800-word essays.*

1. *Purpose*: To outline the steps involved in painting a bedroom.
2. *Purpose*: To tell the story of my first encounter with authority (police, boss, and so on).
3. *Purpose*: To define *affluence*.
4. *Purpose*: To compare this year's holiday (Christmas, Labour Day, July the 1st) with last year's.
5. *Purpose*: To prove that strict discipline of children is the best way to raise them.

EXERCISE 2, VIEWPOINT. *(1) Describe an incident in which you met a friend at an airport, bus station, disco, movie, or the like. Tell of the encounter first from your point of view, then from your friend's. (2) Select some other incident – an argument, a news event – and try narrating it from first a serious, then a humorous perspective.*

EXERCISE 3, DEFINITION. *Most one-sentence definitions follow a three-part order according to which the thing to be defined is stated, then the class to which it belongs, and finally the specific differences that set it apart from other things in the same class. Here are some examples:*

A *car* is a *four-wheeled vehicle* designed *to transport up to eight people from one place to another.*

A *dog* is a *hairy four-legged animal* that *serves primarily as a domestic pet.*

A *house* is a *building with several rooms* in which *one family normally lives.*

A *six-shooter* is a *hand-held weapon* that *fires six shots.*

The third component in these definitions could be expanded or made up of different details, most of which would define the term adequately. The trick is to be as specific as possible in stating differences: note that the definition of a dog could also apply to a cat.

1. Write specific one-sentence definitions of the following words:

soccer	ambivalence	hammer
blender	groupie	fate
pirate	pants	phony

2. The student essay below attempts to define the term *bigot*. What techniques does he use? Does he make clear the distinction between a bigot and, say, a hypocrite? What of the people he chooses as examples of bigots? Would some other term be appropriate for any of these? In the last paragraph does the writer go beyond simple definition? If so what is he saying?

BIGOT

[1] A bigot claims all Indians are drunks. A bigot is a property owner who has no rooms when he has many. A bigot is a wealthy person who has an idea that poor people exist, but really doesn't care as long as they remain separate. The word bigot means these things and more. White bigots, black bigots, rich or poor – bigotry has no racial or economic boundaries. Poor people very often are bigoted against the wealthy. Snobbery and discrimination come to mind when I think of the word bigot. Hatred and contempt also describe it. Fear, though, may be the key word to understanding bigotry; a fear that someone might be bigger, darker, richer, or smarter than one's self. From that initial fear stems all the hatred and contempt most of us try to ignore.

[2] A bigot in today's society may not be too dangerous if he's not in a position of power. He goes through life with fear and hatred inside himself, but often his only outlet is his family. He screams at them about the black people because they won't work, the Catholics because they pray too much, the Jews because of their wealth, and the Polish people because they're dumb. Any person or group is vulnerable to attack from the bigot, ninety-nine percent of the time verbal and, most often, not to their face. This is not to say that a person with these feelings can't cause very real and serious trouble.

[3] In North America's nineteenth century bigotry against native people was, in fact, deadly. Many thousands of people, whites and Indians, were killed during the so-called "Indian Wars." The redman was a savage, a beast, lower than a dog in many people's minds. The white European bigots could not, and would not attempt to understand his religion, the way he dressed, the way he ate his food. Bigotry killed the North American Indian.

[4] In this century too, we have been witness to many such instances of bigotry. Adolf Hitler turned Germany into a nation of bigots and killers the likes of which the world has never seen before. If a person wasn't blond-haired and blue-eyed, with certification to prove his pure Aryanism, his hold on life was tenuous at best. The suffering the Jewish people underwent is unbelievable. Some of Hitler's subordinates have said they didn't really know what was happening, that mass murder was not an official policy of the Hitler regime. Official or not, it caused many millions of people terrible suffering and death. Although millions of black people have not been murdered in the United States, they have suffered both physically and emotionally. Bigotry has not been an official policy of the U.S. government any more than that of Hitler's, yet it has caused the black man to feel he does not belong and is not wanted there.

[5] Bigotry is psychological. Something in our minds tells us that we are right and they are wrong. We cannot control the way someone thinks or feels. We can control actions to a degree – hopefully to a high enough degree to prevent another Indian massacre or Jewish genocide. I

doubt, though, that we can really control bigotry.

[6] I do believe we can fight against it. Individuals must first want to do away with bigotry and then find the roots of their prejudices. When, as individuals, we begin to understand these prejudices, then as groups, we can work to fight bigotry.

[7] Bigotry is like a cancer; it feeds on its victim until both are destroyed. Bigotry and cancer are both ruthless killers, each as deadly as the other. But there is one major difference – the control of cancer is foreseeable.

– Terry Sickel

EXERCISE 4, DESCRIPTION. *(1) Describe a scene that has changed dramatically since you first knew it – a neighbourhood, a house or building, a room. Use metaphors and similes wherever possible to make the description more vivid. (2) Write a description of yourself as if you were the subject of a newspaper article. Try to isolate some feature of your personality – a hobby, something in your appearance – that might make you interesting to a newspaper audience.*

EXERCISE 5, THE BOOK OR MOVIE REVIEW. *Write a short, one-page review of a movie or book you have seen or read recently. Then, compare that movie or book with another by the same director or author. Make a decision about which is better and why. Look over the suggestions for planning and writing in the Comparison and Contrast section.*

EXERCISE 6, DIRECTIONS. *Make a list of some operations you believe you can perform better than anyone else: repairing a stereo, baking bread, restringing and tuning a guitar, hanging wallpaper. Write the first draft of a process paper giving directions so clear that even your instructor might be able to perform the delicate task. Remember the goal of making the paper interesting and readable.*

EXERCISE 7, BEGINNINGS. *Select a subject that you want to use for an essay of persuasion. Write four beginnings for it. With the help of your instructor pick out the most promising one and use it for your paper.*

1. Begin by using an imagined incident that illustrates the point of your paper or out of which a discussion may arise.
2. Begin with evidence of the importance or the timeliness of your subject.
3. Begin with a shock or surprise opening.
4. Begin with a question or a series of questions.

EXERCISE 8, TOPIC OUTLINES. *Select three subjects from the list below and prepare a topic outline to show how a composition might be written on each of the subjects.*

Science fiction movies	Sexism	Urban crime
Canadian socialism	Freedom of speech	Depression
Higher education	Parental power	Rock music

EXERCISE 9, PROOFREADING. *Make a list of the errors you catch in your proofreading. Compare it with a similar list of corrections made by your instructor on your paper. Does this comparison suggest some hints for future proofreading? Are you missing errors of a particular kind?*

EXERCISE 10, ANALYSIS. *Here are two uncorrected student essays that may be analysed in the same way your instructor reads and corrects your work. Consider some of the following questions in a written critique of the papers: Are the subjects adequately focussed and limited? What order of presentation does each writer choose? Does the writer follow the principles of that order? Is the essay coherent? What types of beginnings and endings are used? Does the writer use more active verbs than passive ones? Is there anything in particular that the writer might do to improve the essay?*

Uncorrected Student Essay 1[1]

SKEWED LANGUAGE

''Skewed language'' is defined as biassed or planted language. Many examples of skewed language can be found in English, especially with reference to women. The English

[1]Reprinted by permission of the author, Cheryl Boes.

language was formed to keep women in their inferior or secondary role.

Common examples of occupational names – mailman, policeman, garbageman, fireman – give the impression that women can't hold these jobs. If a woman does hold a job, once thought to be only a man's job, she is labelled with lady or woman followed by the occupational name as in woman doctor or lady engineer.

Our male-dominant standard of English is well illustrated in the words playboy and don juan. The feminine equivalents – loose woman or slut – have completely different connotations. While playboy is not degrading to the males, loose woman is certainly degrading to the females. Another example is the single male, the glamorous bachelor, as opposed to the single female, the old maid or spinster.

The English language also has many words that reduce women to animals. Chick, bunny, and mouse are common examples. Although some expressions for men also refer to animals, they are the big, strong animals like tiger, cat, and fox, which show the dominance of male over female.

Throughout the entire English language, there are many derogatory and degrading words aimed at women but very few, if any, aimed at men.

Uncorrected Student Essay 2[2]

LAW AND DISORDER

To my thinking the movie *Law and Disorder* was written for today's times and people. Most people are becoming more and more concerned with the amount of violence and crimes that occur and the increase of crime each year. There are many ideas as to what can be done to combat crime and protect the citizen and one idea is to form a group and patrol your own neighbourhood. This is the idea the movie used and tried to show what could happen.

The crimes they used were possibly extreme or exaggerated, yet they do happen: a car is parked on a street and in five minutes is completely stripped; a man lowers himself by

[2]Reprinted by permission of the author, Virginia Stoker.

rope from the roof of an apartment building, climbs in an open window, takes the TV, ties it on the other end of the rope and he goes down to the next floor, while the TV goes to the roof. All this happens while the occupant is in the kitchen fixing a sandwich.

The people living in this neighbourhood were getting more furious each time the police were unable to protect them, so they decided to form a group to help the police and patrol their own neighbourhood.

I thought the movie was quite good in pointing out some of the things that could happen. What began as trying to help the police turned into the group trying to be or thinking they *were* the police. Instead of wearing their own clothes they needed uniforms that looked like police uniforms, then they needed to act like policemen so they must drill. It was like watching a group of children so excited about their new game and one of the children has an idea to go one step further and another step until it is not at all what the game originally was. Not being satisfied with walking the streets they purchased an old police car with a siren that they put on top. Now they could ride around like policemen and with the radio go on police calls outside their neighbourhood. They answered a police call and in trying to be regular policemen one of their group was shot and killed. Their police car had been shot at and they were a group of very confused frightened men.

The ending was not at all what they had thought it would be: I think they had hoped to be heroes and instead one person was dead, and I don't think they realized what they had done that caused his death.

To me the show was effective and I don't think it could have ended any other way. It gave the problem, the increase in crime and what we can do about it. It took one of many answers and showed what could happen.

EXERCISE 11, PAPER TOPICS. *These suggested paper topics can be covered in essays of 500–1000 words. Before writing on any of them be sure to review the appropriate section in this chapter. Decide beforehand as well on your purpose, title, and central idea.*

1. Most television programs, especially soap operas, represent a picture of life that contrasts significantly with what we call reality. Analyse one of these programs, pointing out specifically how incidents in it differ from real life.

2. Write an essay in which you convince your reader that automobile companies should produce electric cars; or that businesses and industries should develop and use more underground space; or that the housing industry should build more solar-heated homes. Construct the essay so that the opposing arguments are given due weight.

3. Point out the fallacies in the following statements. Then write an essay on one of them showing how the kind of thinking revealed in the statement is practised in other areas of society.

   The last two times we went to the game the Expos lost. We are not going to any more games so that they will be sure to win them.

   Canadians should abolish the Senate. It has never been any use and never will be any use.

   In order to be an international ''honest broker,'' Canada must withdraw from NATO.

   Experience proves that nice guys finish last.

4. Decide on some event in your recent experience – an accident, a near accident, an argument, a victory in some sport or game – and write an essay detailing its causes and effects. Try to pinpoint the most important cause and effect.

5. Compose an interview with a friend, a famous person, or an imaginary personality. Write the interview as a question and answer exchange, aiming at a full representation of the person's likes and dislikes. Remember that your reader knows next to nothing about your subject.

6. Select a review of a film or book or musical or dramatic performance from some local newspaper or national magazine.

Cut it out and tape it to a sheet of blank paper. Then write a critique of the review, showing what you learned from it, the writer's biases, and your own expectations. Decide whether the reviewer has satisfied your definition of the job.

7. Write closing paragraphs for the two essays that might follow these opening paragraphs. Make some reference to the beginning, but be sure not simply to restate the openings.

> **Many human beings never experience autonomy and self-determination in any meaningful sense. There are intelligible explanations for this: mass starvation, plague, and war. There are other equally devastating but less intelligible situations that prevent the development of full individual personhood. Two such situations are the colour of one's skin and the configuration of one's genitals, known more fashionably as racism and sexism.**
>
> > – Kathryn Morgan, ''The Androgynous Classroom: Liberation or Tyranny?''

> **Peace in our world is seriously threatened, and not only peace but the very life of the human race. If a world war broke out today, we have such weapons that the whole of mankind is in danger of annihilation. It is therefore urgent that young people be educated for peace and universal brotherhood in a radically new way.**
>
> > – Jean Vanier, ''Education Towards Peace and Universal Brotherhood''

8. Think of certain words you hear used with different connotations or shadings of meaning. Write an essay on a particular word or set of words, describing the context in which the meanings occur. Some examples: *boss, nice, mean, funny, beautiful.*

9. Detail the steps in a process that everyone must go through at some time or another. Registering for classes is a good example; applying for a loan is another. In the rest of your essay outline a modification of this process, showing how specific changes would improve it.

10. Write an essay in which you take the position that television news reporting is inferior to newspaper or newsmagazine reporting. Try to think of at least four reasons for your stand and devote a paragraph to each. After completing a first draft, cut the paper into individual paragraphs and rearrange these on a blank sheet of paper. You may want to do this more than once. Was your original structure or ordering better than the later one(s)? Then write a final draft of the paper.

7

WRITING ESSAYS ABOUT LITERATURE AND FILM

Essays about literature and film require the same careful planning, statement of purpose, supported arguments, and coherent organization as essays of persuasion. There are, however, some special features of such critical essays that call for a separate chapter on the subject. The word *critical* in the last sentence underscores the fact that writing essays about literature and film calls for the honing of evaluative, analytical tools. Like the science student looking through his or her first microscope, the beginning critic will have to learn to name what he or she sees and to describe its pattern or design. Both the critic and the scientist will also have to know how to determine whether or not the discovery is worthwhile.

You have no doubt seen at some time a television commercial in which a gray-haired, trustworthy-looking man tells an anxious patient in his most sincere voice that in his medical experience a

239

certain painkiller outperforms all others. While he is delivering this testimonial there appears at the bottom of the screen the announcement: "This is a dramatization." From this statement you learn that the speaker is not a doctor and that the patient is not really sick. In a similar way, literature dramatizes incidents instead of directly stating them, as an essayist would. Poems, plays, novels, films – all of these literary forms subscribe to the same concept of implication; imaginative writers tell stories or describe emotions without forcing them to express explicitly certain morals, or testimonials. This does not mean that literature does not teach us something about life and human behaviour. What we learn, however, comes not from direct pronouncement but by way of developing *themes*, the central or controlling ideas of literature. The first step of the critical writer is to locate these themes and to explain how they function in the work.

Because imaginative writers imply rather than state directly, the beginning critic must read the work or view the film, paying careful attention to its structure. Repeated contact will help make the work less imposing. Once a pattern is discerned – of words, actions, images – the critic must attempt to describe it in his or her own words. This process is called *paraphrase*.

Paraphrase

Paraphrasing a poem is of course less complex than summarizing *War and Peace* or *The Diviners*. In these instances, however, some statement of literal meaning provides the clay with which you will shape your essay. A review of the events in the plot of a novel like *David Copperfield* would prove of special value to your reader in a discussion of some particular scene or character. An essay on a selected poem may well include the paraphrase itself as a means of illustrating features of a difficult passage.

Here is a short passage spoken by one of Shakespeare's great villain heroes, and a paraphrase.

> Life's but a walking shadow, a poor player
> That struts and frets his hour upon the stage
> And then is heard no more.
>
> —*Macbeth*

Paraphrase: Life is like an actor who plays out his short part and then exits.

As you see, the paraphrase guts Shakespeare's lines of their poetic strength and beauty. But a paraphrase is essentially a translation; it is important for the translator to grasp the basic meaning of the passage. Often, unfortunately, the nuances of the original are lost. In the case of a novel, short story, or film, the act of paraphrase involves describing what happens to the main character or characters in the work.

EXPLICATION

Explication is the next step following paraphrase. The word means more than just explaining, although a good explication gives the reader a better understanding of the work. Explication also means "analysis" or "interpretation." It is the writer's chance to look for the implied theme or meaning. In the case of the *Macbeth* passage, a possible explication might be:

> For Macbeth at this point in the play, life has become an illusion that has deceived him, much as an actor deceives an audience about the role he is playing. In Macbeth's case the choice of metaphor is significant, since he now realizes that the Witches have led him to believe incorrectly that he is invincible. This speech marks the fatalism that will direct his behaviour in the final scenes. Macbeth is a victim of equivocation, a major theme in the tragedy.

This explication relates the passage to the speaker's character and indicates how the imagery supports the central idea of the play. The writer has begun a process of interpretation that could lead into other areas as well: the role of the Witches, Macbeth's past behaviour, and his relationship with his wife. Limited by the writer's purpose, explication is really the essence of critical writing. But it cannot proceed until the writer has attempted some sort of paraphrase.

SOME CRITICAL APPROACHES: FORM FIRST

Whether writing about poems, plays, novels, or films, the beginning critic should be aware that there are some standard topics or subjects that might be profitably investigated. Before the actual writing, however, it is important to determine the form or genre of the work you intend to discuss. Once you discover that the poem in question is, say, a sonnet, you will recognize its fourteen lines and particular rhyme scheme as conventions of the form. This discovery will help to avoid the trap of comparing a sonnet to an epic poem or an elegy. A satirical novel such as Mordecai Richler's *The Apprenticeship of Duddy Kravitz* should likewise not be compared to the romantic epic *War and Peace* just because both are novels. Tolstoy's monumental work chronicles the story of a Russian family in the Napoleonic age. Richler, on the other hand, writes about the decline of social values in our society as represented by a ruthless youth's struggle for success. Determining form will help you to understand the boundaries of a particular literary world, leading to comparisons with other worlds of a similar kind. You can get some help for this investigation into form from introductions, book jackets, and histories or anthologies of literature. Some useful books are listed at the end of the chapter.

THEME APPROACH

Unlike the well-controlled persuasion essay you might write for your English course, a work of literature may not be so easily boiled down into a central thesis that can be stated in one sentence. The quote from *Macbeth* that was paraphrased in a sentence implies the theme of illusion and reality, but it also introduces the idea of fatalism or determinism, a theme that especially dominates the close of the action. An effort to locate and state one theme is also likely to distort the work to some degree, leading us to relate everything else in it to that theme.

In addition some poems, like this epigram, are not primarily presentations of themes as much as descriptions of emotions or reactions.

> you fit into me
> like a hook into an eye
>
> a fish hook
> an open eye
>
> > −Margaret Atwood,
> > *Power Politics*

Discussing this poem's imagery would yield considerably more than an analysis of its theme.

To write a successful essay on theme in a literary work or movie, you need to recognize first that the theme you select is likely to be one of several that might be identified. Your task is to convince the reader that *your* theme is significant and essential to an understanding of the work. Shakespeare's *Macbeth*, for example, is a study of a man who becomes so driven by ambition that he ignores all moral restraints and kills the rightful king of Scotland to win the crown. In order to persuade your reader that this is the correct way to read the play, you should begin with the three-step prewriting formula outlined in chapter 5.

Purpose: To convince the reader that the theme of ambition in *Macbeth* best illustrates the fate of the hero and the state.

Title: The Magnetic Crown: Ambition in *Macbeth*

Thesis: Macbeth is so completely blinded by ambition that he violates the significant moral and ceremonial laws that hold society together, destroying himself and nearly destroying the state.

Armed with these guides, you can begin to gather supporting details as you would for any persuasion essay. The Witches tempt Macbeth by promising him the kingship, but Macbeth himself decides to kill the king. Lady Macbeth reinforces Macbeth's ambition and helps him to commit the murder, but after the killing of Banquo, which is Macbeth's idea, she too becomes a victim of ambition. Macbeth murders Duncan while the king is asleep in Macbeth's own castle, thereby violating moral, familial, and social laws and customs. Macbeth's ambition blinds him to the reality that he has no heirs to inherit his tainted crown. He soon experiences the paranoiac fear that tells him other lords – Banquo, Macduff – seek to depose him; as a result, he launches a reign of terror and murder that nearly destroys Scotland. This is obviously a rich vein in the play; its yield gives to the essay the concreteness and evidence that make for good critical writing.

In the process of exploring the theme of ambition you should recognize the existence of other themes in *Macbeth*. For instance, there are references throughout to free will and fate. In fact, some commentators on the play believe the Witches direct Macbeth to kill King Duncan, thereby sealing his fate. Given this reading, the theme of fate or determinism becomes central to the action. While acknowledging this interpretation, however, you might point out that the Witches' prophecy only complements Macbeth's own ambition; the murders of Duncan, Banquo, and others are not controlled by any supernatural force. A sound, thoughtful argument could convince the reader that the theme of ambition is more central to *Macbeth* than any other.

Be sure that the theme you choose is in fact an established pattern in the work. Try as well to be as specific as possible in stating the theme: "Love in *Romeo and Juliet*" is obviously too broad. Such a title will leave the reader asking about the difference between love as a subject and some depiction of love (Shakespeare calls it "star-crossed" in *Romeo and Juliet*) as a theme.

STRUCTURE APPROACH

Any essay about the structure of a literary work or film must pay attention to the elements or parts that make up the work or film. If you choose to write an essay, your task will require analysis of such parts as chapters (novels), scenes (plays or films), stanzas (poems), and a discussion of how they function in the whole design. For example, an examination of the structure of *Macbeth* might reveal the growing isolation of the hero as the scenes in which he appears after the banquet (III.iv) find him alone. Or you might argue that the structure of the plot moves slowly toward greater tension and conflict (called *rising action*) until the climax of the banquet scene, after which events transpire rapidly and the action "falls" to a resolution or dénouement with the killing of Macbeth. Another possibility is to show that the main incident of the final scene – the beheading of Macbeth – is meant to recall the opening of the play, in which the traitor Cawdor, whose title Macbeth inherits, is beheaded. Essays following these patterns of organization demonstrate how the themes of the work are presented through the play's structure or design. An essay on alternating comic and serious scenes in Shakespeare would be concerned with the way a particular mood is created.

There are at least three recognized ways of talking about structure. Concentrating on any or all of these will help you to grasp more firmly just what literary structure is.

1. Setting. Determining where the action takes place will start you thinking about how setting is related to structure. If events begin in one place and the action then shifts to another, the writer may logically discuss how the two settings are similar and different. More particularly, you might compare the way the main character behaves in each setting. In Ernest Buckler's *The Mountain and the Valley*, for example, the main character feels both secure and trapped in the valley, in contrast to his dream of the complete freedom of the mountain top. These contrasting settings are used to organize the plot and themes of the novel. In *Macbeth*, the hero's castle, where much of the action takes place, is a scene of tension and terror that is contrasted with the atmosphere in England, a healthy, well-governed realm. Alternating settings can establish a pattern in which readers observe significant differences or similarities between characters and events. Of special interest is the way in which setting is associated with the main character, how it compares with or even determines his or her own nature.

2. Time Sequences. Events in plays, films, novels, and short stories are narrated chronologically as a rule. A sequence of events covers a period of time with some sense of beginning, middle, and end. Novels like Margaret Laurence's *The Stone Angel* take the reader from the central character's childhood to extreme old age; others are like W.O. Mitchell's *How I Spent My Summer Holidays*, which is concerned with only a short, intense period in the life of a boy as he moves through puberty. The passing of time in *Macbeth* is somewhat indefinite, although we can say with some certainty that Shakespeare attempts to compress time in order to create a fast pace that nicely parallels Macbeth's breakneck rise to power. Through flashbacks authors suspend time to allow for the sketching in of details about character and motivation. A study of time sequence might examine variations in the pace of time's passing, interruptions for flashbacks and their relation to the main time sequence, or gaps in time between events. This latter technique is a favourite one in films, where narration is often not as careful as it is in written fiction.

3. Emotion and Suspense. Imaginative writers and filmmakers often build their works on the principle of suspense, keeping their readers and viewers emotionally involved in the action. One way to achieve this effect is to arrange scenes or chapters so that gradual discovery and suspension of our emotions are achieved. A classical example of suspense is the plot of *Oedipus Rex* by the Greek playwright Sophocles. The hero seeks out the cause of drought and sickness in his kingdom at the opening of the tragedy. As the play progresses we realize that he is the cause of the curse on his land: He has unwittingly murdered his father and married his mother. The perfect example of a philosophical murder story, *Oedipus Rex* reveals parts of its terrible truth through witnesses who are brought in for questioning. The last witness, a shepherd who knows the true story of Oedipus's birth, clinches the case against the king, who then blinds himself in remorse for his deed. Sophocles scores a brilliant coup by making the audience aware of Oedipus's guilt long before he is. This effect is known as dramatic irony, a signifi-cant part of good dramatic structure.

Novelists may manipulate our feelings toward particular characters by skilful arrangements of parts or scenes. In Dickens's *Great Expectations* the hero, Pip, first encounters the convict, Magwitch, in a graveyard. This opening scene of ter-ror is firmly impressed on our minds as Pip describes his fears and feelings of guilt for having helped Magwitch escape. When Magwitch later appears in the novel, emerging almost from the grave, Pip expects him to expose his guilt to the world. In fact, Magwitch turns out to be Pip's unknown benefactor, providing money for his education and career in return for Pip's assistance. Like the hero, we too are surprised and elated because Dickens has prepared us to think of the old convict as selfish and an enemy to happiness. The structure of *Great Expectations* could in fact be described as following a pattern of reversal, with each chapter establishing a mood that is "reversed" or modified in the next. The result is greater pleasure for the reader.

Remember that your evaluation of the structure of a film or literary work will concern how each part (chapter, scene, stanza) contributes to the whole. What is the cumulative effect of the ordering of incidents on the overall work?

Do not simply recount events in the plot and suppose you have written an essay on structure. You must evaluate these events, compare them to others, and point out how the pattern reinforces the themes of the work.

When recounting events in a literary work or film remember to use the present tense: "Macbeth *responds* to Banquo's ghost by *throwing* his goblet at him." Assume that the story is unfold-ing for the first time as you read it, and this perception will prevent you from lapsing into the past tense.

CHARACTER APPROACH

An essay on a character or characters can be both easy to handle and indicative of the author's ability to portray rounded per-sonalities. In essence, such an essay is descriptive, focussing on the details of appearance, manner, and behaviour that are depicted in the work. But the essay goes beyond description and into evaluation when you attempt to prove some thesis about the character. Analysing Macbeth, you might argue that he is a tragic figure because he possesses so many traits of greatness that are eventually destroyed by his ambition. In gathering information about him, you need to consider first his own speeches and actions. The early part of the play, for example, is marked by his serious reflections on the Witches' prophecies. When Lady Macbeth urges him to murder King Duncan, Macbeth delivers speeches in which he depicts the moral horror of such a deed. After the murder, however, his speeches and actions become those of a frightened, hallucinating villain, vowing to destroy all real and imagined enemies.

In addition to Macbeth's speeches and actions, you have his relations with other characters as a means of studying him. His friendship with Banquo seems firm at the play's opening, but soon after Macbeth becomes king the two are separated by mutual suspicion. Macbeth eventually has Banquo killed because he fears the Witches' prophecy that Banquo's heirs will become kings. Macbeth's relationship with Lady Macbeth is probably the most complex and fascinating one of its kind in literature. She at first dominates him, literally shaming him into the murder of Duncan with taunts about his manhood. But with the murder of Banquo we see her influence declining until, overwhelmed by suppressed guilt, she suffers the fate – madness and death – that should have visited Macbeth. He instead grows more isolated and tyrannical.

In any analysis of character, some attempt should be made to comment on the work's main theme or themes. Macbeth's transformation from hero to tyrant can be neatly tied to the theme of ambition, the force that destroys his humane qualities of imagination and compassion. You may also want to say something about how successful the writer is in depicting a believable character. In *Macbeth* the hero could have easily slipped into a stereotyped villain, but Shakespeare takes pains to differentiate him from the stereotype by exploring the inner recesses of his mind. The soliloquy, a speech of self-assessment delivered while the speaker is alone on stage, proves to be a useful device for individualizing character in drama.

POINT OF VIEW

In fiction the author has a choice of ways to narrate the story. The vantage point from which an author presents the actions and characters of a story is called the point of view. Put simply, point of view is determined by the voice telling the story, and a number of questions concerning that storyteller have to be asked by the reader in order to understand a story properly. Does the narrator know everything that is going on in the story and in its characters at all times? Is the narrator's knowledge restricted to one or only a few characters? Is the narrator a reliable source of information and judgement or is he or she blind in some way? Is the narrator outside of the story's events or a participant in them? There are various ways of classifying the answers to these questions. The following are standard points of view that you should be aware of before assessing character in a work of fiction.

Omniscient Narrator. An omniscient narrator knows everything about the characters and events in the story, and is free to move back and forth in place or time, and to shift from one character to another to reveal or conceal their behaviour, motives, thoughts, and feelings. The narrator stands outside the story and uses third person pronouns or proper names to refer to his or her characters. The reader implicitly trusts this narrator's voice and often it will guide the reader by ''intruding'' with evaluations, interpretations, commentary, editorial asides, and judgements. If the narrator does not comment at all, yet tells the story using third person narration, the point of view is sometimes called objective or impersonal or unintrusive, but this point of view is not found in stories very often. Here is an example of an omniscient narrator describing the reaction of her hero who has just lost both a local election and his fiancée. She even ''intrudes'' into the story to summarize one of the major themes of her novel.

> They had little advice for him about his political atti-
> tude, little advice about anything. He noticed that his

presence on one or two occasions seemed to embarrass
them, and that his arrival would sometimes have a disinte-
grating effect upon a group in the post office or at a street
corner. He added it, without thinking, to his general heavi-
ness; they held it a good deal against him, he supposed, to
have reduced their proud standing majority to a beggarly
two figures; he didn't blame them.

I cannot think that the sum of these depressions alone
would have been enough to overshadow so buoyant a
soul as Lorne Murchison's. The characteristics of him
I have tried to convey were grafted on an excellent fund
of common sense. He was well aware of the proportions of
things; he had no despair of the Idea, nor would he despair
should the Idea etherealize and fly away. Neither had he,
for his personal honour, any morbid desires toward White
Clam Shell or Finnigan's cat. His luck had been a good deal
better than it might have been; he recognized that as fully
as any sensible young man could, and as for the Great
Chance, and the queer grip it had on him, he would have
argued that too if anyone had approached him curiously
about it. There I think we might doubt his conclusions.
There is nothing subtler, more elusive to trace than the
intercurrents of the emotions. Politics and love are thought
of at opposite poles, and Wallingham perhaps would have
laughed to know that he owed an exalted allegiance in part
to a half-broken heart. Yet the impulse that is beyond our
calculation, the thing we know potential in the blood but
not to be summoned or conditioned, lies always in the
shadow of the ideal; and who can analyse that, and say, "Of
this class is the will to believe in the integrity of the beloved
and false; of that is the desire to lift a nation to the level of
its mountain-ranges"? Both dispositions have a tendency
to overwork the heart; and it is easy to imagine that they
might interact.

–Sara Jeannette Duncan, *The Imperialist*

Limited Narrator. Sometimes the narrator tells the story in the
third person, but only through the experiences, thoughts, and
feelings of a single character, or at most only a few characters

in the story. The centre of consciousness can be a major or minor character, or a mere witness to the events. The more restricted this point of view the closer the reader comes to experiencing only what the central character experiences. Eventually the narration turns into "interior monologue" or "stream of consciousness," where the author's attitude is increasingly unintrusive. A great many twentieth century writers employ this point of view in telling their stories. Morley Callaghan's *The Loved and the Lost* and most of his short stories use this point of view.

> She seemed so puzzled, so worried and aloof from even the deepest bitterness within him, that George felt impatient, as if it were her fault that the child was sick. For a while he watched her rocking back and forth, making always the same faint humming sound, with the stronger light showing the deep frown on her face, and he couldn't seem to think of the child at all. He wanted to speak with sympathy, but he burst out, "I had to get up because I couldn't go on with my own thoughts. We're unlucky, Marthe. We haven't had a day's luck since we've come to this city. How much longer can this go on before they throw us out on the street? I tell you we never should have come here."
>
> She looked up at him indignantly. He couldn't see the fierceness in her face because her head was against the window light. Twice he walked the length of the room, then he stood beside her, looking down at the street. There was now traffic and an increasing steady hum of motion. He felt chilled and his fingers grasped at the collar of his dressing gown, pulling it across his chest. "It's cold here, and you can imagine what it'll be like in winter," he said. And when Marthe again did not answer, he said sullenly, "You wanted us to come here. You wanted us to give up what we had and come to a bigger city where there were bigger things ahead. Where we might amount to something because of my fine education and your charming manner. You thought we didn't have enough ambition, didn't you?"
>
> –Morley Callaghan, "The Blue Kimono"

First Person Narrator. The point of view of this narrator is usually that of a main character who tells the story using the first-person pronoun *I*. In other words the voice comes from within the story. This *I* should not automatically be taken for the author, nor should it automatically be assumed that he or she is telling the truth. In Gabrielle Roy's *Street of Riches*, the main character Christine's experiences as a fledgling writer living in St. Boniface, Manitoba seem to parallel those of the author. In both fiction and poetry, however, it is probably better to consider the first-person narrator as a character with a life and viewpoint that are separate from those of the author. The main character's way of speaking and behaving will greatly affect the language and style of the work. The unnamed narrator of Margaret Atwood's *Surfacing* uses a quietly desperate style, rich in surrealistic imagery, that conveys the impression of a woman gradually being driven insane by an increasingly mechanized world. Jack Hodgins' character Spit Delaney has a frank style that makes him as intriguing as the story he tells. Although most first-person narrators are major characters, there are some works in which minor characters assume that role. In Robert Kroetsch's *The Studhorse Man*, the narrator Demeter holds a position of relative unimportance compared to the role of *his* hero, Hazard Lepage. An essay on the first-person narrator in a particular novel might usefully discuss how the novel would change should the narration shift to an omniscient or limited point of view. Be careful to determine whether or not the narrator is reliable or trustworthy, and how much the narrator reveals unconsciously in the way he or she presents the story. Alice Munro often creates first-person narrators of psychological complexity who reveal more about themselves, their fears, neuroses, and defence mechanisms, than about others.

> Gabriel told me when I first knew him that he enjoyed life. He did not say that he believed in enjoying it; he said that he did. I was embarrassed for him. I never believed people who said such things and anyway, I associated this statement with gross, self-advertising, secretly unpleasantly restless men. But it seems to be the truth. He

is not curious. He is able to take pleasure and give off smiles and caresses and say softly, ''Why do you worry about that? It is not a problem of yours.'' He has forgotten the language of his childhood. His lovemaking was strange to me at first, because it was lacking in desperation. He made love without emphasis, so to speak, with no memory of sin or hope of depravity. He does not watch himself.

– Alice Munro, ''Material''

Be sure you identify the point of view before beginning to write about a character. The way in which that character has been created will determine his or her role in the work.

IMAGERY APPROACH

As you saw in the discussion of description, imagery refers to the picture-making quality of language. Pictures are made with metaphors and similes, both of which are, in effect, comparisons of one thing to another. Here is a striking simile from *Macbeth*:

> And pity, like a naked, new-born babe
>   striding the blast . . .
> Shall blow the horrid deed in every eye.

The use of *like* or *as* signals a simile. Shakespeare compares pity to trumpet-blowing cherubim spreading word of Macbeth's murder of King Duncan throughout the realm. In order to qualify as a simile the statement has to compare two things that are dissimilar in kind. ''Your car is like mine'' is not a simile; ''Your car is like a metal ladybug'' is a simile. Similes usually limit or refer to only one trait the two things have in common: pity in the *Macbeth* quote has the effect on us of children crying out. Metaphors drop the linking word *as* or *like* – ''Pity *is* a naked, new-born babe'' – and also allow for a greater number of similarities or connotations. Macbeth's ''Life's but a walking shadow'' could mean that life is an illusion or that it is ghostlike, with the connotation of *sinful* or *damned* attached. Both connotations can apply at the same time, since they are not mutually exclusive but in fact complementary.

Here are some examples of similes and metaphors from different kinds of poems:

> His soul would shrivel and its shell
> Go rattling like an empty nut.
>
> > –Archibald Lampman,
> > "The City of the End of Things"

> Unreal   tall as a myth
> by the road the Himalayan bear
> is beating the brilliant air
> with his crooked arms
> About him two men   bare
> spindly as locusts   leap
>
> > –Earle Birney,
> > "The Bear on the Delhi Road"

> a sunken pendulum: *invoke*, *revoke*;
> loosed yon, leashed hither, motion on no space.
>
> > –A.M. Klein,
> > "The Rocking Chair"

> At night his two-finger whistle brought her down
> the waterfall stairs to his shy smile
> which, like an eddy, turned her round and round
> lazily and slowly so her will
> was nowhere – as in dreams things are and aren't
>
> > –P.K. Page,
> > "Adolescence"

Lampman's soulless urbanite in the final city is compared to a hollow nut. Birney catches the mysterious majesty of the bear and the pesky quality of the starving trainers in his arresting simile. Kleine's metaphor suggests the timeless quality of the rocking chair as a static emblem of rural Quebec. The motion of the chair's curved legs becomes that of the pendulum of a grandfather clock. There is motion but it does not go anywhere. Does this suggest that life there is also stifling? Page finds perfect metaphors to suggest the emotional state of adolescents in love. Stairs become waterfalls of smooth and rapid movement and the awkward moment of shyness at the bottom is an eddy that twirls her around and gives the whole experience an illusory quality.

If you are analysing the imagery in a long poem or play or short novel, your best approach is to describe a pattern of such imagery. In *Macbeth*, for instance, blood imagery drenches the play. With what events and characters is blood associated as the play develops? Are there different types of blood images: innocent blood, the blood of traitors, blood lines? Is Shakespeare trying to paint the picture of a hero actually drowning in the blood of his victims? Images depicting the sea, colours, storms, birds, and so forth are common in many works of literature and are usually arranged in a comprehensible design. In some works an image may be repeated without any change in the formula. Papers dealing with repeated images might comment on how repetition transforms the image into a symbol, an action or object that implies a meaning beyond itself. The crown in *Macbeth* comes to symbolize the hero's ambition as we see it used by the Witches to mock his murder of Duncan and Banquo and his usurpation of the throne. Common symbols are flags, roses, swords, crosses, doves, and spider webs.

An essay on imagery or symbolism should attempt to show how the pattern is related to the work's main theme or themes. Blood imagery clearly pictures the results of Macbeth's ambition, especially in the murders of innocents like Banquo and Macduff's wife and children. There is also an element of irony in the pattern, since Macbeth's own blood has not produced a male heir to whom he can pass on his tainted crown. This connection with the main theme should be hinted at throughout the paper, not sprung on the reader in the last paragraph.

STYLE APPROACH

Perhaps the most difficult and yet satisfying critical essay is the study of a particular author's style. This kind of essay is difficult because it requires close reading and listing of qualities. You must pay attention, for example, to a writer's characteristic way of presenting characters, describing scenes, or making sounds. Like the attempt at assessing imagery, the stylistic essay is looking for patterns, an exercise that may well prove tedious when scouring the pages of *War and Peace*. But such an essay can prove especially rewarding when you feel you have unlocked the mystery of a writer's style. Your next encounter with his or her work should be more pleasurable precisely because you know what to look and listen for.

In beginning the essay on style, it is best to choose a representative sample of the work for analysis. A speech or soliloquy in a play, a character description in a novel, a whole short poem – these are manageable selections to study. Your conclusion will suggest how the passage or section is representative of the whole work.

Once you have decided on a sample, the next step is to examine its diction. The words chosen by writers tell us a good deal about their purposes. Formal words and constructions create a slow-paced, distanced tone that colours the way we perceive characters and events. Specific or concrete words create a mood of realism in a work; abstract or general words tend to cast events in a philosophical mould. (The way in which an author arranges words and images in fact creates a world for the literary work or film; this world must be understood on its own terms by anyone attempting to criticize it.) When denotative words predominate, the style is more likely to be descriptive of a material, realistic world; an abundance of connotative words, on the other hand, signals a more poetic, sometimes fantastic setting for events. Even the length of words can establish a particular rhythm that comes to distinguish the work. Consider the effect of the following passages on your ear:

> The small, sleek car sped past and almost blew us off the road. We lost it in the dust cloud raised up ahead. Our rage was spent on two beers at the bar.

> With supercilious pomposity the guardian of morals from our local tabloid unleashed a tirade of devastating adjectives on the inventive but unfortunately inept performance of Molière's satiric comedy by the community repertory company.

The differing sounds and rhythms clearly point to different voices, the latter assuming the stance of an educated, somewhat jaundiced commentator on the arts scene.

After words, sentences should be the next object of study in a paper on style. Questions about length are valid here too: Are the sentences varied in length? Are they predominantly short or long? Do they employ many points of punctuation? You will also want to consider types of sentences. If the author repeats questions, exclamations, or commands, the emerging pattern will affect the work's style in particular ways. Hamlet asks many questions besides "To be or not to be"; most of them are similarly philosophical and hard to answer. As a result the play seems to be full of insoluble puzzles. In poetry and poetic drama, like *Hamlet*, word order will also affect style. Inverted sentences arrest the eye, focussing attention on a particular word: "Fate is the hunter" places greater emphasis on the word *fate* than does "The hunter is fate." Types of sentences give similar clues about style. A string of simple declarative sentences in a novel establishes a mood of reportorial detachment. Sentence fragments – "Not me!" "Never again!" – create a mood of heightened emotion. As in the analysis of words, the central question is, "What pattern emerges in the passage?" Remember too that even though some poetic lines do not contain punctuation, the rules of sentence structure still apply.

Finally, you will want to determine the sound effects in a literary work or film. Poetry and poetic drama depend heavily on language that makes certain sounds, since the words in the work are meant to be spoken aloud. (Poetry should be read aloud to determine sound and rhythm patterns.) To a lesser extent, fiction too depends on sound effects, although the narrative or story-telling purpose keeps the reader moving with language rather than stopping too frequently to listen to it. Sound effects and music obviously play a big part in movies; these features should be considered in any film review that tries to give a full impression of the work.

Two favourite devices of imaginative writers concerned with sound effects are alliteration and assonance. Alliteration is the repetition of words that begin with the same letter or sound. It is an especially effective device for expressing a strongly felt emotion. Read aloud the following passage from F.R. Scott's poem about adolescents in a drug store in the 1940s:

> I swivel on my axle and survey
> The latex tintex kotex cutex land.
> Soft kingdoms sell for dimes, Life Pic Look Click
> Inflate the male with conquest girly grand.
>
> My brothers and my sisters, two by two,
> Sit sipping succulence and sighing sex.
> Each tiny adolescent universe
> A world the vested interests annex.
>
> —F.R. Scott, "Saturday Sundae"

The *s* alliterations in the sixth line are particularly effective in slowing down the pace of the poem as well as capturing the whispered intimacies of the romantic adolescents.

Assonance is the repetition of internal vowel sounds in more than one word. In a poem about the power of poetry itself, Scott demonstrates why poetry will never die through repeating sounds that seem to uplift and contrasting sounds that seem to push down.

> So I know it will survive. Not even the decline of reading
> And the substitution of advertising for genuine pornography
> Can crush the uprush of the mushrooming verb
> Or drown the overtone of the noun on its own.
>
> —F.R. Scott, "Poetry"

These sound effects should be used carefully in your own writing; excessive use of them is often the sign of amateur writing.

As was said earlier, stylistic analysis of any passage should demonstrate how that section is representative of the whole work. You will note too that after the study of diction, sentence form, and sound effects is finished, the critic is obliged to relate these elements to the work's tone. Both tone and style will to a great extent be decided by the genre or form as well. Shakespeare's *Macbeth* is a tragedy, and its diction can be seen to conform to a pattern of formality and seriousness that befits the tragic form.

In conducting your analysis, try to identify the stylistic traits that are unique to the author in question. Do not simply list types of sentences or sound effects. Make the evidence part of a larger generalization or thesis that can be supported.

There are other approaches to critical writing besides those discussed here. The book or film review is treated in chapter 5, ''The Problems of Subject and Focus.'' The persuasion essay is discussed at length in chapter 6. Turn to these sections for further information. You can also consult some of the books listed at the end of this chapter.

The short essay reproduced here illustrates how the analysis of character, imagery, and structure can be employed in the close reading of an individual passage.

HAMLET'S SELF-REVELATION: A READING OF HAMLET, I, v, 95–109

Remember thee?	95
Ay thou poor ghost, whiles memory holds a seat	96
In this distracted globe. Remember thee?	97
Yea, from the table of my memory	98
I'll wipe away all trivial fond records,	99
All saws of books, all forms, all pressures past,	100
That youth and observation copied there,	101
And thy commandment all alone shall live	102
Within the book and volume of my brain,	103
Unmixed with baser matter, yes, yes, by heaven:	104
O most pernicious woman!	105
O villain, villain, smiling, damned villain!	106
My tables, meet it is I set it down	107
That one may smile, and smile, and be a villain,	108
At least I am sure it may be so in Denmark.	109

In this passage from Act I of *Hamlet*, Hamlet is alone on stage immediately after the ghost has left, and so the character addressed is the ghost, at least at first. Actually, the speech is a soliloquy, because Hamlet almost immediately seems to be talking to himself or to the open air. Although he speaks about

From *Rebels and Lovers: Shakespeare's Young Heroes and Heroines*, ed. Alice Griffin (New York University Press, 1976), p. 321.

the ghost, about his mother (who is the "most pernicious woman"), and about his uncle (the "villain"), *the real subject of the speech is himself.* ★ *His thoughts show his disturbed condition, his selection of words indicates his background as a student, and the rhythm in the concluding part of the speech shows his forthcoming preoccupation with the "ills that flesh is heir to."*†

First of all the speech shows that Hamlet has been greatly disturbed by the Ghost's message that Claudius is a murderer. Whereas previously the young prince has been melancholy, feeling the need to do something but with no reasons for action, he is now promising the Ghost to remember him and his desire for revenge. If one assumes that Hamlet is a person of normal sensibility, thoughts of murderous vengeance would necessarily create confusion. Such disturbance, which Hamlet himself feels in his "distracted globe" (97), is shown by his resolution to wipe away "all trivial fond records" from the "table" of his memory (99, 98), and then by his action of writing in his "tables" that "one may smile, and smile, and be a villain" (108). Surely this contradiction between intention and action demonstrates his disordered state.

Just as the contradiction reveals Hamlet's troubled mind, the diction reveals his background as a student and therefore it shows that Shakespeare has completely visualized and perfected Hamlet's character. The words are those to be expected from a student whose mind is full of matters associated with school. *Table, records, saws of books, copied, book and volume of my brain, baser matters, tables, set it down* – all these smack of the classroom, where Hamlet has so recently been occupied. And in lines 96 through 104 there is a complicated but brief description of Renaissance psychology, a subject that Hamlet has just been learning, presumably, at Wittenberg. Briefly, he states that his mind, or his memory, is like a writing tablet, from which he can erase previous experience and literature

---

★ Central idea.
† Thesis sentence.

(the "pressures past" of line 100), and which he can then fill with the message that the ghost of his father has just transmitted to him. Even in the distracted condition of this speech, Hamlet is capable of analysing and classifying what is happening to him. This is the reflexive action of a scholar.

An additional indication of Hamlet's mental condition, perhaps a subtle one but certainly in keeping with Shakespeare's poetic genius, is the rhythm of the speech. The full impact of what Hamlet is saying is that by wiping away all previous experience from his memory, and by thinking only about death and vengeance, his mind is taking a morbid turn. The last part of the speech is rhythmically consistent with this condition. There are many trochaic rhythms, which would have been described in Shakespeare's day as having a *dying fall*. There are thus falling rhythms on

$$\acute{}\ \circ\ \acute{}\ \circ$$
yes, by heaven

and

$$\acute{}\ \circ\ \ \acute{}\ \circ\ \ \ \acute{}\ \circ\ \ \ \ \acute{}\ \circ\ \ \acute{}\ \circ$$
O villain, villain, smiling, damned villain!

The last two lines end with trochees (*villain, Denmark*). This rhythm is unlike most of what went before, but will be like most of what follows, particularly the interjections in the "To be or not to be" soliloquy and the conclusions in that soliloquy (on the word *action*).

Since this passage reveals Hamlet's character so clearly, it is relevant to the rest of the play. From this point onward Hamlet will constantly be spurred by this promise to the ghost, that the ghost's "commandment all alone shall live / Within the book and volume of . . . [his] brain" (102, 103) and Hamlet will feel guilty and will be overwhelmed with self-doubt and the urge for self-destruction because he does not act on this promise. His attitude toward Claudius, which previously was scornful, will now be vengeful. His budding love for Ophelia will be blighted by his obsession with vengeance, and as a result Ophelia, a tender plant, will die. Truly, this passage can be regarded as the climax of the first act, and it points the way to the grim but inevitable outcome of the play.

EXERCISES

EXERCISE 1, PARAPHRASE AND EXPLICATION. *Paraphrase the following poem. Then write a short paragraph of explication. Remember that paraphrasing calls for restating the central idea or theme in other words. Explication requires evaluating any deeper or larger meaning in the passage. Be sure to look up any words you do not understand.*

> This flesh repudiates the bone
>   With such dissolving force,
> In such a tumult to be gone,
>   Such longing for divorce,
> As leaves the livid mind no choice
>   But to conclude at last
> That all this energy and poise
>   Were but designed to cast
> A richer flower from the earth
>   Surrounding its decay,
> And like a child whose fretful mirth
>   Can find no constant play,
> Bring one more transient form to birth
>   And fling the old away.
>
>   –A.J.M. Smith, ''Metamorphosis''

EXERCISE 2, THEME. *Select a short story or poem and write a 500-word essay about its central theme. Show how any lesser themes are related to what you believe is the main theme.*

EXERCISE 3, STRUCTURE. *Select a novel or play and outline its setting, time sequence, and emotional or suspenseful features. Show how these elements are co-ordinated to create the structure of the work.*

EXERCISE 4, CHARACTER. *Select a major character from a novel, play, or film. Identify the point of view employed by the author (director) in presenting the character. Then describe the important ways in which the character is developed: author's description, dialogue, inner monologue, comments by other characters, and so forth.*

EXERCISE 5, IMAGERY. *Write an essay of 500–1000 words on one image pattern in a poem, short story, novel, or film. Make sure you show how this pattern is related to the main theme or themes.*

EXERCISE 6, STYLE. *Analyse the style of the following paragraph. After you have finished commenting on the diction, sentence form, sound effects and rhythm, identify the tone and mood of the passage.*

> Gertrude Stein projected a remarkable power, possibly due to the atmosphere of adulation that surrounded her. A rhomboidal woman dressed in a floor-length gown apparently made of some kind of burlap, she gave the impression of absolute irrefragability; her ankles, almost concealed by the hieratic folds of her dress, were like the pillars of a temple: it was impossible to conceive of her lying down. Her fine close-cropped head was in the style of the late Roman Empire, but unfortunately it merged into broad peasant shoulders without the aesthetic assistance of a neck; her eyes were large and much too piercing. I had a peculiar sense of mingled attraction and repulsion towards her. She awakened in me a feeling of instinctive hostility coupled with a grudging veneration, as if she were a pagan idol in whom I was unable to believe.
>
> –John Glassco, *Memoirs of Montparnasse*

SUGGESTED FURTHER READING

ABRAMS, M.H. *A Glossary of Literary Terms.* 4th ed. New York: Holt, Rinehart and Winston, 1981.

CIRCLOT, J.E. *A Dictionary of Symbols.* Trans. Jack Sage. New York: Philosophical Library, 1976.

GUERIN, WILFRED L., EARLE G. LABOR, LEE MORGAN, JOHN R. WILLINGHAM. *A Handbook of Critical Approaches to Literature*. 2nd ed. New York: Harper & Row, 1979.

HOLMAN, C. HUGH. ed. *A Handbook to Literature*. 3rd. ed. New York: Odyssey Press, 1972.

JAMES, HENRY. *Theory of Fiction*. Ed. James E. Miller, Jr. Lincoln: University of Nebraska Press, 1972.

KENNEDY, X.J. *An Introduction to Poetry*. 3rd ed. Boston: Little, Brown, 1974.

MONACO, JAMES. *How to Read a Film*. New York: Oxford University Press, 1977.

PERRINE, LAURENCE. *Story and Structure*. 5th ed. New York: Harcourt Brace Jovanovich, 1978.

ROBERTS, EDGAR V. *Writing Themes About Literature*. 4th ed. Englewood Cliffs, N.J.: Prentice-Hall, 1977.

WIMSATT, W.K., JR. and CLEANTH BROOKS. *Literary Criticism: A Short History*. New York: Knopf, 1957.

8

THE RESEARCH PAPER

Importance of the Research Paper

The research paper is an important and extended exercise in writing. It is best understood as an essay or report derived from the collection of data by research. Although the preparation of a research paper may depend on concentrated study of books, articles, and reports in the library – the study, in short, of someone else's research – it may be written after almost any kind of information-gathering exercise. Careful observation of your family's patterns of behaviour on rainy days is, in this sense, a form of research.

There are many values and skills to be acquired from writing a research paper:

1. Practice in preparing the term papers that will be required in many of your courses.
2. Acquisition of interesting and perhaps useful information about a special subject.
3. An increase in the ability to distinguish between facts and opinions.

4. An improved ability to *judge* material as well as to find it, to evaluate its worth, to organize it, and to present it in attractive form.

These skills are useful whether you compose a report for your speech class, a speech for a political organization, or an article for the school newspaper.

The Use of the Library

Although differences in size and organization of different libraries must always be taken into account, a study of the resources of a library can still be taken up under three main headings: (1) the holdings files, (2) the general reference library, and (3) the guides and indexes to periodicals and bulletins.

THE HOLDINGS FILES: BASIC GUIDE TO THE LIBRARY

The starting point for exploration of the library is, logically, the card catalogue, which is a collection of 5 x 7 cards, or the microfiche. These list every book (including reference books), bulletin, pamphlet, and periodical the library owns.

The listings are arranged alphabetically according to authors, titles, and subjects. In other words, a large and complete library will have every book listed on at least three separate files. You can therefore locate a book if you know the author's name, or the title, or the subject with which it deals. A listing, however, is no more than a record that the library believes it owns the work in question, and a book on the shelves is worth two in the files.

Magazines and bulletins are usually listed by title – that is, the card catalogue or microfiche will tell you whether or not the library owns a certain magazine or series of bulletins. The listing for a given magazine or bulletin will tell you which volumes are bound and shelved (and usually the call number to be used in asking for them), and which are stacked unbound in a storeroom. In most libraries there will be a duplicate list of periodicals for use in the reference library room. For detailed information about the contents of periodicals, bulletins, and newspapers you will have to consult the periodical indexes. These are listed and explained on pages 278–281.

Here is a typical library card.

```
F1026    Creighton, Donald Grant.
 .C74       The empire of the St. Lawrence. Toronto,
            Macmillan Co. of Canada, 1956.

            441 p.   illus.   24 cm.

            First published in 1967 under title: The com-
            mercial empire of the St. Lawrence, 1760–1850.
            Includes bibliography.

            1. Canada – Hist.   2. Canada – Comm.
            3. St. Lawrence River – Comm.   4. Canada –
            Relations (general) with the U.S.   5. U.S. –
            Relations (general) with Canada.   I. Title.

        F1026.C74   1956       971            57–1322 ‡

        Library of Congress     (3)
```

1. F1026.C74 is the call number, according to the Library of Congress system. (See pages 269–271.)
2. "Creighton, Donald Grant" is the author's name (last name given first). The date of the author's birth (and death) may or may not appear.
3. "The empire of the St. Lawrence . . . 1956" gives the title of the book, the place of publication, the publisher, and the copyright date. On this line you may also find the author's name repeated, the writer of a foreword, preface, or introduction.
4. The next line explains that the book contains 441 pages, illustrations, and that the shelf size (height on the shelf) of the book is 24 centimetres. Added information, such as the book's original title and that it contains a bibliography, comes next.

5. The titles near the bottom of the card tell under what subjects the book can be found in the holdings files. You can find this work by looking under Canada – History: Canada – Commerce; St. Lawrence River – Commerce; Canada – Relations (general) with the U.S.; United States – Relations (general) with Canada; and under the book's title.
6. At the bottom of the card the Library of Congress and the Dewey Decimal call numbers are both listed: F1026.C74 and 971.
7. ''Library of Congress'' indicates that the Library of Congress has a copy of the book.
8. The numbers and letters at the lower right are for the use of librarians in ordering copies of this book. They are of no use to the general user of the card catalogue.

The card just examined is an author card. A title card is just like an author card, except that the title is typewritten at the top.

```
F1026          Empire of the St. Lawrence

  .C74    Creighton, Donald Grant.
                The empire of the St. Lawrence. Toronto,
          Macmillan Co. of Canada, 1956.

                441 p.   illus.   24 cm.

                First published in 1967 under title: The com-
          mercial empire of the St. Lawrence, 1760–1850.
          Includes bibliography.

                1.  Canada – Hist.   2.  Canada – Comm.
          3.  St. Lawrence River – Comm.   4.  Canada –
          Relations (general) with the U.S.   5.  U.S. –
          Relations (general) with Canada   I.  Title.

          F1026.C74   1956        971              57–1322  ‡

          Library of Congress (3)
```

A subject card is an author card with the subject typed, usually in red, above the author's name at the top.

Usually, all the other information is the same as on the author card. It should be kept in mind that library systems are in the process of changing. Library of Congress cards now contain an ISBN number or the number of a particular book given to it by its publisher for ordering purposes. The format of card entries is also changing to allow computers to read them. If a library makes up its own cards, rather than purchasing them from the Library of Congress, some of the above-mentioned information may be missing.

To find information about a certain periodical consult your library's Serial Record. This listing will tell you where to find the periodical in the library and how many and which volumes are available.

Call Numbers. A call number is a symbol or group of symbols used by a library to designate a particular book. It consists frequently of two parts: the first, or upper, is the classification number, the second, or lower, the author and book number. The call number is typed on the upper left-hand corner of the card-catalogue card, on the spine or binding of the book, and often inside the book's front or back cover. In most libraries, before you may take out a book, you must fill out a call slip. On this slip should appear the call number, the name of the author, and the title of the work. Your signature and whatever supplementary information the library requires complete the call slip.

For the undergraduate, a knowledge of the systems used in devising call numbers is relatively unimportant. To satisfy a natural curiosity on the part of many students, however, the following brief explanation is given.

Two classification systems are used by libraries in this country: the Library of Congress system and the Dewey Decimal system.

The Library of Congress System. The Library of Congress system, found more frequently in academic libraries than in public libraries, uses the letters of the alphabet, followed by additional letters and Arabic numerals, as the basis of its classification.

A   General works
B   Philosophy – Religion
C   History – Auxiliary sciences
D   History and topography
E and F   American history
G   Geography – Anthropology
H   Social sciences
J   Political science
K   Law
L   Education
M   Music
N   Fine arts
P   Language and literature
Q   Science
R   Medicine
S   Agriculture
T   Technology
U   Military science
V   Naval science
Z   Bibliography and library science

The following table shows the larger subdivisions under one of these main classes:

G Geography – Anthropology

G   Geography (General)
GA   Mathematical and astronomical geography
GB   Physical geography
GC   Oceanology and oceanography
GF   Anthropogeography
GN   Anthropology – Somatology – Ethnology
         Ethnogeography (General)
         51–161   Anthropometry – Skeleton – Craniometry
         400–499   Customs and institutions (Primitive)
         537–686   Special races
         700–875   Prehistoric archaeology

GR   Folklore
GT   Manners and customs (General)
GV   Sports and amusements – Games
         201–547   Physical training
         1580–1799   Dancing

The Dewey Decimal System. The Dewey Decimal system, devised by Melvil Dewey, uses a decimal classification for all books. The entire field of knowledge is divided into nine groups, with an additional group for general reference books. Each main class and subclass is shown by a number composed of three digits.

000	General works	500	Natural science
100	Philosophy	600	Useful arts
200	Religion	700	Fine arts
300	Sociology	800	Literature
400	Philology	900	History

The following table shows the first subdivision under the literature class and the beginning of the intricate system of further subdividing under the 820 group.

800   Literature
         819   Canadian
         820   English
                 821   English poetry
                 822   English drama
                         822.3   Elizabethan drama
                                 822.33   Shakespeare

830   German
840   French
850   Italian
860   Spanish
870   Latin
880   Greek
890   Minor literatures

THE REFERENCE LIBRARY

The reference library consists of all the general reference works, such as encyclopaedias and dictionaries, and collections of pamphlets, bibliographies, guides, maps, and pictures that are to be consulted for some specific information rather than to be read in their entirety. Reference books ordinarily may not be taken from the library. The following list of reference books should be a starting point for your exploration of possible subjects. It is wise to know what they are, where these books are shelved, and how they can be used to the best advantage. The date given is usually the date of the latest revision. In this rapidly changing world, the date of publication may be very important in a reference book.

General Encyclopaedias. A student using the *Britannica* and the *Americana* should consult the annual supplements, the *Britannica Book of the Year* and the *Americana Annual*, for additional information

> *Encyclopaedia Britannica.* 30 vols., 1975. Chicago: Encyclopaedia Britannica, Inc. Since 1940 the *Britannica* has been kept up to date by continuous revisions. The 15th ed. is divided into a macropedia (19 vols.), consisting of long, fully detailed articles, and a micropedia (10 vols.) of dictionarylike format. Both are arranged alphabetically. A single-volume propedia, or index, is arranged according to topic. The micropedia and propedia may be used as indexes to macropedia articles.

> *Encyclopedia Americana.* 30 vols. New York: Americana Corporation. Like the *Britannica*, the *Americana* is now kept up to date by continuous revision. Hence the date is necessary with any reference to it.

> *Collier's Encyclopedia.* 24 vols., 1973. New York: Crowell Collier, and Macmillan Publishing Co., Inc. Continuously revised. Although written in a popular style designed for the general rather than scholarly reader, it is objective and authoritative.

Encyclopedia Canadiana. 10 vols. 1970. Toronto: Grolier. Not revised but contains some entries on Canadian topics not found in other encyclopaedias.

Special Encyclopaedias. A special or limited encyclopaedia is available for almost any subject of importance that one can think of. You may find a long list by looking under "encyclopaedias" in the most recent annual volume of the *Cumulative Book Index*. Many of these special encyclopaedias, once useful and authoritative, have not been revised recently. The information they contain is now dated. Others are valuable as historical records. Here are a few examples of this type of reference book:

The Catholic Encyclopedia. 15 vols. New York: McGraw-Hill Book Company, 1967. Although this work deals primarily with the accomplishments of Roman Catholics, its scope is very general. It is useful for subjects dealing with mediaeval literature, history, art, and philosophy.

The Jewish Encyclopedia. 12 vols. New York: Funk & Wagnalls, 1925.

McGraw-Hill Encyclopedia of Science and Technology. 15 vols. incl. yearbooks. New York: McGraw–Hill Book Company, 1960, 1966, 1971.

Encyclopedia of World Literature in the Twentieth Century. 3 vols. New York: Frederick Ungar Publishing Co., 1971.

Yearbooks. In addition to the general yearbooks listed here, there are yearbooks for many specialized fields. See the *Cumulative Book Index*, *Books in Print*, or *Canadian Books in Print* for titles.

Britannica Book of the Year. Chicago: Encyclopaedia Britannica, Inc., 1938 to date.

Americana Annual. New York: Americana Corporation, 1923 to date.

Chambers' Encyclopedia Yearbook. London: International Learning Systems Corporation Limited, 1970 to date.

World Almanac and Book of Facts. New York: The New York World-Telegram and Sun, 1868–1967; Newspaper Enterprise Association Incorporated, 1967 to date.

Information Please Almanac. New York: Macmillan Publishing Co., Inc., 1947–1959; McGraw-Hill Book Company, 1960; Simon & Schuster, Inc., 1961 to date.

Economic Almanac. New York: National Industrial Conference Board, 1940 to date.

Statesman's Year-Book. London: Macmillan & Co., Ltd.; New York: St. Martin's Press, Inc., 1864 to date.

The Official Associated Press Almanac. New York: Almanac Publishing Company Incorporated, 1970 to date. (First published as *The New York Times Encyclopedia Almanac*.)

Canada Year Book. Ottawa: Ministry of Supply and Services Canada, 1905 to date.

Canadian Almanac and Directory. Toronto: Copp Clark Pitman, 1847 to date.

Canadian Annual Review of Politics and Public Affairs. Toronto: University of Toronto Press, 1960 to date.

Guides to Reference Books. The following are the principal bibliographies of reference texts.

BARTON, MARY NEILL, and MARION V. BELL. *Reference Books: A Brief Guide*. 7th ed. 1970.

The Bibliographic Index. 1937 to date.

GATES, JEAN KAY. *Guide to the Use of Books and Libraries*. 2nd ed. 1969.

JARVI, EDITH I. *Guide to Basic Reference Materials for Canadian Libraries*. 4th ed. 1974.

RYDER, DOROTHY E. *Canadian Reference Sources, A Selective Guide*. 2nd ed. 1981.

SHORES, LOUIS. *Basic Reference Sources: An Introduction to Materials and Methods*. 1954.

WINCHELL, CONSTANCE M. *Guide to Reference Books*. 8th ed. 1967.

A World Bibliography of Bibliographies. 4th ed., 5 vols. 1965–1966.

The Harper Encyclopedia of Science. Rev. ed. 1967.

Constance Winchell's *Guide* offers the best source of reference books in your field of interest. More specialized bibliographies and indexes can also be found in this volume.

Biographical Information. Biographical information can also be secured with the help of various periodical indexes (such as the *Readers' Guide to Periodical Literature*) and in very compressed form in your own desk dictionary.

Dictionary of American Biography. 20 vols., plus 3 supp. vols. New York: Charles Scribner's Sons, 1928–1973.

Dictionary of National Biography. 22 vols., plus 7 suppl. vols. London: Oxford University Press, 1885–1971. The word *national* is sometimes confusing to students; it refers to the ''nationals'' of the British Empire, now known as the British Commonwealth of Nations.

Current Biography: Who's News and Why. New York: H. W. Wilson Company, 1940 to date. Published monthly, with six-month and annual cumulations.

Webster's Biographical Dictionary. Springfield, Mass.: G. & C. Merriam Company, 1971, 1976. A one-volume pronouncing biographical dictionary of over 40 000 names. It includes living persons.

Who's Who in America. Chicago: A. N. Marquis Company, 1899 and biennially to date.

Who's Who. London: A. & C. Black, Ltd.; New York: Macmillan Publishing Co. Inc., 1849 to date.

Who's Who in Canada. Toronto: International Press, 1910 to date.

Canadian Who's Who. Toronto: University of Toronto Press, 1982.

Dictionary of Canadian Biography. 11 vols. and index. Toronto: University of Toronto Press, 1000–1890.

The Macmillan Dictionary of Canadian Biography. 4th ed. Toronto: Macmillan, 1979.

Biography Index. New York: H. W. Wilson Company, 1947 to date. This is a guide to biographical information in books and magazines.

Dictionaries and Books of Synonyms. The following books are useful for study of the changing meanings of words and for the discovery of synonyms.

The Canadian Dictionary for Schools. Toronto: Collier Macmillan Canada, Inc., 1981.

New Standard Dictionary. New York: Funk & Wagnalls, 1935 to date.

New Century Dictionary. 3 vols. New York: The Century Company, 1927–1933. Based on the original *Century Dictionary*, 12 vols., 1911.

Oxford English Dictionary. New York: Oxford University Press, 1933. A corrected reissue of *A New English Dictionary on Historical Principles*, 1888–1933. The purpose of this work is to give the history of every word in the English language for the past 800 years. It contains many quotations illustrating meanings of words in various periods and full discussions of derivations and changes in meanings and spellings.

Dictionary of American English on Historical Principles. 4 vols. Chicago: University of Chicago Press, 1936–1944. This is especially useful to the student who wishes to learn the historical changes in the use and meaning of words in American English.

Gage Canadian Dictionary. Toronto: Gage Publishing Limited, 1983.

Webster's New Dictionary of Synonyms. Springfield, Mass.: G. & C. Merriam Company, 1968. A dictionary of discriminated synonyms with antonyms, analogues, and contrasted words.

HAYAKAWA, S.I. *Modern Guide to Synonyms and Related Words.* New York: Funk & Wagnalls, 1968.

KLEIN, ERNST. *A Comprehensive Etymological Dictionary of the English Language.* 2 vols. Amsterdam, New York: Elsevier Publishing Co., Inc., 1966–1967.

PARTRIDGE, ERIC. *A Dictionary of Slang and Unconventional English.* 2 vols. New York: Macmillan Publishing Co., Inc., 1967.

Roget's International Thesaurus. 4th ed. New York: Crowell, 1977.

Roget's II, The New Thesaurus. Boston: Houghton Mifflin, 1980.

Gazetteers and Atlases. In a world of rapidly changing national boundaries and of former colonies emerging as independent nations, gazetteers and atlases are out of date almost as soon as they are printed. Most of the following works, however, are kept up to date by reasonably frequent revisions. Check the date on the book you are using.

The Columbia Lippincott Gazetteer of the World. A revision of *Lippincott's Gazetteer* of 1905. New York: Columbia University Press, 1962.

Rand McNally Commercial Atlas and Marketing Guide. Chicago: Rand McNally Company.

Encyclopaedia Britannica World Atlas. Chicago: Encyclopaedia Britannica Company, 1959. Rev. annually.

National Geographic Atlas of the World. 3rd ed. 1970.

The Times Atlas of the World. Sixth edition 1980. Reprinted 1981.

Books of Quotations. When you are in doubt about the source or wording of a passage that you can only vaguely recall, search out the complete passage in a book of quotations. These volumes are thoroughly indexed by key words.

BARTLETT, JOHN, and E.M. BECK. *Familiar Quotations.* 14th ed. Boston: Little, Brown and Company, 1968.

COLOMBO, JOHN ROBERT, ed. *Colombo's Canadian Quotations.* Edmonton: Hurtig, 1974.

HAMILTON, ROBERT M. and DOROTHY SHIELDS. *The Dictionary of Canadian Quotations and Phrases.* Rev. and enl. Toronto: McClelland and Stewart, 1979.

STEVENSON, BURTON. *The Macmillan Book of Proverbs, Maxims, and Famous Phrases.* New York: Macmillan Publishing Co., Inc., 1941.

_____. *The Home Book of Quotations.* 10th ed. New York: Dodd, Mead and Company, 1967.

The Oxford Dictionary of Quotations. 2nd ed. Toronto: Oxford University Press.

GUIDES AND INDEXES TO PERIODICALS AND BULLETINS

Magazines and Bulletins. Indexes to magazines, bulletins, and newspapers are usually shelved in the reference room of the library.

When searching for something published in a magazine, you need to know two things: (1) Does the library subscribe to that periodical? (2) In what issue was the article published? The answer to the first question is on a card, found in either the general catalogue or an additional special file in the reference room. For an answer to the second question, look into a periodical index. (Your reference librarian can help you to locate these resources.)

Bulletins are listed in most indexes. In compiling your bibliography remember that a bulletin is treated as a periodical if it is published at regular intervals (that is, as a series), and as a book if it is a separate, single publication.

There is a special index for material published in newspapers. See page 281.

Poole's Index to Periodical Literature, 1802–1881, and supplements from 1882 to 1906. A subject index only. Materials such as poems and stories are entered under the first word of the title. Only volume and page numbers are given; dates are excluded.

Reader's Guide to Periodical Literature, 1900 to date. Entries are under author, title, and subject. Besides volume, paging, and date, it indicates illustrations, portraits, maps, and other materials. Since for the student seeking a general topic this is the most important of the indexes, a sample of its entries follows:

Acid rain

Acid precipitation: what is it doing to our forests? G. Wetstone and S. Foster. bibl f il *Environment* 25:10-12+ My '83

Acid rain: now it's threatening our forests [study on Camel's Hump Mountain, Vt.] N. Tripp. il pors *Blair Ketchums Ctry J* 10:63-70 My '83

Phenomena, comment and notes. J. P. Wiley, Jr. il *Smithsonian* 14:24+ My '83

Laws and regulations

The complex challenge of controlling acid rain [with editorial comment by Alan McGowan] S. L. Rhodes and P. Middleton. bibl f il *Environment* 25:inside cover, 6-9+ My '83

Study criticizes U.S. acid rain policies [study by Gregory S. Wetstone and Armin Rosencranz] I. Peterson. *Sci News* 123:231 Ap 9 '83

Acne

Acne and the adolescent, J. P. Comer. il *Parents* 48:109 My '83

Acoustics, Architectural

Adjustable acoustics derive from two electronic systems [Silva Concert Hall, Eugene, Or.] il *Archit Rec* 171:130-3 My '83

Acquired immunodeficiency syndrome *See* AIDS

Acquisitions, Museum *See* Art galleries and museums – Acquisitions

ACS *See* American Chemical Society

Actions and defenses
> *See also*
> Damages
> Libel and slander
Everybody is suing everybody. il *Changing Times* 37:76 + Ap. '83
Activated carbon *See* Carbon, Activated
Actors and actresses
> *See also*
> Motion picture actors and actresses
> Television performers
Actors and actresses, Handicapped
In the image and spirit of Terry Fox, amputee Eric Fryer runs to
stardom. R. Bricker. il pors *People Wkly* 19:46-8 My 30 '83

Specialized Periodical Indexes. These include the following:

The Canadian Periodical Index, 1938 to date. A serial list of
publications in Canadian periodicals that includes an index
to the *Financial Post*.

Canadian Government Publications, from 1953 on a monthly
catalogue.

Canadian Book Review Annual, from 1973 on.

The Canadian Essay and Literature Index, from 1973 on.

A Bibliography of Canadian Bibliographies, 2nd ed. 1972.

Social Science and Humanities Index (formerly the *International
Index to Periodicals*), 1907 to date. This is the best index to
periodical journals. It also indexes some foreign-language
journals, especially those in German and French.

Agricultural Index, 1916 to date.

Art Index, 1929 to date.

Biography Index, 1947 to date.

Book Review Digest, 1905 to date.

Education Index, 1929 to date.

Index to Legal Periodicals, 1908 to date.

Music Index, 1949 to date.

Public Affairs Information Service, 1915 to date. Indexes, periodicals, books, documents, and pamphlets relating to political science, sociology, and economics.

Quarterly Cumulative Index Medicus, 1927 to date. *Index Medicus*, 1879–1926. An author and subject index to periodicals, books, and pamphlets in the field of medicine.

Index to Newspapers. *The New York Times Index* can be used as an index to any daily newspaper in the United States, since the same stories will probably be found in all daily papers on the same day they appear in the *Times*. The London *Times Index* is a good source for articles of all kinds.

Canadian News Facts. Contains an index.

New York Times Index, 1913 to date.

Index to The Times [London], 1906 to date.

The Research Paper

The research paper, variously known as the investigative essay, the term paper, or the research essay, is an exposition, based on research in a library, presenting the results of careful and thorough investigation of some chosen or assigned subject. You will no doubt also have occasions to write term papers based not on library research but on laboratory experiments, questionnaires, or your own critical reactions to something you have read; papers of that sort are organized and written like any other expository paper. Some English departments require a long analytical discussion based on material collected and printed in what is often known as a source book or casebook. This type of paper, which is sometimes called the controlled-research or controlled-sources paper, solves certain problems inherent in the research assignment, such as the need to plumb the library or assemble original data. Where the controlled-sources method is used, the instructor's directions should be followed exactly. The information that follows applies primarily to papers based on library investigation.

Summarized here are the values or purposes of the research paper:

1. It will teach you how to use the library efficiently.
2. It will acquaint you with the methods of scholarly documentation – that is, the use of bibliography and footnotes.
3. It will increase your ability to take usable notes.
4. It will teach you how to organize and combine material from a number of different sources.
5. It will give you practice in presenting material in a way that will appeal to your readers.

The research paper can be a project full of frustrations, however, unless you follow orderly procedures. Below is a commentary on the various steps that constitute an orderly, efficient approach to the job.

DECIDE ON A GENERAL SUBJECT OR FIELD OF INVESTIGATION

As soon as the research paper is assigned, many students will ask themselves: "Now what subject do I know something about?" A major in English may want to investigate some author or literary movement. A student in forestry may be especially eager to investigate the new uses of forest products. A student of home economics may wish to write on nutrition or consumer redress. In some ways this attitude is commendable; it approaches in method the theory of the "special topics courses" – the independent investigation in depth of some special field related to a student's major interest. But in other ways this attitude is a mistake. A student should indeed be interested in the subject of the investigation, but that interest may as well involve the thrill of exploring an unfamiliar field.

Of course, if the subjects are assigned, the problem of choice does not exist; but if the student has a choice, either unrestricted or limited, the choice should be based on a knowledge of what is desirable and what must be avoided. The following kinds of subjects are not workable; they lead only to frustration:

1. Subjects that are too broad. Broad or general subjects are starting points. They must be limited or narrowed to usable dimensions.
2. Subjects on which little has been published anywhere.
3. Subjects on which the local library has little material.
4. Subjects that are so technical that the writer cannot understand the material, much less present it intelligibly to others.
5. Subjects that are too narrow or too trivial for a paper of the suggested length.
6. Subjects indistinguishable from those selected by other students.

The following suggestions might prove helpful to you when you are searching for a subject:

1. Something related to the course you are taking or expect to take, such as literature, history, business, or political science.
2. Something coming out of your experience, such as your work during summer vacations, your travel or stay in a foreign country, the occupations of your parents. Remember, however, that these are only the starting point for your library work.
3. Something related to your hobbies, your special talents, or your reading interests, such as photography, archaeology, exploration, sports, aviation.

MAKE A PRELIMINARY CHECK OF THE LIBRARY AND DO SOME GENERAL READING

Before making a final decision on the general subject it is best to spend an hour or two browsing in the library to see whether the subject will be satisfactory and to get an idea of how it can be limited. First look in the holdings files. Then check through some of the periodical indexes to ascertain the extent of the available published material in the selected field. Notice in what types of periodicals the information is to be found, and make a preliminary check, either through the general holdings files or through a special list of periodicals, to see which of the sources are avail-

able in the library. Look in the *Britannica* to see what it has
on the topic. If there is only a limited amount of information
on hand and several people want access to it simultaneously,
efforts at research will run into frustrating delays.

LIMIT THE SUBJECT

After selecting a general field of interest, you will, with the help
of your instructor, select some part or aspect of it that can be
effectively presented in the given space and time. If you are
interested in Canadian literature, you may decide to write about
E.J. Pratt or Margaret Atwood. You may find it convenient to
limit your subject still further and to investigate the early poems
of Pratt or the feminist tendencies expressed in the works of
Atwood. These are merely suggested topics. The variety of possible topics is vast. How you limit a broad subject depends
partly on the time or the space allowed, partly on the thesis of
the paper, partly on the extent of available material. A scholarly probing of a very minor area is one thing; a more general
presentation of facts, such as might be read before a club or a
seminar, is another. In choosing a subject, always remember that
it is impossible to narrow or limit a subject by excluding details. A research article should be interesting. Interest comes
from the concrete details, the examples, and the imaginative
touches in the writing.

The following lists show how two general fields can be narrowed down to topics that can be presented adequately in the
time and space prescribed:

General Subject: Movies

1. Hollywood stars
2. Famous directors
3. Horror movies – their history
4. Québecois films
5. Novels into films
6. The art movie
7. The history of film technology
8. The gangster film

9. Problems of distribution of Canadian films
10. Silent comedies

General Subject: Warfare

1. Caesar's battles
2. The militia in Canada
3. The strategy of siege
4. Air battles of World War I
5. World War II generals
6. War in literature
7. Tragic Canadian campaigns
8. Modern weapons of war
9. Canadian conscription crises
10. Nuclear arms limitation

PREPARE A WORKING BIBLIOGRAPHY

A bibliography is a list of books, articles, bulletins, or documents relating to a given subject or author.

When you begin working on a research paper, arm yourself with a supply of 3 × 5 cards or slips of paper. On these cards make a list of references – one and *only one* to each card – that you hope will be useful. Collect the references from the holdings listings, the encyclopaedias, and the periodical indexes. Since there is always a great deal of wastage and frustration in defining a specific area of research, take out insurance by getting more references than you expect to use. As you proceed with your reading, refine the bibliography by adding new references and by discarding those you find useless.

Bibliographic Forms. It is unfortunate that bibliographic forms have not been standardized as completely as have the parts of an automobile. Recently, however, the Modern Language Association has moved toward standardization in the general field of literature, language, and the social sciences. The Association's most recent publication on bibliographic forms is called the *MLA Handbook for Writers of Research Papers, Theses, and Dissertations*. As its long title indicates, this handbook may be used by undergraduates, graduates, and professionals in the preparation of research papers and theses. The forms of bibliographies and footnotes used here are based on the *MLA Handbook*, insofar as the recommendations of the MLA are applicable to undergraduate work.[1]

(There are other forms used for bibliographies and footnotes, however, and your instructor may well recommend modifications of the MLA style. Use the form requested.)

Every bibliographic reference consists of the three parts necessary for a complete identification of the printed work used, and these parts are generally arranged in this order:

1. *The author's name.* (Write the last name first only where lists are to be alphabetized. If an article or pamphlet is unsigned, begin with the title.)

2. *The title.* (If it is a book, underline the title. If it is an article, essay, poem, short story, or any subdivision of a larger work, enclose it in quotation marks.)

3. *The facts of publication.*
   a. For a book, give the place of publication (with the abbreviated province, if needed for clarity, as in *Sidney, N.S.*), the name of the publisher in full, and the date.
   b. For a magazine article, give the name of the magazine, the volume number, the date, and the pages.
   c. For a newspaper article, give the name of the newspaper, the date, the section if the sections are paged separately, and the page.

---

[1] *The MLA Handbook for Writers of Research Papers, Theses, and Dissertations* (New York: Modern Language Assn., 1977).

SAMPLE BIBLIOGRAPHY CARDS
The sample bibliography cards that follow illustrate the arrangement of items and the punctuation in various types of references.

Article in an Encyclopaedia
Initials of the author identified in vol. I. Date of copyright from back of volume. Title of article in quotes. Underline title of reference book.

> Atkinson, Richard J. C.
> "Stonehenge." Encyclopaedia Britannica. 1958, XXI, 440–441.

Book by a Single Author
Copy call number. Underline title of book.

> HC115
> .J6C3
> 1977
>
> Johnson, Harry Gordon
>
> The Canadian Quandary; Economic Problems and Policies
>
> Toronto: McClelland and Stewart, 1971.

Book by Two or More Authors
All names after the first are in normal order.

> HF5415
> .14C3
>
> Leighton, David S., and Donald H. Thain.
>
> Canadian Problems in Marketing
>
> Toronto: McGraw-Hill, 1959.

Book Edited by More Than Three Persons

et alii ("and others") abbreviated *et al.* (Do not underline.)

PS8071 .K6L5 1976	Klinck, Carl Frederick, et al., 3 vols. Literary History of Canada; Canadian Literature in English 2nd ed. Toronto: University of Toronto Press, 1976.

Book Edited

PS8537 .C6A6 1972	Scott, Duncan Campbell Selected Stories of Duncan Campbell Scott. Ed. and intro. by Glenn Clever. Ottawa: University of Ottawa Press, 1972.

Signed Magazine Article

Beer, etc.

Whittingham, Anthony

"Beer: an industry comes alive."

Maclean's. Aug. 15, 1983, pp. 18–21.

Unsigned Article

Cruise Missile Testing in Canada
'Researcher' pours red paint on copy of the Constitution.
Globe and Mail Jl. 23 '83

" 'Researcher' pours red paint on copy of the Constitution."
The Globe and Mail, July 23, 1983, p.1

Newspaper Article

Larue-Langlois, Jacques: Montreal se gave de jazz. illus.
J1.2, 1983, p.11

Larue-Langlois, Jacques

"Montreal se gave de jazz. . . ."

Le Devoir, July 2, 1983, p.11

READING AND TAKING NOTES

It is a good idea, before you begin to read and take notes, to collect a few fairly promising bibliography cards. Take your cards with you to the library. Look up several of your references. You might start with the encyclopaedia articles, or with books that give an overview of your subject. The aim in this reading is to develop a preliminary understanding of the subject you are interested in exploring. Read for general information. While exploring, note those topics that seem to be most closely related to your particular subject. If your subject is the problem of distribution of Canadian films, be sure to record information about U.S.-owned theatre outlets, independent owners, and the history of our branch-plant economy. These topics, properly arranged, will become your first rough outline. They will be the headings to use on your note cards when you begin taking notes.

Reading and Skimming. The tortures of research, the dead ends, the crucial articles that turn out to be irrelevant, the books that cannot be located, plague everyone. But there will be fewer frustrations and less wasted time if you remember that what you have learned about writing must apply also to your reading. Good writing produces work organized so that its contents are evident quickly, easily, without confusion, without wasted effort. Those who write books, chapters, essays, or articles in magazines follow the same principles of writing that you have learned –

so that *you* may get the information you want, easily, quickly, without confusion, without wasted effort. Here are some aids to quick reading and comprehension:

1. In a book examine first the table of contents, preface, foreword, or introduction, the index (if it has one), the chapter headings, and the topics of the lesser divisions.
2. In an essay or article look for a formal statement of plan or purpose at the beginning. If it is a rather long essay or article – one of those five-part essays used by magazines for serious discussions, for example – look at the beginning of each part for a hint of the contents.
3. Glance through the essay, reading a topic sentence here, another one there, until you come to what you want. This process is called skimming.

Evaluating Your Sources. To expect a student writing his or her first research paper to have the experience necessary to evaluate all sources is not fair or reasonable. But any student can learn a few hints or signs that will help distinguish the totally unreliable from the probably reliable. The student should first realize that not all that gets into print is true. Some – perhaps most – of it is as true and as reliable as honest and informed men and women can make it. Some of it is mistaken or biassed opinion. The following suggestions will help in the evaluation of sources:

1. The first aid is the date of publication of the book or article. In some fields, such as chemistry, physics, and medicine, information even a few months old may be outdated. Try to get the most recent facts possible.
2. To a certain extent, judge the information by the authority of the publication in which it appears. The *Britannica*, for instance, selects its authors with more care than does a newspaper.
3. A long, thorough treatment of a subject is probably more accurate than a short treatment of it, or a condensation.
4. Finally, if it is possible, find out something about the reputation of the author. Obviously a careful checking of authori-

ties is a necessity in a scholarly thesis written for publication, and a desirable but often unattainable ideal in a term paper. In practice, however, a good library can usually be trusted to winnow out most of the chaff before it buys. When in doubt ask your librarian for help.

The Topic Outline. Once the dimensions of a subject area have been established by preliminary exploration, it is time to organize the subject according to a topic outline. A topic outline, however, should consist of more than a simple record of information; it should also begin to sift the information in terms of what an intelligent, mature person approaching the matter with an open mind will most appreciate being told. A writer must always keep the reader in mind. The information that is actually available is, of course, the primary restriction on any topic outline. From that point the topic outline is the result of selecting material appropriate to the writer's objective and the reader's interest. "Selecting" is the key word. A tabulation of everything ever thought about a subject is no more a topic outline than is a list embracing every conceivable perspective some imaginary reader might like to see explored. The writer must pick and choose, add to and discard from the working outline, until the paper is set in its final form. But if the first topic outline is bound to undergo change, it is nonetheless important as a necessary guide for notetaking. It is therefore better that its preliminary form include too much than too little.

Use of Note Cards. When you go to the library you should have with you a generous supply of note cards. These may be either the 3×5 cards that you use for your bibliography or some slightly larger ones, such as the 4×6 size. If you cannot obtain cards, cut notebook paper into quarters to make slips approximately 4×5 inches in size. Just as carry-on baggage should not be stowed in an aircraft's baggage rack, notes should not be written in a notebook. One loose piece of paper to each note is the only format permitting easy and frequent rearrangement.

Methods of Identifying Notes. Notes must be identified if you are to avoid confusion later on. Two simple methods of identifying notes are presented here:

1. As you take notes, write at the top of a card the topic under which the information falls. At the bottom of the card write an abbreviated reference to the source of your information. This reference may consist of the author's last name, an abbreviated title, and the exact page reference.
2. The second method is to number all the bibliography cards. Any number system will do as long as the numbers are not duplicated. Then instead of the reference at the bottom of the note card, write the number of your bibliography card and the page number. Of course, whichever method is used each note card must relate to a topic in the working topic outline.

Be sure to use the method that is recommended by your instructor.

The Form of Notes. Sample note cards are given on pages 293–294, but before you study them, consider the following suggestions for note-taking:

1. Most notes will be in the form of a summary. Get what is essential and get it accurately, but do not waste words. In order to avoid any chance of inadvertent plagiarism, try to paraphrase what you read – that is, try to use your own words, not the words of your source. But dates, figures, and such matters must obviously be quoted accurately.
2. If you wish to quote the exact words of an author, copy your material in the form of direct quotations. Ordinarily you should not use direct quotations from your sources if a summary will serve. But if you wish to preserve the words of your source because of unusually apt or precise language, or for some other adequate reason, quote your source exactly. If you leave out a part of a quoted sentence, indicate the omission by means of spaced periods (. . .) called ellipsis points or suspension points. Use three spaced periods, leaving a space

between the word and the first period, if you omit words in the sentence, and four spaced periods (which include the period ending the sentence) if your omission follows a complete sentence. If you omit a paragraph or more, use three spaced periods centred on the card and in a line of their own, with space above and below the ellipsis.

3. Let your first unbreakable rule be: "One topic to a card." Do not include in your notes on the same card material relating to two or more topics. You may have as many cards as you wish covering the same topic, but take care to label each card and cite the exact source of your notes on each card.

4. Make your notes accurate and complete enough to make sense to you when they become cold.

5. Use headings or topics that represent actual divisions of your outline. Too many topics will merely result in confusion. Let the working outline be your guide.

6. Finally, remember that every note card must have three pieces of information: (1) the heading or topic, which shows you where the information belongs; (2) the information itself (in quotation marks if you use the words of your source); (3) the exact source of the material (including page reference).

II, B. Phrases, Clichés

Phrases of Shakespeare's creation:
"tower of strength"
"yeoman service"
"to the manner born"

Gordon, The English Language, p. 31

II, A. Words, Figurative Use

   Shakespeare was the first writer
to use "cap" in the sense of taking off
or touching one's cap as a token
of respect.

Brewer, <u>Dictionary of Phrase and Fable</u>, p.185

Plagiarism. In writing a paper based on research, it is very easy to fall into unintentional plagiarism. Therefore, you should understand exactly what plagiarism is, and how it can be avoided. The procedure outlined in this chapter should help you to steer away from borrowing without giving proper credit through careful note-taking. In taking notes be sure to rephrase the author's material in your own words; do not merely alter a word here and there. The danger is that if you do alter only a few words, the language of your source will carry over into the final paper. To prevent this transference, rephrase and summarize in your notes. You will naturally do more rephrasing when you write your first draft and the final draft, thus reducing the possibility of copying. Since plagiarism can be a serious offence (in some cases students have been expelled for committing it), ask your instructor to explain his or her definition of the word, and to give you assistance in any doubtful instances.

PREPARE THE FINAL OUTLINE

For most of you, the final outline is not the one you will write the paper from. In other words, the outline is usually in a state of flux until the paper itself is finished. It is subject to change until the last moment. If something that looked good at first later seems to be out of place, throw it out and improve the outline. The outline is a working blueprint, a simplified diagram of your paper, but it is no help to anyone if it forces you to construct something that at the last moment you feel is wrong. Change it if it needs changing.

For the conventions of the formal outline, turn back to chapter 5. Then examine the outline preceding the sample research paper in this chapter.

WRITE A FIRST DRAFT OF THE PAPER

In the process of writing a paper based on research in the library, most writers – whether students or professionals – work up the outline slowly and gradually as they collect notes. The whole process is one of synthesis, of gradual putting together, of sifting and rearranging, which of course includes throwing away unusable material as well as filling in unexpected gaps. It is time to begin writing when the working outline adequately defines the limits of the paper's content and when an approach to the subject, and possibly to the reader, is clear. It may be that you even have thought of an interesting beginning. So, take your note cards and outline at this point, and, on the table in front of you, spread out your note cards for your first section. Read them over to freshen in your mind the sequence or flow of thoughts – and then you are on your own.

As you write, whenever you come to borrowed material, either quoted or paraphrased, include the reference in parentheses in the right place in the text or between horizontal bars running from margin to margin, the first immediately below the material. Later, copy your footnotes, in the approved form, at the bottom of each page as you prepare the final draft of your paper.

When you quote verse, you may run two lines together in your quotation if you indicate the end of a line by a slash (/), but if you quote more than two lines you should centre the quotation on the page. If you quote prose of some length, you should separate the quotation from your text by indention. No quotation marks are used when quotations are marked by indentions. Ask your instructor if single or double spacing is required for indented quotations. Study the sample research paper at the end of this chapter for examples of these conventions.

WRITE A FINAL DRAFT WITH FOOTNOTES

The Final Draft. Go over your first draft carefully before adding the footnotes and copy it for final submission. Keep the following principles in mind: (1) unity and direction of the paper as a whole; (2) interest, supplied by fact and example; (3) organization of the paper as a whole and of the separate paragraphs; (4) correctness of sentence structure; and (5) correctness of punctuation and spelling.

Footnotes: Where Needed. Whether in a term paper or in a scholarly research article, footnotes are required:

1. To acknowledge and identify every direct quotation. Quoted material should always be quoted exactly, word for word, except where deletions are indicated, and either enclosed in quotation marks or indented. Footnotes are not used with familiar sayings or proverbs; everyone knows that these are quoted. (Expressions such as ''all the world's a stage'' or ''all that glitters is not gold'' are examples. But be careful to avoid these clichés; the research paper, like any other essay, requires aptness and freshness of language.)
2. To acknowledge and identify all information that has been used in the paper or thesis in paraphrased, reworded, or summarized form. Of course, facts of general knowledge need not be credited to any one source.
3. To define terms used in the text, to give additional information that does not fit into the text, and to explain in detail what has been merely referred to in the text.
4. To translate unusual foreign phrases.

Numbering and Spacing Footnotes. To indicate to the reader that a footnote is being used, place an Arabic numeral immediately *after* the material referred to and a little above the line. Do not put a space before the number or a period after it, either in the text or in the footnote. Place the same number *before* and a little above the line of the note at the bottom of the page. Each note should be single-spaced, and there should be one line of space between notes.

Footnotes should be numbered consecutively, starting from *1*, in a paper intended for publication; in a typed or handwritten paper, however, it is often required that they be numbered beginning with *1* on each page. Some instructors and editors prefer that footnotes appear on a separate sheet(s) at the end of the essay. Use the style your instructor recommends.

The Form of Footnotes. The first time you use a footnote to refer to any source, give the same information that is given in the bibliographic entry, and the exact page from which your information is taken: the author's name (but in the natural order, *not* with the last name first), the title of the work, the facts of publication, and the exact page reference. The punctuation in the footnote is changed in one important respect – instead of periods, as in the bibliography, commas and parentheses are used to separate the three parts of the reference. Later references to the same source are abbreviated. If only one work by an author is used in your paper, the author's name with the page reference is enough. If more than one work by the same author is used, the author's name and a shortened form of the title (with exact page reference, of course) will suffice. Book publishers' names are given in the shortest intelligible form – *Collier Macmillan*, not *Collier Macmillan Canada, Inc.* – when they are included.

The forms illustrated here are those recommended by the *MLA Handbook* (1977), with the addition of the publishers' names. For scientific papers the forms are slightly different, and the student who writes papers for publication in scientific journals should follow the rules set up by those journals.

MODELS FOR FOOTNOTES – BOOKS

Books by One Author

[1]Dennis Lee, *Savage Fields, An Essay in Literature and Cosmology* (Toronto: Anansi, 1977), p. 64.

[2]Laurence Ricou, *Vertical Man/Horizontal World* (Vancouver: University of British Columbia Press, 1973), p. 106.

Later References

[3]Lee, p. 96. (The MLA recommends use of *p.* or *pp.* [*pp.* is the plural abbreviation] only with works of a single volume. Otherwise it is omitted.)

[4]Ricou, *Vertical Man*, p. 132.

Two or More Authors

[5]Paul Wonnacott and Ronald Wonnacott, *Economics* (New York: McGraw-Hill, 1979), p. 45.

Edited Book

[6]Christopher R. Reaske, ed., *Seven Essayists: Varieties of Excellence in English Prose* (Glenview, Ill.: Scott, Foresman, 1969), p. 75.

Book Edited by More Than Three Editors

[7]M. H. Abrams et al., eds., *The Norton Anthology of English Literature* (New York: Norton, 1968), I, 33.

Reprinted Book

[8]L. C. Knights, *Drama and Society in the Age of Jonson* (1937; rpt. New York: Norton, 1968), pp. 146–149.

Book Review

[9]John Mills, rev. of *The Mangan Inheritance* by Brian Moore, *The Fiddlehead*, 126 (Summer, 1980), 123–127.

Dissertation

[10]Douglas O. Spettigue, "The English-Canadian Novel; Some Attitudes and Themes in Relation to Form," Diss. University of Toronto, 1966, p. 69.

Translated Work of Two or More Volumes

[11]H. A. Taine, *History of English Literature*, trans. H. Van Laun (New York: 1889), IV, 296.

MODELS FOR FOOTNOTES – ARTICLES

Article in a Journal

[12]Cindy Nagel, "Psychological Androgyny – An Exploration," *Canadian Women's Studies*, 3 (1981), 51–56. [Note that *p*. or *pp*. is not used for page numbers.]

Article in an Encyclopaedia

[13]Richard J. C. Atkinson, "Stonehenge," *Encyclopaedia Britannica* (1958), XXI, 440.

Article from a Monthly Magazine

[14]George Woodcock, "Seven Burmese Days," *The Canadian Forum*, July 1983, p. 15.

Article in a Weekly Magazine

[15]Peter C. Newman, "Oracle of the Computer Age," *Maclean's*, 8 Aug. 1983, p. 34. [When the volume number is not given, the page number is identified by *p*. or *pp*.]

Unsigned Magazine Article

[16]"The Aircraft that Comes in a Crate," *Canada Commerce*, May 1983, p. 23.

Signed Newspaper Article

[17]Catherine Harris, "How to size up where you stand on inflation," *The Financial Times*, 29 May 1982, p. 1 cols. 1–4.

Article in an Edited Collection

[18]W.H. New, "Sinclair Ross's Ambivalent World," in *Writers of the Prairies*, ed. Donald G. Stephens (Vancouver: University of British Columbia Press, 1973), p. 184.

MISCELLANEOUS

Interview

[19]Nikki Abraham, personal interview on dance administration, Edmonton, Alberta, 19 Feb. 1983.

Quotation Cited in a Secondary Source

[20]Gourmet Fields, "The Most Delectable Food I Ever Tasted," as quoted in *W. C. Fields by Himself*, ed. Ronald J. Fields (Englewood Cliffs, N.J.: Prentice-Hall, 1973), pp. 4–5.

Article Reprinted in a Collection

[21]E.K. Brown, "To the North: A Wall against Canadian Poetry," *Saturday Review of Literature*, 29 April 1944, pp. 9–10, rpt. in *Responses and Evaluations: Essays on Canada*, ed. and intro. David Staines (Toronto: McClelland and Stewart, 1977), pp. 78–79.

Film

[22]*The Taming of the Shrew* (1966), dir. Franco Zeffirelli, s. Elizabeth Taylor, Richard Burton. USA/Italy: Royal Films International F.A.I. Prod. [There is as yet no standardized form for footnoting films. The above citation includes as much information as is available, though the main elements are the title, date of release, director, country, and production company.]

Recording

[23]Stan Rogers, "The Field Behind the Plough," *Northwest Passage* (Fogarty's Cove Music, 1983).

Roman Numerals. Because Roman numerals have a restricted use, students are sometimes unfamiliar with them. The following brief explanation may be helpful:

The key symbols are few in number: 1 = I, 5 = V, 10 = X, 50 = L, 100 = C, 500 = D, 1000 = M.

Other numbers are formed by combining these symbols. The

three main principles involved are as follows: (1) A letter following one of equal or greater value is added value. (2) A letter preceding one of greater value is subtracted value. (3) When a letter stands between two of greater value, it is subtracted from the last of the three and the remainder is added to the first. Try this explanation with the following examples:

Rule 1

2 = II	20 = XX	200 = CC
3 = III	30 = XXX	300 = CCC
6 = VI	60 = LX	600 = DC
7 = VII	70 = LXX	700 = DCC

Rule 2

4 = IV	40 = XL	400 = CD
9 = IX	90 = XC	900 = CM

Rule 3

19 = XIX	59 = LIX	1900 = MCM

Abbreviations in Footnotes. Although the number of abbreviations used in research papers at the graduate-school level is large – and often confusing to the lay reader – only a few are of immediate concern here.

anon.   Anonymous.

c., ca.   *Circa*, "about." (used with approximate dates.)

cf.   *Confer*, "compare." (should not be used when *see* is meant.)

ch., chap.   Chapter.

Chs., chaps.   Chapters.

col., cols.   Column, columns.

ed.   Edited, edition, editor.

e.g.   *Exempli gratia* [ĕg · zĕm′plī grā′shĭ · à], "for example."

et al.   *Et alii* [ĕt ā′lĭ · ī], "and others."

f., ff.   And the following page (f.) or pages (ff.).

ibid.   *Ibidem* [ĭ · bī′dĕm], "in the same place." (*Ibid.* refers to the note immediately preceding. *The MLA Handbook* recommends substituting either the author's name or an abbreviated title; either is unambiguous and almost as brief as *ibid.*)

i.e.   *Id est*, "that is." Do not use for "e.g."

l., ll.   Line, lines.

loc. cit.   *Loco citato* [lō′kō sī · tă′tō], "in the place cited." (*Loc. cit.* refers to the same passage cited in a recent note. It is used with the author's name but is not followed by a page number.)

op. cit.   *Opere citato* [ŏp′ĕ · rē sī · tā′tō], "in the work cited." (*The MLA Handbook* calls this "the most abused of scholarly abbreviations," and recommends instead the use of the author's name alone or with an abbreviated title.)

The Fair Copy. After you have finished your final draft, you should prepare a clean copy for submission. Chapter 6 gives some general rules that you should follow unless your instructor has some other preference. The sample research paper at the end of this chapter will also assist you.

PREPARE A FINAL BIBLIOGRAPHY

Your final bibliography should include all the articles and books cited by your paper in the footnotes, plus whatever additional source information your instructor specifies. A bibliography can be prepared quickly and simply by gathering the bibliography cards for the footnotes in the final draft and arranging the citations taken from them in alphabetical (index, not dictionary) order by author, or by title when no author is given.

To alphabetize titles in index order, remember that (1) initial articles (*a*, *an*, *the*) are disregarded and (2) alphabetization is by word, with short forms of the same word coming first no matter what letter the second word starts with. For instance, *Montreal* always precedes *Montrealers*:

Montreal: Days of Adventure
Montreal: The Fast Pace
Montreal Audiences
Montreal Critics

To alphabetize names in index order, you will also need to bear in mind a few variations from dictionary order. *Mc-* and *M'-* are alphabetized as if spelled *Mac-*. When two authors have identical last names, alphabetize by first names first, second names next: *Norman, Marie B.* precedes *Norman, Mary A.* An initial takes precedence over a spelled name that begins with the same letter, and a last name followed by a single initial takes precedence over a last name followed by two initials: *Norman, M.* precedes *Norman, M. B.*, and both precede *Norman, Mary A.* Use the titles (or dates, if titles are identical) to alphabetize a number of works by the same author writing alone. When there are collaborators, use the following order: (1) single author; (2) author and collaborator; (3) author "et al."; (4) title; (5) date, with the earliest first:

JONES, A. B. *My Life and Times.* Edmonton: Jones Publishing Company, 1984.

_____ and TOM SMITH. *Friendly Enemies.* Edmonton: Jones Publishing Company, 1984.

_____ et al. *Relatives.* Edmonton: Jones Publishing Company, 1984.

_____ et al. *Topical Essays.* Edmonton: Jones Publishing Company, 1983.

_____ et al. *Topical Essays.* Edmonton: Jones Publishing Company, 1984.

The form of the individual entries has already been treated on pages 287–289. See also the bibliography accompanying the sample paper that follows.

SAMPLE OUTLINE AND RESEARCH PAPER

The following sample outline and essay are reproduced here, not as perfect models to imitate, but as examples of conscientious and competent work.[2] (The student has used a *sentence* outline here; for a sample of the *topic* outline, turn back to p. 178.)

Words, Words, Words:
Shakespeare's Contribution to Our Language

Thesis Sentence: Although Shakespeare is widely recognized as a literary genius, his work as well constitutes a major contribution to our language, giving us the words to create satisfying images and to express insights into human nature.

I.   Shakespeare's vocabulary and the language richness of his age created the right atmosphere for his contribution.
   A.   Shakespeare's vocabulary was large and diverse.
      1.   General estimates put it at 20 000 words.
      2.   About 90% of his vocabulary was made up of native words.
   B.   The Elizabethan age was one in which the language changed rapidly.
      1.   The Elizabethans were language conscious – they loved sermons and speeches – and Shakespeare took advantage of this condition.
      2.   Shakespeare was also part of the transformation from Middle to Early Modern English.

II.   Shakespeare was the inventor of many words and phrases.
   A.   He used words to which he gave original connotations.
      1.   Greek and Latin derivatives like ''obscene'' and ''pedant'' were given special meanings.
      2.   Ordinary words like ''bump'' and ''dwindle'' are attributed to him.
      3.   Figures of speech were given meanings – ''coxcomb'' meaning ''fool'' – that they retain today.

---

[2] Reprinted by permission of the author, Jennifer Borron.

        4. Shakespeare invented many compound words – "hot-blooded," "hell-black" – that have continued in use.

  B. Many new phrases were introduced in his works.

        1. Phrases like "heart of gold" have been repeated so much that they are now regarded as clichés.

        2. Certain phrases – "beat it," "fall for it" – have been twisted into slang.

        3. Some clichés have achieved the status of proverbs: "the devil can quote scripture."

        4. We now use certain quotations – "Beware the Ides of March" and "What's in a name?" – as signs of literary sophistication.

III. Shakespeare's works are the sources of expressions that have become identified with character or social types, books, and derivative plays.

  A. Shakespeare's individualized characters have been transformed into stereotypes.

        1. "Romeo and Juliet" is the tag for stereotyped young lovers.

        2. "Shylock" is used as a derogatory label for money-lenders.

  B. Book titles often have their origins in lines from Shakespeare.

        1. The Sound and Fury was taken by Faulkner from Macbeth.

        2. Brave New World is a line from The Tempest.

  C. Adaptations of the plays have provided new, well-recognized expressions.

        1. Kiss Me, Kate is based on The Taming of the Shrew.

        2. West Side Story is a musical version of Romeo and Juliet.

IV. Shakespeare should be recognized as the writer who has most strongly influenced today's language.

  A. His works continue to have widespread popularity, especially as sources of quotations.

  B. In a sense, the wheel has come full circle, since Shakespeare was equally influential in forming the language of his own age.

Words, Words, Words:
Shakespeare's Contribution to Our Language

By
Jennifer Borron

English 120–B
August 1, 1980

Words, Words, Words:
Shakespeare's Contribution to Our Language

As we know it today, English is one of the richest languages in the world. Studies of its evolution have shed light on the number of literary figures who have given so much of their vocabulary to us; they are responsible for much of this enrichment. Included in these ranks are names like Chaucer and Milton. However, the one name that stands out with unequalled greatness in linguistic contribution is William Shakespeare.

No other person has had such influence on the way a language is spoken or written. Henry Bradley confirms this claim in The Making of English: ''Shakespeare has no equal with regard to the extent and profundity of his influence on the English language.''[1] Bradley's opinions do not stand alone in the field of literary criticism and the study of the history of the English language. James C. Gordon, who has written extensively on the etiology of English, regards Shakespeare as the greatest single benefactor of our language. Furthermore, he considers Shakespeare's works ''so familiar to so many that our cultivated tradition, both literary and colloquial, is studded with . . . phrases of his creation.''[2] The extent of the research done on Shakespeare's use of words and phrases illustrates his great reach into almost every profession dealing with language.

Why has Shakespeare had such an impact on how we use our language? Largely the answer lies in the size of his vocabulary, which is generally accepted as consisting of about twenty thousand words. Not only was he an ingenious inventor, twisting meanings to create entirely new meanings or turning nouns into verbs, he also had a command of word use in the writings of certain authors before and during this time. Shakespeare's knowledge of classical and foreign literary sources furthered the success of his creativity in writing. Yet despite this acquaintance with foreign and classical works, the semanticist Mario Pei proposes that ''his vocabulary is about ninety percent native, . . . [giving] the world a full realization of the potentialities of . . . English . . . .''[3] Because of Shakespeare's extensive resources, he is one of the heaviest contributors to the language's vocabulary, but Pei admits ''it is often difficult to distinguish between the words he accepted and gave currency to, and those he personally coined.''[4] An article dealing with Shakespeare's vocabulary in the literary journal, <u>Notes and Queries</u>, assumes that once a word was part of his vocabulary, it was never lost.[5]

Shakespeare's enrichment of our tongue also stems from the period of time in which he lived. Shakespeare wrote most of his plays during the reign of Queen Elizabeth, the Elizabethan Age. The primary characteristic of the age was a sort of "language-consciousness,"[6] which allowed men like Shakespeare to lay the foundations of Modern English. The Elizabethans were frequently exposed to sermons and public speeches, which stimulated their interest in the sound and sense of the language. James D. Gordon speculates that Shakespeare knew of this consciousness and took advantage of it when writing.[7] His awareness of the effect of language went along with what is called in <u>The Riverside Shake-speare</u> "the fundamental state of the language, which was just ripe for Shakespeare's formative use of it."[8] The Elizabethan Age was in fact in the transitional period between Middle and Modern English. Gordon, in <u>The English Language: An Historical Introduction,</u> calls Shakespeare's language "Early Modern English."[9] Using Shakespeare as an example of a writer who contributed to the change of the language from one period to another illustrates his importance in the history of English.

According to Stuart Robinson, a good part of Shakespeare's "legacy to the language" comes from his supremacy in word-making.[10] A brief survey of the <u>Oxford English Dictionary</u> leaves one astonished at the number of quotations indicating William Shakespeare as the first user of a given word. Some words can be easily recognized as his inventions – the compound form "star-crossed," for example – but others give no indication of their originator.

Many Greek and Latin derivatives were introduced for the first time in Shakespeare's plays. L. K. Barnett's book, <u>The Treasure of Our Tongue</u>, cites a long list of words that entered English in this manner: "accommodation," "apostrophe," "frugal," "pedant," and "premeditated," to name a few. Other classical words that Shakespeare popularized are: "assassination," "dexterously," "dislocate," "indistinguishable," "misanthrope," "obscene," "reliance," and "submerged."[11] In <u>Origins of the English Lan-guage</u>, Joseph M. Williams asserts that "Shakespeare's use of new words illustrates an important point in connection with them. This is the fact that they were often used, upon their first introduction, in a sense different from ours, closer to their etymological meaning in Latin."[12] Whether or not Shakespeare had an intimate knowledge of Latin is not known, but we do know he had a poet's sense of the appropriate word for the feeling or idea he was trying to convey.

Shakespeare not only borrowed and made familiar words of classical origin, he is also credited with a lengthy list of ordinary words. According to G. Blakemore Evans, editor of The Riverside Shakespeare, "It was he who introduced such ordinary words as 'lonely' and 'laughable,' invented such onomatopoeic vocables as 'bump,' borrowed from their classical cognates 'monumental' and 'aerial,' not to mention 'critic' and 'pendant,' without which his students would be at a loss."[13] George H. McKnight attributes to Shakespeare: " 'dwindle,' 'credent,' 'baseless,' 'multitudinous,' and 'courtship.' "[14] James Gordon adds " 'control,' 'countless,' and 'exposure.' "[15] Since the words were drawn from his plays, it is easy to see how "ducat" was extracted from Shylock's exclamation in The Merchant of Venice[16] and "confectionary" was drawn from the name "Count Confect" in Much Ado About Nothing.[17] This list seems to substantiate an impressive contribution, but it must be remembered that these words are known as Shakespeare's, as is the case with any other author, only because they have not been found in any previous works, not because he first used them in his writings.

Although the group is smaller, figurative words used by Shakespeare have carried into modern English the meaning he originally intended them to have. For example, Brewer's Dictionary of Phrase and Fable lists the verb "to cap. To take off, or touch one's cap to, in token of respect; also to excel."[18] This meaning, Brewer adds, comes from Hamlet (II, ii): "as in 'on fortune's cap we are not the very button.' "[19] Thus it is used by Shakespeare to refer to a mark of excellence. Similarly, "to beetle" and "to bone," meaning "to overhang" and "to filch," are attributed to Shakespeare's Hamlet.[20] Asimov's Guide to Shakespeare states that Shakespeare gave the word "coxcomb" the figurative connotation of "fool" that it still retains.[21]

It was fashionable in Shakespeare's day to create certain new words by hyphenating others. One can imagine the large number of compounds that appeared in Modern English at that time. Mario Pei submits a list of compound words, such as " 'foam-girt.' 'heartsick,' "needlelike,' 'everburning,' 'lacklustre,' 'hot-blooded,' and 'hell-black,' "[22] that can be traced directly to Shakespeare.

Although word contributions are important pieces of evidence of Shakespeare's gift to the language, Bradley believes "the greatness of his influence [lies] in the multitude of phrases derived from his writing."[23] For the most part these phrases were introduced through his plays, very few coming from his sonnets and long poems. Over the centuries they have been quoted and alluded to so much that Shakespeare's phrases have turned into clichés.

The OED defines a cliché as "the French name for a stereotype block."[24] In English the term has come to refer to phrases that are well worn from repetition. With this definition a seemingly endless list of clichés are noted as Shakespeare's phrases. Among the more familiar expressions, Pei lists " 'heart of gold,' 'the naked truth,' foregone conclusion,' 'to break the ice,' 'to breathe one's last,' 'to tell the world,' 'to wear one's heart on one's sleeve,' and 'the milk of human kindness.' "[25] James Gordon lists other phrases of Shakespeare's creation, such as " 'tower of strength,' 'yeoman service,' and 'to the manner born.' "[26]

It seems reasonable that the better-known plays would produce a greater number of phrases which have become clichés. Such is in fact the case. From Julius Caesar comes "dish for the gods," "lean and hungry look," "live-long day," and "it's Greek to me."[27] Mark Antony's speech to the crowd at Caesar's funeral has become so familiar that we use "lend me an ear" to signify "pay attention to what I am about to say."[28] Hamlet is so well known that " 'flaming youth,' 'not a mouse stirring,' 'to smell to heaven,' " not to mention "something rotten in the state of Denmark," have all become common phrases.[29] From Othello we extract the phrase "crocodile tears." Isaac Asimov declares, "Any mention of crocodiles would irresistibly bring tears to mind, for the most famous . . . legend concerning [the animal] is that it sheds tears over its prey while swallowing it."[30] Hence the expression connotes a form of hypocritical sorrow. The theme of Othello is one of hypocrisy and jealousy alike. When Iago declares, "O beware, my lord, of jealousy!/It is the green-eyed monster, which doth mock/The meat it feeds on" (III.iii.165–67), we have Othello becoming a victim of jealousy, popularly identified with the phrase itself.[31]

Some slang phrases have resulted from corruptions of Shakespeare's clichés. From A Golden Book of Phrases, Stuart Robinson compiles examples like: " 'beat it,' 'done me wrong,' 'fall for it,' 'not in it,' and 'not so hot.' "[32] One would certainly not imagine Shakespeare as the originator of these expressions, and we are also likely to think of someone else as the source of "swear a mild oath by the dickens."[33]

The proverbial phrase is another form of cliché, examples of which we can find in Shakespeare. The proverb and cliché are similar, although the proverb tends to convey a more heavily moral message. In the case of Shakespeare, his "aphorisms have turned into proverbs: 'the devil can quote scripture,' and 'misery makes strange bedfellows' come, with slight modification, from The Merchant of Venice (I.iii.98) and The Tempest (II.ii.40) respectively."[34] Another, more famous proverb from The Merchant of Venice warns us, "All that glitters is not gold."[35] Shakespeare not only coined phrases that became clichés and slang expressions, his language also imparted to us his wisdom concerning human nature.

Many other Shakespearean phrases have become familiar to us as direct quotations. The Oxford Dictionary of Quotations devotes a large section to Shakespeare's writings. Our speech would be incomplete without the flavouring of his phrases, which have become favourites of rhetoricians and orators who call upon them to express ideas more eloquently. Quoting Shakespeare is considered a sign of literary sophistication. Our public speech would certainly lack some of its character could we not recall the soothsayer's words in Julius Caesar (I.i.18) exclaiming, "Beware the ides of March,"[36] or Banquo's prophecy in Macbeth (I.iii.123), "the instruments of darkness tell us truths. . . ."[37] Without Shakespeare young lovers would not be able to express the intense emotion echoed in Juliet's "What's in a name? That which we call a rose/By any other name would smell as sweet" (II.ii.42–43).[38] Neither could actors refer to the Seven Ages of Man nor boldly exclaim: "All the world's a stage,/ And all the men and women merely players" (As You Like It, II. vii.129–130).[39]

From Shakespeare's cast of "players" have emerged stereotypes, a phenomenon comparable to the transformation of his original phrases into clichés. Romeo and Juliet stand among the ranks of the world's great lovers, and we picture Caesar through Shakespeare's portrayal of the character, rather than through historical accounts that more accurately portray him. " 'Benedick,' the name of Shakespeare's bachelor par excellence . . . has undergone only very slight modification in coming to represent a '(newly) married man.' "[40] Isaac Asimov affirms that "Shylock" is not a Jewish name, nor was there ever a Jew named "Shylock," but the characterization of the man is so powerful that Shakespeare's invention has entered into English as the name for any grasping, hard-hearted creditor.[41]

Furthermore, Shakespeare has entered our lives in ways more subtle than direct contributions. Knowledge of his works has led authors like William Faulkner and Aldous Huxley to borrow his words for titles of their books. Faulkner extracted a line from Macbeth for the title The Sound and Fury[42] and Huxley mined Miranda's speech in The Tempest (V.i.183–184) for his book, Brave New World.[43] The rhyme "Jack and Jill" bears a striking resemblance to a passage in A Midsummer Night's Dream, and King Lear is said to have inspired Robert Browning's Gothic poem "Child Harold to the Dark Tower Came."[44] Cole Porter named his musical version of The Taming of the Shrew, Kiss Me, Kate, after Petruchio's words in that same play; Romeo and Juliet's saga was transported in its entirety to New York City of the 1950s in West Side Story.

Viewing Shakespeare's works as a whole, it is not possible to comprehend just how great a part he plays in our speech and writing. It is not until we divide into categories the mass of information that has been collected dealing with his influence on language that we begin to realize the extent to which our imaginations are possessed by him. Looking at the contributions from a literary perspective barely touches on Shakespeare's effect on the English language. Words and phrases of his creation can be added to a list that includes examples of his influence on syntax, grammar, and the evolution of spelling changes in English. While his works have taken on the reputation of literary classics, they should also be studied as sources of words and phrases that are still in use and applicable to our time.

Over the course of history, English has undergone a series of changes. Each has enriched and expanded our language to the point that it is one of the most widely spoken tongues in the world. As the British Empire grew, so did the language, along with an awareness of its writers. Today this awareness has grown to the point that Shakespeare is synonymous with the brilliance of the English language. His profound influence on that language is evidenced daily in ordinary conversation. As he himself said, "The wheel has come full circle."

Footnotes

[1]Henry Bradley, The Making of English (London: Macmillan and Co., Ltd., 1904), p. 153.

[2]James D. Gordon, The English Language: A Historical Introduction (New York: Thomas Y. Crowell Company, 1972), p. 31.

[3]Mario Pei, The Story of the English Language (London: George Allen and Unwin, Ltd., 1967), p. 61.

[4]Pei, p. 61.

[5]Edward Slater, ''Word Links with The Merry Wives of Windsor,'' Notes and Queries, 22 (Apr. 1975), 169.

[6]Pei, p. 58.

[7]Gordon, p. 31.

[8]G. Blakemore Evans, ed., The Riverside Shakespeare (Boston: Houghton Mifflin, 1974), p. 8.

[9]Gordon, p. 103, n. 2.

[10]Stuart Robertson, The Development of Modern English (New York: Prentice-Hall, Inc., 1936), p. 400.

[11]Lincoln Kinnear Barnett, The Treasure of Our Tongue (New York: Knopf, 1964), p. 151.

[12]Joseph M. Williams, Origins of the English Language: A Social and Linguistic History (New York: The Free Press, 1975), p. 288.

[13]Evans, p. 11.

[14]Gordon, p. 31, n.1., citing George Harley McKnight, Modern English in the Making (New York: Appleton-Century-Crofts, 1925), p. 188.

[15]Gordon, p. 31, n.2.

[16]Isaac Asimov, Words from History (Boston: Houghton Mifflin Co., 1968), p. 69.

[17]Isaac Asimov, Asimov's Guide to Shakespeare, 2 vols., (New York: Avenel Books, 1978), I, 557.

[18]E. C. Brewer, ed., Dictionary of Phrase and Fable (New York: Harper & Row, 1970), p. 185.

[19]Brewer, p. 184.

[20]Brewer, pp. 95, 133.

[21]Asimov, Guide, I, 593.

[22]Pei, p. 61.

[23]Bradley, p. 153.

[24]The Compact Edition of the Oxford English Dictionary, 2 vols., (New York: Oxford University Press, 1971), I, 496.

[25]Pei, p. 143.

[26]Gordon, p. 31.

[27]Pei, p. 143.

[28]Brewer, p. 359.

[29]Gordon, p. 31.

[30]Asimov, Guide, I, 353.

[31]Evans, p. 24.

[32]Robertson, p. 470.

[33]Evans, p. 11.

[34]Evans, p. 11.

[35]Brewer, p. 472.

[36]The Oxford Dictionary of Quotations, 2nd ed. (London: Oxford University Press, 1955), p. 448.

[37]The Oxford Dictionary of Quotations, p. 456.

[38]The Oxford Dictionary of Quotations, p. 477.

[39]The Oxford Dictionary of Quotations, p. 427.

[40]Thomas Pyles, The Origins and Development of the English Language (New York: Harcourt Brace Jovanovich, 1971), p. 307.

[41]Asimov, Guide, I, 510.

[42]Evans, p. 25.

[43]Evans, p. 24.

[44]Asimov, Guide, II, 36.

Bibliography

Asimov, Isaac. Asimov's Guide to Shakespeare. 2 vols. New York: Avenel Books, 1978.

———. Words from History. Boston: Houghton Mifflin Co., 1968.

Barnett, Lincoln Kinnear. The Treasure of Our Tongue. New York: Knopf, 1964.

Bradley, Henry. The Making of English. London: Macmillan and Co., Ltd., 1904.

Brewer, E. C., ed. Dictionary of Phrase and Fable. New York: Harper & Row, 1970.

The Compact Edition of the Oxford English Dictionary. 2 vols. New York: Oxford University Press, 1971.

Evans, G. Blakemore, ed. The Riverside Shakespeare. Boston: Houghton Mifflin, 1974.

Gordon, James D. The English Language: A Historical Introduction. New York: Thomas Y. Crowell Company, 1972.

McKnight, George Harley. Modern English in the Making. New York: Appleton-Century-Crofts, 1928.

The Oxford Dictionary of Quotations. 2nd ed. London: Oxford University Press, 1955.

Pei, Mario. The Story of the English Language. London: George Allen and Unwin, Ltd., 1967.

Pyles, Thomas. The Origins and Development of the English Language. New York: Harcourt Brace Jovanovich, 1971.

Robertson, Stuart. The Development of Modern English. New York: Prentice-Hall, Inc., 1936.

Slater, Edward. "Word Links with The Merry Wives of Windsor." Notes and Queries, 22 (Apr. 1975), 169–71.

Williams, Joseph M. Origins of the English Language: A Social and Linguistic History. New York: The Free Press, 1975.

WRITING
AND
REVISION

9

GRAMMAR AND USAGE

---

§ 1. Sentence Fragments

Fragmentary sentences should be avoided in expository writing.

A grammatically complete sentence is a pattern of communication in words that is based on a verb with its subject. The essential core of a complete sentence is at least one verb with its subject or subjects. Structurally the sentence must be an independent unit, capable of standing alone. Dependent units, such as phrases, clauses, appositives, and similar groups of words, are not sentences, and should not be written as sentences. When any of these dependent units is written and punctuated as a sentence, it is called a *sentence fragment*.

INEFFECTIVE SENTENCE FRAGMENTS

An *ineffective sentence fragment* may be revised by (1) attaching the fragment to the sentence with which it logically belongs, (2) completing its form by adding the necessary words, (3) rewriting the passage.

The four main types of ineffective sentence fragments are listed below and their corrections indicated by examples:

1

1a.   A dependent clause should not be written as a complete sentence.

If you remember that a dependent clause usually begins with a connective that relates it to the main clause, you can guard against some types of fragments. For adjective clauses look for the relative pronouns *who, which,* and *that,* and the relative adverbs *when, where,* and *why.* For adverb clauses look for the subordinating conjunctions *after, although, as if, because, before, if, since, though, unless, when, where,* and *while.* Noun clauses are almost never miswritten as fragments. Another helpful fact to remember is that the fragment usually *follows* the main clause, to which it may be joined in correction.

Fragment
He spent his life preaching social justice. *Which was a startling concept in his day.*

Revision
He spent his life preaching social justice, which was a startling concept in his day. [Add fragment to main clause.]

Fragment
The animosity that his ideas excited is incredible. *Although a few brave men praised him.*

Revision
The animosity that his ideas excited is incredible, although a few brave men praised him. [Add clause to sentence.]

Fragment
The officer came to the alley where the man was last seen. *And where the stolen jewellery was probably hidden.*

Revision
The officer came to the alley where the man was last seen, and where the stolen jewellery was probably hidden. [The second *where*-clause also modifies *alley*.]

1b. A verbal or a prepositional phrase should not be written as a complete sentence.

Fragment

The two boys took the first trail to their left. *Hoping it would take them to a river.*

Revisions

The two boys took the first trail to their left, hoping it would lead them to a river. [Join phrase to main sentence.]

The two boys took the first trail to their left. They hoped it would lead them to a river. [Supply subject and verb to make the fragment a sentence.]

Fragments

They trudged along the trail all day. *Without a rest. Without stopping to eat what food was left.*

Revision

Without a stop to rest or to eat what food they had, they trudged along the trail all day. [You may also revise by putting the prepositional phrases after the main clause.]

Fragment

The sports complex made the team very popular. The number of fans leaping from hundreds to thousands in two years. [This is a participial phrase, of the special type called the absolute phrase. See page 99.]

Revision

The sports complex made the team very popular. The number of fans leaped from hundreds to thousands in two years. [Change the participle to a verb to make a complete sentence. You may also join the phrase to the main clause.]

1c. An appositive phrase should not be written as a complete sentence.

Guard against this fault especially when the phrase is introduced by such words as *namely*, *for example*, *such as*, and the like.

1

Fragment
Some games are called contact sports. *Namely, football, basketball,* and *hockey.*

Revision
Some games, namely football, basketball, and hockey, are called contact sports.

Fragment
New problems face the student entering college. *Such as budgeting money and time for study.* [*Budgeting* is in apposition with *problems.*]

Revision
New problems, such as budgeting money and time for study, face the student entering college. [Place the appositive near *problems,* not at the end of the sentence.]

Fragment
We found the case transferred to Juvenile Court. *A development that completely puzzled us.* [*Development* is in apposition with the whole idea expressed in the main clause.]

Revision
We found the case transferred to Juvenile Court, a development that completely puzzled us. [Add the appositive to the main clause.]

1d. Any verbless piece or fragment of a sentence, whether you can classify it or not, should not be allowed to stand as a sentence.

Some fragments are written because the writer was in too much of a hurry to think; others are written because the writer has carried over into writing the exclamatory nature of very informal speech. The following examples will make the point clear:

Fragments
Just a lazy weekend vacation. No work. No worries. That's what he promised me.

Revisions

Just a lazy weekend vacation with no work or worries – that's what he promised me. [The dash indicates a sharp break in the construction.]

What he promised me was a pleasant weekend vacation, with no work and no worries.

Fragment

Unexpectedly I dropped in on her daughter. *Just a friendly call, no party.* [The writer of this was making notes, not sentences.]

Revision

Unexpectedly I dropped in on her daughter. I intended this to be just a friendly, informal call. [Make a sentence out of the fragment.]

Fragments are allowable when reproducing conversation or when asking or answering questions. Since these situations occur mainly in novels or short stories, expository writers should be wary about their appearance in essays. For example, the asking and answering of rhetorical questions in an argumentative essay creates a sort of bogus dialogue that can wear the reader's patience thin:

How often should the president answer letters? Always. When? As soon as all the evidence is in.

It may be strategic to quote a patch of dialogue for illustration's sake, especially if you are trying to convey a particular mood for a scene you are describing.

EXERCISES

EXERCISE 1, RECOGNIZING SENTENCE FRAGMENTS.
Copy the following sentences. Some of them are complete. Some are fragments. If a sentence is complete, underline its subject once and its verb twice. If the group of words is a clause, encircle the subordinating connective. If it is a verbal phrase, encircle the verbal.

1

1. *Lives of Girls and Women* being Alice Munro's first really successful book.
2. Although she had already been a published writer.
3. A native of Huron County, Ontario, she wrote about the things she knew best.
4. Many of the residents of her home town were very indignant.
5. Resenting what they felt were slurs against their way of life.
6. They complained that her novel was not a true picture of the town.
7. That her characters were caricatures and the town a monstrosity.
8. Insisting that her family, neighbours, and friends are not models for her stories.
9. Returning, in 1976, to marry and settle in her old home town.
10. "Some core of you never changes," she said.

EXERCISE 2, ELIMINATING SENTENCE FRAGMENTS.
In some of the following word groups you will find sentence fragments. Eliminate each fragment either by joining it to the main clause or by rewriting it as a complete sentence. Be able to tell whether rule 1a, 1b, or 1c applies.

1. Last summer, while marching in an anti-cruise missile demonstration, we passed by my old neighbourhood. Which I had not seen since I was a boy.
2. The little park, once known as Balfour Park, is now expanded and known as Lester B. Pearson Park. Names of parks being subject to change.
3. The neighbourhood is not exactly modern, as some say. Neither does it have many new developments.
4. The march to the city hall took us through many neighbourhoods. The streets at times hilly and crowded but never difficult to walk on.
5. I was excited at the numbers and enthusiasm of the protestors. Included among them infants and pensioners.
6. I saw an old friend, acting as a marshal. Which she had done in demonstrations when we were students.

7. Her face showed at once that she had aged and gained weight. And her hair, although cut short, having turned gray.

8. She said she was glad to see us, and after the speeches would take us out for dinner. Which was an offer that we accepted with many thanks.

9. Talking with an old friend revives old memories. Such as earlier student anti-war protests, parties, and music.

10. Leaving her that night, we felt that she was leading a happy, useful, and rewarding life. An observation that we spoke about during most of the next day.

§ 2. Run-on Sentences

When two or more complete sentences are combined in a single sentence, they must be properly separated from one another.

A sentence made up of two or more independent, co-ordinate clauses, properly joined and punctuated, is called a *compound sentence*. (See page 104.) The usual means of joining these independent clauses are (1) a semicolon, (2) a conjunction, (3) a comma and a conjunction, (4) a semicolon and a conjunction. (See also §§ 13 and 14.)

2a. The comma splice or comma fault may be corrected in several ways.

The use of a comma to join independent, co-ordinate clauses is called a *comma splice* or a *comma fault*. It should be avoided. A comma splice may be corrected in one of the following ways. The student should choose the method of revision that produces the most effective sentence.

1. The comma splice may be corrected by *subordinating one of the two independent sentences*. (If you put both statements in the same sentence, you must believe that one is closely related to

2   the other. A subordinate clause can express this relation specifically.)

Splice
We all went home after the picnic, it had started to rain.

Better
We all went home after the picnic because it had started to
rain.

Splice
The food was fine except for the salad, I didn't like it.

Better
The food was fine except for the salad, which I didn't like.

2. The comma splice may be corrected by *inserting a co-ordinating
conjunction after the comma*. (These conjunctions are *and*, *but*,
for, *or*, *not*, *yet*.)

Splice
We were looking for a shady spot, we couldn't find one.

Better
We were looking for a shady spot, but we couldn't find one.

3. The comma splice may be corrected by *using a semicolon
instead of a comma if the sentences are close enough in meaning to
be combined into a compound sentence.*

Splice
We finally found a satisfactory place, it was breezy but quiet.

Better
We finally found a satisfactory place; it was breezy but quiet.

If you wished instead to subordinate, then the sentence would
look like this:

We finally found a satisfactory place, which was breezy but
quiet.

4. The comma splice may be corrected by *using a period to separate the two co-ordinate clauses*. In simple examples, such as the ones discussed here, the danger of this alternative is a series of very short sentences that look choppy.

Correct but Choppy
We finally found a satisfactory place. It was breezy but quiet.

Note that the choice of a solution for the run-on sentence, like all choices in writing, can affect the tone of the statement. In the last revision above, the choice of two very short sentences makes the speaker sound matter-of-fact and distanced, almost like a police officer reporting details of an investigation. The decisions you make about grammar relate directly to the way your words affect the reader.

Legitimate Comma Junctions

The use of a comma to join co-ordinate clauses is more common in novels, stories, and some types of journalistic writing than in expository prose. The clauses so joined are likely to be short and simple, and are most likely to occur in the following situations:

1. *When the clauses are arranged in the "a, b, and c" order.*

Examples
The shrubs were leafy and well-shaped, the walks had been carefully raked, and the fountain shone in the sunlight.

The dog growled, the cat spat, the mouse fled.

The batter swung, the catcher dove, and the ball rolled to the backstop.

2. *When the series of statements takes the form of a climax.*

Examples
I came, I saw, I conquered.

The sun is growing warm, frogs are waking in the marshes, planting time will soon be here.

2

3. *When the statements form an antithesis, or are arranged in the "it was not merely this, it was also that" formula.*

Examples

It was more than just murder, it was a massacre.

To give in to them now not only would mean defeat, it would mean accepting their savage way of life.

Two familiar situations in writing invite the comma splice. One such danger point is immediately following tags such as *he said* in dialogue.

Dialogue

"That's right," said Paul. "I'd almost forgotten her name." [A period is the usual punctuation, although a semicolon is occasionally used.] "No one remembers the good things I have done," she complained; "no one ever does." [Semicolon used here.]

"Yes, I know, sir," said Tony. "I warned him to be careful." [Period used here.]

The other danger concerns conjunctive adverbs such as *however*, *moreover*, and so on.

Adverbs

The prisoner told a long story of atrocities; however, his companion did not agree with his version of what had happened to them. [Use a semicolon before the conjunctive adverb. By using a semicolon and relocating the adverb within the second clause, you can achieve a smoother transition: ". . . atrocities; his companion did not agree, however, with his version . . ."]

When I registered for engineering, I had two high school subjects to make up; moreover, I had forgotten most of the algebra I ever knew. [Use a semicolon before the conjunctive adverb.]

2b. The fused sentence may be corrected by the same methods as the comma splice.

The fused sentence is one in which two sentences are run together with no punctuation at all between them. It is an extreme example of the same carelessness that produces the sentence fragment and the comma splice.

In the following pairs of sentences, the first is a fused sentence and the second a unified one. Notice how familiarity with sentence combining techniques like subordination can help you out of such corners.

> At first I wondered if I should speak to her she seemed to be so wrapped up in her thoughts.
>
> She seemed so wrapped up in her thoughts that at first I wondered if I should speak to her. [Subordination]

> I almost decided to walk by and pretend I did not see her she might think I was intruding.
>
> Fearing that she might think I was intruding, I almost decided to walk by and pretend not to see her. [Subordination]

> I was lonesome I decided to speak and I said hello in a weak voice.
>
> As I was lonesome, I decided to speak to her, and I said hello in a weak voice. [Subordination]

EXERCISES

EXERCISE 1, SUBORDINATING CLAUSES. *Correct each of the following sentences by subordinating one or more of the run-on co-ordinate clauses.*

1. Some people like an ocean voyage in winter, they want to escape the frost and snow at home.
2. A few are likely to be bored on a ship it is such a closed-in community.
3. The weather may be fine for days, however, it may change abruptly, everyone gets seasick.

2

4. The food is usually rich and plentiful, it would be a crime not to enjoy it.

5. Deckchairs are the rule in sunny weather, in bad weather one stays below.

6. Who would not appreciate seeing the islands of the West Indies, we have heard so much about them?

7. The stewards on shipboard are uniformly pleasant and efficient, they have been so well trained, they know exactly what to do.

8. Vacations at sea are within the reach of many people today they were a luxury for a privileged class not so very long ago.

9. Air travel is much faster, of course, nevertheless a week on a ship can be far more restful.

10. Most people are glad to get home, however, you can tell by looking at their happy faces as they step ashore.

EXERCISE 2, SUBORDINATING WITH PHRASES AND APPOSITIVES. *Revise each of the following sentences by using subordination of a rank below that of a subordinate clause (a phrase or an appositive).*

1. Success in life, they say, requires two principal qualities, they are perseverance and innate talent.

2. This is like most such generalizations it is hard to put to practical use.

3. A person has perseverance, or innate talent, how can you distinguish?

4. Many people apparently have perseverance and talent, they still do not conspicuously succeed.

5. Such statements are misleading they are so simple, they sound falsely profound.

6. Luck must have something to do with success, ask any millionaire about it.

7. Money seems to be the only measure it is the one most people accept.

8. There are only three recognized classes of successful people in Canada they are corporation executives, politicians, and sports stars.

EXERCISE 3, REVISING AN INFORMAL PARAGRAPH.
Here is a paragraph composed in a style approximating informal speech. Rewrite it by revising its fragments and run-on sentences in any way you think appropriate.

3

I'm disgusted with him. The liar. Telling me all the time how honest he was, too. He wanted to borrow my car, I knew he didn't even have a licence, his roommate told me that. I should have said no to him, I know I should. Right to his face. I'm soft-hearted, you know how I am. In spite of all past disappointments. I wonder where my car is, it's been quite a long time now. That thief.

Notice again, as you do this exercise, how the tone changes with the changes in grammar. Is the speaker in your revision more angry than the original speaker, or less? Is the speaker closer to the imaginary listener, or further away?

§ 3. Subject–Verb Agreement

A verb must agree in number with its subject.

Once it is understood that a singular verb matches a singular noun and a plural verb a plural noun, there is nothing very difficult in recognizing that "The *boys are* playing in the yard" is standard English, whereas "The *boys is* playing in the yard" is not. As long as subject and verb lie close together, and it is obvious whether the subject is singular or plural, there should be no problem in applying the principle of agreement in number. Confusion arises when the complexity of a sentence or the peculiarity of a subject obscures the immediate relation between subject and verb. Problems in agreement fall into three main categories:

1. When several other words intervene between the subject and verb, or when the word order is unusual, the writer or speaker may forget for the moment just what the subject is and so make an error.

2. When the subject seems to be simultaneously singular and plural – "everybody," "gymnastics," "the whole family," "either of us," "a group of people" – or when its number seems to be a matter of choice, the writer can easily become confused over the number to be reflected in the verb.

3. Because usage differs according to situation or occasion, the writer may not know which rule best suits a given occasion. The forms recommended in this book, however, are appropriate and correct in all varieties of English – formal or informal, written or spoken. In very informal situations, other forms may *also* be current.

3a. Plural words that intervene between a singular subject and its verb do not change the number of the subject.

Examples

The *racket* of all those engines *was* deafening. [*Racket was*, not *engines were.* "Of all those engines" is a phrase modifying *racket*, and this of course does not make *racket* plural.]

One of the many techniques she explained to us *was* that of repelling. [*One* technique *was repelling.*]

3b. When words are added to a singular subject by *with*, *together with*, *as well as*, *in addition to*, *except*, and *no less than*, the number of the subject remains singular.

Examples

The *teacher*, as well as the principal, *was* exonerated. [*Teacher was*]

The *boy*, together with three companions, *was* discovered the next day. [*Boy was*]

These expressions may be logically considered as introducing modifiers of the subject. They do not have the force of *and*, which is the word that compounds a subject and makes it plural.

3c.   In sentence patterns that depart from the typical subject-verb-complement order, watch for the following situations in particular.

1. The Subject Following the Verb. Mental transposition into normal order will clarify agreement of subject and verb.

Examples

Scattered over the floor *were* the *remains* of the evening's feast. [*Remains were scattered*]

Browsing peacefully in her vegetable garden *were* a large *elk* and three mule *deer.* [*Elk and deer were*]

2. Introductory *It*. Introductory *it*, as in "It is the people who matter," is always followed by a singular verb, no matter whether the noun that follows is singular or plural. *It* in such cases is an expletive, often called the *preparatory subject*, preparing the way for the real subject to come. Nevertheless it controls the verb. No one would say, "It are the people." (The preparatory subject is often used as a carry-over from spoken English. In the first example below note how much more direct the statement becomes after eliminating "It is . . . that" and rearranging word order: "We must consider her happiness." When you find yourself using the "It is" or "There are" constructions to excess, try rephrasing your sentences without them.)

Examples

It is her *happiness* that we must consider. [*It is happiness.* But try rephrasing: *We must consider her happiness.*]

It is the *colleges* that must take up the burden. [*It is colleges.* Rephrased: *Colleges must take up the burden.*]

3. Introductory *There*. In present-day English, usage seems to be divided in regard to the number of the verb when the preparatory *there* introduces a sentence.

In sentences in which the noun that follows the verb is *plural,* most writers and speakers will use a plural verb.

Examples

There *are*, if I counted right, exactly *thirteen* persons at this table. [*Persons are*]

There are, you must admit, several *degrees* of guilt. [*Degrees are*]

4. Introductory *What*. *What* as a preparatory subject may be either singular or plural according to what the writer means. If it serves in the sense of *the one thing that*, it is singular, and the only caution to observe is that all related verbs should respect its singular status – even when its subjective complement consists of more than one thing.

Example
What is interesting about this model *is* the seven speed settings available. [*The one thing about this model is. . . .*]

It is usually clear when *what* must be plural.

Example
For *what are* doubtless good reasons, responsibility for maintaining the reservoir has been transferred from the Sewage Authority.

Even with logic on your side, it is advisable to avoid constructions like the following:

Pterodactyls were not birds; *what* they were *was* reptiles. [Balance is preserved by saying simply, ". . . they were reptiles."]

When the subject following the verb consists of a number of nouns, the first of which is singular, there is a tendency to make the verb singular.

Examples

In a club like ours, there *is* one president, one meeting place, and one set of rules for everyone.

At the party, where there *was* a great guitarist and a good selection of wine, we saw several old friends.

There *is* enough gold and silver in those hills to make digging worth your time.

3d. The verb agrees with its subject, not with its subjective complement.

If the difference in number between subject and complement produces an awkward sentence, it is better to rewrite.

Right
The one last *object* of her love *was* three Siamese cats. [Not *object were*]

Rewritten
She had nothing left to love except her three Siamese cats.

Right
Our *worry was* the frequent storms that swept the lake. [Not *worry were*]

Rewritten
We worried because storms frequently swept the lake.

3e. A compound subject joined by *and* takes a plural verb.

Do not be distracted by unusual word order or by intervening phrases.

Examples
The *rest* of the manuscript and the *letter* from Whitney *seem* to have been destroyed in the fire. [Not *seems*]

A heavy *coat* or *windbreaker* and a fur *cap are* recommended as additional equipment. *Are* both an *overcoat* and a *parka* necessary? [Not *overcoat and parka is*]

When several singular subjects represent the same person or thing, however, a singular verb is used.

Examples
Our *ally* and *neighbour* to the south, the United States of America, *maintains* a quiet border.

My *friend* and *colleague* Paul *races* cars as a pastime.

3   Notice the difference that an article (*a, an, the*) can make.

Examples

The blue and gold sweater is very attractive.
The blue and the gold sweaters are very attractive.

A red and white rose is in bloom.
A red and a white rose are in bloom.

3f.   When subjects are joined by *neither-nor, either-or, not only-but also*, the verb agrees with the nearer subject.

When both subjects are singular, the verb is singular; when both subjects are plural, the verb is also plural. But when one subject is plural and the other singular, *formal usage* prescribes that the *nearer subject* dictates the number of the verb. In informal usage there is a tendency to make the verb *always plural*. One way to avoid an awkward sentence – as well as an awkward decision – is to recast the sentence entirely.

Formal

Neither the *students* nor their *teacher is* adequately prepared.

Neither *you* nor *I am* going there now.

Informal

Neither the *students* nor their *teacher are* adequately prepared.

You and *I aren't* going there now.

Recast

Both the *students* and the *teacher are* inadequately prepared.

You aren't going there now and neither *am I*.

3g.   After *each, every, each one, everyone, everybody, anybody, nobody, none, either*, and *neither* the singular verb is used in formal English.

Examples

Each of us *is* willing to pay *his* or *her* share of the expenses.

3

[Note that *his* or *her*, referring to *each*, is also singular.]

Every soldier *knows his* or *her* duty.

Has anyone seen her?

I wonder if *anybody knows* who wrote the song.

The rule as stated here represents the practice of most writers. Exceptions can easily be found, in both formal and informal writing. In an attempt to interpret usage, it is said that the *intention* of the writer determines whether the singular or the plural is to be used. But that is a razor-edge distinction for a student to make. When you say, "*Each* of the boys *tells* a different story," the choice is clear, but it is a less obvious matter of right between "*None* of the boys is telling the truth," and "*None* of the boys *are* telling the truth." You may justify the first as formal usage and the second as informal usage. The simplest solution is to say, "All the boys are lying."

3h. **With a collective noun a singular verb is used when the group named by the noun is regarded as a unit; a plural verb is used when the noun is regarded as indicating the individuals of a group.**

Common collective nouns that are tricky are *class, band, number, family, group, public, committee*.

Examples

The *number* of failures *was* surprising. [*The number* is usually construed as a single unit.]

A *number* of students *are* failing this term. [*A number* refers to individual items or members of a group and is therefore plural.]

The whole *family is* here. [The modifier indicates that *family* is considered as a single unit.]

The *family are* all attending different churches. [Here the reference is to the individuals of the family.]

Since there is considerable range for individual choice in the use of collective nouns, *consistency* must be the student's guide. Once you have spoken of a group as a single unit, you should not, without some explanation, refer to it as a plural.

3

Examples

The *platoon are* removing their knapsacks. *They are* getting ready for a mock charge.

The *class was* assembled promptly and proceeded with *its* assignment.

3i. **When the subject is a title, the name of a book, a clause, a quotation, or some other group of words expressing a single idea, the verb is singular.**

Examples

A Sadness of Spacemen is a collection of Robert Priest's poems.

All men are created equal is a statement of dubious truth.

This rule also applies to expressions signifying number, quantity, distance, time, amount, or extent. When the subject is expressed as a unit, the verb is singular.

Examples

Twenty years is a long time to wait for an editor to make up his mind.

Five hundred words is long enough for most daily essays.

Thirty miles is a tiring day's run.

But when the amount is meant to be made up of separate units, the plural verb is used.

Examples

The first *ten years* of every marriage *are* the hardest.

There *are five hundred words* in the essay.

3j. **Several words ending in -*s* are governed by special rules of usage.**

A number of nouns ending in -*ics* are considered singular when they refer to a branch of study or a body of knowledge (*linguistics, physics, mathematics, civics, economics*), but are usually plural when they refer to physical activities, qualities, or phenomena (*acoustics, acrobatics, tactics, phonetics, athletics*).

Other words likely to cause trouble are listed below.

Usually singular: *news, measles, mumps, gallows.*
Usually plural: *scissors, riches, slacks, means, falls* [water].
Either singular or plural: *headquarters, politics, sports.*

3k. **A singular verb is used with a relative pronoun referring to a singular antecedent, and a plural verb is used with a pronoun referring to a plural antecedent.**

Examples

It is important to associate with *students who are* honest. [*Who* refers to *students*, a plural noun.]

He is the only *one* of the family *who intends* to go to college. [*Who* is singular because it refers to *one*.]

Now notice the difference between the last example above and the following construction: "He is one of those boys who are always getting into trouble." If you shift this about to read, "Of those boys who are always getting into trouble, he is one," you can see that *who* refers to *boys* and is therefore plural. But in practice the singular verb is very common, especially in speech: "He is one of those boys who is always getting into trouble."

EXERCISES

3

EXERCISE 1, RECOGNIZING SUBJECTS AND VERBS. *Some of the difficulty with agreement, as we have seen, is simply a matter of making sure just what the subjects and verbs in sentences are. In the following sentences write* S *above each subject and* V *above each verb.*

1. As he said, there were a police officer and a crowd of people in front of our house.
2. The police officer, as well as most of the crowd, was looking up at the sky.
3. One of several things that I worried about was a fire.
4. Neither burglars nor a fire is ever far from a homeowner's thoughts.
5. Every one of my neighbours is worried about fires.
6. My friend and neighbour George swears that we have poor fire protection.
7. Smoke, as well as fire and water, causes much damage to a burning house.
8. Looking up toward the treetops in front of our house were three small boys.
9. The number of people inspecting our residence was growing steadily.
10. The news that finally reached us was reassuring; the excitement was about a kitten frantically trying to descend from its perch on a tall tree.

EXERCISE 2, CORRECTING ERRORS IN SUBJECT-VERB AGREEMENT. *Correct the errors in each of the following sentences. Tell what rule applies.*

1. The outcome of all those meetings and conferences were the appointment of a committee.
2. In colleges and in governments there is usually a type of person that love to serve on committees.
3. This committee, with the dean of administration, serve as a check on the other committees.

3

4. There seems to be several explanations why this was called a standing committee.
5. If my mathematics is correct, this committee sat from two to six the first day.
6. Four hours are a long time for a standing committee to sit.
7. Each of the members have a different cause to champion.
8. Neither the dean nor the chairperson admit saying, "A camel is a greyhound designed by a committee."
9. One man complained that the acoustics in the auditorium was poor.
10. The outcome of all their deliberations were that the questions under discussion should be referred to a new committee.

EXERCISE 3, RECOGNIZING AND CORRECTING ERRORS IN AGREEMENT. *Some of the following sentences contain errors; some are correct. Point out each mistake that you find, correct the sentence, and tell what rule applies.*

1. The teacher remarked that his use of obscenities were unfortunate.
2. Either you or I am going to tell him to watch his language.
3. Linguistics are not exactly his strong point; he is much better at athletics.
4. Athletics, whether you believe it or not, do require some skilled teaching.
5. The salary of a football coach, fifty thousand a year, is much more than the average professor earns.
6. There seems to be several reasons why this is so.
7. The public know that a good fullback is hard to find, and it is willing to pay the price required.
8. But many a good fullback were lost to the world because he could not pass his entrance examinations.
9. My uncle is one of those who do not believe that a knowledge of poetics is useful in a business office.
10. After his long career as a little-known author, one of his novels were made into a motion picture.

§4. Pronouns

4 **Be careful to use the right form of the pronoun.**

Nouns in modern English change their form for the plural and for the possessive. Plurals are discussed in § 19. The possessive forms are discussed in § 15. There are very few problems connected with the form changes of nouns.

Some pronouns, however, change their forms for person, number, and case, and thereby cause the student of the English language numerous difficulties. In English there are three cases: the *nominative* or *subjective*, the *possessive*, and the *objective*. There are also three persons: the *first* person indicates the speaker; the *second* person indicates the one spoken to; the *third* indicates the one spoken about.

The forms of the personal pronoun are shown in the table below:

Singular Number

	FIRST PERSON	**SECOND PERSON**	**THIRD PERSON**		
			Masc.	*Fem.*	*Neuter*
Nominative:	I	you	he	she	it
Possessive:	my, mine	your, yours	his	her, hers	its
Objective:	me	you	him	her	it

Plural Number

	FIRST PERSON	**SECOND PERSON**	**THIRD PERSON**
Nominative:	we	you	they
Possessive:	our, ours	your, yours	their, theirs
Objective:	us	you	them

The relative and interrogative pronoun *who* has only three forms:

Nominative:	who, whoever
Possessive:	whose
Objective:	whom, whomever

There are also a number of *indefinite* pronouns, such as *another, anybody, anyone, anything, both, each, either, everybody, everyone, everything*, *few*, *many*, *neither*, *nobody*, *none*, *one*, *somebody*, *someone*.

The intensive pronouns (used for emphasis) and the reflexive pronouns (used to point the action back toward the subject) are *myself*, *himself*, *herself*, *itself*, *yourself*, *yourselves*, *ourselves*, *themselves*. Be careful not to overuse these intensive pronouns.

4

Intensive
The general *himself* gave the order. I *myself* will carry it out.

Reflexive
"You can easily hurt *yourselves*," I said, but they picked *themselves* up.

Misused

Everyone, including *myself*, was surprised by the announcement. [The objective case, *me*, is appropriate.]

My wife and *myself* were invited to Harry's party. [My wife and *I*]

NOMINATIVE CASE

4a. The nominative case is used when the pronoun is the subject of a verb.

You should watch out for three trouble spots in connection with the use of the nominative case:

1. A parenthetical expression, such as *they think*, *they say*, *we believe*, etc., between *who* (*whoever*) and the verb may confuse the writer.

Examples

Jones is one senior who we think could teach this class. [Not *whom we think*, but *who could teach*]

A young man who we believe was the driver of the car is being held. [Not *whom we believe*]

Who did you say brought us these cherries? [Not *whom did you say*]

We agreed to accept whoever they thought was the best fore-man. [Not *whomever*]

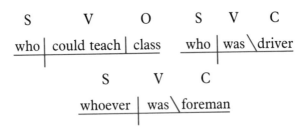

2. The fact that a *who* or *whoever* clause follows a preposition may lead the writer into using the wrong case.

Examples

Send a card to *whoever* asks for one. [Not to *whomever*. *Whoever* may seem to be attracted into the objective case by its position after the preposition. But it is the subject of the verb *asks*. The whole clause is the object of the preposition.]

Settle the question with *whoever* wrote the report. [Not *with whomever*, but *whoever wrote*]

3. In clauses of comparison, with *than* and *as*, the nominative is used with the implied verb.

Examples

She can usually see more in a painting than *I* [can see].

No one knows that better than *she* [knows it].

Few can play as well as *they* [do] on that field.

Comparison between two clauses, the verb of one of which is implied, constitutes what is called an *elliptical* sentence.

4b. In standard literary English, the nominative-case form is used when the pronoun is a subjective complement after the verb *be*.

In conversation, "it's me" is generally accepted, and in most conversational situations "it's *I*" or "it is *I*" would sound affected and silly. As for "it's *us*" or "it's *them*," probably the best advice – *in conversation* – is to follow your ear and your sense of propriety. You should do the same when writing dialogue. Outside quotation marks, however, standard written English requires the nominative in all such uses.

4

Examples

It is *we* who must bear the burden of the tax program, even though it was *they* who initiated it.

It was *he* (or *she*) who made the plans for the rained-out picnic.

POSSESSIVE CASE

4c. The apostrophe is not used with personal pronouns to form the possessive case; the apostrophe is used, however, with those indefinite pronouns that can be used in the possessive.

The possessive forms of the personal pronouns are *my, mine, your, yours, his, her, hers, its, our, ours, their, theirs*.

The possessive forms of the indefinite pronouns are *anybody's, anyone's, everybody's, nobody's, no one's, one's, somebody's*.

Wrong

The furniture is *their's*, but the house is *our's*.

The bush is dying; *it's* leaves are covered with volcanic ash.

Right

The furniture is *theirs*, but the house is *ours*.

The bush is dying; *its* leaves are covered with volcanic ash.

Note carefully the distinction between *it's*, which means *it is*, and *its*, which is the possessive form of *it*. Note also that when *else* follows the indefinite pronoun, such as *anybody, somebody, someone*, the apostrophe and *s* are added to *else*, not to the pronoun.

Right

It's [contraction of *it is*] *anybody's* guess *whose* [possessive form of *who*] car will win the race.

4

Would you like to ride in somebody *else's* car?

It is best to trust someone *else's* judgement on Mulroney's leadership.

4d. In standard English the general practice is to use the possessive form of the pronoun when it precedes a gerund.

Please note that *general* does not mean *universal*. It means, "Most do; some don't." It is easy enough to find exceptions in the writing of reputable authors.

Examples

I cannot understand *his refusing* to do that for me.

Her driving off so abruptly was hard to understand.

I told them about *your resigning* from office.

In these sentences the verbals *refusing*, *driving*, *resigning* are gerunds. They are used as object, as subject, and as object of a preposition, in that order. When the verbal is a participle, however, the objective case is correct.

Examples

We saw *them waving* a white flag. [Them in the act of waving]

I found *him using* my typewriter. [Him in the act of using]

With nouns introducing or modifying gerunds, usage varies. There are situations in which the possessive is desirable; there are others in which it is difficult or clumsy, and therefore it gives way to the objective.

Examples

The family resisted the idea of Keith's *leaving* home.

The prospect of *nations fighting* one another is again conceivable.

It was hard to imagine so many *buildings being constructed*.

4e. Instead of the apostrophe-*s* form, the *of*-phrase may be used to show possession when the situation calls for it.

1. Ordinarily, the *of*-phrase is used for inanimate objects: "the back of the building," "the top of the heap," "the hem of the dress" (not "the dress of my sister"). However, notice such forms as "in an hour's time" and "a week's pay." In some cases either form may be used; in other cases only one form is possible.

2. The *of*-phrase may also be used when the simple possessive form would separate a noun from its modifier.

Example

The trustworthiness of a man who never thinks twice is highly questionable. [Not "The man's trustworthiness who never thinks . . ."]

The reassurances of a driving instructor who doesn't own a car are difficult to accept. [Not "The driving instructor's reassurances who doesn't . . ."]

The double possessive is a construction long established in standard English.

Examples
friends of Kara's   that old passion of mine   a colleague of his

OBJECTIVE CASE

4f. The objective case of the pronoun is used when the pronoun is the direct or indirect object of a verb or verbal.

Direct Object
We liked *him*. Paul called *her*. The plumber tried to pay *him*.

Punishing *him* did little good. The attorney-general indicted *them*.

4   **Indirect Object**
     The lawyer's wife served *them* their dinners. I offered to find *him* a good lawyer.

The need for the objective case in a pronoun object that immediately follows a verb or verbal is easy to recognize. A fault is obvious in sentences such as "I saw *she* at the game" and "My father bought *we* a new surfboard." Three kinds of construction, however, may pose some difficulty.

1. *Who* and *whom* may be confused when they appear out of their normal subject-verb-object pattern. In questions, *who* beginning the sentence is used in informal speech for both the subject and the object forms, but formal writing requires *whom* as object.

Conversational

Who did you want to see?

I'd like to know *who* they're going to elect.

Formal

Whom can we trust at such a moment in history? [We can trust whom.]

Franco was the one *whom* they finally selected. [They selected whom.]

2. When the pronoun is the second of two objects connected by *and*.

Examples

The pilot told John and *me* to make the decision to jump. [Not John and I]

Everyone was astounded when the bowlers' association chose for membership both *her* and *me*. [Not her and I]

3. When the pronoun is the object of an implied verb, after *than* and *as* in clauses of comparison.

Examples

He always gave Jack more attention than [he gave] *me*.

Mary told me more about her secret life than [she told] *him*.

By reviewing paragraph 3, §4a, you can observe the difference when the nominative pronoun is used as the subject of the implied verb in similar constructions:

Example

Mary told me more about her secret life than *he* [told me about his].

4g. The objective case form is normally used when the pronoun is the object of a preposition.

Here again trouble arises not when the pronoun immediately follows a preposition, as in "I said to *her*" [not, of course, to *she*], but when the pronoun comes before its preposition or when it is the second of two objects.

Examples

It is difficult to predict *whom* the people will vote for. [For *whom*]

Whom could we turn to at a time like this? [To *whom*]

There was some controversy between *him* and *me*. [Not *him and I*]

Informal, conversational usage accepts *who* as the objective form, especially in questions, in which the pronoun may begin a sentence or a clause, such as "*Who* did you call for?" or "*Who* are you talking to?" But it is *not* acceptable, in either speech or writing, to use a nominative pronoun linked with a noun in the objective case, as in "of we citizens" or "between we men and women." Be wary, in fact, of using these constructions in formal writing, even with the proper objective pronoun. "A body of us citizens went to see the mayor" is not a very effective, serious sentence. "We concerned citizens went to see the mayor" is a better sentence.

4h. **The objective case is proper when the pronoun is the assumed subject or the complement of the infinitive** *to be.*

Examples

Everyone wanted *him* to be the leader of the shark-hunting trip.

The woman whom I thought to be *her* turned out to be someone else.

4i. **A pronoun should agree with its antecedent in number, gender, and person.**

The antecedent of a pronoun is the word or words to which the pronoun refers. If the antecedent is singular, the pronoun should be singular; if it is plural, the pronoun should be plural.

Examples

First one woman cast *her* vote.

Then three men cast *their* votes.

An old man cast *his* vote.

Mary and her lamb had left *their* house early.

We prefer to speak to *you, who are* the president.

Here as elsewhere, when questions of usage arise, there must be a distinction between what is customary in formal usage and what is accepted in conversational, informal situations. The problems of agreement in certain typical trouble spots that often require more than one kind of answer are as follows.

1. In situations that call for more or less formal English, it is customary to use a singular pronoun to refer to any of the following: *anybody, anyone, everyone, everybody, nobody, no one, somebody, someone, person.*

In informal English, especially in conversation, these words, although they take singular verbs, are quite generally felt to be collectives (plural in sense), and the pronouns referring to them are often plural. In addition, all sorts of special situations arise. For instance, *each*, *every*, *everybody*, *everyone* have a general meaning of "all, or a group, but taken individually." Apparently it is the "group" sense that is dominant in influencing the number of the pronoun referring to one of these words. In some situations, such as in this sentence, "Everybody started to laugh, but in a moment *they* realized that the speaker was not joking," the singular form just would not make sense.

Formal Agreement

England expects every man to do *his* duty. [No question of gender here]

Often Accepted in Conversation

Somebody must have left *their* coat here after the party.

Everyone ought to feel that *their* vote really counts.

By "often accepted," however, we do not mean universally accepted, even in conversation, and in any case a stricter agreement is found in formal written English.

2. Either a singular or plural pronoun may be used to refer to a collective noun, depending on whether the noun designates the group as a whole or the members of the group. *Consistency is the governing principle.* The construction should be either singular or plural, but not both.

Inconsistent

The cast is giving *their* best performance tonight. [The verb is singular but the pronoun is plural.]

The team *is* now on the floor, taking *their* practice shots at the basket. [Again, verb and pronoun indicate a shift in number.]

Consistent

The cast is giving *its* best performance tonight.

The team *are* on the floor now, taking *their* practice shots.
[The team is thought of as being more than one person.]

Other collective nouns to watch for are *faculty, legislature, student body, union.*

3. Traditionally, one of the masculine pronouns – *he, his, him* – has been used to refer to an unspecified or hypothetical person who may be either male or female, or to one of these "group taken individually" words.

Everybody was requested to put *his* loose change in the basket.

Every *author* is responsible for proofreading *his* book.

This practice, though still common, has come under criticism for unnecessarily excluding from consideration half of the species – women. To overcome this problem, many writers now use the construction *he or she.*

Everybody was requested to put *his or her* loose change in the basket.

Another alternative is to use a plural construction.

All *authors* are responsible for proofreading *their* books.

Never use the shorthand device *he/she.* It has no spoken equivalent and reveals the writer as someone who has no concern for the sound of words. For useful and sensible suggestions on how to avoid sexism in language, see *The Handbook of Nonsexist Writing* by Casey Miller and Kate Swift.

4. In modern usage, the relative pronoun *who* is used to refer to persons and occasionally to animals, but *whose* may refer to persons, animals, or things, especially when *of which* produces an awkward construction. The relative pronouns *that* and *which* may refer to persons, animals, places, things, and ideas.

Examples
My brother, *who* is an art critic, particularly admires modern painting. It is a taste *that* I cannot understand. He once gave me a painting, *which* I hung upside down in my room. It is a

masterpiece *whose* meaning is obscure, at least to me. But my best friend, *whose* critical taste I admire, thinks it is magnificent. Taste in art is something *that* I find hard to fathom.

For at least a century many writers have used *that* and *which* interchangeably as relative pronouns, often making their choice on the assumption that *which* is somehow more refined than *that*. Between the two words, however, there is a distinction that precise writers should observe. *That* is a *restrictive* relative pronoun. It introduces a clause that particularizes or identifies the antecedent so that the antecedent may not be mistaken for anything else.

Example

Bring me the umbrella *that* is drying in the hall. (There may be half a dozen umbrellas lying around, but I want only the one *that* is drying in the hall.)

In a *non-restrictive* clause, one that adds information about an antecedent but does not single the antecedent out, *which* is the proper, formal relative pronoun.

Example

Bring me my umbrella, *which* is drying in the hall. [*Drying in the hall* is one of many details – colour, size, style – the speaker might have offered. Note too that a non-restrictive clause, unlike a restrictive one, is usually enclosed by commas.]

See "A Guide to Usage," page 555.

5. Pronouns used in apposition are the same case as their antecedents.

Examples

The reward was divided among us three, George, Tom and *me*. [Not *I*]

They had told *us* – *him* and *me* – to report to headquarters immediately.

EXERCISES

4

EXERCISE 1, CASE OF PRONOUNS. *In the following sentences, tell whether each of the italicized pronouns is used as the subject of a verb, the complement of a verb or verbal, or the object of a preposition.*

1. *I* wonder whether *you* will walk downtown with Harris and *me*.
2. *We* must visit a lawyer *whom we* talked to last week.
3. *I* usually try to bring along *whoever* wants to come, if *he* asks *me*.
4. *Neither* of *us* is quite sure what the lawyer wants *us* to do.
5. *Who* else do *you* suppose would care to come with *us*?
6. A woman can often be of assistance to *us* men in such cases if *she* wishes.
7. *It* was *she* who helped *us* last time.
8. *Everyone* knows a lawyer can be difficult for those of *us* victims who are unsure of *themselves*.
9. If *he* says, "Try to remember *whom* you met that day," I am likely to forget *whoever* it may have been.
10. *You* are more quick-witted than *I*, so come along.

EXERCISE 2, CORRECTING PRONOUN ERRORS. *Correct every error in the use of pronouns in the following sentences. Assume that your corrected sentences are to appear in an essay, not in informal conversation.*

1. Lorraine, who is more energetic than me, is the person they should have for the job of president.
2. We voters, of course, are the only ones who's preference matters.
3. Of all we people whom I think should be available for office, Lorraine is the first who comes to mind.
4. But the whole question, as I say, is up to we voters, who will cast our ballots on Friday.
5. When a person casts their ballots, they have to consider very carefully who they should vote for.
6. At any rate Lorraine is the person whom I feel sure will be most adequate to serve us all, and everybody will be pleased with their new leader.

7. If I were her I would be overjoyed at their showing so much confidence in me.
8. Yesterday a member said to Lorraine and I that they would probably give her or me their vote.
9. You probably know to who I am referring.
10. No one could be more pleased by such information than me, who is always eager to serve.

EXERCISE 3, FORMAL AND INFORMAL ENGLISH. *For each of the following sentences, provide two versions, one of which can be, but need not necessarily be, the form given here. One version should be appropriate to conversational speech, and one appropriate to graceful, formal, written English. In some cases (as in the first sentence), you should revise wording that may be formally correct but that is awkward or stuffy. In some cases you may feel that your two versions should be identical; after all, good written prose and good conversation may employ in very many instances exactly the same language. Do not be afraid to remove pronouns altogether in the interests of realistic speech or graceful prose.*

1. It is I who am best prepared of all those whom you have available for the task which we have been discussing.
2. I wonder who he's talking to – me?
3. One should not exaggerate one's virtues in order to impress one's listener with one's superiority.
4. Who is it? It is I.
5. Some people whom I know intimately are likely to assert that which they know with altogether too much passion.
6. Everybody has their own opinion about that.
7. I wonder who he's going to call on next.
8. Somebody left their raincoat on this rack; he will have to come and get it.
9. Those to whom I have spoken on the subject which is before us have made the point that all is lost which is not pursued vigorously, and I am bound to agree with their opinion.
10. Whoever I need, I get.

§ 5. Adjectives and Adverbs

5 **Distinguish between adjectives and adverbs and use the correct forms of each.**

Adjectives modify nouns. Adverbs modify verbs, adjectives, other adverbs, or groups of words, such as phrases and clauses, even when they are whole sentences. One superficial sign of distinction between the two is that most adverbs end in -*ly*. A few adjectives, such as *friendly* and *lovely*, also have the -*ly* ending, and a number of common adverbs, such as *fast, far, here, there, near, soon,* do not. Usually these are not hard to recognize.

Adjective

That's a *friendly* gesture.

He is a *violent* man.

She is a *lazy* person.

Adverb

Butter it *only* on one side.

She learns *fast*.

I shook him *violently*.

He sat *lazily* in the sun.

The wine should arrive *soon*.

Of course, the difference between adjectives and adverbs depends not on a distinctive form or ending but on the way the words function in sentences. Thus a number of familiar words are used as either adjectives or adverbs, depending on their function. In the following list note that *when the word modifies a noun, it is used as an adjective; when it modifies a verb, an adjective, or another adverb, it is used as an adverb.*

Examples

	ADJECTIVES	**ADVERBS**
deep	We dug a *deep* well.	He dug down *deep*.
early	I am an *early* bird.	They sent us home *early*.
fast	He is a *fast* walker.	He walks much too *fast*.
little	It is a *little* game.	The game is *little* understood.
right	I wish I had the *right* answer.	I wish I could do it *right*.

5

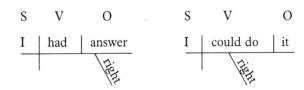

5a. The clumsy or awkward use of a noun form as an adjective should be avoided.

In our flexible language, as has been seen, words commonly used as nouns can also function as adjective modifiers, as in a *bird* dog, a *house* cat, an *ivory* tower, an *iron* rod, a *silk* dress, a *flower* pot, the *Victoria* streets, the *boat* people. These are natural and legitimate uses. The objection is to awkward or ambiguous uses, as in the following examples:

Awkward

We heard a communism lecture.

It was really a heart attack sign.

She's really a fun person to be with.

Better

We listened to a lecture explaining communism.

It was a symptom of a heart attack.

You'll have a lot of fun in her company.

5b. Use the adjective after certain linking verbs, such as *be*, *become*, *appear*, *seem*, *prove*, *remain*, *look*, *smell*, *taste*, *feel*.

5

A *predicate adjective* describes the subject.

The woman was *quiet*. [The *quiet* woman]

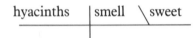

The little boy appears *happy*. [The *happy* little boy]

Hyacinths smell *sweet*. [*Sweet* hyacinths]

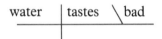

This water tastes *bad*. [*Bad* water]

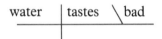

The report proved *true*. [*True* report]

With some of the verbs, when the word in the predicate refers to the manner of the action and not to the subject, it is, of course, an adverb, and the adverb form must be used.

Examples

The Martian appeared *unexpectedly*.

The man felt *carefully* for the door.

She looked *quickly* at me.

We tasted the water *suspiciously*.

5c. Use the adverb form for a word that modifies a verb, an adjective, or another adverb.

Adverb Modifying a Verb

He dresses *well* [not *good*], but his manners are poor.

During the summer I improved my tennis game *considerably*. [Not *considerable*]

Although she talks *cleverly* [not *clever*], her arguments are shallow.

Adverb Modifying an Adjective

My uncle was *really* [not *real*] happy to see us again.

It was *awfully* [not *awful*] generous of you to help us out.

Adverb Modifying Another Adverb

He slid down the hill *considerably* [not *considerable*] faster than he had crawled up.

She *almost* [not *most* or *mostly*] always jogs before breakfast.

Most of the difficulties centre in a few words, of which the following are typical: *bad – badly, good – well, sure – surely, real – really, most – almost, awful – awfully, considerable – considerably*.

The words *most* and *almost* present a special problem. In formal usage, *almost* is the accepted modifier in such expressions as: almost all were saved; summer is almost here; we almost never see him; almost everyone respects her. But in informal conversation, *most* is widely used in those situations. In your writing it is best to follow formal usage.

5d.   Certain colloquial uses of adjective and adverb should be avoided: *type*, *like*, *-wise*.

Undesirable

This *type* screw won't go into that *type* wood.

Hers is not a power-*type* serve.

Better

This kind of screw will not go into that kind of wood.

Hers is not a powerful serve.

Undesirable

I slid down the hill *like*, and then I saw this, *like*, glow in the sky.

It was *like* hours, you know, before the bus came.

Better

I slid down the hill, and then I saw a glow in the sky.

It was hours before the bus came.

Undesirable

Moneywise I was in favour of it, but *companywise* I was against it.

Timewise we were in real trouble.

Better

The proposal was good financially, but I disapproved of it in the interest of the company.

We had almost no time left.

5e. **When an adverb has two forms (the short and the -*ly* forms), any difference in their use or meaning is determined by idiom.**

The following adverbs – and a few others – have two forms:

bright – brightly	high – highly	near – nearly
cheap – cheaply	late – lately	right – rightly
close – closely	loose – loosely	tight – tightly
deep – deeply	loud – loudly	wrong – wrongly

The adverbs in these pairs are not always interchangeable. Nor is there any quick and easy way of learning how to distinguish them in meaning and function. Using them in sentences, as in the following, will help.

IDIOMATIC	**INEFFECTIVE IDIOM**
Lately the son has been staying out late.	Late the son has been staying out lately.
The dog crept close to me.	The dog crept closely to me.
Nobody was near.	Nobody was nearly.
He was highly respected.	He was high respected.
The woman slowly opened the door.	The woman slow opened the door.

5f. Observe the distinction between the comparative and the superlative.

The positive form of an adjective or adverb assigns a quality to the word it modifies, as in "a *big* bed," "he walked *rapidly.*" The comparative degree is formed by adding *-er* to the positive or by using *more* or *less* with the positive, as in "a *bigger* bed," "he walked *more rapidly*" (not *rapider*).

The superlative degree is formed by adding *-est* to the positive form, or by using *most* or *least* with the positive. The superlative degree ranks the modified word highest or lowest in a class. It implies that there are at least three things in a class: "a *big* bed," "a *bigger* bed," "the *biggest* bed." [See also § 33.]

The comparative degree, then, is used when referring to two persons or things; the superlative degree is used when three or more persons or things are involved.

Comparative

She was *taller* than her brother.

Of the two boys, John was the *more intelligent* and the *more co-operative*.

She learned *faster* than I [not me].

Superlative

She was the *tallest* person on the basketball team. [More than two]

John was the *most intelligent* and the *most co-operative* boy in school. [Highest in a group consisting of more than two]

She learned *fastest* of us all.

5 Some words are compared irregularly:

many	more	most		much	more	most
bad	worse	worst		good	better	best
little	less *or* lesser	least		well	better	best
little	littler	littlest				

Adjectives of more than two syllables rarely take *-er* and *-est* to form comparatives and superlatives. Forms such as *famouser* or *magnificentest* are not modern English. Do not use comparative or superlative forms of adjectives that name qualities thought of as absolute, such as *more perfect*, *most perfect*, *most unique*.

In modern English one does not combine two superlatives to form a kind of super-superlative. The same principle applies to comparatives.

Wrong
That is the *most unkindest* thing you could have said.

Right
That is the *most unkind* thing you could have said.

Wrong
He finally reached the *more remoter* regions of the country.

Right
He finally reached the *remoter* regions of the country.

EXERCISES

EXERCISE 1, RECOGNIZING ADJECTIVES AND ADVERBS.
Copy the following sentences. Underline each adjective once and each adverb twice.

1. Her spirits were high because the sun shone bright on her graduation day.

2. You may be right, but the little boy climbing the mountain does not appear lazy.
3. The aged teacher was considerably provoked because the bright students protested loudly against the assignment.
4. When he awoke after a deep sleep, he noticed that the cold morning air smelled fresh and sweet.
5. All decisions regarding high policy must be carefully scrutinized to see whether they are right or wrong.
6. Then, too, a lively conversation with the kindly old man was an awfully pleasant price for a delicious dinner.
7. The room smells stuffy, the milk tastes sour, the oil-cloth feels gritty, the toast appears sooty, and the prospect for a happy day looks poor.
8. The housekeeper is coming early, I am sure, because everything looks wrong in my room.
9. Really, I feel well, although I did not sleep well last night.
10. Things look bad everywhere today.

EXERCISE 2, CORRECTING ADJECTIVE AND ADVERB
ERRORS. *Correct the error in the form or use of the adjective or adverb in each of the following sentences.*

1. In the window he saw a coat that was richer and luxuriouser than anything he could imagine.
2. His manners were gentlemanly and he spoke friendly to me, but I could not trust him with the gun in his hand.
3. All the players felt unhappily after losing the game, and the alumni sure felt bad about it too.
4. You have been so good to me that I feel cheaply because I cannot repay you.
5. Lately she has taken to driving her sports car real fast.
6. I am most ready; my paper is near finished.
7. There is considerable merit in your paper ideawise, but structurewise it is badly arranged.
8. When I compare it with the one written by Anne on paperweights, it is real hard to say which is worst.

9. He held the bat closely to his chest and then hit the ball highly in the air.
10. Sit tight; the doctor is near ready to see you.

6

EXERCISE 3, CHOOSING CORRECT ADJECTIVE AND ADVERB FORMS. *In each of the following sentences select the correct form of the adjective or adverb.*

1. I was (really carefully, real careful, really careful) about mounting the horse with red in his eye.
2. In spite of his education, he still does not read (well, good).
3. We drove (slow and careful, slowly and carefully) over the icy roads.
4. When we lost our way, Tracy (sure, surely) felt (bad, badly).
5. Like most careful persons, she takes her driving (real serious, really seriously).
6. Eugene is the (tallest, taller) of the two forwards on the team.
7. Alice did (good, well) on her English test.
8. Tony is (carefuller, more careful) than Eugene.
9. Eugene's history essay was (more perfect, more nearly perfect) than Tony's.
10. Harriet looked (curious, curiously), but actually she was only amused.

§ 6. Verb Forms

The appropriate form of the verb should be used.

A student who is uncertain about the right form of a verb turns to the dictionary for help. A dictionary gives what are known as the *principal parts* of a verb, or as many of them as are necessary. Verbs are *regular* or *irregular*, and this distinction controls the amount of information that the dictionary gives. The regular verbs form their past tense and their past participle by adding *-d*, *-t*, or *-ed* to the present: "I *looked*," "I *have looked*." Therefore only one part (*look*) is sufficient. But the irregular verbs change the present stem form to make the past tense and the past participle: "I *lie* on the floor," "I *lay* on the floor," "I *have lain* on the floor." The dictionary gives as many principal parts as are necessary to indicate all the forms of the verb – or its *conjugation.* In the case of *lie*, the dictionary lists all the principal parts – namely, the past tense, the past participle, and the present participle. When the dictionary does not list the past participle of an irregular verb, it is assumed that it is the same as the past tense, as in "I *lead*," "I *led*," "I *have led.*"

An abridged conjugation of the verb *take* follows. For other forms and their uses, see §6a. The principal parts of *take* are *take*, *took*, *taken*, *taking.*

6

Indicative Mood

ACTIVE VOICE		PASSIVE VOICE	
Singular	Plural	Singular	Plural
PRESENT TENSE			
I take	we take	I am taken	we are taken
you take	you take	you are taken	you are taken
he takes	they take	he is taken	they are taken
PAST TENSE			
I took	we took	I was taken	we were taken
you took	you took	you were taken	you were taken
he took	they took	he was taken	they were taken
FUTURE TENSE			
I shall (will) take	we shall (will) take	I shall (will) be taken	we shall (will) be taken
you will take	you will take	you will be taken	you will be taken
he will take	they will take	he will be taken	they will be taken

PRESENT PERFECT TENSE

I have taken	we have taken	I have been taken	we have been taken
you have taken	you have taken	you have been taken	you have been taken
he has taken	they have taken	he has been taken	they have been taken

PAST PERFECT TENSE

I had taken	we had taken	I had been taken	we had been taken
you had taken	you had taken	you had been taken	you had been taken
he had taken	they had taken	he had been taken	they had been taken

FUTURE PERFECT TENSE

I shall (will) have taken	we shall (will) have taken	I shall (will) have been taken	we shall (will) have been taken
you will have taken	you will have taken	you will have been taken	you will have been taken
he will have taken	they will have taken	he will have been taken	they will have been taken

IMPERATIVE FORMS: take, be taken

INFINITIVE FORMS: to take, to have taken, to be taken, to have been taken

GERUNDS: taking, having taken, being taken, having been taken

PARTICIPLES: taking, taken, having taken, being taken, having been taken

TENSES

6a.   The correct tense forms of the verb should be used.

1. The Present Time. Present time may be expressed by three main verb forms. The *simple present* tense form usually expresses general or habitual action: "I *work*," "he *teaches*," "she *lives* in Judique," "they *drive* a Mazda." To express action as going on at the present time we use the *progressive* form of the present: "I *am working*," "he *is teaching*," "she *is living* in Judique," "they *are driving* a Mazda." There is also a present auxiliary form, "do," which is used for emphasis (I *do work*), for negations (she *does* not *teach*), and for questions (*does* she *live* in Judique?).

2. The Past Time. Past time is usually expressed by the *past tense*, as in "I *studied*," "she *played* the piano," "he *taught*," "I *worked*." Past time may also be indicated by the present tense form (called the *historical present*), as "The captain *looks* at me, and I *stare* back at him, and he *says* to me . . ." It is a device that should be avoided in writing, except as part of dialogue, or in narrative writing that expresses vivid feelings and sense impressions.

3. The Perfect Tenses. The *present perfect* tense shows that an act has been completed prior to the present.

Examples

The attendants *have taken* all the tickets.

All the tickets *have been taken*.

The *past perfect* tense shows that an act was already completed before some specified or understood time in the past.

Examples

I *had heard* about the crash before you told me.

He *had* already *paid* his respects to the deceased.

The *future perfect* tense, which is less common than the others, indicates a future act as having already taken place, in relation to some specified or understood time in the future.

Examples

He *will have counted* the money by the time the police arrive to collect him.

By late this afternoon the money *will have been counted*.

4. The Future Time. Future time may be indicated in several ways. It may be indicated by the *present tense with an adverb or an adverbial phrase of time*.

Examples

6

We *arrive* in Regina in *thirty minutes*.

Our wedding *takes* place *next June*.

The future may also be indicated by using *going to* or *about to* with the verb.

Examples

We *are going to stay* overnight in Saskatoon.

He is *about to declare* himself a candidate.

Shall – Will, *Should – Would*. Finally, and most obviously, the future may be indicated by using *shall* or *will* with the verb. Attitudes toward the use of *shall* and *will* have provoked controversy because the words are another illustration of the language in rapid change, and when usage changes quickly, controversy often arises. But the distinction between *shall* and *will*, once considered vital to educated English, now no longer seems so important. In modern informal speech, most people use *will* and *would* (or the contractions *I'll*, *he'll*, *he'd*, *you'd*) for all expressions of the future, and many do the same in writing. Others, at least in writing, use *shall* and *should* for the first person singular and plural, and *will* and *would* for the second and third persons. Once again, these seemingly trivial choices have their effect on tone: to maintain the *shall – will* distinction is to add a slight touch of traditional formality to the style.

Those who do maintain the distinction observe, in general, the following rules: for simple future, *shall* with the first person, *will* with the second and third persons; for the emphatic future, *will* for the first person, *shall* for the second and third persons.

Examples

I shall discuss the uses of verbs, and you will write the appropriate forms.

You will have to study diligently if you are to put them to good use.

In asking questions, *shall* is ordinarily used with the first and third persons and *will* with the second person when a request for permission is implied: "*Shall* I wrap it up for you?" "*Shall* he take you home?" "*Will* you do it?" A note of formality may be imparted to a question if the speaker uses the form that is anticipated in the answer: "*Shall* you be at the meeting?" "I *shall*."

To express habitual or customary action, *would* is generally used in all three persons; *should*, however, may be found in the first person.

Examples

She *would* read in the library instead of playing tennis with her friends.

He *would* sit in his rocker and knit all day long.

I *would* [should] be grateful for your advice.

Should is often used in the sense of *ought*, although in some sentences *ought* may imply a slightly stronger sense of obligation.

Examples

He really *should keep* his mouth shut. [He ought to . . .]

The policy *should have been defined* long before this. [The policy ought to have been defined . . .]

You *ought* to stop throwing cream pies at celebrities.

Sequence of Tenses. Use the tenses that show the correct relation of time between the main verb and the subordinate verb. When, for example, a verb indicates action that took place before the action of the main verb, and the main verb is in the past tense, then the subordinate verb must be in the past perfect tense.

Examples

After I *had talked* with him for a while, he *was* more agreeable.

When they *had run* ten miles, they *decided* to stop.

6   Be careful to use the correct tense of infinitives and participles. Notice in the following examples that the time indicated by the verbal is always in relation to the time expressed by the main verb. That is, a present infinitive indicates the same time as the main verb, even when the main verb is past.

Examples

I was very pleased *to hear* from you. [Not *to have heard*]

She intended *to go* home, but she did not make it. [Not *to have gone*]

With participles, a past tense of the participle must be used to indicate a time previous to the main verb.

Examples

Having played tennis all day, we were tired. [Not *playing*]

Talking as we walked along, we soon arrived at the cliff's edge. [Not *having talked*]

Careless Shifts in Tense. In telling a story or recounting an event, it is undesirable to shift from past to present or from present to past unless there is a real change in time of the action being described. For this reason the historical present should be used with care. (See also §§ 31 and 33.)

Careless Shift

I *went* out the door and *walked* slowly down the street, where the traffic *seemed* even more noisy than usual. Suddenly a man *approaches* me from an alley. "Look!" he *says*, and *forces* a piece of paper into my hand; but when I *looked* at it I *saw* nothing. I *continued* my walk.

The Subjunctive

6b. The subjunctive mood is used in a number of situations in formal writing.

The only uses of the subjunctive the student need be concerned about in speech and writing are the following:

6

1. In *if*-clauses expressing doubt or impossibility of the condition (usually referred to as ''condition contrary to fact'').

Examples

If she *were* here, you would not dare insult her.

Were he with us today, he would be gratified at this scene. [This word order has a somewhat old-fashioned ring.]

Were we to pursue the investigation, you would soon become uneasy.

Note that when the condition is *not* contrary to fact, the subjunctive is not used.

Examples

Either he was here or he was not. If he was here, then he must know that his stereo was stolen.

If she did go swimming, she must have noticed the piranhas.

2. In *that*-clauses expressing a wish, request, or command.

Examples

The president has ordered that all prisoners *be* treated equally.

I demand that he *come* here at once. [Again, note the relative formality of these sentences using the subjunctive. *Compare:* I want him to come here at once.]

3. In main clauses to express hope, wish, or prayer, usually in traditional and stereotyped patterns.

Examples.

The Force *be* with you.

Long *live* rock and roll!

"The rules *be* damned!" shouted the losing coach.

With regard to the form of the verb, we can say that for most verbs the subjunctive form differs from the indicative in only the third person singular of the present tense.

6

INDICATIVE		**SUBJUNCTIVE**	
I take	we take	if I take	if we take
you take	you take	if you take	if you take
he takes	they take	if he take	if they take

[*If* here is only an indicator of the subjunctive mood. *Should* is also sometimes used for the same purpose.]

Examples

We recommend that he *take* the entrance examination.

The remark about his hairpiece could hurt, should he *take* it the wrong way.

The verb *to be* is a special problem. The problem may be simplified by saying that the subjunctive of *to be* uses:

1. *Be* in all forms of the present tense.
2. *Were* in all forms of the past tense.
3. *Have been* in all forms of the present perfect tense.

Examples

Be it ever so noisy, there is no place like the dorm.

Were you as busy as I was at that moment, you would not have asked me to help you.

VOICE

6c. The passive voice of the verb should not be overused.

In most writing, and especially narrative and descriptive writing, the active voice is preferred as more direct, vivid, and emphatic than the passive voice. It is obviously simpler and clearer to say "I hit the intruder on the nose" than "the intruder was hit on the nose by me." But the passive voice has its legitimate uses, as the first sentence in this paragraph should testify. It is useful when the action of the verb is more important than the doer, the doer of action may not be known, or when the writer may wish to place emphasis on the recipient of the action rather than on the doer.

6

Examples

Twenty thousand dollars was collected from a number of sources.

Another man was fired last night.

All the bridges were destroyed during the war.

It is not the passive voice in itself that is objectionable – it is the overuse or misuse of it. Constant repetition of passive verbs can create an effect of deadness in the action of the prose, as if nothing *did* anything but instead sat around waiting for something *to be done to it.*

The passive voice becomes the scapegoat if not the actual criminal when there is a shift in point of view in a group of sentences. Notice what happens in the following sentences:

Confused

One person may be writing a letter; a book absorbs the attention of another. As usual someone sat in her chair sound asleep. Constant whispers could have been heard by the lecturer. [The effect here is similar to that found in a carelessly edited film, where an actor exits screen left and reappears screen right without any visible reason for the flip. Continuity is lost.]

Consistent

During the lecture, one person is writing a letter; another is reading a book. As usual someone sits sound asleep. Several people are whispering constantly.

The passive voice, on the other hand, may be useful in enabling a writer to maintain one point of view through several sentences.

Shift in Point of View

She sat absorbed in her book. A frown could be seen on her face. Then a long whistle from outside interrupted her thoughts. She glanced in annoyance toward the window. Then she smiled as if what she saw there amused her. It was Spot, the whistling beagle.

Consistent Point of View

As she sat there frowning, absorbed in her book, her thoughts were interrupted by a long whistle from outside. Annoyed, she glanced through the open window. Then she smiled at what she saw there. It was Spot, the whistling beagle.

EXERCISES

EXERCISE 1, PRINCIPAL PARTS. *With the help of your dictionary find the principal parts of the following verbs. List the form given, the past tense, the past participle, and the present participle or gerund; for example,* begin, began, begun, beginning.

bear	dive	know	raise	spring
blow	drink	lay	ride	sting
break	drive	lead	ring	swim
bring	eat	lend	rise	take
burst	get	lie	set	throw
buy	go	lose	shake	wake
choose	grow	prove	sink	write

EXERCISE 2, TENSES. *Make necessary corrections of tenses in the following sentences.*

1. I was eager to have learned German since I planned to go to Berlin.
2. I told everyone I bought my ticket two days before.

3. Learning the language in a few weeks, I was ready to go at last.
4. I should have purchased a round trip ticket, but I failed to do so.
5. Will you be in Berlin at any time this summer?
6. The year before, I had travelled in England so that I could have spent some time with a friend of mine in London.
7. Shall I try it once more?
8. By midnight we shall have reached our first destination.
9. I was pleased yesterday to have heard from you at last.
10. Knowing what a good correspondent you are, I look forward to hearing from you soon.

EXERCISE 3, THE SUBJUNCTIVE. *In the following sentences select the correct forms from those given in parentheses.*

1. I requested that an invitation (be, is, was) sent to them immediately.
2. We all wish we (are, were) with you at this time.
3. He demanded that their rock throwing (cease, ceased, ceases) at once.
4. We suggested that he (withdraw, withdraws) these demands.
5. He looks as if he (is, were) angry, but one cannot be sure.
6. I know he (is, were) angry because I heard him swear.
7. My suggestion is that he (bring, brings) you along with him.
8. Finally someone made the motion that the whole discussion (is, be, was) dropped.
9. If Jack (is, were) here at last, you (should, would) not treat me this way.
10. Since Jack (is, were) here at last, you will not treat me this way.

EXERCISE 4, PASSIVE AND ACTIVE VOICE. *In the following sentences change the passive constructions to active ones where appropriate. Remember that there are some legitimate uses of the passive.*

1. I am seen at the corner disco every night.
2. Another operator was fired last night for playing Glenn Miller records.
3. Bernie Lablatt attracts everyone's attention when he dances with Natalie Strobe.

4. Frantic whispers can be heard by the manager when the chandelier stops spinning.
5. I was bumped into at least twice by Carole Pope.
6. All the wooden tables were imported from France.
7. A smile could be seen on Lorna's face when they showed the clip from *Disco Drive-in*.
8. At least ten thousand dollars is made there every night.
9. Claude claimed that illegal sales were taking place downstairs.
10. In her usual witty way Mindy observed that a swinging time was had by all.

10

MECHANICS

§ 7. Manuscript: Form and Revision

7a. In the preparation of manuscript, follow standard procedures and any special instructions given you by your English instructor.

1. *Use standard typewriter paper or, for handwritten papers, the 8½ × 11 ruled paper.* Most English departments require composition students to use regulation typewriter paper, unruled if essays are typewritten, ruled if essays are handwritten.

2. *Write legibly.* If you write by hand, make your writing easy to read. Write with a good pen and use black or dark blue ink. Do not use red, violet, or green ink. Form all letters distinctly, especially those that might be confused with other letters. Dot your *i*'s and cross your *t*'s. Do not decorate your letters with unnecessary loops and flourishes. Indicate paragraphing clearly by indenting about an inch.

3. *Type legibly.* If you use a typewriter, see that the ribbon is fresh and the type clean. Adjust your margin properly. *Always*

double-space your typing. Space five spaces for paragraph indentions, one space between words, and two spaces after the end punctuation of a sentence. If you must delete material, use one of the convenient correction tapes or liquids. *If you must cross out any considerable portion of your material, type your page over again.* Never begin a line with a punctuation mark, such as a comma, a period, a question mark, or an exclamation point, that belongs at the end of the preceding line.

4. *Label your essays correctly.* Use the method of labelling papers recommended by your instructor. Follow his or her instructions exactly. Never write on the back of the paper.

5. *Be careful about the correct placement and capitalization of the title.* Write the title on the first line of the first page only, or about two inches from the top of the sheet. Centre the title on the page. Capitalize the first word and all important words in the title; the usual practice is to capitalize all nouns, pronouns, verbs, adverbs, and adjectives, and all prepositions that stand last or contain more than five letters. Do not underline the title or enclose it in quotation marks, unless the title is a quotation, and you wish to emphasize that it is quoted. Do not use a period after it, but you may use a question mark or an exclamation point if the sense of the title calls for either of these marks. Leave a space of about an inch between the title and the first line of your essay. Do not repeat the title on succeeding pages.

6. *Use proper margins.* Leave margins of an inch at the top and at the left of each page. Do not crowd your words at the right or at the bottom of the page. Some instructors like a wide margin at the right as well as at the left of the page so as to have room for comments and corrections. After the first page, begin writing on the first line.

If you are quoting verse, centre your quotation on the page and follow the line arrangement of the poem from which you are quoting. *No quotation marks are needed.* If the quotation does not end a paragraph, begin the next line of your composition flush with the left margin.

7. *Make deletions and corrections clearly.* Parentheses and brackets are never used to delete or cross out a word. These marks have other uses.

To delete material, draw a horizontal line through it. In typing, material may be deleted by some kind of liquid white-out or correcting tape.

If you wish to insert a correction in your text, mark the point of insertion with a caret (∧) and write the inserted material above the caret.

7b. Revise your manuscript carefully, both before you hand it in and after it has been returned to you for correction.

1. *Go over the first draft of your paper and copy it for final submission.* In revising your first draft, you should consider the following checklist:

  a. Has the paper an objective, a central idea, a direction?
  b. Is the content made interesting by facts and examples?
  c. Is the organization, in the whole paper and in the separate paragraphs, as logical as possible?
  d. Are there obvious errors in sentence structure to correct, such as the period fault, the comma splice, failure of verbs and subjects to agree?
  e. Are the punctuation and spelling correct?

2. *Revise your paper carefully after the instructor has returned it to you.* Make every correction indicated or suggested by your instructor. If he or she refers you to a book section, first study the section carefully to see how it applies to your error. Then, in pencil or a distinctive colour of ink, draw a horizontal line through the word or words you wish to cancel, and, in the space above, between the lines, write the revised version. If for any

reason you do not have the time to revise the returned paper, at least make sure that you know what the faults indicated are and how you would revise them had you the time.

On pages 380–381 are two paragraphs of prose filled with elementary errors. The instructor has used section numbers from this book to show the student where each kind of error is discussed and the correction explained. If the instructor had wished to be more explicit, he or she would have underlined the points of error.

On pages 382–383, the same selection appears. This time the instructor has used correction symbols, according to the system of this book. The student has revised the sentences, in response to the instructor's corrections, by writing between the typewritten lines.

If your instructor indicates by a note or a comment in the margin that some part of your page is confused, undeveloped, or illogical, rewrite the section criticized. Whenever the revision is short, you may write between the lines. When you rewrite a number of sentences or paragraphs, however, you should first make your corrections on the face of your manuscript, and then recopy the entire page.

3. Once you have revised a page or an entire essay, it is a good idea to ask your instructor's opinion of the revision. Of course, the instructor may require you to hand in the revision, in which case consultation is an even better idea.

Why College?

12   Why did I come to college. That is a hard

 2   question, it cannot be answered in a few words.

19   From one point of view, it seems abserd that I

         should be here without knowing why I am here.

15/19   Its true my parents allways wanted me to go to

         college. They probably never quite analysed their

reasons for wanting me to go. They wanted me

| to better myself. To learn a profession or a

|| trade. They felt that a well educated person

6 would be able to lead an easier life than they

29/6/13 lived. Knowing the hard life they lived their 7

attitude seems reasonable to me. From another

13 point of view however, it seems logical to me

that I should come to college to find out why I

came to college. I am not sure that I can find

all the answers. My college work may give me

| one answer to my question. Or maybe several of

37 the many possible answers. While I do not

expect to find all the answers, after my years

19 here I may know more definately what the

question means.

28 I have talked with other first-year students

19 about their reasons for comeing to college. They

21 have many solutions. Most of them talk about

| economic security. Which of course is a

legitimate objective. Others talk about a life of

25 service to others. If you talk long enough about

the subject, you will hear about cultivation of

the mind and the emotions. These are ideas I

will try to discuss here.

Sample Essay Marked
by the Instructor

Why College?

Ques. Why did I come to college/? That is a hard

RS question, ~~it~~ *which* cannot be answered in a few words.

Sp From one point of view, it seems ~~abserd~~ *absurd* that I

should be here without knowing why I am here.

Pn/Sp It's true my parents ~~allways~~ *always* wanted me to go to

college. They probably never quite analysed their

reasons for wanting me to go. They wanted me

PF to better myself/ ~~To learn~~ *by learning* a profession or a

Pn trade. They felt that a well-educated person

Tnse
Dng would be able to lead an easier life than they *have*
Tnse
C lived. ~~Knowing~~ *Because I know* the hard life they *have* lived, their

attitude seems reasonable to me. From another

C point of view, however, it seems logical to me

that I should come to college to find out why I

came to college. I am not sure that I can find

all the answers. My college work may give me

PF one answer to my question/ ~~Or~~ *or* maybe several of

Gl the many possible answers. ~~While~~ *Although* I do not

expect to find all the answers, after my years

Sp here I may know more ~~definately~~ *definitely* what the

question means.

Sub. ~~I have talked~~ *As I talk* with other first-year students

Sp/Ex about their reasons for ~~comeing~~ *coming* to college/, ~~They~~ *I*

Ex

OF

encounter many ideas.
~~have many solutions.~~ Most of them talk about
which
economic security/, ~~Which~~ of course is a
legitimate objective. Others talk about a life of

Nd
Rep

humanity
service to ~~others.~~ If you talk long enough about
the subject, you will hear about cultivation of
the mind and the emotions. These are ideas I
will try to discuss here.

8

Sample Essay as Corrected
by the Student

§ 8. Capitals

A *capital letter* is a kind of punctuation mark, designed to draw
the reader's attention to itself for a particular reason. These reasons have been formalized so that there is justification for the
appearance of every capital. They should not be abused by
overcapitalization.

8a. **Capitalize the first word of every sentence, including
fragments punctuated as sentences, and the first word
of any group within a sentence that is understood as a
sentence in its own right.**

Examples

What now? Who knows? Nobody.

He replied, "There is little hope left."

The main question is, When do we eat?

Do *not* capitalize the first word of (a) an indirect quotation,
(b) a direct quotation that is a structural part of the new sentence in which it is quoted, (c) the part of a direct quotation

that follows dialogue tags such as *he said*, unless the part begins a new sentence.

Examples

Everyone said that the statement was untrue. [Indirect quotation. *Compare*: Everyone said, "The statement is untrue."]

Some people feel, like the singer in Joni Mitchell's song, that they've "seen life from both sides now." [Direct quotation made a structural part of the new sentence]

"I wish I could tell you," he added, "what I really mean about that."

In quoting poetry or any other document, follow the original exactly in respect to capitalization. In writing out a title, capitalize the first word and all other words except conjunctions and prepositions of less than five letters. An exception is a short preposition ending the title, which should be capitalized: *When the Lights Were Turned On*. For further information on the special problems of titles, see § 10a.

8b. Proper nouns and adjectives are capitalized.

A *proper noun* names some particular person, place, or object; a *common noun* indicates one of a class of persons, places, or objects. In practice the distinction is usually not difficult to discern.

Capitalize:

1. Names of persons, places, buildings, ships, and so on: John H. Farley, Manitoba, the Royal Ontario Museum, the *Bluenose*, Vaughan Township, Israel.
2. Names of political and geographical divisions if they are part of a proper name: Union of South Africa, Northwest Territory, Dominion of Canada. [But *not*: a union of states, the territory toward the northwest]
3. Names of historic events or epochs: the Middle Ages, the Black Death, World War I, the Depression.

4. Names of nationalities, religious groups, and languages: English, Mormon, Slavic, Japanese. [Note that these can be used either as nouns or as adjectives.]
5. Adjectives derived from proper names: Byronic, Freudian, Scottish. [A few adjectives, used in special senses, such as *roman* or *italic* type, are often considered common rather than proper.]
6. Names of organizations: Canadian Union of Public Employees, the Red Cross, Congress of Industrial Organizations, United Nations, Phi Beta Kappa.
7. Days of the week, names of the months and of particular holidays: Easter, Good Friday, Canada Day, the second Monday in March.

As a rule, difficulties arise only when the same word is used both as a proper noun and as a common noun; some of these difficulties are discussed in §§ 8c and 8d below.

8c. Any title used preceding a name or as a substitute for the name is capitalized.

A *title* is always capitalized preceding a name.

Examples
Captain Townsend; Prince Philip; Pope John Paul II; Premier William Bennett; *but* William Bennett, the premier of British Columbia.

Notice that these words are *not* capitalized when they are not used as a title for a particular, named person. The article *a* is usually a signal that a common noun follows.

Examples
A queen's consort is usually a prince.

He was promoted to captain.

When will they elect a new pope?

He is a good prospect for a vice-president's position.

Abbreviations after a name, such as Esq., Ph.D., M.D., F.R.S., are usually capitalized and not spaced. The following, however, are correct either with or without capitals: Jr., jr., Sr., sr. (*and note also* No., no.; A.M., a.m.; P.M., p.m.). Be consistent.

8d. Common nouns are capitalized only when they are used in the sense of proper names.

1. Capitalize *North*, *South*, *East*, *West*, *Northwest*, *Far East* only when these words refer to specific geographical divisions. Do not capitalize them when they refer to directions.

Examples

The West is gaining industrially at the expense of the East.

I turned south at the crossroads.

She lives north of the city.

2. Capitalize the words for educational and other institutions only when they are a part of some name, not when they are used as common nouns.

Examples

The school was near Toronto General Hospital, not far from the University of Toronto.

I attended high school there. It was called Beaverbrook High.

Many universities are looking for a good president.

I would like to work for the National Museum of Man or the National Gallery of Canada, but not all museum work interests me.

3. Capitalize the names of particular courses of study, such as *Mathematics 120*, *Physical Education 485*. But do not capitalize such terms when they are used to refer to general areas of learning: *mathematics, physical education, history, law*. Remember, however, that names of nationalities and languages are always capitalized: *French history, English literature, Mexican art*.

4. Capitalize words denoting family relationships (*mother, father, uncle, grandfather*) only when these words stand for an individual who is called by that name. Again, be alert for the signal of a common noun, such as an article or possessive preceding the word.

Examples

A mother is often a twenty-four-hour labourer. My mother was such a person. One day I said to her, "Do you work as hard as Grandmother did, Mother?" She only replied that mothers have always worked hard. She is definitely a candidate for the women's movement.

The dictionary can often be useful in determining standard practice of capitalization. But in most doubtful cases, as these examples illustrate, it is necessary to recognize just how a word serves in a particular context.

EXERCISES

EXERCISE 1, SUPPLYING CAPITALS. *Copy the following sentences, supplying capitals when necessary.*

1. hockey is a popular sport in almost all communities in canada.
2. there are teams in all regions of the country, from as far east as newfoundland to as far west as british columbia.
3. twenty years ago, canadian boys dreamed of playing for the toronto maple leafs or the montreal canadiens.
4. now young players from the west cheer on the edmonton oilers or the winnipeg jets, and the quebec nordiques rival the canadiens in popularity in the east.
5. most n.h.l. players are canadians and many of them learned their skills through playing on frozen lakes in the prairies, northern ontario, or quebec.
6. in 1972, the whole country was united behind the canadian all-star team that played an exhibition series against an all-star team from the soviet union.

7. most people were surprised when the soviet players came so close to winning this unofficial world championship.
8. now canada and the soviet union frequently play exhibition series, the most popular of which is the canada cup.
9. most players consider it an honour to represent their country, although n.h.l. players believe the timing of the tournament is not favourable to them.
10. many fans still maintain that the winner of the stanley cup is the true world champion.

EXERCISE 2, SUPPLYING CAPITALS. *Here is a piece of administrative English, of the sort that might appear on a college bulletin board. Again, supply capitals where necessary, and only where necessary.*

registration for the fall term will take place in walker hall from monday at 9 a.m. till wednesday at 4 p.m. all students will bring high school records and identification cards with them. the following courses will not be offered this year: economics 130, english 110, french 111, chemistry 120. students expecting to major in physical science should see professor adkins. those expecting to enter law school must elect political science 430. please talk without delay to the professor who has been designated as your adviser.

---

§9. Abbreviations and Numbers

9a. In ordinary writing, abbreviations are usually avoided (with a few standard exceptions).

The following are usually written out, although in footnotes, bibliographies, tabulations, and addresses they may be abbreviated to conserve space:

1. Names of countries and provinces: Canada [not *Can.*], Alberta [not *Alta.*].
2. Names of the months and days of the week: September [not *Sept.*], Monday [not *Mon.*], Friday [not *Fri.*].

3. Christian names: Charles [not *Chas.*], Robert [not *Robt.*], Edward [not *Edw.*].
4. Names of college courses, titles of professors, and other words frequently abbreviated in campus conversation: professor [not *prof.*], educational psychology [not *ed. psych.*], political science [not *poli. sci.*].
5. The titles *The Reverend* [not *Rev.*] and *The Honourable* [not *Hon.*], at least in formal situations. These titles are used with the person's full name, not with just the last name.
6. The following words: *number, volume, chapter, page, and [not &], street, avenue, manufacturing, company, mountain, Christmas.*

Poor

He was looking forward to Xmas vacation next Dec.

Better

He was looking forward to Christmas vacation next December.

Poor

This class meets on Tues., Thurs., and Sat.

Better

This class meets on Tuesdays, Thursdays, and Saturdays.

Poor

He worked in T.O. for Collier Macmillan.

Better

He worked in Toronto for Collier Macmillan Canada, Inc. [Remember that sometimes a company name is properly composed of abbreviations and ought to be written accordingly, e.g., Collier Macmillan Canada, Inc. As there may be a legal reason for the use of abbreviations in company names, try to find out what the company's letterhead says and use that.]

Poor

Some day she hopes to be a prof. of poli. sci.

Better

Some day she hopes to be a professor of political science.

Poor
Wm. and Chas. live on Jerome Ave., near Dilmore St.

Better
William and Charles live on Jerome Avenue, near Dilmore Street.

The following abbreviations are customary and appropriate:

1. Titles before proper names: *Dr.*, *Mr.*, *Mrs.*, *Ms.*, *M.*, *Messrs.*, *Mme.*, *Mlle.*

2. Certain designations after names: *Jr.*, *jr.*, *Sr.*, *sr.*, *D.D.*, *M.D.*, *Ph.D.*

3. With dates only when necessary for clearness: *A.D.* and *B.C.*: Octavian lived from 63 B.C. to A.D. 14. (Note that B.C. follows the year, A.D. precedes it. It has been argued by some people that the abbreviations *B.C.* and *A.D.* do not represent a true, universal reckoning of history. The alternatives proposed are *B.C.E.* (Before the Christian [or Common] Era) and *C.E.* (the Christian [or Common] Era).

4. Certain expressions usually abbreviated in informal and in technical writing, though written out when a more formal effect is desired: *i.e.*, *e.g.*, *viz.*, *etc.* These actually stand for *id est*, *exempli gratia*, *videlicet*, *et cetera*, but they are written out as *that is*, *for example*, *namely*, *and so forth*.

5. Names of government agencies and certain other well-known organizations: TVO, CIDA, NATO, CUPE. Note that the last three of these are pronounced as single words, rather than as series of letters. Abbreviations pronounced as words are known as *acronyms*. Note also the omission of periods. When in doubt about the punctuation, consult your dictionary.

Observe that it is not customary to space after periods within most abbreviations, except that initials representing names *are* spaced: A. L. Jones.

9b. There is no universal standard for writing numbers. Follow the style preferred by your instructor.

One common system is for numbers between one and ten to be spelled out and numbers above ten to be written in figures. When a number begins a sentence, however, spell the number out, no matter what it is.

Eight hundred and sixty-seven candidates ran for parliament.

9

Numbers that appear in close proximity and in the same context should be treated consistently.

She bought four apples, seven oranges, eighteen figs, and twenty-seven butter tarts.

but

Sixty-seven men, 59 women, and 11 children completed the marathon. (A number opens this sentence.)

Round numbers are usually spelled out.

Jane's essay traced two thousand years of political developments.

The rock concert attracted three hundred thousand people.

9c. Figures are used for the following:

1. Dates: March 20, 1984, *not* March twentieth, nineteen hundred eighty-four. [Note that the day of the month is separated from the year by a comma.]

2. Street and room numbers: 415 State Street; *not* four hundred fifteen State Street; Union Hall 216, *not* Union Hall two hundred sixteen.

3. Page numbers: page 334; *not* page three hundred thirty-four.

4. Decimals, percentages, mathematical and technical statistics: 0.7, *not* zero point seven; 27%, *not* twenty-seven percent; $1/25$, *not* one twenty-fifth.

It is still common to see large numbers whose units are separated by commas. Metric number style, which uses a space instead of a comma, is becoming increasingly popular.

10 927 354

EXERCISES

9

EXERCISE 1, CORRECTING ABBREVIATION ERRORS.
Correct the errors in the use of abbreviations in the following sentences.

1. Our route took us through Man., Ont., and Que.
2. The Stoic philosopher Seneca lived from 4 B.C. to 65 A.D.
3. This author was not born until after 1917 A.D.
4. English lit and math are my best courses.
5. We were in B.C. for the rock festival.
6. Thos. Jones took me to the game with Hancock Hi.
7. I think that our chem labs are poorly designed.
8. One of the profs there said they were firetraps.
9. Professor L.B. White and Doctor A.G. Black are my chem lecturers.
10. Rev. Holmes was our convo speaker

EXERCISE 2, IDENTIFYING ABBREVIATIONS. *Identify each of the following abbreviations. Consult your dictionary.*

1. ad lib	6. ESP	11. UNESCO
2. CBC	7. f.o.b.	12. S.R.O.
3. ACTRA	8. q.v.	13. CRTC
4. CLC	9. TNT	14. CNIB
5. colloq.	10. S.J.	15. op. cit.

EXERCISE 3, SPELLING OUT NUMBERS. *In the following sentences circle the numbers that should have been written out in words.*

1. He will inherit the estate when he reaches the age of 21.
2. The estate consists of a ranch, some stocks, and $35 600 in bonds.

3. Brenda was given an expensive car on her 18th birthday.
4. Her sister Diana, who is 16, is in love with a boy 3 inches shorter than she.
5. Margaret's birthday parties are poorly attended, for she was born on December 26, 1950.
6. Although a member of the 4-H Club for 6 years, she does not know what the four *H*'s stand for.
7. Timmy, an 8th grader, told her his scholastic average for 2 years is 86.55.
8. He has just bought a 90mm lens for his Exakta, which is a 35mm single lens reflex camera.
9. In 1940 McMillan and Abelson produced element 93, named *neptunium* after the planet Neptune.
10. 36 men can be housed in the dormitory at 218 South 36th Street.

§ 10. Italics

Italics are used to set words apart in a variety of situations.

The word *italics* refers to print. In handwriting or in typing, a word to be understood as in *italics* is underlined.

Typewritten

In the May 1983 issue of <u>Books in Canada</u> there is a review of Leon Rooke's <u>Shakespeare's Dog.</u>

Print

In the May 1983 issue of *Books in Canada* there is a review of Leon Rooke's *Shakespeare's Dog.*

In business letters, instead of being underlined, the words are usually typed in capitals, as: BOOKS IN CANADA, SHAKE-SPEARE'S DOG.

Usage varies greatly in regard to the use of italics. The principles of usage in this section refer to more or less formal usage. If you are writing for publication, the only sure guide is the style sheet of the publication you are aiming at.

The following rules are usually observed in college papers of a formal nature.

10a. When referred to in formal writing, titles of books, plays, newspapers, magazines, musical compositions, and works of art as well as names of ships are usually underlined in manuscript and printed in italics.

10

Examples

Obasan	*Saturday Night*
Le Devoir	the *Queen Elizabeth II*
Michelangelo's *Pietà*	Beethoven's *Missa Solemnis*

Quotation marks are generally used for titles of chapters or subdivisions of books and for titles of short stories, magazine articles, newspaper articles, and short poems.

Examples

Some of the stories in Alice Munro's *The Moons of Jupiter*, such as "Mrs. Cross and Mrs. Kidd" and "The Accident" appeared previously in magazines like *Toronto Life* and *Tamarack Review* before being published in book form.

The Belleville *Intelligencer* ran a story titled "Gone With the Wind" about tornado damage.

The definite article *the* and the name of the city before the title of a newspaper are usually not italicized: the Ottawa *Citizen*. Some periodicals, however, prefer the italicized article: *The New Yorker*. [Note that *The* in such use requires a capital.]

10b. Foreign words and phrases that have not been Anglicized are italicized (underlined) when used in writing.

A number of terms pronounced like foreign words are nevertheless considered so much a part of our language that italics are *not* used. Examples include: *cliché*, *staccato*, *blitzkrieg*. Some dictionaries will tell you whether a word is still considered foreign and therefore must be italicized. Different dictionaries use different symbols for this purpose.

10c. **In formal writing, words, letters, and figures, referred to as such, are usually italicized.**

You have seen this procedure exemplified many times in this book, where italics have been used to mark off a word being discussed *as a word*. But in informal writing, quotation marks may be used for the same purpose. As always, be consistent in the form selected. In definitions, the word to be defined is commonly set in italics (underlined) and the definition is enclosed in quotation marks.

Formal Style

One of the best-known supporters of spelling reform was the English writer George Bernard Shaw, who, to point out the irregularity of our spelling, humorously suggested the word *fish* should be spelled *ghoti*, combining the *gh* from *cough*, the *o* from *women*, and the *ti* from *nation*.

Informal Style

Many people confuse ''imply'' and ''infer.''

The European ''7'' is written differently from ours.

10d. **Italics may be used to give special emphasis to a word or phrase.**

The use of italics or underlining for emphasis can be badly abused in formal writing, where it is likely to appear as a weak effort to give importance to words that ought to be important without such mechanical help. Furthermore, excessive underlining has associations with trivial dialogue, often of a juvenile flavour. (''Hey, *man*, you should have seen those *wheels*. I mean you should have *seen* them. *Outasight!*'') In a similar way, italics have been used by some novelists to suggest the up-and-down stresses of emotional speech.

Example

Toby laughed his puzzled, whim-destroying laugh. "Is
that all there is to it, Dave?" he said. "Is *that* all we're
going way up there for?"

"I guess," David said.

"It isn't like it was a *real* mountain," Toby said. "What
makes you think it's so wonderful?"

– Ernest Buckler,
The Mountain and the Valley

10   But in formal exposition, it is conventional to use italics for
emphasis far more sparingly, usually only when the sentence
would not be immediately clear without them.

Example

In philosophy, intuitive knowledge carries little weight. What is
needed is *formal* proof, proof that has no personality.

EXERCISES

EXERCISE 1, ITALICS AND QUOTATION MARKS. *Copy the
following paragraph, underlining for italics and adding quotation marks
where necessary. Use the formal conventions.*

Webster's New World Dictionary, like other such works, includes
helpful lists of synonyms for many familiar words. Listed under
crowd, for example, you will find throng, multitude, swarm, mob,
host, and horde, with precise differences indicated. An introductory
article called Guide to the Use of the Dictionary is of further
assistance to the reader searching for a mot juste. A subsection of
this article, titled The Synonymies, treats antonyms as well, and
concludes: "the antonym sad heads a synonymy that includes
melancholy, dejected, depressed, and doleful, all antonymous to
happy."

EXERCISE 2, ITALICS AND QUOTATION MARKS. *Copy the following paragraph in the same way, underlining for italics where necessary and adding quotation marks in the proper places.*

Hugh MacLennan's position as one of Canada's pre-eminent novelists is unquestioned. Yet his career began inauspiciously. As a young man he had failed to have published two novels that had international themes, so he decided to write a specifically Canadian novel. The result was Barometer Rising, a novel that has as its centre the Halifax explosion of 1917, and which is widely read even today. MacLennan's reputation was established. Perhaps his most famous novel is Two Solitudes, a story of the conflict between French- and English-speaking Canadians and the tragic consequences of that conflict. The novel struck a chord in Canadian readers and the phrase two solitudes became, and still remains, a shorthand description of one of the most serious social and political problems the country faces. What makes his success with this novel all the more remarkable is that when he wrote it, MacLennan was an outsider – one of les Anglais – from Cape Breton, and a relative newcomer to Quebec. Nearly forty years after his first novel, Hugh MacLennan published Voices in Time, a story of a post-nuclear-war world. It has achieved high praise and popularity, and, as one critic remarked, to be doing your best work in your middle 70s seems a happy fate.

§ 11. Syllabication and Hyphens

11a. The awkward division of a word at the end of a line of handwritten or typewritten manuscript should be avoided.

In printed matter, where a perfectly even right-hand margin is customary, we have become accustomed to a number of word divisions at the ends of lines. In handwritten or typewritten papers, however, it is usually unnecessary to divide many words. For clearness and ease in reading, it is wise to observe the following advice about dividing words at the end of a line:

1. Never divide words of one syllable, such as *eighth*, *rhythm*, *signed*, *burned*. Note that the *-ed* ending in the past-tense form must not be split off as a syllable.
2. Never divide a word so that a single letter is allowed to stand by itself, either at the end of a line or the beginning of the next line, as in *a- / mount*, *a- / round*, *e- / lope*, *greed- / y*, *read- / y*.
3. Try to avoid dividing proper names, as in *Ed- / ward*, or *John- / son*.
4. Try not to separate a name and the initials that go with it, as in *J.J.- / Robinette*.
5. Try to avoid dividing the last word of a paragraph or a page. In print such a division is often necessary, but in manuscript it can be easily avoided.

11b.   If a division of a word is necessary, the division should be made between syllables and a hyphen placed at the end of the line.

Assume that your reader is pronouncing your sentence aloud and divide words so that both parts are pronounceable. You must divide correctly between syllables and your best resource in doing so is your dictionary, where syllables are clearly indicated. The following advice should be of additional help:

1. Divide compound words on the hyphen, and try to avoid a second hyphen: *self- / evident*, not *self-evi- / dent*; *college- / trained*, not *col- / lege-trained*.
2. In words with prefixes, divide on the prefix: *non- / sensical*, *pre- / caution*, *ante- / diluvian*. Note that these words are ordinarily written solid; they are not hyphenated compounds.
3. In words with suffixes, divide on the suffix: *child- / ish*, *dog- / like*, *youth- / ful*, *fall- / ing*, *yell- / ing*.
4. As a rule, when a word contains double consonants, divide between the two consonants: *ac- / com- / mo- / date*, *in- / ter- / ro- / gate*. In such examples as *fall- / ing* and *yell- / ing*, however, the rule about double consonants conflicts with the rule about suffixes; the rule about suffixes takes precedence.

11c. Two or more words forming a compound adjective preceding a noun are hyphenated.

Examples

A broad-shouldered, long-legged man; a rough-looking centre; ready-made opinions; a twin-screw engine; in up-to-date condition; a well-travelled highway; a two-thirds majority; an old-fashioned soda; a three-dog night; the Russo-Finnish border.

When a compound modifier consists of two or more words with a common beginning, the following style is used: *A three- or four-room addition, paid in five- and ten-dollar bills.*

The following are usually not hyphenated: compound modifiers that follow the noun; compounds in which an adverb ending in *-ly* is used.

Examples

The man was well known for fiddling. [We met a well-known fiddler.]

His information was up to date. [He planned an up-to-date revision of the book.]

It was a loosely worded statement. [Her explanations were loosely worded.]

In order to express certain ideas more emphatically, professional writers may sometimes invent their own hyphenated phrases. While this practice has the stylistic advantage of grabbing the reader's attention, it is best for beginning writers to follow it sparingly.

Example

This habit of the I-want-it-and-I-want-it-now buying public leads many record producers to turn out popular-but-slick albums. [Would *spoiled* or *catered to* work better than the compound modifying *public*? Isn't the second compound more descriptive than the first?]

11d.   Compound numbers from twenty-one to ninety-nine are hyphenated.

Examples

Twenty-seven dollars, thirty-four inches

Fractions, when used as modifiers, are hyphenated. When one of the terms of the fraction is already a compound, however, no additional hyphen is used, as in *four twenty-fifths*, *twenty-one fortieths*. Such simple fractions as *one half*, *two thirds*, and so on, are often written without a hyphen, but *one-and-a-half* always follows the hyphenated form.

11

Examples

The bill was finally passed by a two-thirds majority.

One half of the pie was already eaten.

Paul normally employs about one one-hundredth of his brain.

11e.   Hyphens are used with the following classes of compound words.

1. With prefixes *ex-* (in the sense of "former") and *self-*: *ex-president*, *ex-minister*, *self-regard*, *self-help*, *self-pity*.
2. When two functions that are usually distinct are united in one person or thing: *cleaner-polisher*, *secretary-treasurer*, *publisher-editor*, *city-state*.
3. With prefix *semi-* when second element begins with *i*: *semi-independent*, *semi-invalid*, *semi-retired*.
4. With suffix *-like* when first element ends with *ll*: *bell-like*; when first element is a proper noun: *Canadian-like*, *Garbo-like*.
5. With groups making or containing prepositional phrases: *son-in-law*, *man-of-war*, *jack-in-the-pulpit*.
6. To prevent confusion with similar words: *re-form* [to form again], *reform* [to change or amend]; *re-count* [to count anew], *recount* [to tell]; *re-creation* [a second creation], *recreation* [play, sport, diversion].

7. When the second element of a compound word is a proper noun: *anti-American, pre-Renaissance, pro-Russian.*

When in doubt about the correct form of a compound, consult *The Canadian Dictionary for Schools*, the *Gage Canadian Dictionary*, the *Oxford English Dictionary*, or *Webster's New Collegiate Dictionary.*

EXERCISES

EXERCISE 1, SYLLABICATION. *Indicate which of the following words you should not divide at the end of a line. Show how you would divide the others. Give your reason in each case.*

1. agreed	6. sorely	11. brushed
2. precedence	7. speedy	12. elect
3. pre-eminent	8. unit	13. bankbook
4. through	9. across	14. squeezed
5. thorough	10. action	15. stringy

EXERCISE 2, COMPOUND WORDS. *With the aid of a dictionary determine which of the following should be written solid, which with a hyphen, and which are separate words.*

1. air raid	16. good bye
2. air raid shelter	17. half brother
3. all inclusive	18. half crazed lion
4. all right	19. half written theme
5. ante date	20. partly written paper
6. ante bellum	21. in as much as
7. anti climax	22. infra red
8. any body	23. north west
9. basket ball	24. post office
10. book store	25. score board
11. by law	26. text book
12. by pass	27. inter collegiate
13. post Renaissance	28. under graduate
14. dining room	29. week end trip
15. every thing	30. well made car

11

PUNCTUATION

The purpose of punctuation is to help make clear the meaning of printed or written language.

To some degree punctuation symbolizes the pauses in oral speech, but it does so crudely and artificially. It is still useful to read a sentence aloud with attention to its meaning, and punctuate the pauses you hear in your own voice. But correct punctuation has also come to reflect the grammatical structures of sentences, as well as the particular conventions of the age. Therefore, a comma does not always represent a drop or pause in the speaking voice, and the various marks of punctuation do not consistently distinguish among the various subtle drops that our voices so naturally perform. Like most other conventional patterns of behaviour, the conventions of punctuation have to be learned.

The practice of writers has been codified into a number of rules or principles of punctuation. These rules or principles govern a very large number of typical situations in writing. At times, however, certain marks are optional, depending on the writer's particular attitude toward what he or she is saying and on decisions of publishers. On the whole, nevertheless, college students can have success if they follow codified usage. When in genuine doubt, resort to common sense.

Punctuation, then, is not simply a series of rules: *it offers one more way of clarifying expression*. Even in the many situations where one has a choice – for example, to include a comma or leave it out – one's choice need not be arbitrary. The rhythm of one's prose style will be very largely controlled by the use or omission of punctuation marks where no rule clearly applies.

§ 12. End Punctuation

THE PERIOD

12a. **A period is used after a declarative or imperative sentence, or after an indirect question, but not after a direct question.**

12

Examples

I had no idea where I had been or how I got there. [Declarative]

Always know where you are. [Imperative]

The legislature asked how the firm spent the money. [Indirect question]

The legislature asked, "How have funds been dispersed?" [Direct question, ending with a question mark]

Note the difference, in the last two examples, in the way the human voice is used. At the end of the indirect question there is a drop in voice level characteristic of all declarative sentences. But a rise in pitch at the end of a sentence – How have the funds been dispersed? – is usually a sign of a question, to be symbolized by a question mark.

12b. **Most of the common abbreviations require a period.**

Examples

Mr., Mrs., Ms., Dr., St., Jr., a.m., B.C., P.E.I.

Increasingly, the period is not used with certain groups of letters or acronyms standing for organizations or government agencies. Note that the letters are written without spacing.

Examples

UN, USSR, TVO, CRTC, CUPE, RCMP.

Usage is divided in regard to some of the older abbreviations consisting of the initial letters of words, though the tendency is toward omitting the period. Consult your dictionary when in doubt.

Examples

Y.M.C.A. *or* YMCA; r.p.m. *or* rpm

12c. **Spaced periods (ellipsis marks or suspension points, usually three within a sentence, four at the end of a declarative sentence to include the necessary closing period) are used to indicate the omission of words from a quoted passage, or pauses or hesitation in dialogue.**

Example

The present order is marked by glaring inequalities of wealth and opportunity. . . . Power has become more and more concentrated into the hands of a small irresponsible minority of financiers and industrialists. . . . Our society oscillates between periods of feverish prosperity . . . and of catastrophic depression . . . these evils can be removed only in a planned and socialized economy . . . .

–Regina Manifesto of the CCF

THE QUESTION MARK

12d. **A question mark is used after a direct question but not after an indirect question.**

Note the distinction in voice level discussed under § 12a. Most of our problems in using the *question mark* are mechanical ones, involving other punctuation surrounding the mark in special cases.

Examples

What if I'm wrong? was the question Lawrence asked himself as his pencil put deep lines into the manuscript. [A question mark is used at the end of an interrogative part of a sentence.]

Who was it who said, "If you can't beat 'em in the alley, you can't beat 'em on the ice"? [The question mark is placed inside quotation marks only when it is part of the quoted material.]

As she stood knee-deep in mud, she remembered her mother's dying words, "Where is the light?" [A question mark ends the sentence if the last part is a quoted question.]

12

A single question mark is used after a double question – that is, a quoted question following a question. (See also § 16.)

Example

Who wrote "Where have all the aardvarks gone?"

A question mark within parentheses may be used to indicate doubt or uncertainty about the preceding figure or fact. This is a conventional practice in the case of a doubtful birth or death date.

Example

Lucien Botha was born in 1779(?) and died in 1859.

The use of a parenthetical question mark to indicate irony is the mark only of immature writing.

Poor

We had a great(?) time at that party.

A question mark is often used after commands or requests phrased as questions if a formal effect is desired, but a period is used for a less formal effect. A convenient test, once again, is to read the sentence aloud, checking for the rise in pitch characteristic of the last syllable of a question.

Formal
May I ask the entire pitching staff to reassemble here at four o'clock?

Less Formal
Will all the hurlers meet here again at four o'clock, please.

THE EXCLAMATION POINT

12e.   An exclamation point is usually used after an expression that indicates strong feeling or emotion.

The student's temptation often is to overuse the *exclamation point*, creating a breathless or overexcited style not unlike that produced by an overuse of italics. (See § 10d.)

Examples

"Good Lord!" he gasped in amazement.

It is difficult to see how anyone in their right mind could have concluded *that!*

Oh, this is unforgiveable!

The hours dragged on at a turtle's pace. He had read every *Maclean's* in the waiting room. This was the last time he would come to this doctor! What a way to treat a loyal dog lover!

EXERCISE

EXERCISE, END PUNCTUATION IN DIALOGUE. *In the following dialogue, supply commas, periods, question marks, and exclamation points where they are necessary. Be careful to place punctuation correctly in relation to quotation marks.*

1. "Did you know the ending would turn out that way" asked Dr Fisher

2. "No I didn't" she replied

3. The doctor asked her what other movies she had seen lately

4. "Oh not many" she said "Have you seen anything like this before"
5. "What makes you ask that" he replied
6. "Do you know who said 'Movies are getting better' " she asked
7. "Who was it that used to ask 'Why not try a good movie tonight' "
8. "Watch out" he shouted suddenly as they attempted to cross the street in front of the theatre
9. "Wasn't that Mr Wells in his MG Wow That was too close for comfort"
10. "I wonder" he observed "when the streets will ever be safe for pedestrians"

13

§ 13. The Comma

Of all the marks of punctuation, the *comma* has the widest variety of uses. Probably because the comma is used in so many situations, any attempt to codify the practice of writers and to state usage in terms of definite principles must give due weight to the exceptions. Yet, however important the differences of practice are, to the student the most important thing is that there is such a large area of agreement. Most of the uses of the comma can be stated in terms of principles that reflect what most writers are doing.

The student should always remember, however, that these descriptions of usage must be interpreted with a little common sense. It is true, for instance, that writers place a comma after an introductory clause or phrase if they feel that this sentence element is not an integral part of the main clause – that is, if it is not closely restrictive – but no rule, only common sense, can tell a student when this clause is restrictive or non-restrictive.

Generally, punctuation tends to be *close* (that is, with a liberal use of commas) in serious or formal writing, where precision is vital. It tends to be *open* (that is, using a minimum of punctuation) in informal description and narration and in journalistic writing.

Although the primary function of punctuation is to help make meaning clear, punctuation has another function, a rhetorical one. The comma – and to a certain extent the semicolon – may be used to indicate the degree of pause or emphasis or rhetorical balance or contrast of ideas. The important fact still remains, however, that before a writer can make punctuation a stylistic resource he or she must first become familiar with the general practice of writers.

Because of its wide variety of uses, the comma may appear to some a subject of puzzling complexity, although at times it is hard to see why young people, who speak familiarly of isotopes and learn to operate computers, should be bowled over by so simple a thing as a comma. At any rate, it is possible to simplify a simple subject further by dividing all comma uses into two groups. In one group we have the *to separate* uses; in the other group we have the *to enclose* uses.

A TABLE OF COMMA USES

Usually to Separate	Usually to Enclose
13a. main clauses	13h. non-restrictive clauses
13b. elements in series	13i. parenthetical elements
13c. co-ordinate adjectives	13j. absolute phrases
13d. words that may be misread	13k. appositives
13e. introductory modifiers	13l. words in direct address
13f. transposed elements	13m. dialogue guides
13g. mild exclamations, etc.	13n. dates and addresses

13a.   A comma is ordinarily used to separate co-ordinate clauses joined by *and, but, for, or, nor,* except when the clauses are short and closely related in meaning.

A writer is safe to apply this rule rather strictly in formal writing. At the same time it must be acknowledged that the use of a comma to separate main clauses has become almost optional. Journalistic writing discards the comma in this situation except to prevent misreading. At the formal level, the general practice is to omit the comma when the subject of the sentence does not change after the first clause. If there is any other clearly defined practice to help the beginning student, it is that the comma is obligatory before *for* (to prevent confusion with the preposition *for*) and recommended before *but*.

> Since 1867, successive Canadian governments have tried to solve the problem of French- and English-Canadian relations, and in 1984 the problem remains unsolved. [comma before *and*]

> The difficulties of adolescence are essentially one, for they all have at their core the longing to find meaning in life. [Comma before *for*]

> The brilliance of a nova at its peak is usually not sufficient to make it visible to the naked eye, but supernovae surpass in brilliance the brightest of ordinary stars and some of them can be observed in full daylight. [Note that no comma is used before *and* because the subjects of the last two clauses are felt to be closely related.]

13b. Commas are used to separate words, phrases, or clauses in a series.

A *series* must have at least three members; usually the last is joined to the other by *and* or *or*. It is at this point, the point of the conjunction, that usage differs. Although the comma is generally used, some writers do omit it.

> People today are so insecure that their aspirations are to find a secure job, buy a house, and have a good pension plan – all before they're thirty! [Series of predicates]

> The crunch of skates on the ice, the terse shouts of the players, the echo of the puck bouncing off the boards, and the dying and rising roar of the crowd brought back Marcel's happy memories of boyhood visits to the Forum on Saturday nights. [Series of nouns]

13c.   Commas are used to separate consecutive adjectives preceding the noun they modify when the adjectives are co-ordinate in meaning.

The comma is correct only when the adjectives are *co-ordinate* – that is, when each of the adjectives refers directly and independently to the same noun. When an adjective modifies the whole idea that follows it, it is not separated by a comma. If you can substitute *and* for the comma, the comma is correct. Note in the following examples that *and* would be a natural substitute for each comma used:

> with slow, powerful strokes . . . these cold, treeless heights . . . the still, dimly lighted street . . . this bold, gleaming structure . . . his exuberant, energetic brother . . . their dull, inglorious lives . . . the muddy, tired, discouraged soldiers

A safe practice is to omit the comma with numerals and with the common adjectives of size and age:

> the little old lady from Pasadena . . . a tired old senior citizen . . . the spreading chestnut tree . . . a large red-haired woman . . . four tiny black dots

More generally, a comma should not be used when one of two adjectives associated with a noun modifies the other adjective or the other adjective and the noun together.

Examples
Ground roast coffee . . . dark brown earth . . . pure spring water . . .

13d.   The comma is used to separate words and phrases that might be incorrectly joined in reading.

This rule applies to the following situations:

1. When the conjunctions *for* and *but* might be mistaken for prepositions.

> The performer waited in anxious silence, for the messenger

seemed to be in a desperate hurry. [Waited in anxious silence for the messenger?]

All hands slid down the ropes, but one sailor seemed to be caught in the rigging. [All slid down the ropes but one sailor?]

2. When a noun might be mistaken for the object of a verb, verbal, or preposition that precedes it.

After washing, the doctors filed into the dining tent. [*Not* After washing the doctors]

Before starting to eat, the chaplain bowed his head in prayer. [*Not* Before starting to eat the chaplain]

Above, the sun burned a dull red; below, the sand radiated heat like a furnace. [*Not* Above the sun . . . below the sand]

When we left, the Bickersons were still playing their endless game of pinochle. [*Not* When we left the Bickersons]

13e. Ordinarily, a comma is used to set off a modifier that precedes a main clause, especially when the introductory element is long and not closely connected with the main clause in meaning, and when it is not *restrictive*.

In punctuating modifiers that precede the main clause you should depend on your good sense as well as on rules. You should decide whether or not the sentence will be clearer with the introductory modifier set off by a comma. The length of clause alone will not prescribe when to use a comma and when not to use it. Frequently very short clauses are set off for emphasis. In general, if the introductory element is not clearly restrictive, put a comma after it. The following distinctions will help you:

1. Use a comma when you begin with a fairly long (usually over five words) non-restrictive adverbial clause:

When it came time to pack up the weapons, we discovered that one of the grenades was missing.

Because the car's wheels should touch the pavement, your Jaguar should not be pushed over 180 kilometres per hour.

If we are not six feet tall, we can at least console ourselves with the knowledge that we are not three feet tall.

2. Use a comma to set off an introductory participial phrase modifying the subject or an introductory *absolute phrase* (see "Parts of Speech," page 99):

Having paid in full his debt to society, the ex-convict was bitter at not being able to get a job.

The fire being over, the students returned to the classroom. [Absolute phrase]

3. Set off short introductory prepositional phrases only when they are definitely non-restrictive, such as *transitional phrases* (see "Parts of Speech," page 97).

No Comma

Up to this point we are on safe ground.

During the ceremony a dog strayed into the room.

In the spring the ground is covered with poppies and beer cans.

Comma Used

In addition, such experiences are educational.

Of the small islands, the nearest is heavily populated.

In the first place, his idea for dog galoshes is not new.

Long introductory prepositional phrases may be set off if the writer believes that a comma is an aid to clearness:

After being made an Officer of the Order of Canada in 1973, Christopher Pratt was elevated to the higher rank of Companion in 1983.

4. A short introductory clause is usually not followed by a comma. It may, however, be set off for greater emphasis or for clearness.

When he gives us a test he usually leaves the room. [Informal]
If the deputy comes I will tell him to look for you in the shop.
[Informal]

13f. **A comma, or commas, may be used to indicate transposed or contrasting sentence elements.**

Examples

A boy, thin, ragged, and very frightened, had wedged himself behind the grate. [*Note:* A, thin, ragged, and very frightened boy had. . .]

Inequality, by arousing jealousy and envy, provokes discontent.
[*Not transposed:* Inequality provokes discontent by arousing jealousy and envy.]

She insisted on blue, rather than white, gowns and tuxedoes.
[Contrasting sentence elements]

13

13g. **Commas are used to set off mild exclamations, sentence adverbs (i.e., which modify the entire sentence), and the responsives *yes* and *no* when they begin a sentence.**

Examples

Yes, she assigned another essay for Friday.

Evidently, you will not have the paper ready for her.

Unfortunately, I will have to stay up all night to write it.

Mary said, ''Well, what excuse can I give her?''

Oh, you will think of something to say before Friday.

13h. **Commas are used to set off non–restrictive clauses. They are not used to set off restrictive clauses.**

If the distinction between restrictive and non-restrictive clauses is not already clear to you, think of restrictive clauses as ''identifying'' or ''pointing-out'' clauses. A restrictive clause helps to locate or identify its antecedent. It says to the reader, ''I mean this particular person or object, and no other.'' It is close to its antecedent in meaning, so close that it cannot be separated from it by a comma. A non-restrictive clause does not point out or identify; it merely gives additional information about its antecedent.

Restrictive Clauses

The board decided in favour of another candidate *who has had more experience*. [Not just another candidate, but one with more experience]

The teenager *who has a hobby* will never be lonely. [Not any teenager, but that particular kind of teenager]

Please bring me the book *that you see lying on the table.* [That particular book and no other]

Non-restrictive clauses

The board decided in favour of Ms. Rossi, *who has had more experience.* [The name identifies the person; the clause does not need to identify or point out.]

Terry Fisher, *who has a hobby*, will never be lonely. [The name identifies him.]

Please bring me David Richards's *Lives of Short Duration, which you see lying on the table.* [The title identifies the book.]

Astronomy, *which is the study of heavenly bodies*, is a fascinating subject. [*Astronomy* identifies itself. It does not need a clause to tell which particular astronomy.]

My father, *who had not heard the question*, shook his head in silence. [A person has only one father. The clause cannot help identify him.]

Participial phrases may be either restrictive or non-restrictive, depending on the meaning intended.

Restrictive

The young woman *standing near the door* is waiting to register. [That particular young woman]

13

A book *written by that author* is bound to be interesting. [Phrase points to a particular kind of book – one written by that author.]

Non-restrictive

Honor Miller, standing there by the door, is waiting to register. [Name identifies her.]

Raising his rifle quickly, he fired at the moving object. [Nothing in the phrase helps to identify the person.]

13i. **Commas are used to set off parenthetical elements (interrupters), or words, phrases, and clauses used to explain, to qualify, or to emphasize.**

In a sense, several of the sentence elements discussed under other rules are "interrupters" in that they tend to break or interrupt the normal flow of a sentence, but strict classification is not here important. The parenthetical elements dealt with here may be classified as follows:

1. Conjunctive adverbs, such as *however, therefore, moreover, furthermore*, when they are used within the clause. In any style, an epidemic of *moreover*'s and *furthermore*'s is as bad as a plague of *and*'s and *but*'s.

Examples

An institution, *therefore*, may fail because its standards are too high.

In truth, *however*, it was probably not known until after the bodies were discovered.

Do not use a conjunctive adverb to force a connection. "She ate too many hot dogs; consequently, she was sick" is nauseous in more ways than one.

2. Directive and qualifying words and phrases. Some of the most common of these, such as *also, perhaps, indeed, too, at least*, may, in informal writing, be considered as close modifiers and therefore not set off by commas. Others are usually set off.

Examples

All of this, *of course*, is theory.

Her theory, *unluckily*, was disproved by the events that followed.

He would become, *in short*, a delinquent of the worst kind.

3. Parenthetical phrases and clauses. Most of these are parenthetical comments, but some are adverbial clauses that interrupt the sentence flow.

Examples

This, *I suppose*, is the essence of juggling.

Our interpretation of his motives is, *I think*, totally unfair.

If you must take risks on the lake, see to it that, *whenever storm warnings are up*, you at least have a life preserver on the boat.

It should be noted here that three types of punctuation are used with parenthetical elements. Parentheses are used for the most distant, dashes for something a little less distant, and commas for interrupters most closely related to the rest of the sentence. For a further discussion see §§ 17 and 18.

Examples

The *Star Wars* cast *(a strange collection of men, women, and machines)* has managed to hold together through many films without appearing to age.

It isn't that the scene offends him, but he feels that he – *the shark's main course* – should have something to say about how the sequence is shot.

In painting, *especially modern painting*, it is sometimes difficult to distinguish between the Norse helmet and the woman's form.

13j. Commas are used to set off absolute phrases when they occur within the sentence.

Example

She stood there, *her damp face glowing with happiness*, and asked us all to be seated.

13k. Commas are used to set off appositives.

An *appositive*, or a word in apposition, is used to limit or qualify the meaning of another word, to stand for it, to add to its meaning, or to emphasize it. The name *appositive* refers to the fact that a word and its appositive stand side by side. Most appositives – with the exception of some types listed below – are to be set off by commas.

Examples

Stan Perkins, the *foreman* of the plant, was hurt yesterday. [Appositive with modifiers]

Other animals, such as the giraffe, camel, and brown bear, use a different type of locomotion. [Appositive introduced by *such as*]

As he skated past the blueline one final opponent, *a big, burly defenceman*, *a mean-looking man*, stood between him and the net.

Welles, a *director of considerable merit*, had to borrow large sums of money in order to transform *Othello*, *full of special scenery and lighting effects*, into a film with nightmarelike dimensions.

But do *not* use commas with many common expressions in which the appositive and its substantive are so close that they are felt as a unit:

Jack the Ripper, Jack the Giant-killer, Henry the Eighth, my son Harold, William the Conqueror, the word *appositive*, the novelist Atwood.

Participles and occasionally adjectives may be placed for greater emphasis or for variety after the words they modify. When so placed they are said to be in the appositive position and are therefore set off by commas. See also § 13f.

Examples

During a pause in the game, one of the fans, *devotedly cynical*, shouted mock encouragement at the pitcher.

A sound, *loud and high-pitched like a jet engine's scream*, escaped from her throat.

The shot, *slow and tantalizing*, was typical of Lafleur's shooting style, *the mark of a seasoned, devious veteran*. [Adjectives in the appositive position and then a substantive appositive]

13

Appositives may also be enclosed in parentheses or set off by dashes to indicate a greater degree of separation, if such distinction is desired. (See §§ 17 and 18.) Sometimes dashes are used because of the presence of several commas.

Example

After every significant wave of repression – Hungary in 1956, Czechoslovakia in 1968, Chile in 1973, Vietnam in 1980 – Canada has benefited from the vitality and creative energy of political refugees.

Appositives are sometimes introduced by such words as *that is*, *namely*, *such as*, *for instance*, *for example*, and the like. In long, formal sentences these words may be preceded by a colon or a semicolon. In ordinary writing, both formal and informal, *namely*, *that is*, *for example*, and *for instance* are usually preceded and followed by commas. *Such as* is not followed by a comma.

Examples

Short prepositions, such as *in*, *on*, *to*, *for*, are not capitalized in titles.

We know that white light – light from the sun, for example – is really a mixture of light of all colours.

There is only one proper thing for a driver to do when the car dies, namely, put up the hood and take a nap.

13 l. Commas are used to set off substantives used in direct address.

Examples

Professor Holmes, your lectures are a constant delight to your class. [To begin a sentence]

Read the poem, *Mr. Taylor*, and tell me if it means anything to you. [Within the sentence]

"Please change places with me, *Helen*," I asked. [With quotation marks]

13m. An explanatory clause such as *he said* (a dialogue guide), when it interrupts a sentence of dialogue, is set off by commas.

13

Examples

"For your next project," said the instructor, "you will write an essay about the Blarney Stone."

Sean McCarthy raised his hand and said, "Did you know that Cormack McCarthy, one of my ancestors, built Blarney Castle in 1602?" [Dialogue guide begins sentence]

"Most tourists," explained Eric Swensen, "do not know that the real Blarney Stone is impossible for them to reach."

"They are allowed to kiss a substitute stone," he added. "It works just as well." [Dialogue guide at end of one sentence and before the second sentence]

Also see § 16 for placing of quotation marks in relation to commas.

13n. Commas are used to separate elements in dates and addresses that might otherwise be confused.

Examples

Ms. Janice Irons, 27463 Rockland Road, St. John, New Brunswick E2J 2N9

Mr. L.P. Friend, 6423 Jade Avenue, Nanaimo,
British Columbia V9T 2R1

March 17, 1981 [The comma is necessary only to separate 17
from 1981. If the date is written European style, 17 March 1981,
there is no need for a comma; nor is there in the absence of the
day of the month, March 1981. A comma should be used after the
full citation of month, day, and year: "On March 17, 1981, the last
prisoners. . . ."]

William Shakespeare was born on April 23, 1564, in
Stratford-upon-Avon, England.

Caution

13

No comma is needed following the year if only that date is
cited: "He was married in 1582 to Anne Hathaway."

EXERCISES

EXERCISE 1, NON-RESTRICTIVE CLAUSES. *Punctuate each
non-restrictive clause in the following sentences.*

1. I remembered that this was the day when every student was to
   be prepared for the worst.
2. Every year we have a homecoming day when everybody tries to
   impress parents and other visitors.
3. I awakened Toby Blair who was my roommate so that he would
   have time to dress more formally.
4. His everyday outfit which consists of jeans and a sweater seemed
   hardly appropriate.
5. His father and mother of whom he was very proud were coming
   to visit us.
6. We found them a room at the Green Mountain Inn where most
   of the alumni liked to stay.
7. I did not think that my parents who were vacationing in Mexico
   would come for the reunion.
8. I am happy to have a roommate whose parents adopt me on
   occasion.

9. I know a student who gets letters and cheques from two sets of parents.
10. This weekend which we spent with Toby's parents was a happy one.

EXERCISE 2, USING COMMAS AND SEMICOLONS. *Punctuate each of the following sentences. Decide whether to use a comma, a semi-colon, or no mark at all. Be able to justify your decision.*

1. I have considered going into social work but my mother has tried to discourage me.
2. My mother is a practical person and she thinks that I am too young to know my mind.
3. I know something about the work for I have studied sociology and made trips to the provincial institutions.
4. During the summer I worked in the Red Cross office and I enjoyed the work.
5. A friend of mine is a social worker and I have occasionally gone with her on her trips.
6. Her work is very interesting for it introduces her to all sorts of people.
7. She visits poor and hungry families but she does not actually take them baskets of food.
8. Sometimes she comes home very angry for she has no patience with drunken spouses.
9. She makes a careful study of each case and then she recommends the most suitable kind of assistance.
10. At times the Red Cross gives immediate help and then the happiness of the needy family is a welcome reward to the case worker.

13

EXERCISE 3, WORDS IN SERIES. *In the following sentences insert commas where they are necessary.*

1. W.O. Mitchell was born on March 13 1914 in Weyburn Saskatchewan.
2. After three years at college he took a disastrous trip to Europe: he was robbed two hours after docking in London arrested in

Paris for running over a policeman and then himself run over by a streetcar in Soissons.

3. As a young man he held a variety of odd jobs including high diver at a carnival seller of classified ads and door-to-door encyclopaedia salesman.

4. His humour irreverence and affection for ordinary people are apparent in his Jake and the Kid stories.

5. These stories were so popular that they appeared individually in *Maclean's* magazine were dramatized on the CBC and some of the best ones were collected in a book that won the Leacock award for humour in 1962.

6. From his boyhood in Saskatchewan he found the raw material for such characters as Jake Trumper Colonel Hepworth and Old Man MacLachlin.

7. *Jake and the Kid Who Has Seen the Wind* and his most recent novel *How I Spent my Summer Holidays* are probably W.O. Mitchell's best-known and best books.

8. Although *Who Has Seen the Wind* is the best-selling novel in Canadian history W.O. Mitchell still must rely on teaching the lecture circuit and writing stage plays to make a living.

9. With his long unkempt hair his bushy eyebrows and mustache and his folksy philosopher image Mitchell reminds many people of the American writer Mark Twain.

10. In 1973 he was awarded two honorary doctorates in literature was made an Officer of the Order of Canada and had *The Vanishing Point* published.

EXERCISE 4, INTRODUCTORY ELEMENTS. *In each of the following sentences decide whether the introductory phrase or clause is to be followed by a comma or not.*

1. If a blind poet had not written a long poem about it few modern readers would have heard about the Trojan War.

2. Because the wife of a Spartan king ran off with a young Trojan many warriors perished before the walls of Troy.

3. Although the Homeric account may be the romantic version of the story the real cause of the war may have been political and economic rivalry.
4. After the sudden elopement of Helen and Paris the friends of King Menelaus of Sparta assembled to avenge the insult.
5. Having discovered a just cause to do what they liked to do even without cause the Greek heroes assembled at Aulis for the expedition.
6. Excited by hopes of an easy victory and thoughts of rich plunder the avengers gathered 100 000 men and 1 186 ships.
7. Unlike modern wars in which everybody loses ancient wars could often be profitable to the victors.
8. Ten long years having been wasted before the walls of Troy both sides were willing to try any stratagem to win or call the war off.
9. Deciding to put their faith in trickery instead of bravery the Greeks built a large hollow horse and pretended that it was an offering to their gods.
10. Convinced by a Greek spy that the horse would make them invincible the Trojans dragged it into the city and with it enough armed Greeks to open the gates of the city to the invaders.

13

EXERCISE 5, DATES AND ADDRESSES. *Copy the following sentences. Insert commas where they are needed.*

1. Our friends used to live at 28 Dunlop Street Stewarton Nova Scotia but they recently moved to 31 Armour Place New Dundee Ontario.
2. John A. Macdonald was born in Glasgow Scotland in 1815 and died in Ottawa Canada on June 6 1891.
3. Malcom Lowry was born in Merseyside England on July 28 1909 but lived in Dollarton British Columbia from 1940 until 1954.
4. Mary's new address is 12 Whiteford Avenue Toronto Ontario M6G 2H9.

5. All questions should be addressed to 1250 Gervais Drive North Hamilton Ontario L6A 2W3.

EXERCISE 6, COMMAS AND RULES. *Copy the following sentences. Supply every missing comma and tell what rule of usage applies.*

1. If you have never heard of Milton Acorn you have missed knowing about one of Canada's most unusual poets.
2. Milton Acorn was born in 1923 in Charlottetown and although his career as a poet began in Montreal he is still closely associated with Prince Edward Island.
3. A carpenter by trade he decided to take up the literary trade of poetry and so one day he simply sold his carpentry tools and began to make his living from his pen.
4. He has defined himself as a revolutionary poet – in the political not the poetic sense – and at one time or another he has been a member of almost every left-wing group in Canada.
5. He is passionately concerned with the oppression of working people socialism Canadian nationalism and poetry.
6. In 1975 he won the Governor General's Award for poetry for his book *The Island Means Minago* a collection of poems about P.E.I.
7. In 1970 he did not win the Governor General's Award and his fellow poets incensed at what they considered a terrible injustice presented him with an anti-Governor General's Award the Canadian Poetry Award and named him the People's Poet.
8. For many years Milton Acorn lived in a small room in the Waverly Hotel which is located in a run-down section of Toronto.
9. Even physically – with his unkempt hair plaid shirt old trousers and sneakers – Milton Acorn looked the cantankerous outsider.
10. In 1982 after five years of silence and many more years of personal turmoil he published *Captain Neal MacDougal & The Naked Goddess* a collection that some have said is the best work he has ever done.

EXERCISE 7, ALL USES OF THE COMMA. *Punctuate the following sentences. Tell what rule or principle of usage applies to each comma that you use.*

1. At the desk sat a slender red-haired woman who gave us more cards to fill out.
2. As we watched the woman reached for the telephone dialed the number and asked for somebody named Monty.
3. Her soft pleading voice dripping with honey she spoke words that would have melted a traffic constable's heart.
4. My companion Paul Biggs a graduate of U.B.C. knew her for they had worked at the same summer resort in Quebec.
5. Quebec with hills lakes and rolling rocky scenery is a popular vacation spot.
6. As he confided to me in whispers they had picnicked swum hiked and ridden horseback together over the famous Long Trail but their bridle paths as he said never became a bridal path to the altar.
7. Monty an elusive sort of character if we might judge from the overheard conversation finally agreed to some tentative arrangement.
8. The crisis having been postponed for the time the woman turned her attention to us and to her work.
9. She accepted our cards and with a fluttery momentary smile tossed them into a box.
10. "If you should ask me which I hope you don't" said Paul "I would tell you that our applications will never reach the manager."

13

§ 14. The Semicolon

14a. **A semicolon is used between the main clauses of a**
compound sentence when they are not joined by one
of the co-ordinating conjunctions.

In weight, or length of pause, a *semicolon* is more than a comma
and less than a period. The period separates sentences. The semicolon separates main clauses within a sentence. Its frequent use
marks a dignified formal style, implying relatively long, balanced sentences, and for this reason an abundance of semicolons in an informal paper should be viewed with suspicion. On
the other hand, the semicolon provides an excellent substitute
for weak conjunctions between co-ordinate clauses, and it can
often strengthen structures that are clearly parallel. It is in general an important device in developing a firm, economical style.

Ordinarily a semicolon should not be used to cut off a phrase or a
dependent clause from the main clause.

Examples of Incorrect Use

In these days, as writing grows increasingly brisk if not openly
journalistic; one sometimes wonders what has happened to
the good old semicolon.

She was habitually critical of me; because my manners, she
said, were like those of the inhabitants of a zoo.

Notice, however, that substituting the semicolon for the subordinating conjunction, when the relationship between the clauses
is implicit, can give a stylistic advantage.

Examples

She was habitually critical of me; my manners, she said, were
like those of the inhabitants of a zoo.

The vastness of the country has had a powerful effect on the
Canadian character; our much-deplored timidity may simply
be a subconscious response to the overwhelming size of the
land.

Rich people are not always happy; wealth brings as many problems as pleasures.

No author is solely responsible for the contents of a book; many unheralded people put a great deal of their time and talent into the successful completion of a publishing project.

When a pitcher sees a batter at the plate he thinks of a strike-out; when a batter sees a pitcher on the mound he thinks of a home run; when a umpire sees them both he thinks of trouble.

Often the verb in the second or third clause may be unstated, but understood to be the same as the verb in the first clause.

Example

Westerners dismiss the federal government by calling it Eastern-controlled; the Quebecois by calling it English-controlled; and the rest of Canada by calling it bureaucrat-controlled.

14

14b. **A semicolon is used between the co-ordinate clauses of a compound sentence with one of the following conjunctive adverbs:** *therefore, however, hence, accordingly, furthermore, nevertheless,* **and** *consequently.*

In modern prose, however, it is more common to find the conjunctive adverb placed within the second or third clause and enclosed in commas than to meet it as a conjunction at the beginning of its clause.

Examples

He had worked in the foreign service for two years without leave; hence he was tired and frightened almost beyond endurance.

He had worked in the foreign service for two years without leave; he was, consequently, tired and frightened almost beyond endurance.

From a running start Lance launched his body into a vigorous racing dive; however, he was about thirty feet from the pool at the time.

14c. **A semicolon is used in place of a comma when a more distinct pause than the comma would give is desirable.**

14d. **Semicolons are used to separate series when members of the series have internal commas.**

Example

Two new features of the PG2732 are its information-gathering capabilities, now standard in most comparable machines; and its self-starting component, an addition that makes the PG2732 unique in the field.

14

You may sometimes find published writers using the semicolon in ways that violate Rule 14a above. Although such exceptions do exist, they should not give you justification for adopting them in classroom work. Follow the rules outlined here as closely as possible.

EXERCISE

COMMAS VERSUS SEMICOLONS. *In the following sentences, determine appropriate punctuation to be used in the places marked by brackets. Would you use commas, semicolons, or no punctuation at all?*

1. His hair was white and stood up wildly on his head [ ] nevertheless I was struck by a singular neatness in his appearance.
2. It was due, I suppose [ ] to his lofty stature and immaculate dress [ ] no doubt he has a careful attendant looking after him.
3. Like all distinguished men in political life [ ] he spoke with assurance, even with arrogance [ ] yet I could not help sensing some anxiety in his behaviour.
4. I walked up to him then [ ] and held out my hand [ ] but he evidently failed to recognize me.
5. When a man has the weight of nations on his shoulders [ ] he may be forgiven for overlooking individuals [ ] but I admit I was angry.

6. It is one thing to be dignified and detached [] it is quite another to be downright rude.
7. I had arrived early [] as was my habit [] I therefore felt privileged to depart without delay.
8. The affair was not the worst I have ever endured [] but it was nearly so [] at such times one wishes one could escape at any cost.
9. Once I had arrived at the entrance [] however [] there was no turning back.
10. When I go to a place like that [] I go gladly [] when I return [] I come home even more gladly.

§ 15. The Apostrophe

15

15a. **An apostrophe and -*s* are used to form the possessive of a noun, singular or plural, that does not end in -*s*.**

Examples

A man's will, women's rights, children's toys, a dog's life, the sun's rays, the earth's surface, Irene's husband, my mother-in-law's views.

When two or more names joined by *and* are represented as joint owners of something, in ordinary usage the last name alone takes the apostrophe.

Examples

Meier and Frank's store, Swenson and Carmody's Machine Shop, Nancy and Sally's mother, Larson, Jones, and Marshall's antique shop, Jon and Lorna's affairs.

But when separate ownership is meant, the apostrophe follows each noun. Of course, when both nouns and pronouns are used, the pronouns take the possessive-case form.

Examples

Nancy's and Sally's clothes are strewn all over the bedroom.

Mr. Marshall's and Captain Ford's egos were badly damaged in the collision.

Mr. Danby said that his, his wife's and his daughter's possessions were saved before the ship sank.

15b.   The apostrophe alone is used to form the possessive of a plural noun ending in -s.

Examples

Workers' rights, three months' wastes, students' diseases, the Smiths' house, foxes' tails.

15c.   The apostrophe with -s is used to form the possessive of singular nouns ending in -s, if the resultant form is not unpleasant or difficult to pronounce.

Examples

James's cycle, Keats's poems, Jones's office; *but*: for goodness' sake, for conscience' sake, Demosthenes' orations.

15d.   An apostrophe with -s is used to form the possessive of certain indefinite pronouns.

Examples

Anybody's game, somebody's hat, everybody's business, one's ideas, somebody's coat, another's turn.

The apostrophe should not be used with personal pronouns to form the possessive. See §4c, ''Pronouns.''

Examples

If this coat isn't yours [not *your's*], it's probably hers [not *her's*].

The decision is ours [not *our's*].

The two dogs are theirs [not *their's*].

It's only a puppy; its [not *it's*] bark is worse than its [not *it's*] bite.

15e. An apostrophe is used to indicate the omission of letters or figures.

Examples
Hasn't, doesn't, weren't, o'clock, it's [it is], I'll, class of '84.

15f. An apostrophe and -*s* are used to form the plurals of figures, letters, and words referred to as words.

Examples
You have not dotted your *i*'s or crossed your *t*'s.

Your *m*'s, *n*'s and *u*'s look alike.

He used too many *and*'s and *but*'s in his paper.

Be careful not to make your *3*'s look like *8*'s.

His jeans are more appropriate for the 60's than the 80's. [In formal writing, decade references should be written out: sixties, eighties.]

Note that only the figures, letters, and words are set in italics. The *'s* are set in roman type. Some publications omit the apostrophe in these situations, but there may be confusion in a sentence like this: In his handwriting the *i*s and *u*s are but a wavy line.

15g. The apostrophe is often omitted in names of organizations, associations, buildings, etc.

Examples
The Authors League, Farmers Market, Ontario Teachers College, Mathematics Teachers Association, St. Elizabeths Hospital.

EXERCISES

EXERCISE 1, USE OF THE APOSTROPHE. *Copy the following sentences. Insert an apostrophe wherever it is correct.*

1. "Its almost ten oclock," said Toms cousin, "and hes not in sight yet."

2. "I wouldn't worry," replied Maries mother. "Theyre very busy now at Smith and Elberlys Department Store this season."

3. "Were hungry, Mom," said little Edie. "Arent you going to make us a sandwich?"

4. "Mind your *p*s and *q*s, young lady, and youll earn your *A*s and *B*s," remarked Marie apropos of nothing.

5. "If Dads not here pretty soon," said Tom, "hell be here in time for tomorrows breakfast."

6. "Its all in the days work. Once he took the Smiths ocelot to the doctors and decided to sit up all night with it," said Marie.

7. "Youre joking, of course," replied Tom. "You know that its leg was broken."

8. "Well, for heavens sake," exclaimed Maries mother, "it was somebody's responsibility, wasnt it?"

9. "Mother, did you say 'for Keats sakes' or 'for Keatss sakes'?" asked Marie. "Theres a fine difference, you know."

10. "I think everybody's so hungry theyre getting silly," said Tom. "Whos going to make some hamburgers for us?"

15

EXERCISE 2, POSSESSIVE FORMS. *Write the possessive singular and the possessive plural of each of the following. Example:* child, child's, children's.

1. boy	11. attorney
2. baby	12. fox
3. Smith	13. wolf
4. mother-in-law	14. Powers
5. he	15. wife
6. goose	16. Berry
7. it	17. writer
8. woman	18. she
9. Williams	19. sailor
10. Allen	20. kangaroo

§ 16. Quotation Marks

16a. **Double quotation marks are used to enclose a direct quotation in dialogue and in reproducing short passages from other writers.**

Examples of Dialogue

Talking quietly as they left the concert hall, the two couples were discussing the difference between modern dance and ballet.

"That concert was a good example of why I prefer modern dance to ballet," said Charles.

"What do you mean?" asked Kate.

"They danced about important things, about things that mean something, not about frivolous things like nutcrackers or swans," he replied.

"Yes," said Frances, "but modern dance has no sense of humour and takes itself far too seriously. Ballet has a better sense of fun."

"Ballet is for rich people and modern dance is for everyone," offered Hari.

"Well, I disagree," countered Frances. "I like ballet and I'm not rich."

Note that in dialogue a new paragraph is used with every change in speaker.

The writer must be careful not to leave out one set of quotation marks. Quotation marks come in pairs, one set at the beginning and one set at the end of every quoted part.

Wrong

"I have never really liked potted beef, said King Henry. It frequently gives me heartburn."

Right

"I have never really liked potted beef," said King Henry. "It frequently gives me heartburn."

A familiar error in citing passages from others is to begin a quotation that never ends. By failing to close the quotation with the appropriate second set of marks, the passage from the quoted author and the comment by the quoting writer can become thoroughly confused.

Wrong
King Henry once observed, ''I have never really liked potted beef. It frequently gives me heartburn. This remark has often been misquoted.

If a quotation consists of several sentences, the quotation marks are placed at the beginning and at the end of the entire quotation, not at the beginning and end of each separate sentence in that section.

16 ''I think we would have been killed, Ray,'' said Angela, ''if the guards hadn't arrived then. Sir,'' she continued, ''our thanks to you, and your men, for coming when you did. Another five minutes and I'm sure you would only have found our dead bodies.''

If a quotation consists of several paragraphs, quotation marks are placed before each paragraph but at the end of the last paragraph only. This convention applies to a continued speech by one speaker. If the speaker changes, his words are placed in a new paragraph or paragraphs. Short descriptive, narrative, or explanatory passages may be paragraphed with dialogue, especially if they are placed between sentences of dialogue spoken by the same person.

A quoted passage of several lines of prose or poetry – not a part of dialogue – may be indicated by indention. In typing it is often typed single-spaced; in print it may be set in smaller type than the rest of the text. No quotation marks are needed when indention is used.

No quotation marks are used with an indirect quotation.

Direct
''Yes,'' I said to him, ''it's all right.''

"I am relieved to hear it," he replied.

Indirect

I told him it was all right.

He said he was relieved to hear it.

16b. **Single quotation marks are used to enclose a quotation within a quotation.**

Example

"Finally," she said, "I just turned to him and shouted, 'Leave me alone, won't you?'" [Note the position of the quotation marks in relation to other marks.]

16c. **Quotation marks are used to enclose quoted titles of stories, poems, chapters, and other subdivisions of books. (See § 10.)**

16d. **Quotation marks are often used to enclose words referred to as words.**

Italics are used for this purpose, however, when the style is formal, although writers are not consistent in this practice. In informal writing, quotation marks are usually more common. See § 10c.

Example

He was no doubt angry when sportwriters described him and his play in words such as "showboat," "hot dog," and "bush."

16e. **Quotation marks are used to enclose words used in a special sense.**

Often quotation marks are used to indicate to the reader that the writer is using the words in an ironic sense.

Examples

National greed has disguised itself in arguments that "infla-tion" forces prices skyward. [The writer does not think that in-flation is the cause.]

The press secretary claimed that the jungle village had to be "demolished" in order to be "saved." [The writer points out the obvious contradiction in the choice of words.]

Don't overuse quotation marks in an apologetic or self-conscious way, enclosing slang or other expressions that you feel may be inappropriate. If they are inappropriate, you should find better ones. If they are appropriate, they need no apology.

Wrong

He is often the victim of unhappy "attachments."

The "street cops" are watching for illegal sales of Chateau-Gai wines.

Hers is a "star-type" figure and personality.

Right

He is often the victim of unhappy attachments. [The attempt at irony fails here.]

The undercover police are watching for illegal sales of Chateau-Gai wines. [Do not try to bring in a slang term under cover of quotation marks.]

She possesses the figure and personality of a star. [Avoid using -*type* constructions, especially as modifiers of nouns.]

16f.   Quotation marks are often used to enclose the defi-nitions or meanings of words spoken of as words.

In Old English the word *man* simply meant "person" or "human being" and not just "male human." The word *wer* meant "adult male" and *wif* meant "adult female." *Weapman* meant "adult male person" and *wifman* meant "adult female person."

See also § 10c.

16g. Commas and periods are always placed inside quotation marks.

This rule is a printers' convention. The period and the comma are the two marks that occupy the lower half of a line of print; all other marks – the colon, the semicolon, the question mark, and the exclamation point – stand the full height of the line. To have a comma or a period trail out beyond quotation marks looks bad. Remember the convention: periods and commas are *always* placed inside quotation marks. See § 16b for an example.

16h. The question mark, the semicolon, and the exclamation point go inside quotation marks if they belong to the quoted part. They go outside if they do not belong to the quoted part.

Examples

16

Did you hear him say, "I won't go"? [The question mark belongs to the main clause, or the entire sentence. Hence it stands at the end. But notice that no period is used in addition to the end punctuation.]

"Well, we'll see about that!" she exclaimed in anger.

"Gentlemen," said the colonel, "sometimes duty and the needs of the country require difficult actions"; in other words, kill all the prisoners.

16i. For dialogue guides (such as *he said*) with quoted dialogue, use the punctuation that the structure of the sentence calls for.

Example

"The price is not a matter of profit," he said, stiffly; "it is a matter of principle." [Notice the semicolon to separate co-ordinate clauses in a compound sentence of dialogue. Most writers use a period and a following capital letter instead of a semicolon in this sort of construction. See § 16a for other examples of punctuating dialogue.]

The general practice is not to use a comma before a quoted part that is woven into the sentence or before a title. This is logical enough: note that the voice makes little or no pause before reading such quotations.

Examples

Her Volkswagen was the kind of car that "spends more time in the shop than on the road." She was sure that before the car was ready to drive again repairs would "cost a fortune."

We must have read "A Vagabond Song" every year I was in high school.

16   EXERCISES

EXERCISE 1, COMPOSING A PARAGRAPH WITH QUOTATIONS. *Copy out a paragraph of formal prose that interests you. Then write your own paragraph of comment, in which you quote three or four short phrases from the original, punctuating properly as you do so.*

EXERCISE 2, QUOTATION MARKS AND PARAGRAPHING. *Copy the following, punctuating and paragraphing correctly.*

The man shuffled in, head down, eyes averted, not wanting to see or be seen. What's with him? I whispered. Lost his job. Laid off over a year ago. Took it hard. But Pete, I said, that happens all the time now. There's more than a million like him. It's not his fault. No, but he's a proud man. He always worked hard, paid his own way, and asked for no favours. He can't understand how this could happen. He doesn't say much, but you can tell he feels worthless and even guilty. I raised my glass to my lips but couldn't take my eyes off the man. He didn't look much over forty. I felt a sudden small fear in my chest. Come on, Harry. Let's go. I picked up my change and stood up.

§ 17. Colon and Dash

THE COLON

**17a.   The colon is used to separate an introductory
statement from a list of particulars.**

The *colon* is a mark of emphatic separation and should not break
grammatically related elements apart: should not divide a verb
from its object, an object or subject from its appositives. Whatever precedes the colon, then, must constitute a grammatically
complete clause or statement.

Ruptured Sentence

In the kitchen drawer she kept: a hammer, a screwdriver, a
pair of pliers, some assorted nails, and a pneumatic drill. [A
hammer . . . drill are all objects of *kept*. No punctuation is necessary
to announce them.]

Complete Clause Introducing a List

In the kitchen drawer she kept a few household tools: a hammer, a screwdriver, a pair of pliers, some assorted nails, and
a pneumatic drill.

Exception: a list set out in tabular form introduced by an
incomplete clause.

If you can answer my questions, I would like to know:
1. how often you teach the course,
2. what textbook you usually use,
3. how many students normally enroll in the course,
4. what kind of textbook you consider acceptable,
5. whether you feel the enclosed book might prove a useful
   substitute for the text you now use.

These clauses begin with a lower case letter and are closed with
commas. If even one of the clauses contained internal commas,
it would be necessary to close each with a semicolon to avoid

confusion. As the clauses in this case are considered part of the sentence beginning with "If you can answer," the last one terminates with a period. When every clause in a list is a complete one, as those in the example are not, the usual practice is to treat each as an individual sentence beginning with a capital and ending with a period. *The art is to compose the list so that its punctuation is consistent.*

17b. A colon introduces a long quotation.

Much of Crad Kilodney's humour rests on his sense of the absurd:

> Monday: I wrote several poems about sex. They were full of nostalgic, understated awe and unfamiliar words I found in an advanced chemistry book. Readers would be intimidated by my above-average capacity for experience.
>
> Tuesday: I interrupted the hockey team's practice to speak to them about Picasso's life and work. I told them his life was interesting and so was his work. They said no one had ever told them these things before.
>
> Wednesday: I picked up a derelict on Adelaide Street and bought him a hamburger in exchange for his life story. This was better than communicating with extraterrestrials.
>
> Thursday: I looked at a sewing machine in order to discover its Cosmic Meaning. Sure enough, it had one. I wrote it down.
>
> – Crad Kilodney, "My Re-creation of the World"

17

17c. The colon may be used to separate main clauses when the second amplifies, restates, or interprets the first.

Example

The R.C.M.P. commander met for two hours with the Prime Minister; he told the country's leader what he wanted to hear: that the Mounties were ready at a moment's notice to destroy the alien saucers.

17d. In a formal business letter the colon rather than a comma is used after the salutation.

Dear Mr. Crushbum:

    The longline panty-girdle manufactured by your company, Binding Foundations, Incorporated, contains several serious defects. . . .

THE DASH

17e. The dash is used to indicate a sudden, abrupt break in thought or structure.

Examples

The last shot – a rocket from our left-winger – was so powerful that the goalie – an experienced but cocky type – did not realize it was in the net until ten seconds after the red light blinked.

''I wish – I wish you'd let him know – please do – it was an accident.'' [In dialogue to give the effect of hesitation]

''I don't know whether she would like – '' [Speech abruptly broken off]

17f. The dash is used for an explanatory or parenthetical phrase or clause that breaks into the normal flow of the sentence.

Three kinds of marks may indicate parenthesis – *the comma, the dash,* and *marks of parenthesis.* The degree of separation indicated by these marks varies from the lightest, for which commas are used, to the most definite and the most formal, for which parentheses are used.

Examples

There may be a better guitarist somewhere – in a small, obscure Spanish village – but when Segovia begins his performance you believe you are hearing notes and harmonies that can only be called divine.

17g.   The dash is used to introduce or to set off a long, formal appositive or summary.

Examples

There is no other dog in the world to match the Afghan hound – for elegant beauty, for friendliness, and for blinding speed.
[Introducing an appositive]

Many obstacles – poor management decisions, intolerable working conditions, outmoded and dangerous equipment, and inadequate pay – stand in the way of workers doing a good job.

The dash may occasionally be found before such words as *namely* and *that is* introducing an appositive. See also § 13k.

Example

The board of directors – that is, its most powerful and influential members – seemed determined to accumulate as much power as was legally permitted.

A dash may be used before such words as *all* and *these* introducing a summary, or summarizing appositive, after a series. The occasions for this use of the dash are infrequent.

Examples

Pop quizzes, dances, new friends, Frisbee contests – all these should be a part of your first college year.

Good acting and a fast-paced plot – these are the key elements of a successful adventure film.

Caution: The dash must not be used indiscriminately for all other marks of punctuation. It should be saved for its special function, so that it will be effective when it is used.

§ 18. Parentheses and Brackets

PARENTHESES

18a. **Parentheses are used to enclose material that is supplementary, explanatory, or interpretive.**

In theory, the general principle is that commas set off material that is fairly close to the main meaning of the sentence (see § 13i); dashes set off material more distant in meaning (§ 17g); and marks of parenthesis are used to indicate the most distant parenthetical relation. In practice, however, there is considerable variety among modern writers in the way parentheses are used. One traditional function is to enclose an explanation, a definition, or a set of examples to clarify a particular reference.

Example

In their book, *None is Too Many: Canada and the Jews of Europe 1933–1948* (the title comes from the reply of a senior Canadian official to the question of how many death camp survivors would be allowed into the country), Irving Abella and Harold Troper prove that anti-Semitism governed Canadian immigration policy during the years of the Holocaust.

Sometimes parentheses may be used to introduce a comment by the author that draws the reader's attention to some particular device of style.

18b. **Parentheses do not obviate the need for other punctuation in the sentence.**

An expression enclosed in parentheses may be part of a clause, and the clause, including the parenthetical remark, must close with the appropriate punctuation, which is set *outside* and *after* the parentheses.

Examples

Routine maintenance of an automobile can be carried out by numerous agencies (a dealership, a service station, or the owner), but when the car's guarantee is at stake only work done by the dealer will be acceptable. [The comma necessary between independent clauses joined by a conjunction must follow . . . *owner*).]

What she referred to as "the statue's boots" were, in fact, greaves (armour for the shins). [The period follows . . . *shins*).]

Occasionally a parenthetical expression is a separate sentence adding information to the sentences preceding and following it. In such cases the parentheses *enclose* all punctuation, and the expression begins with a capital.

Example

The British shows broadcast on Canadian television are not representative of the British public's lust for highbrow social drama. (One of the most popular programs in England is *Dallas*.) They do demonstrate a typically British knack for adding a successful veneer of professional and technical refinement to a crude and ready-made commonplace, in this case the genre of soap opera.

BRACKETS

18c. Brackets are used to enclose corrections, interpolations, and supplied omissions added to a quotation by the person quoting.

EXERCISES

EXERCISE 1, THE COLON AND THE SEMICOLON. *Copy out from any sample of formal modern prose five sentences in which colons are used. In which of these sentences could semicolons be used instead? What effect would such a substitution have on the meaning or the tone of each sentence?*

EXERCISE 2, THE COLON. *Write out three sentences of your own illustrating the use of the colon as a formal introduction, in the manner described in § 17a. Then write out three others in which the colon is used to separate independent clauses (§ 17c).*

EXERCISE 3, PARENTHESES, BRACKETS, DASHES. *From one of your textbooks copy five sentences in which parentheses or brackets are used. Try substituting dashes for the parentheses and brackets. What is the effect on meaning and tone?*

EXERCISE 4, THE DASH. *Try writing a letter in which you use no punctuation at all except dashes and periods. What is the effect on tone: that is, what kind of voice do you hear uttering these words? What kind of person speaks in this way?*

EXERCISE 5, CORRECT PUNCTUATION. *Select the best punctuation for the sentences below. Dashes are appropriate for a sudden, abrupt break in thought; parentheses enclose material that is supplementary or explanatory; and brackets are used to enclose corrections or supplied omissions. Insert punctuation in place of the carets.*

1. Her reasons were simple but compelling ˄ 1 ˄ he didn't tolerate her friends; ˄ 2 ˄ he never let her have the car; and ˄ 3 ˄ he vacationed alone for three months out of the year.
2. Alden Nowlan ˄ 1933–1983 ˄ wrote a poem called "The Middle-Aged Man in the Supermarket," which today is widely admired by middle-aged men.
3. Few people realized it was he ˄ Jesse James ˄ until the train had completely stopped and men were reaching for their guns.
4. They found the Lincoln the next morning with its engine ˄ how amazing! ˄ resting in the back seat.
5. There will probably not be many people eating those mushrooms ˄ commonly called "toadstools" ˄ now that the coroner's report is published.

18

12

SPELLING

§ 19. The Spelling Problem

As everyone knows, many words in English are not spelled the way they are pronounced. That is why spelling our language is so difficult.

Consider the problem of the foreign speaker who runs up against the various pronunciations of just one small group of letters: *-ough* in *cough*, *dough*, *rough*, *bough*, *through*. The exchange student from France, coming to Canada to improve her English accent, sees a headline on the front page of a newspaper: EXHIBITION PRONOUNCED SUCCESS. ''Ah, this fantastic language!'' she exclaims in utter discouragement, but without surprise.

There was a time, several centuries ago, when writers gave little thought to using the right letters in their words. Some writers, Shakespeare for instance, appear to have spelled their own names in several different ways without a second thought. Our modern attitude toward standardized spelling, however, is very different. Almost everyone – not just your English instructor – takes spelling seriously. One reason is that, unlike most matters of language, spelling is an area where there is usually a Right or Wrong, and it is tempting to make much of someone else's errors when you know they are really errors. There is even an economic importance in trying to learn to spell; employers everywhere assume that poor spelling is a sign of stupidity or illiteracy. They probably reason, rightly or not, that carelessness in spelling is a visible, measurable sign of carelessness in other, more important things. Spelling is something that shows. And because it does show, because it can be easily seen and easily judged, it has become one of the first tests of a person's education and fitness for a job.

What to Do About the Problem. Learning to spell requires memorizing the letters of virtually every word encountered in reading so that it may be reproduced correctly in writing. Most of us, however, have something better to do with our lives, so it is fortunate that there are a few systematic approaches to the process and one invaluable resource. These aids do not let us out of the duty to practise spelling words, to memorize a substantial list of essential ones, and to recognize when we need to investigate the spelling of an unfamiliar word rather than just to have a shot at it, but they do give us a method to pursue.

A good beginning is *to learn a basic list of words* that involve spelling problems. Such a list appears in the next few pages. As memories are fallible, misspellings of even familiar words occur in many writers' first drafts, but if work with the list does not engrave the word on the mind well enough for automatic use, it may yet fix the form in the subconscious so that a misspelling can be recognized after the act of composition. All written work should be proofread, and it is in this process that vague uneasiness at the shape of a word often signals the need for a recheck and correction.

19

Learn words, then, for two purposes: to spell them correctly and to recognize when they are spelled incorrectly. As for proofreading (best accomplished by having someone read aloud a carbon copy while you check the original), remember that there is no easier way to cite a writer for error than to pick out his or her bad spelling. The instructor who discovers numerous spelling errors in a paper would not be human if the frustration at correcting them did not adversely affect his or her appreciation of the entire work.

Knowing something of the analysis of words helps. To understand prefixes and suffixes and roots and stems increases vocabulary and contributes to the small set of rules applicable to spelling. Realize that *ante-* means "before" and *anti-* "against" and there is less probability that *antecedent* will be spelled as though it meant "something against going" rather than what it does mean, "something that goes before." Many English words are descendants of classical Greek and Latin words, to which they bear a more or less recognizable kinship. Other words have drifted into our usage from French, Italian, German (old and new), Spanish, North American Indian, Sanskrit, Hebrew – from, in effect, practically the whole family of languages alive and dead. As the root language of an English word is likely to follow a reasonably phonetic spelling, a spelling in which letters have consistent sound values, knowing what the original or root word is will suggest the spelling of most of its derivatives. Learning the meaning of a word as well as its derivation can aid the student in making that word part of his or her list of frequently used words.

19   *Learning words in terms of their syllable divisions* is another practical tool for mastering spelling. It forces concentration on the letters in the word and breaks down the number of letters to be learned at one time.

There are, too, some mechanical steps toward better spelling. The most effective one is the personal list of the writer. When a spelling error is pointed out, *write down the correction* (there is nothing like co-ordinating hand, eye, and brain to impress the memory) and compile a list of such corrected errors. Keep the list in alphabetical order, make it out on file cards, or simply jot down additions as they arise. Keep the list active and file it where you can refer to it now and again. Some people treat the list like a parole sheet and note the number of offences connected with it. The best system is the one *you* find easiest to follow consistently.

There is one invaluable tool. Find a respectable dictionary and use it. Most dictionaries are well made, so don't be afraid of wearing yours out. Look words up in it whenever you are uncertain of their spellings or meanings, and when looking up a word take note of some of the incidental information given. A good desk dictionary gives not only the spelling of a word, its pronunciation and all its standard modern meanings and uses, but its syllabification, its derivation, and its archaic and colloquial (informal) meanings. For some words the dictionary lists synonyms (words that mean almost the same thing) and antonyms (words with an opposite meaning) as well as giving alternative spellings when they are common enough to present a chance of confusion. The greater the detail with which a word is first investigated, the more likely the word and its spelling are to be remembered. Whatever you do, avoid the easy rationalization: "But how can I find the word in my dictionary if I don't know how to spell it?" You can come close enough.

For more on the use of the dictionary, see chapter 2.

Finally, there are a few spelling rules that seem to apply. They are introduced after the list of commonly misspelled words.

19a. The following is a list of words often misspelled by college students.

19

1. abbreviate
2. absence
3. absorption
4. absurd
5. accidentally
6. accommodate
7. accompanying
8. accomplish
9. accumulate
10. accustom
11. achievement
12. acknowledge
13. acquaintance
14. acquire
15. acquitted
16. across
17. additionally
18. address
19. aggravate
20. all right
21. almost
22. although
23. altogether
24. always
25. amateur
26. among
27. analysis
28. analyse
29. annual
30. answer
31. apartment
32. apology
33. apparatus
34. apparently
35. appearance
36. appropriate
37. arctic
38. argument
39. arising
40. arrangement
41. ascend
42. association
43. athlete
44. athletics
45. attendance
46. audience
47. auxiliary
48. awkward
49. bachelor
50. balance
51. barbarous

52. becoming
53. beginning
54. benefited
55. biscuit
56. boundaries
57. brilliant
58. bureau
59. business
60. cafeteria
61. calendar
62. candidate
63. carburetor
64. career
65. category
66. certain
67. changeable
68. changing
69. characteristic
70. chosen
71. commission
72. committed
73. committee
74. comparative
75. competitive
76. compulsory
77. conceivable
78. conference
79. conferred
80. conqueror
81. conscience
82. conscientious
83. conscious
84. continuous
85. convenient
86. courteous
87. criticism
88. criticize

89. curiosity
90. cylinder
91. dealt
92. decision
93. definitely
94. describe
95. description
96. despair
97. desperate
98. dictionary
99. dilapidated
100. disagree
101. disappear
102. disappoint
103. disastrous
104. discipline
105. dissatisfied
106. dissipate
107. doctor
108. dormitory
109. eighth
110. eligible
111. eliminate
112. embarrass
113. eminent
114. enthusiastic
115. environment
116. equipment
117. equivalent
118. erroneous
119. especially
120. exaggerated
121. exceptionally
122. exhaust
123. exhilarate
124. existence
125. experience

126. explanation
127. extraordinary
128. extremely
129. familiar
130. fascinate
131. February
132. foreign
133. frantically
134. fraternities
135. generally
136. government
137. grammar
138. guard
139. guidance
140. height
141. hindrance
142. humorous
143. illiterate
144. imaginary
145. imagination
146. immediately
147. impromptu
148. incidentally
149. incredible
150. indefinitely
151. indispensable
152. inevitable
153. infinite
154. intellectual
155. intelligence
156. intentionally
157. interesting
158. irrelevant
159. irresistible
160. knowledge
161. laboratory
162. legitimate

19

163. lightning
164. literature
165. loneliness
166. maintenance
167. manoeuvre
168. marriage
169. mathematics
170. miniature
171. mischievous
172. necessary
173. nevertheless
174. noticeable
175. nowadays
176. oblige
177. obstacle
178. occasion
179. occasionally
180. occurred
181. occurrence
182. opportunity
183. optimistic
184. original
185. outrageous
186. pamphlet
187. parallel
188. particularly
189. pastime
190. permissible
191. perseverance
192. perspiration
193. physically
194. picnicking
195. politics
196. practically
197. precedence
198. preference
199. preferred
200. prejudice
201. preparation
202. prevalent
203. privilege
204. probably
205. professor
206. prominent
207. pronunciation
208. prove
209. quantity
210. recognize
211. recommend
212. reference
213. referred
214. regard
215. repetition
216. representative
217. restaurant
218. rhythm
219. rhythmical
220. ridiculous
221. sandwich
222. schedule
223. secretary
224. separate
225. siege
226. similar
227. simultaneous
228. soliloquy
229. sophomore
230. specifically
231. specimen
232. speech
233. strictly
234. surprise
235. temperament
236. temperature
237. thorough
238. throughout
239. tragedy
240. tries
241. truly
242. Tuesday
243. unanimous
244. undoubtedly
245. unnecessarily
246. village
247. villain
248. weird
249. whether
250. writing

19

19b. The following spelling rules will help you to remember how certain words are spelled.

1. A word ending in silent -e *generally drops the* -e *before a suffix beginning with a vowel letter . . .*

DROP -*e*

admire	+ able	= admirable	desire	+ ous	= desirous
admire	+ ation	= admiration	dine	+ ing	= dining
amuse	+ ing	= amusing	explore	+ ation	= exploration
arrange	+ ing	= arranging	fame	+ ous	= famous
arrive	+ ing	= arriving	imagine	+ able	= imaginable
believe	+ ing	= believing	imagine	+ ary	= imaginary
care	+ ing	= caring	love	+ able	= lovable
come	+ ing	= coming	lose	+ ing	= losing
deplore	+ able	= deplorable	move	+ able	= movable

but it retains the -e before a suffix beginning with a consonant letter.

RETAIN -*e*

arrange	+ ment	= arrangement	hate	+ ful	= hateful
care	+ ful	= careful	like	+ ness	= likeness
force	+ ful	= forceful	move	+ ment	= movement

But after c *or* g, *if the suffix begins with* a *or* o, *the -e is retained to indicate the soft sound of* c *or* g.

19

RETAIN -*e*

advantage	+ ous	= advantageous	outrage	+ ous	= outrageous
change	+ able	= changeable	peace	+ able	= peaceable
courage	+ ous	= courageous	service	+ able	= serviceable
notice	+ able	= noticeable			

2. In words with ie *or* ei *when the sound is long ee, use* i *before* e *except after* c.

i BEFORE *e*

achieve	chief	pier	shriek
apiece	field	pierce	siege
belief	fierce	priest	thief
believe	frieze	relieve	wield
besiege	grief	reprieve	yield
brief	niece	retrieve	
cashier	piece	shield	

EXCEPT AFTER *c*

ceiling	conceive	deceive	receipt
conceit	deceit	perceive	receive

Exceptions: either, neither, financier, weird, species, seize,
These may be remembered by arranging the words in a sentence: "Neither financier seized either species of weird leisure."
The so-called seed words can be easily remembered. For those who cannot memorize, a careful reading of the list will suffice:

1. Only one word ends in -*sede*: supersede

2. Three words end in -*ceed*:   exceed
                                                 proceed
                                                 succeed

3. The rest end in -*cede*:

accede	precede
cede	recede
concede	secede
intercede	

19

3. Words of one syllable or words of several syllables with the accent on the last one, and that end with a single consonant preceded by a single vowel, double the final consonant before a suffix beginning with a vowel is added.

Now this looks like a formidable rule to unravel. Let us see what it involves. In the first place, it applies to short words such as *get, swim, drop, drip*. In the second place, it applies to longer words in which the accent is on the final syllable, such as *refer, begin, equip*. Examine the illustrations below to see what happens:

drop [word of one syllable] + ed [suffix beginning with a vowel] = dropped.
control [accented on the last syllable] + ed [suffix] = controlled.
benefit [not accented on last syllable] + ed [suffix] = benefited.
confer [accented on last syllable] + ed [suffix] = conferred.
confer [notice the shift in accent] + ence [suffix] = conference.
defer [accented on last syllable] + ed [suffix] = deferred.
defer [notice the shift in accent] + ence [suffix] = deference.

SUFFIX BEGINS WITH A VOWEL

One Syllable

brag	– bragging	man	– mannish
cram	– cramming	plan	– planning
drag	– dragging	snap	– snapped
dun	– dunning	sin	– sinning
drop	– dropped	stop	– stopped
cut	– cutting	quit	– quitting
bid	– bidding	rob	– robbed
flag	– flagged	stab	– stabbed
get	– getting	whip	– whipped
clan	– clannish	sad	– saddest

Accented on Last Syllable

admit'	– admitted	equip'	– equipped
begin'	– beginning	commit'	– committee
commit'	– committed	occur'	– occurrence
concur'	– concurring	submit'	– submitted
confer'	– conferring	compel'	– compelled

19

Not Accented on Last Syllable

prefer	– preference	benefit	– benefited
refer	– reference	profit	– profitable
happen	– happened		

SUFFIX BEGINS WITH A CONSONANT

sad	– sadness	sin	– sinful
fat	– fatness	equip	– equipment
woman	– womanhood	profit	– profitless

4. A noun ending in -y preceded by a consonant forms the plural in -ies; a verb ending in -y preceded by a consonant forms its present tense, third person singular, in -ies.

ENDING IN -*y* PRECEDED BY A CONSONANT

baby, babies	sky, skies	pygmy, pygmies
marry, marries	copy, copies	fly, flies

ENDING IN -*y* PRECEDED BY A VOWEL

attorney, attorneys   valley, valleys   delay, delays
destroy, destroys   enjoy, enjoys   chimney, chimneys

Note: Some other rules for forming plurals are as follows:

5. *For most nouns, add* -s: boys, girls, houses, ideas, aches, pains.

6. *For nouns ending with a sound similar to* s, *add* -es: birches, foxes, boxes, classes.

7. *For nouns ending in* -f, -fe, -ff, *use* -s *or* -ves: chief, chiefs; staff, staffs, staves; wife, wives; sheriff, sheriffs; elf, elves; dwarf, dwarfs, dwarves.

8. *For nouns ending in* -o *add* -s *or* -es: solo, solos; echo, echoes; potato, potatoes; motto, mottos, mottoes; tomato, tomatoes; alto, altos; hero, heroes.

9. *Some nouns have irregular plurals:* foot, feet; mouse, mice; goose, geese; ox, oxen; woman, women; axis, axes; basis, bases; datum, data; locus, loci; formula, formulas, formulae.

19

   But Mr. and Mrs. Berry are *not* "the Berries," but "the Berrys"; and Mr. and Mrs. Wolf are *not* "the Wolves," but "the Wolfs." Mr. and Mrs. Jones are still "the Joneses."

EXERCISES
Rewrite the following paragraphs, correcting the misspelled words.

EXERCISE 1.

   It has often occured to me that any foreign envirement begins to look familiar after sufficient experiance. In the beginning one may believe that a foriegn land is wierd or even barberous. But it is noticable that in the end one usually consedes the virtues of strangeness. What is outragous is to persist in repititions of embarassing criticisms that are definitly eroneous.

EXERCISE 2.

One chilly Febuary day, three sophmores were sitting in their dormitery discussing one of the campuses most prominant proffessors. They sprawled on separate bunks in their room, occassionally engaging in arguement about the professor's appearance and achievements.

"I went to see his secretery last Tuesday," one student remarked. "I think she's more intelactual than he is."

"I disagree," said another. "But why is he so predjudiced against fraternities?"

"Anyway," said the third, "I've always prefered a conference with the secretary. It's a priviledge to talk to her."

EXERCISE 3.

The most interesting knowledge is likely to seem irrevalent on its first occurence. Many have benefitted from explanations that at first seemed throughly and unnecessarily ridiculous. I recomend that you sieze consiously every ocasion for learning, even if your committment to grammer may be comparitively unenthusiastic.

19

EXERCISE 4.

The weather exceded our expectations. After arriveing we got out the bats, balls, and gloves, and began a carful search for our playing feild. The brief search ended when we stoped near an open acre of flatland under clear skys. No one remembers just when the mosquitos struck, but the Terries and the Jones' were the first to run for cover. The biting ended only after every picnicer was completely immersed in water. That was truely an unforgettable Sunday.

§ 20. Similar Forms

Distinguish between words similar or identical in sound but different in meaning.

The following list is merely a checklist for quick reference. If you need more than this list can give you, refer to your dictionary. You should also look at examples of similar forms in the "Guide to Usage."

accent. Emphasis or stress; to stress. [You accent the wrong syllable.]

ascent. Climbing; a way up. [The ascent of the cliff was difficult.]

assent. To agree; agreement. [He finally gave his assent to the plan.]

accept. To take something offered; to agree to; to approve; to believe. [He accepted the gift. I accept your interpretation.]

except. To leave out; to exclude. [All except the cook were rescued.]

admittance. Permission to enter a place. [The sign read, "No admittance."]

admission. Admitting to rights and privileges; the price of being allowed to enter. [No admission was charged.]

advice. Counsel given to encourage or dissuade. [He offers advice without charge or invitation.]

advise. To give advice to; to suggest. [I would advise you not to jump.]

affect. To influence; to pretend; to assume. [His threats do not affect me.]

effect. To perform; make happen. [The attorney effected a reconciliation.] *Effect*, not *affect*, is used as a noun. [What *effect* did your words have on him?]

all ready. Everyone is ready. [They were all ready.]

already. By this time. [They had already eaten breakfast.]

allusive. Making a casual but significant reference to. [The poem was highly allusive and hard to follow.]

elusive. Difficult to grasp; tending to slip away. [The idea seems at first elusive. The panther is an elusive prey.]

illusive. Deceptive; unreal or illusory. [His visions of a similar solar system proved illusive.]

altar. Place of worship. [They knelt before the altar.]

alter. To change. [Do not alter any part of my criticism.]

ante. Before. [This song is of ante-Beatle vintage.]

20

anti.   Against; opposed to. [I poured some antifreeze into the radiator.]

breath.   Air drawn into lungs. [We need a breath of fresh air.]

breathe.   To take a breath. [We cannot breathe in this room.]

censure.   Blame; condemn; criticize severely. [They voted to censure the general.]

censor.   To oversee morals and conduct; to examine and make changes. [Three women will censor all motion pictures.]

charted.   Mapped or diagrammed. [The Arctic is still not fully charted.]

chartered.   Hired; granted certain rights. [We chartered a boat.]

choose.   To pick out, select. [Will she choose me again?]

chose.   Past tense of *choose*. [They chose a new secretary.]

cite.   To quote or use as example. [Did he cite any authorities?]

site.   Location. [This is a good site for our church.]

sight.   Vision; to see. [His sight was keen. At last we sighted land.]

coarse.   Rough; crude. [coarse food; coarse manners; coarse sand]

course.   Direction; path; series; order. [a course of study; of course]

complement.   That which completes. [a subjective complement]

compliment.   Praise; a polite and flattering comment. [He paid her a compliment.]

20

consul.   Government official appointed to look after foreign business interests.

council.   A group; an assembly. [We will call a council of the elders.]

counsel.   Advice; one who advises; a lawyer. [Give her good counsel. The accused has a right to counsel.]

decent.   Proper, respectable; modest; adequate or satisfactory. [His suit was decent for a change. The performance was decent.]

descent.   Any downward motion; decline or deterioration; lineage. [rapid and steep descent; descent of morals; of aristrocratic descent]

dissent.   To differ in opinion; to withhold approval. [He held it essential to dissent from the popular view.]

detract.   Take away. [Its sordid history detracts from its beauty.]

distract.   Draw away; disturb. [The noise distracts me. Do not distract my attention.]

elicit.   To draw out, evoke. [She tried to elicit a response to her proposal.]

illicit.   Not permitted, unauthorized. [There are laws against illicit gambling in this province.]

eminent.   Distinguished. [The eminent sculptor spoke briefly.]

imminent.   About to happen. [War seems imminent.]

immanent. Existing within; inherent. [God's presence is immanent in the world.]

formally. In formal manner. [He was formally welcomed by the mayor.]

formerly. In the past. [Formerly, no one had greeted him.]

hoards. Stores; collections. [The police found hoards of stolen stereos.]

hordes. Crowds; groups of nomads. [the barbarian hordes; hordes of tourists]

imaginary. Existing in the imagination. [Her life is full of imaginary troubles.]

imaginative. Having imagination; able to imagine. [She is a very imaginative woman.]

implicit. Absolute, implied. [implicit obedience to orders; implicit approval]

explicit. Distinctly stated; definite. [He gave us explicit directions.]

incredible. Unbelievable. [Your story is incredible.]

incredulous. Unwilling to believe. [He was incredulous when I told my story.]

irrelevant. Not to the point. [His question is irrelevant.]

irreverent. Lacking reverence or respect. [His action was irreverent.]

20

loose. Not fastened; careless; not confined. [Tie up your loose shoe strings. There is too much loose talk here. Your dog is loose again.]

lose. To mislay; to fail to win; to waste. [She lost her keys again. We may lose this game yet. Put your loose cash away or you will lose it.]

principal. Chief; most important; chief person; chief teacher. [the principal of a school; the principal actor; the principal occupation; paying something on the principal as well as the interest]

principle. A truth; a belief; a scientific rule. [He is a man of high principles.]

prophecy. A prediction made under divine influence (noun).

prophesy. To predict the future under divine influence (verb).

regretful. Feeling full of regret. [He was very regretful about his bad behaviour.]

regrettable. Expressing disappointment. [His behaviour was regrettable.]

rend. To tear apart; to disturb. [The silence was rent by a frightening roar.]

render. Make; give; represent; play or sing. [You will render a service. The judge rendered his decision.]

respectfully.   With respect. [Speak to your teacher respectfully.]

respectively.   Each in turn or in order. [His three sons, Igor, Dmitri, and Ivan, were 18, 21, and 25 respectively.]

stationary.   Not movable; not changing. [a stationary engine; a stationary enrollment; a stationary income]

stationery.   Writing materials. [Please let me have some stationery; I wish to write a few letters.]

straight.   Not curved; upright; continuous; direct. [The road is straight. Come straight to the point.]

strait.   Narrow; strict; restricting. [a strait jacket; a strait passage; the Straits of Magellan; the Straits of Gibraltar]

undoubtedly.   Beyond a doubt. [She was undoubtedly correct.]

undoubtably.   No such word.

20

13

WORDS AND PHRASES

§21. Diction

Use words that convey your meaning exactly and idiomatically.

Chapter 2 spoke of the *denotation*, or literal meaning of a word, and of the *connotation*, or associated meaning of a word. If a word in your essay has been marked "D" or "Diction," you should first consult a dictionary to see that its denotation is clear. The solution to a problem of denotation may simply be to choose a different, more accurate word. But if the word is guilty of vague or inappropriate connotation, the only answer is to define its meaning or give examples.

21a. Key words that may be understood in more than one sense should be carefully defined.

Most of the words that you use in writing and speaking will do well enough without being defined. The least tricky words are the names of specific persons or objects, such as *Karen Kain*, *laboratory*, *Peggy's Cove*, a *Polaroid camera*, although each may arouse emotional reactions that colour its meaning. More tricky are the words that refer to things or qualities that have been a part of the daily life of many generations, such as *dog*, *cat*, *war*, *generous*, *honest*, *selfish*, and so on. Usually the meaning of the word is defined well enough by the *context* (i.e., the sense of the words around it) in which it is used. Nothing of vast importance is lost through a lack of exact communication. But something of vast importance *is* at stake when people use such words as *radicals*, *reactionaries*, *liberals*, *realistic*, *democratic people*, *peace-loving*, *aggression*, *freedom of speech*. Terms such as these must be defined or qualified.

Examples

Radicals are taking over local government. [Who are these "radicals"? What is their political persuasion?]

People like John Wayne movies no matter what the subject. [Which "people"? Are they the same people who demand "all power to the people"?]

He is into *aggression* as a means of solving his problems. [Does he simply punch those he doesn't agree with in the nose?]

21

21b. Words used in an inexact sense should be checked and restudied with the help of a dictionary.

Most of us learn new words as we need them, without much help from vocabulary improvement schemes. All of us depend heavily and very often on the context, on approximations, for meanings. Here and there we miss the point – sometimes by a narrow margin, sometimes by a wide one. Here and there someone catches us up. It would be naive to assert that a dictionary can solve all your problems with the meanings of words. But here are a few examples to show how a dictionary can serve you:

The doctor decided to try an *explanatory* operation first. [That sounds reasonable, but is that what she actually decided to try?]

The music served to *diverge* my thoughts to more pleasant things. [Here the writer was trying for a word that sounded like this one, and, in a vague way, meant something like it.]

She was listening *intensely* to the lecture. [The right word here is *intently*.]

21c. Vague, blanket words should be replaced with more precise words.

This statement refers primarily to such words as *deal*, *factor*, *stance*, *thrust*, *line*, *point of view*, *angle*, *proposition*, *impact*, *interface*. It refers also to any word that you have used because you were in a hurry and it was easier to use a vague word than to think of a more exact one.

Inexact and Wordy
Did you *get his deal* about wanting to go into something *along the line* of engineering?

Better
Can you understand that he wants to study a branch of engineering?

Inexact
An exciting *factor* of our summer vacation was a trip to Japan.

Better
An exciting event of our summer vacation was a trip to Japan.

Inexact
I never could decide what his *angle* was from the *point of view* of making high grades.

Better
I never could decide what his thoughts (ideas) were about making high grades.

Inexact
The sphere *impacted* on the *interface* between the audience and the green, flat surface.

Better
The ball bounced off the wall in left field.

Remember that although you may get away with using blanket words in speaking they are all too noticeable in writing.

21d. A writer should guard against the right word taking an unintended meaning in the context.

A serious writer should guard against unintentional humour. Bloopers (or malapropisms), either the natural or the synthetic variety, are of course the stock-in-trade of the gag writer or the television comedian. Here are some examples of unintentional slips:

Blooper
The writer made the poem more effective by the use of metaphors and illusions.

Correction
The writer made the poem more effective by the use of metaphors and allusions.

Blooper
Finally, at midnight, I sat down to learn my history.

Correction
Finally, at midnight, I sat down to study my history assignment.

21

Blooper
Every time he opens his mouth, some fool speaks.

Correction
Every time he starts to speak, some fool interrupts him.

Blooper
The book is obscene and difficult to reprehend.

Correction
The book is obscure and difficult to comprehend.

EXERCISES

EXERCISE 1, ASSOCIATED MEANINGS. *Which words in the following groups of words suggest an unfavourable attitude and which suggest a favourable attitude?*

1. Teacher, tutor, professor, counsellor.
2. Police officer, cop, pig, traffic officer.
3. Dainty, fragile, delicate, weak, flaccid, spineless.
4. Woman, female, chick, broad, girl.
5. Mixture, mess, jumble, patchwork, blend, alloy.

EXERCISE 2, EXACTNESS. *Point out every instance of inexact use of words in the following sentences and suggest a revision.*

1. The long arm of television permeates all of the civilized world.
2. In this poem the author tells about England's downfall from a leading country.
3. Judge Brand ordered the man to disabuse his wife and children.
4. The effect of the poem depends on what the reader divulges from it.
5. In order to solve their curiosity they must read the story to the end.
6. He quickly built a shelter to shed the rain off his precious equipment.
7. He describes in a realistic way about the things he has experienced in the slums.
8. My problems are more of an uncertainty, like being able to place a comma in this place or a semicolon in that place.
9. My hobby includes time, work, and expense.
10. As I am a seldom reader of poetry, I did not enjoy this book.
11. The story centred around life in Stornoway.
12. He confused Joan for Ellen when he saw her on the street.
13. Harley told us to precede with filling the hot tub.
14. Even George, who's I.Q. is embarrassingly low, could understand the morale of the film.
15. That behaviour doesn't conform to passed practice.
16. They played too loosely and ended up loosing the game.
17. With his dyeing words he complained about the colour they died his shirt.
18. It was the right devise but it blew up too soon.
19. Her reason for missing the plane was because the cab took her too the train depot.
20. It was an accident irregardless of what you say.

21

§ 22. Appropriateness

Use words that are in keeping with the subject of your paper, with the occasion, and with the readers you are addressing.

Many of the papers that you write for your courses are informal; some are formal. You should always remember that the terms *informal* and *formal* are relative – not absolute. Each covers a wide range. Obviously, you will probably never try to write with the formality of Pope John Paul, or Eugene Forsey, or Winston Churchill addressing Parliament; you may, however, approach the style of a present-day historian or critic or essayist. Examples of different styles can be found throughout this book.

When you write a serious discussion of a serious subject, you should use language that is dignified but not pretentious or affected. If the occasion is informal, you write in an informal, easy manner – remembering always that as there are degrees of formality so are there degrees of informality. The informality that runs to slang or vague terms has little place in school work. Intelligent people have different styles of writing at their command just as they have clothes appropriate for different occasions. A man does not attend a formal dinner in sweater and slacks, or a football game in a tuxedo, unless he is determined to make a spectacular and probably unfavourable impression. There *are* rules and conventions in the use of language, just as there are conventions governing social behaviour everywhere else – at a dinner table, at a football game, on a street corner, anywhere. Good sense is the best rule of conduct.

Here are a few examples of failure in appropriateness.

Inappropriate in Formal Writing
Poor
Until the government provided loan guarantees, the trucking company was going down the tubes.

Better
Until the government provided loan guarantees, the trucking company was near insolvency.

Poor

A year later the company went belly up anyway.

Better

In spite of this help, the company went bankrupt a year later.

Inappropriate in Informal Writing

I certainly hope you are having a good time at school this year *and realizing your potential for intellectual growth and development.* [Say *and getting a lot out of it.*]

He told me what to do and *I accomplished the operation.* [Say *I did it.*]

She was *informed* that *one did not have to prevaricate* in order to *advance one's cause.* [Say "she was told that she didn't have to lie to get ahead."]

22a. In serious writing, inappropriate slang should be avoided.

Slang has often been defined as a kind of made-to-order language, characterized by extravagant or grotesque humour. This is by no means a complete or all-inclusive definition of slang, nor is an all-inclusive definition important in this book. Not even the editors of dictionaries agree on what is slang and what is not. *The Canadian Dictionary for Schools* lists the following, among others, as examples of slang: *rod* [revolver, pistol], *rap* [to arrest, hold; to converse informally], *nut* [a crazy person], *savvy* [understanding, to understand], *dumbbell* [a stupid person]. In other dictionaries you may find other words listed as slang.

22

Slang is usually inappropriate in serious or formal writing, but some writers use it with telling effects. Writers who strain to avoid slang may still err by using stilted, general, vague, and pompous words under the impression that a simple and direct style is not good enough for important ideas.

22b. A mixture of the colloquial and the formal styles is usually inappropriate in serious writing.

Most dictionaries use *colloq.* as a usage label for certain words and phrases. *Colloquial* means informal, or characteristic of a conversational style, as opposed to a formal, literary style. In the past, many people believed that *colloq.* implied a condemnation of a word or phrase, in spite of the fact that editors of dictionaries were careful to define the word correctly in the vocabularies and in the explanatory notes. Scholars, lexicographers, and linguists have pointed out that every educated person uses colloquial English, and, what is important to remember, he or she uses it correctly in appropriate situations.

EXERCISES

EXERCISE 1, APPROPRIATENESS. *Some of the following italicized expressions are appropriate in serious writing; some are not. With the help of your dictionary, decide which are more appropriate in colloquial than in formal situations.*

1. We are determined to *face up to* this monstrous foe with all our hearts.
2. Finally, after many years of service, the old crate *gave out.*
3. The trusted servant, we discovered, had *made off* with our two cameras.
4. He was to board a plane at ten, but none of his friends was there to *see him off.*
5. The man was instructed to *sing out* if he saw any prowlers.
6. Within a year the young man *had run through* his inheritance.
7. At the end of the year he felt that it was not easy to *take off and leave* his new friends.
8. The principal was trying to find out who had *put him up to it.*
9. His arrogance was something no one was willing to *put up with.*
10. Nobody expected her to *carry on so* when she heard that her daughter had eloped.

EXERCISE 2, FORMAL AND INFORMAL EXPRESSIONS. *Give the formal equivalent of each of the italicized expressions.*

1. *to back down*
2. He's *into* Zen these days
3. to *go him one better*
4. *How come?*
5. He *got busted* during the raid.
6. You'll *get your cut!*
7. He *fed* his new date *a line.*
8. That music really *moves* me.
9. Give him his *walking papers.*
10. *Stick around* for a while.

22

§ 23. The Idioms

23a. Use idiomatic English.

An idiom is an expression peculiar to a given language. It cannot usually be translated word-for-word into another tongue, though its sense can often be rendered by an equivalent idiom native and natural to that tongue. Created out of the day-to-day living of ordinary people, idioms are often irrational, racy, and lively with images. Many of them have originated in someone's clever and original metaphor, which then became "dead" as it was repeated by other people. "You said a mouthful." "He was beside himself with worry." "Who slipped up?" "Water off a duck's back." "I'm getting my act together." As these examples suggest, idioms are often colloquial or slang, though not necessarily so.

Even more than other elements in the language, idioms change status constantly as they come into or go out of fashion, or as they become respectable in formal English or fall into disrepute. In fact such change has become so rapid and complex in our time that the editors of the latest unabridged *Webster*'s have dropped most of their notations of *slang* and *colloq*. Even your desk dictionary, however, can be very useful in listing the various idioms formed from ordinary single words. Many idiomatic phrases have grown up around the verbs of everyday living – *go, do, catch, get, make, take,* and so on.

The student's difficulties in handling idioms are likely to be of two kinds. First, trouble occurs in sensing the status of a particular idiom. A student might, for instance, go so far as to write, in a formal essay, and with no humorous intention, "This flipped me!" In this case, of course, the writer has failed to recognize the highly colloquial and ephemeral quality of that expression. Or the student might say, in a serious descriptive essay, "It rained cats and dogs," thus failing to recognize that this particular idiom has long been a very tired cliché. (Clichés are treated more fully in § 25.) The best guard against errors of this kind is constant reading, writing, and listening, with an

23

awareness of how different kinds of expressions are acceptable in different situations.

A second source of student difficulty with idioms might be called a failing of the ear – that is, the student may forget just how an idiom is said in English, and that there is seldom much justification for the phrasing of idioms. The problem is most severe in the case of prepositions, as the subsection immediately following will show.

23b. Observe the idiomatic use of prepositions after certain verbs, participles, adjectives, and nouns.

The following list will not take the place of an unabridged dictionary. It will serve merely as a check list to put you on your guard. Consult the dictionary for more complete information.

abstain from
accede to
acquiesce in
acquit of
addicted to
adept in
adhere to
agree to (a thing)
agree with (a person)
agreeable to
angry at (a thing)
angry with (a person)
averse to
capable of
characteristic of
compare to (for illustration)
compare with (to examine qualities)
concern in (interest in)
concerned for (troubled)
concerned with (involved)
concur in (an opinion)

concur with (a person)
desire for
desist from
devoid of
differ about
differ from (things)
differ with (a person)
different from
disagree with
disdain for
dissent from
distaste for
empty of
envious of
expert in
foreign to
guard against
hint at
identical with
independent of
infer from
initiate into

23

inseparable from
jealous of
obedient to
oblivious of
preparatory to
prerequisite to
prior to
proficient in
profit by
prohibit from
protest against

reason with
regret for
repugnant to
sensitive to
separate from
substitute for
superior to
sympathize with
tamper with
unmindful of
vie with

It is characteristic of English that an idiom may have several meanings, and that it may shift into a new part of speech. The professor *makes up* a roster of students, and the *makeup* of the class displeases her. A lady *makes up* her face, which is to say she applies *makeup*. I *make up* a funny story, which then appears *made-up*. Idioms such as these, composed originally of a verb and an adverb, quickly become nouns in our language, as the following short list will suggest:

blowup
carry-over
cookout
countdown
drive-in

rundown
runaround
runaway
turnover
upkeep

Many nouns so formed are obviously of recent origin: *cookout*, *countdown*, *drive-in*. Do not hesitate to make use of such new terms, in spite of their predominantly informal quality. In the list above, for example, almost every term is at least conceivably appropriate in almost any context.

On the other hand, the temptation to transform certain nouns into verbs should be resisted, especially when the nouns are not concrete. "He wanted to know whether or not to *prioritize* the items" is a sentence that sounds pretentious. *Impact*, *interface*, *input*, *author*, *craft* are examples of words that work best as nouns.

EXERCISES

EXERCISE 1, IDIOMS. *In your dictionary find the idioms listed under several of the following words. You will find idiomatic phrases printed in boldface type, usually after the synonyms. Bring to class a number of these for discussion. Try to decide why some are marked* colloq. *and some are without a label.*

eat	go	head	mouth	stand
foot	hand	heart	pick	take
get	have	horse	run	word

EXERCISE 2, MISUSE OF IDIOMS. *Rewrite the following paragraph, correcting the misuses of idiom.*

He was superior than all of us, or so he thought, but his bragging was no substitute of ability. He felt himself independent from the rest of us, though he was usually agreeable with going along with the majority. I was often angry at him, since he differed from me so often. When he left he showed no concern with the way others felt. He was entirely oblivious to public opinion. We were all very surprised and jealous of him when he was elected president.

EXERCISE 3, IDIOMATIC PREPOSITIONS. *Supply the idiomatic prepositions as required in the following sentences.*

1. Since I was so concerned (   ) my business at that time, she was concerned (   ) my health.
2. At that period we differed (   ) almost everything.
3. She especially differed (   ) me about money matters.
4. Finally we separated (   ) one another.
5. Neither of us, however, proved to be capable (   ) living alone.

23

§ 24. Conciseness

Avoid using more words than are necessary for the adequate expression of your thought.

The stylistic fault of *wordiness* has been the concern of writers and speakers for many centuries. Wordiness has been called by many names – verbosity, prolixity, diffuseness, circumlocution, periphrasis. By any name, wordiness simply means the use of more words than you need in a particular situation. To achieve conciseness, you must ask whether every word you write is doing its work, carrying its proper load of meaning, and helping its fellow workers with their loads.

Do not mistake brevity for conciseness. A sentence is not concise if it lacks the necessary words for clear communication. Cutting out words in a good essay might also cut out of it those qualities that make it good – strength, variety, maturity, grace, wit, even accuracy.

Study the following sets of sentences. Do you see what is meant by conciseness?

1. Whenever anyone called for someone to help him do some certain thing, Jim was always the first to volunteer and lend his help for the cause.
2. Whenever anyone called for help, Jim was always the first to volunteer.

1. This spirit of co-operation is essential and necessary for anyone to have in order to get along with other people, and this is a quality that Jim had.
2. Jim had the spirit of co-operation that is necessary if one wishes to get along with people.

1. Jim was one of those people of whom there are few in this world like him.
2. There are few people like Jim.

1. Forestry is placed in the top position among resource industries in Canada from the standpoint of importance.
2. Forestry is the most important resource industry in Canada.

1. To consider self-perpetuation or to consider its alternative, these are the fundamental parameters of the interface.
2. To be or not to be, that is the question.

This section will concern itself with several kinds of wordiness to be avoided by the writer who hopes to be concise, direct, and to the point.

24a. Avoid careless repetition of the same word.

Careless repetition of a word weakens the effectiveness of a sentence and is often a symptom of wordiness. The fault may be corrected by using synonyms, by using pronouns, or by completely rewriting the sentence.

Poor
I have been asked to write on a controversial subject that has been the subject of controversy among historians for years. That subject, as you have probably guessed, is none other than how to account for the rise of Hitler's Germany. The rise of Hitler's Germany has fascinated me for a longer time than I can remember.

Better
I will try to account for the rise of Hitler's Germany, a controversial subject that has fascinated me for some time.

24

Poor
He felt that the remark about his reputation would do great damage to his reputation.

Better
He felt that the remark would do great damage to his reputation.

The importance of avoiding awkward repetition must not distract the writer from the possibilities of *repetition for emphasis* – a valuable device for securing certain kinds of attention from the reader.

In the following excerpt, George Woodcock repeats the word *freedom* (and its variant *free*) to emphasize the benefits of anarchism, which he maintains is the most desirable political arrangement for modern states.

> Anarchists do not advocate political freedom. What they do advocate is freedom from politics, freedom from the institution of government, freedom from coercion, freedom from the law's interference in the lives of individual men and women, freedom from economic domination and inequality. The last is perhaps the most important, in that economic freedom, the satisfaction of man's physical needs for food, clothing, shelter, and all the other material needs of a civilized life, is necessary before any man can begin to be free.
>
> – George Woodcock, ''The Rejection of Politics''

The speech-making style in this selection suggests that repetition is a characteristic device of oratory. For serious defences of concepts like free speech or freedom of religion, such a style is obviously indispensable.

Repetition can also prove effective in establishing an ironic tone, as illustrated in this example:

> The reviewer described Lawson's performance as ''competent.'' Indeed, her performance in over twenty sold-out concert halls could be termed ''competent,'' and there is little doubt that the standing ovations and insistent demands for encores were the result of ''competent'' playing. One can only hope that Lawson will be equally ''competent'' on her next tour.

24

Quotation marks are required to achieve the desired effect, which can be especially appealing to your reader. By saving such ammunition for just the right battle, however, you avoid the danger of wasting it in sniperlike exchanges.

24b. Avoid repetition of words with the same meaning (tautology).

Wordy

The analysis was *thoroughly and wholly complete.*

All the requirements of *frank* and *honest candor* made his speech popular.

The *basic fundamental essentials* of a college education are *simply* and *briefly* these.

He woke up at six *a.m. this morning.*

There is no need to change pilots *at this point in time.*

Many clichés, particularly those picked up from legal jargon, are tautologies: *Null and void, cease and desist, swear and affirm.*

24c.   Avoid the double *that* before a clause (pleonasm, a grammatical tautology).

I was very glad that when I came into the house that I found everything in order. [Omit the second *that*.]

The author feels that it is only *Last Train From Kapuskasing* that many critics regard as her sole great work. (The author feels that many critics regard *Last Train From Kapuskasing* as her sole great work.)

24d.   Avoid roundabout expressions (circumlocution or periphrasis).

Wordy
The reason why I was so upset was because she seemed so angry with me. [reason – why – because] [I was upset because she seemed so angry with me.]

24e.   Avoid the overuse of intensives and other modifiers.

It is wise to question critically all modifiers (adjectives and adverbs), because it is often through these words that wordiness gets a foothold. The so-called intensives – *very, much,* and so on – are likely to weaken a sentence.

Wordy
They were absolutely so much astonished to find so very much still to do that they were absolutely speechless. [They were

speechless with astonishment to find so much still to be done.]

She was completely and totally pleased by the very fine report that the children gave her. [She was pleased by the children's fine report.]

Officials were really very pleased to find the documents that they thought had been stolen. [Officials were pleased to find the documents . . .]

24f. Avoid repetition of similar sounds.

The awkward repetition of similar sounds in prose may seriously distract your reader from what you are trying to communicate. Consider the following examples:

The *loss* of the *toss* meant that the *Trackers* could not be *attackers*. (Because they were losers of the toss, the Trackers began the game on defence.)

To *relent* to the *extent* that you lose your *rent* deposit is unwise. (Giving in at this point may mean the loss of your rent deposit.)

The stock of refrigerated Snickers bars was ve*ry* near*ly* comp*lety* dep*le*ted. (The stock of refrigerated Snickers bars was almost gone.)

It is *common* for the *nom*inating *comm*ittee to res*pond* the next day. (The nominating committee usually reports the next day.)

24

24g. Avoid officialese (also called "gobbledygook").

The language of bureaucratic, government, and military life is seldom concise. You will find many examples of wordiness. Note especially, in such writing, the overuse of passive verbs (see §6c) and a fondness for abstract nouns. A similar kind of stuffiness infects the report writing of committees – writing created, that is, by more than one author. Extracurricular student writing is not always free from the wordiness of hot air, too. See your student newspaper.

The following notice, posted on schools in Toronto, is a good example of officialese:

Entry upon this school site for any purpose inconsistent with the education act is prohibited.

The average person encountering this sign would probably first feel intimidated, then confused, and finally obliged to go to the library to study the education act and decide if their intentions were consistent with the aims of the act.

A more helpful notice might read:

Please do not enter unless you are on school business.

24h.   Avoid "fine writing."

"Fine writing" is not, as the phrase seems to indicate, good writing. It is flowery, artificial, overblown writing. In an effort to be literary, writers load their style with too many adjectives and adverbs, with big words, awkward repetitions of high-sounding phrases, foreign language phrases, and trite figures of speech. (See also § 25c.) "Fine writing" is often the result of an overcomplicated sentence structure. Its effect is that of a voice that sounds pompous and stuffy, and no sensitive reader will listen to such a voice for very long.

Examples

Heller's style is marked by a certain dementia praecox that lends sparkle to the demimondes he creates.

Her *Weltanschauung* could be described in no other way than by pointing to the *Weltschmerz* expressed by her heroines.

Below is a parody of the prose style of Henry James, which illustrates many of the faults of "fine writing."

> Author Winner sat serenely contemplating his novel. His legs, not ill-formed for his years, yet concealing the faint cyanic marbling of incipient varicosity under grey socks of the finest lisle, were crossed. He was settled in the fine, solidly-built, cannily (yet never parsimoniously, never niggardly) bargained-for chair that had been his father's, a chair that Author Winner himself was only beginning to think that, in the fullness of time, hope he reasonably

might that he would be able (be possessed of the breadth and the depth) to fill. Hitching up the trousers that had been made for his father (tailored from a fabric woven to endure, with a hundred and sixty threads to the inch), he felt a twinge of the sciatica that had been his father's and had come down to him through the jeans. Author Winner was grateful for any resemblance; his father had been a man of unusual qualities; loyal, helpful, friendly, courteous, kind, obedient, cheerful, thrifty, brave, clean and reverent; in the simplest of terms: a man of *dharma*.

– Felicia Lamport, ''By Henry James Cozened''

EXERCISES

EXERCISE 1, AWKWARD REPETITIONS. *In the following sentences, underline the awkward repetitions and examples of wordiness. Then rewrite the sentences, making them more concise by cutting or other revision.*

1. The several features of the situation were complex, and altogether the situation was complicated because of the many elementary elements involved.
2. It was perfectly clear that if she had come along with you as your companion that she would have been welcome.
3. I need hardly say to you all at this time and place that the very great economic loss is a serious source of loss to us all.
4. The chief significant reason why the economy failed was on account of an economic imbalance in the balance of trade.
5. I told him about the courses we were taking, French and history and so on and so forth, so he would get a good idea of the curriculum in which we take courses.
6. He had an arbitrary, set, inflexible rule for everything that he did, and for anything on which he had made up his mind it was very difficult to persuade him otherwise.
7. I really mean it, I certainly was relieved to make that discovery, to my real relief.

24

8. Unless a person is thoroughly and completely prepared, both mentally and psychologically, the chances of success in marriage are dim, doubtful, and obscure.

9. In regard to this matter of your new insurance policy, please be advised that your new policy is being taken up in a matter of approximately a week or thereabouts.

10. Without any doubt it is very true and unarguable that this great nation of ours is very ready to prepare to defend itself to the very last puck.

EXERCISE 2, OFFICIALESE. *Here is an example of officialese, not much exaggerated. Rewrite in plain English.*

It is desired by the administration at this particular time that students refrain and desist from the excessive noise and jostling that has characterized their behaviour in halls and corridors during recent occasions that I have observed. The magnitude of the noise involved has reached a degree where, in some cases of particularly recalcitrant offenders, the awarding of the degree in June may be jeopardized. All faculty personnel are enjoined to be alert to transmit to this office any flagrant discrepancies of this sort that may come to their attention from time to time.

§ 25. Vividness and Metaphor

25a.   Try to use words and phrases that give life and freshness to your style.

There are many ways to make a style vivid. Some of them were discussed in previous sections under the headings of "concreteness" and "conciseness." This section considers a few other devices available to the writer who wishes to create fresher, livelier language. First, you should be aware of the possibilities for freshness in the various parts of speech – nouns, modifiers, verbs. Second, you should see the possibilities in figurative language, or metaphor, although you must be aware of the dangers of metaphor, particularly since so much figurative language has been used before and has lost its freshness. Finally, you must recognize the related problem of overused language generally: the problem of triteness and clichés.

1. *Specific rather than general nouns will help to produce a vivid style.* When you write, "I heard a bird singing," your words may call up a definite sense image in the mind of your reader – or they may not – but you do not know what that image is. If instead of "bird" you say "canary" or "robin," your reader will at least make an effort to recall or imagine the song of a canary or a robin. Whenever you use a specific noun, you make it easy for your reader's mind to create a specific image. Word images direct the picture-making that goes on in your reader's brain.

2. *Try to use strong, picture-making adjectives and adverbs.* (See also § 21.) No part of speech is more likely to turn blue and rot than a flat, uninspired adjective or adverb. You say, "That was a good lecture," when you mean that it was witty, or stimulating, or instructive, or entertaining. You say "She is a nice person," when you mean that she is friendly, or sympathetic, or generous, or loyal, or modest, or conventional. You can find many adjectives that are more accurate and more vivid than *nice, cool, heavy, big, easy, hard*. A book of synonyms will help you find them.

It is a good idea to be on guard against all weak, overused adverbs, such as *very, pretty, rather, little*. Often a weak verb-adverb group can be replaced more effectively by a single strong verb. Note the following examples:

He ran quickly. [He fled, sprinted, jogged, rushed, surged, dashed.]

He was breathing rapidly. [He was panting, blowing, wheezing, puffing, gasping.]

She cut through it. [She pierced it, sliced it, tore it, split it, ripped it.]

He threw it down violently. [He hurled it, flung it, heaved it, pitched it.]

25

3. Try replacing general or colourless verbs with more specific and descriptive verbs. Here are some examples.

He moved toward the door. [He crept, sneaked, crawled, strolled, sidled, inched, drifted toward the door.]

She spoke several words. [She whispered, roared, shouted, hissed, mumbled, muttered several words.]

We put it on the truck. [We tossed, lifted, pitched, threw it on the truck.]

She got on the horse. [She scrambled, leaped, jumped, vaulted on the horse.]

25b. Figurative language can be used to add freshness to your style.

Some people feel that figurative language is a bit insincere, a little phony perhaps, good enough for poetry but out of place in honest prose. The truth is that all writing, from the deeply serious or reverent to the lightest, uses metaphor. Our daily talk is salted with figures of speech. We meet metaphors in our reading and take them as they come, hardly realizing what they are.

Although all figurative language is usually called metaphorical, some elementary distinctions are useful. A *metaphor* is a figure that likens one thing to another by saying that one thing *is* another: "Life's but a walking shadow, a poor player" . . . "all the world's a stage" . . . "a critic is a legless man who teaches running" . . . "a camel is a greyhound designed by a committee" . . . "an Edsel is a lemon" – these are metaphors. When the likeness is actually expressed by the use of *as* or *like*, the metaphor becomes a *simile* "All the world is *like* a stage" . . . "insubstantial *as* a dream" . . . "the water lay gray and wrinkled *like* an elephant's skin" – these are similes.

Figures of speech are best observed in context, where they look at home, as in the following selections.

Moonlight butters the whole Iowa night. Clover and corn smells are thick as syrup. I experience a tingling like the tiniest of electric wires touching the back of my neck, sending warm sensations through me. Then, as the lights flare, a scar against the blue-black sky, I see Shoeless Joe Jackson standing out in left field. His feet spread wide, body bent forward from the waist, hands on hips, he waits. I hear the sharp crack of the bat, and Shoeless Joe drifts effortlessly a few steps to his left, raises his right hand to signal for the ball, camps under it for a second or two, catches it, at the same time transferring it to his throwing hand, and fires it to the infield.

– W.P. Kinsella, *Shoeless Joe*

I could hear our house cracking its knuckles once in a while, the way it does at night, and Jake snoring gentle and the wind in my window screen and the frogs in our slough sort of stitching the quiet. Prairie gets real still at night.

– W.O. Mitchell, "A Deal's A Deal"

She peels potatoes – the scene flashed before me like an old filmstrip from childhood. How often I had seen her peel things, potatoes for her family, apples for Amande and me. The peel would fall over her wrist in one continuous strip, so thin I would watch spellbound for it to break. It never did, until the apple was pared clean. When, finally, she presented it to me on her great brown hand, it no longer seemed like an apple at all; it was a sculpture of an apple, so lovingly had its nature been understood. And the peel would lie coiled on the newspaper at her feet, beautiful as newly woven ribbon.

– Ebbitt Cutler, *I Once Knew an Indian Woman*

25c.   Metaphors and other phrases that have become trite should be avoided.

Trite expressions, whether they were once metaphors or not, are also called *hackneyed phrases* or *clichés*. At one time they may have been apt or witty and appropriate, but now, because they have been used so often, they are stale and flat. They put off the reader. The following list may help to put you on your guard:

acid test
after all has been said
all in all
all work and no play
among those present
ardent admirers
as luck would have it
at a loss for words
at one fell swoop
avoid like the plague
beat a hasty retreat
beggars description
better half
better late than never
blissfully ignorant
bolt from the blue
breathless silence
budding genius
busy as a bee
by leaps and bounds
caught like rats in a trap
checkered career
conspicuous by his absence
course of true love
discreet silence
doomed to disappointment
drastic action
dull, sickening thud
dyed in the wool
each and every one
easier said than done
equal to the occasion
face the music
fair sex
familiar landmark
favour with a selection

festive occasion
few and far between
goes without saying
gridiron warriors
grim reaper
holy bonds of matrimony
in all its glory
in the last (or final) analysis
irony of fate
justice to the occasion
last but not least
leaves speechless
long-felt need
meets the eye
method in his madness
monarch of all he surveys
mother nature
motley crowd
needless to say
nipped in the bud
none the worse for wear
no sooner said than done
partake of refreshments
play with fire
pleasing prospect
pot luck
powers that be
presided at the piano
proud possessor
psychological moment
reigns supreme
rendered a selection
riot of colour
ripe old age
sadder but wiser
shadow of the goal posts

25

silence reigned supreme
specimen of humanity
sumptuous repast
sweat of his brow
table groaned
tempest in a teapot
tired but happy
troubled waters
untold wealth
vale of tears
venture a suggestion

[make a] virtue of necessity
water over the dam or under
  the bridge
wee small hours
wends his way
where ignorance is bliss
with a vengeance
with bated breath
words fail to express
worked like a horse
wrought havoc

EXERCISES

EXERCISE 1, WRITING FOR VIVIDNESS. *Rewrite the following paragraph. Pay special attention to the verbs, adjectives, and adverbs, and try to make use of metaphors or similes where they can be made appropriate.*

The boy walked home from school very slowly. It was April, and he observed as he went the various signs of the spring season. As he approached his own house, he paused to speak to his neighbour, who was working on his lawn. Finally he turned and walked indoors, for he was hungry.

EXERCISE 2, CLICHÉS AND TRITE PHRASES. *Now rewrite this passage again, this time using as many clichés and trite phrases as you can.*

26

§ 26. Reference of Pronouns

26a. **The antecedent of a pronoun in a sentence should be immediately clear to the reader.**

As a rule, pronouns should have definite antecedents and should be placed as near their antecedents as possible. The hedging in this last sentence, represented by the phrase ''as a rule,'' refers to two or three special situations. First, there are a number of idiomatic phrases in which a pronoun has no visible antecedent, such as *it rained last night*; *it's the climate*; *it is time to go home*. There is no lack of clearness in these sentences. Second, the pronoun *you*, in the sense of *one*, or a *person*, has wide currency in informal written and spoken English, and occasionally in good formal writing. Third, the pronouns *which*, *this*, *that* may refer to an idea or fact expressed by a whole clause or a sentence, or by a part of a clause, if the reference is unmistakably clear. These last, however, present a greater risk than the previous two idioms. Even when the reference *is* unmistakably clear, *which*, *this*, or *that* may be weaker than some more specific noun.

In good writing, the meaning of a sentence should be clear on the first reading. If the reader has to hesitate, to search for the substantive (i.e., a noun or anything that functions as a noun) to which the pronoun refers, or to puzzle over which of two possible antecedents it does refer to, the sentence is inept.

Indefinite
She saw a play at the new Plymouth Theatre, but later she was not able to remember it very well. [What could she not remember, the play or the theatre?]

Clear
At the new Plymouth Theatre she saw a play that she later was not able to remember very well.

or
She saw a play at the new Plymouth Theatre, but later she was not able to remember the building very well.

Indefinite
Since my grandfather was a doctor, it is not surprising that I have chosen *that* for a career. [The antecedent of *that* is only vaguely implied.]

Clear
Since my grandfather was a doctor, it is not surprising that I have chosen medicine for my career.

26

It is usually awkward to have a pronoun refer to an antecedent in a subordinate position, such as the object of a preposition. The reader will instinctively associate a pronoun with the most prominent substantive in the clause he or she has just read. The result is confusion – possibly a momentary confusion but still an undesirable one.

Confusing
Conscientious doctors do attempt to quiet the fears of their patients; they are often better able to face their symptoms as a result. [The reader will hesitate at "they are," because "Doctors" still appears to be the subject of the sentence.]

Clear
Conscientious doctors do attempt to quiet the fears of their patients, who are often better able to face their symptoms as a result.

As long as they occur close together in the same sentence, a pronoun and its antecedent may change places, the pronoun coming first.

Example
Although she was an intelligent woman who could have been "successful," Maria refused to be subservient to her incompetent and patronizing employer.

26b. The reference of a pronoun should not be ambiguous. 26

Ambiguous
The title of the book was so dramatic that *it* was a great help in remembering *it*. [Does the first *it* refer to the title, or to the drama of the title? Does the second *it* refer to the book, or to the title of the book?]

Clear
I remembered that book easily because of its dramatic title.

Ambiguous
The players and umpires know one another well and sometimes they call them by their first names.

Clear
Players who know umpires well sometimes call them by their first names.

Ambiguous
Leonard told his brother that he did not yet know the game thoroughly.

Clear
As Leonard admitted to his brother, he did not yet know the game thoroughly.

or
Leonard charged his brother with not knowing the game thoroughly.

It is clumsy to resort to a parenthetic repetition of the anteced-ent after a pronoun. When you find yourself painted into this corner, revise the sentence according to one of the models listed here.

Awkward
Leonard told his brother that he (Leonard) did not yet know the game thoroughly.

26c.   In formal writing, the indefinite reference is less common than in informal writing and in speech.

26 This stricture refers to two particular situations: (1) the use of the indefinite *you* to mean *one*, *a person* and the indefinite *they* to mean *people*, and (2) the use of *this*, *that*, and *which* to refer to a clause, sentence, or a general idea.

1. The indefinite *you* and *they* are common in speech and in many forms of informal writing; they are less appropriate in formal writing. Guard against making their use a habit, especially in papers of explanation.

Formal
First the seed is scattered evenly over the ground; then the soil is raked lightly and firmed with a roller. [Note the passive voice here.]

Informal

First you scatter the seed; then you rake it in and firm the soil with a roller. [Or "First scatter the seed; then rake it in and firm the soil with a roller." *You* is understood.]

Formal

When a player hits a slapshot, he should bend his knees and follow through completely.

Informal

When hitting a slapshot, you should bend your knees and follow through completely.

2. A pronoun may have a clause or a sentence for its antecedent; it may even refer to a thought expressed by a part of the preceding sentence. As long as the reference is unmistakable, the sentence is clear. But the careless writer may fall into the habit of stringing together a series of *this-*, *that-*, and *which-* clauses without worrying about either clearness or exactness. When the writer has doubts about the clearness or definiteness of an antecedent, he or she can sometimes summarize the idea of the clause referred to by an expression such as *this truth*, *this condition*, *a circumstance which*, and so forth. The sentence should be rewritten if the result is still unsatisfactory.

Notice that the references are clear in the following sentences.

Clear

I have finished my work at last. That should satisfy the boss.

He recommended that I write to the secretary, which I did without delay.

If you have decided to speak out on this issue, it should be done quickly.

Now notice the vague references in the following sentences.

Vague

The antismoking campaign in England, which had such little effect, has cost a good deal of money and energy, and this leads to pessimism about our own campaign.

26

Clear
The expensive and energetic antismoking campaign in England has had little effect, a result that leads to pessimism about our own campaign.

Vague
The fish are kept alive and fresh in glass tanks, and it also attracts people which helps the business considerably. [What do *it* and *which* refer to?]

Clear
The fish are kept alive and fresh in glass tanks. The display of live fish helps business by attracting people to the place.

Vague
No one knew what the president would do about this, but it was clear that it had to be settled by an executive decision.

Clear
No one knew what the president would do about this strike, but some form of executive decision was needed to settle it.

26d. **The careless use of *same*, *such*, *above*, and *said* as reference words often produces an awkward sentence.**

These words are used as reference words in legal or technical writing; in ordinary writing they should be avoided, not because they are incorrect but because they usually lead to awkwardness of expression. Use one of the common pronouns (*it*, *them*, *this*) or the name of the thing to which you refer.

Poor
I stood there holding the monkey wrench and oil can in my hands. The foreman ordered me to return the same to the engine room.

Better
I stood there holding the monkey wrench and oil can in my hands. The foreman ordered me to return the tools to the engine room.

Poor
The significance of said decision is not yet fully comprehended.

Better
The significance of this decision is not yet fully comprehended.

Poor
Please return same to me by bearer.

Better
Please return it [or name the object] to me by the bearer of this note.

Poor
The above is a complete refutation of their arguments.

Better
The facts mentioned completely refute their arguments.

26e. **A pronoun should agree with its antecedent in number, gender, and person.**

For a discussion of the agreement of pronouns, see § 4i.

Poor
Every student is required to bring their books.

Better
Every student is required to bring his or her books.

Poor
A team that loses most of its games may owe its failure to the fact that they do not have a good coach. [You must be consistent. If you begin by considering *team* as singular, you must continue to refer to it as one unit.]

Better
A team that loses most of its games may owe its failure to its lack of a good coach. [Or, more simply, "may owe its failure to poor coaching."]

26

26f.   It is usually considered awkward to begin an essay with a reference to the title.

It is better to repeat the words of your title in your first sentence than it is to refer to your title with a pronoun. For example, if your title is "Coming About in a Smaller Boat," do not begin your paper, "This is difficult for the beginning sailor to learn." Say instead, "The beginning sailor will have some difficulty learning how to come about in a small boat." (The writer would do well, in fact, to lead up to a reference to the subject with a more intriguing opening altogether. This one is flat. When taking an essay test, however, in which the question must be incorporated in the answer, and where there is little time for stylistic nicety, the first sentence of the response might well rephrase the question as a beginning for the argument.)

EXERCISE

EXERCISE, FAULTY REFERENCE. *In each of the following sentences underline the pronoun or pronouns with faulty reference. Rewrite each sentence so as to correct the error.*

1. The baggage was loaded onto a small handcart which was the only way to get it through the crowded airport.
2. I worked for the college physics department last year, washing equipment for them and cleaning their laboratories.
3. He told me all about it, and very well too. It was something I would like to have done myself.
4. The history of this community goes back to the seventeenth century which makes a visit well worth while.
5. The obligations of an army sergeant are that of any leader in a small group.
6. While a person would suppose that she wanted nothing else in life, you could be very wrong about this.
7. The wealth of the country is controlled by a few who live in the city, which is usual in such societies.

26

8. Every player must learn his signals which will make an efficient and co-ordinated team.

9. He laughed at what I had said. This was amazing.

10. Everybody knows the reason why the economy is in such poor shape. It is a source of dismay to us all.

11. In *Being There*, the gang that threatened Chance did not understand how silly their threats sounded.

12. There seems to be no general agreement on this, but attitudes are changing.

13. Between you and me, Charles doesn't know the first thing about good music.

14. Anybody can stand up and state their views on abortion.

15. This is the decision that led to the defeat, and that ended the war.

§27. Proper Arrangement

The parts of a sentence should be so arranged that the meaning of the sentence is clear at the first reading.

Since English is not a highly inflected language (i.e., not one in which words change form to reflect grammatical relations), the meaning of an English sentence depends largely on the arrangement of the words in it. The reader naturally assumes that the parts of a sentence that are placed next to each other are logically related to each other. You must therefore be careful to arrange words in a sentence in such a way that its meaning will be clear on the first reading. The rule that will guide you may be stated in two parts: (1) place all modifiers, whether words, phrases, or clauses, as close as possible to the words they modify; (2) avoid placing these elements near other words they might be taken to modify.

27

27a. In formal writing, place adverbs logically.

Let us use *only* as an illustration of what happens when idiom contradicts logic. Logically, an adverb should be placed near the word it modifies; idiomatically, it is often placed elsewhere. For instance, would you say, "We have room for only two more," or, "We only have room for two more"? The person with a logical mind says that "only" modifies "two"; the person who prefers the second form answers that idiom does not pay much attention to logic. Both forms are used. The second is used generally in speech, in a great deal of informal writing, and often in formal writing. The first is used by writers and speakers who are disturbed by the logic of the second.

Common in Speech

He *only* worked half a day.

Everyone is *not* honest.

The child *hardly* ate any food.

She *just* took one apple.

He *almost* weeded the whole garden.

More Logical in Writing

He worked *only* half a day.

Not everyone is honest.

The child ate *hardly* any food.

She took *just* one apple.

He weeded *almost* the whole garden.

27

27b. Avoid ambiguous placement of phrases.

There is no exact position in a sentence that phrases must always occupy; the best rule to follow is to keep them away from words they must *not* be understood to modify. The result of such misplacement is often unintentionally humorous.

Misplaced
He began to lose his desire to reach the summit *after a time.*

Better
After a time he began to lose his desire to reach the summit.

Misplaced

I was dressed and ready to start climbing *within an hour.* [Does the phrase refer to *being dressed* or to *starting to climb*?]

Better

Within an hour I was dressed and ready to start climbing. [*Or*] I was dressed *within an hour* and ready to start climbing.

Misplaced

Economic sanctions would work against Argentina *without doubt.*

Better

Without doubt economic sanctions would work against Argentina.

27c.   Avoid ambiguous placement of clauses.

Clauses, like phrases, may be placed wherever they seem to fit in a sentence – except near words they can be mistaken to modify.

Ambiguous or Ludicrous

I hid the ring in my pocket *that I intended to give to her.*

Better

The ring *that I intended to give to her* I hid in my pocket. [*Or*] I hid in my pocket the ring *that I intended to give to her.*

27d.   Avoid squinting modifiers.

Modifiers so placed in a sentence that they may be understood with either the preceding or the following words are called *squinting modifiers.* As a rule, it is better not to try to cure the fault by means of punctuation.

Squinting

I firmly decided *the next day* to start studying.

Clear

I firmly decided to start studying *the next day.*

27

Squinting
After we had stopped at a service station *with the help of the attendant* we found our position on the map.

Clear
After we had stopped at a service station, the attendant helped us to locate our position on the map.

Squinting
The girl who had sat down *quickly* opened her textbook.

Clear
The girl who had sat down opened her textbook *quickly*.

27e. Use the split infinitive only to avoid awkwardness.

Placing an adverbial modifier between the sign *to* and the verb of an infinitive results in what is traditionally known as a "split infinitive" ("to quickly walk" *splits* the infinitive *to walk*; "to walk quickly" is a better arrangement). The split infinitive is no longer considered one of the capital crimes of composition – if it ever was. It is not true that the parts of an infinitive are inseparable. But since a split infinitive still causes many people (especially composition instructors) discomfort, it is better not to split infinitives too rashly or frequently. A good rule to follow is this: place the adverbial modifier between *to* and the verb of an infinitive only when such an arrangement is necessary to avoid an awkward phrase. Here are some examples: "to even wish," "to seriously cripple," "to further confirm," "to utterly forget," "to further complicate," "to first consider." Remember that these are exceptions to the rule.

27

27f. Avoid the awkward separation of any words that normally belong near each other.

Words that usually belong near each other are subject and verb, verb and object, the parts of a verb phrase, noun and adjective modifier, and noun and appositive.

Awkward

Mr. Justice Ivan Rand, in a thoughtful consideration of the issue, dissented. [Subject and verb split by long phrase]

Better

Mr. Justice Ivan Rand dissented in a thoughtful consideration of the issue.

Awkward

Finally, we caught, after sitting in our rowboat for four hours, a small salmon. [Verb and object split]

Better

Finally, after sitting in our rowboat for four hours, we caught a small salmon.

Awkward

After it got dark, the girls bedded down beside a stream, wet, tired, and discouraged.

Better

After it got dark, the wet, tired, and discouraged girls bedded down beside a stream. [Or] After it got dark, the girls – wet, tired, and discouraged – bedded down beside a stream.

EXERCISES

EXERCISE 1, ELIMINATING SPLIT INFINITIVES. *Improve each of the following sentences by eliminating an awkward split infinitive.*

27

1. I hope to some day in the near future visit Paris again.
2. You should now begin to methodically and carefully budget your time for study.
3. If you care to remain in college, you must plan to quickly change your habits.
4. Your first concern should be to not carelessly waste your time.
5. If you really care to materially improve your grades, you should promise to immediately give up your trips to the bar.

EXERCISE 2, CORRECTING MISPLACED ELEMENTS. *Point out the misplaced element in each of the following sentences. Then show how the sentence can be improved. Do not use punctuation as a means of correcting an error in arrangement.*

1. We decided at nine o'clock to call him at his home.
2. Taking too many vitamin pills frequently causes excessive smiling.
3. Her dropped packages were collected before any had been stepped on by the bus driver.
4. The goalie returned to the team after two days' absence on Friday.
5. Paul, not wishing to prolong the argument far into the night, agreed to wash my car.
6. To be misunderstood often is the fate of an original lover.
7. The departing train brought thoughts of distant friends to the poor girl rumbling over the high bridge.
8. Our teacher has many theories about things that are different.
9. The sheriff was stabbed while sleeping by an unknown person.
10. He needs someone to show him how to put his affairs in order badly.

§ 28. Dangling or Misrelated Modifiers

28

28a. Awkward dangling modifiers should be avoided.

There is considerable difference of opinion among educated people over the use of what is traditionally known as the ''dangling modifier.'' Some say that it should be called the ''misrelated modifier,'' for instead of dangling it actually attaches itself too easily to the wrong word. When it does, especially when it results in confusion or in unintentional humour, it is bad. When it calls attention to itself and away from the intended meaning of the sentence, it is bad. One might add that it is wrong because so many educated persons have been taught to regard it as a careless way of writing.

Here are some examples of dangling participles, the most common error in this category. Notice that the phrasing often results in unintentionally ludicrous meanings.

Walking along the quiet street, the houses looked old and comfortable.

While waiting for the coffee to warm, the cereal boiled away.

Strewn on the floor in large piles, he glanced idly through the remains of his books.

I had a summer job that year, thereby enabling me to return to school. [This is more awkward than plain wrong. Who or what enabled me to return to school?]

In addition to participles, infinitives are sometimes left dangling. The problem here is that there is no visible subject of the infinitive in the sentence.

To see this view properly, the sun must be shining. [Does the sun see the view?]

To succeed in business the basic facts of economics are apparently not always necessary.

In each of these sentences, it does not matter whether the phrase dangles because it is not attached where it should be or is misrelated because it attaches itself where it should not be. Each sentence is awkward or misleading.

A dangler may be corrected in three ways: (1) by changing the phrase to a clause, (2) by providing a noun or pronoun to which the dangler can properly attach itself, or (3) by reordering the sentence.

28

Examples

As I walked along the quiet street, the houses looked old and comfortable.

While I waited for the coffee to warm, the cereal boiled away.

He glanced idly through the remains of his books, which were strewn on the floor in large piles.

The money I made on a summer job that year enabled me to return to school.

To appreciate this view properly, one should see it when the sun is shining.

In order to succeed in business, it is apparently not always necessary to know the basic facts of economics.

Note that the absolute phrase does not dangle. In the absolute phrase the word that the participle attaches itself to is in the phrase itself.

Examples

The day's work being over, we returned to town.

The guests having arrived, the dog headed downstairs.

Three more girls, their wet hair plastered down over their eyes, stumbled into the classroom.

It may be helpful to think of the participle as a kind of preposition in such sentences as these:

Considering the size of the house, it seemed remarkably cheap.

Judging by his voting record, he is a responsible alderman.

A slight shift in phraseology, however, produces a dangler, even though the meaning is essentially unchanged:

28

Viewing his voting record, he is a responsible alderman. [The sentence suggests that the alderman is responsible, and he is viewing his voting record.]

Certain idiomatic phrases, especially those that express a general action and those that serve as directive and transitional links, are always acceptable in either formal or informal situations. These are phrases like *generally speaking*, *looking at it from another point of view*, *taking everything into consideration*, *provided that*, *failing*, and others that are similar.

Examples

Failing agreement, the meeting was adjourned.

Generally speaking, the worse a pun is, the better it is.

28b. **A sentence with any sort of expression, such as a phrase or an appositive, that is not easily understood with the rest of the sentence is awkward and usually misleading.**

Illogical

A gentleman farmer, his wardrobe ranges from faultlessly tailored suits to four-buckle rubber boots. [The expression *a gentleman farmer* seems to be in apposition with *wardrobe*.]

Revised

As he is a gentleman farmer, his wardrobe ranges from faultlessly tailored suits to four-buckle rubber boots.

Illogical

After five years in a city school, a country school presents many problems in adjustment. [One naturally associates the opening phrase with *a country school*.]

Revised

A person who has spent five years in a city school encounters many problems in adjustment when transferring to a country school.

Illogical

When only a few years old, Yakland's president was indicted for bribery and extortion.

Revised

When Yakland was only a few years old, its president was indicted for bribery and extortion.

The dangling or misrelated modifier, as can be seen from the examples offered, is a stylistic mistake. If it causes confusion, even momentary confusion, or if it is associated with an unintentionally humorous image, it is undesirable.

EXERCISE

EXERCISE, CORRECTING DANGLERS. *Some of the following sentences are correct, while some contain objectionable danglers. Pick out the faulty sentences and correct them.*

1. Buying her ticket at the box office, she walked into the opera house.
2. While waiting to be seated, the usher approached her.
3. He delayed taking her ticket, thus causing a small traffic jam.
4. Seated at last, she glanced through her program.
5. The opera, based vaguely on Shakespeare, was the famous *Falstaff.*
6. One of Italy's most beloved composers, the music was by Verdi.
7. The curtain having gone up at last, she sat back in her seat feeling thoroughly relaxed.
8. While sitting there quietly, the stage exploded with excitement.
9. To see an opera at its best, the scenery too must be appreciated.
10. Rising at the intermission, she strolled into the outer lobby.
11. She heard a familiar voice, thereby meeting an old friend.
12. Being an old opera lover, they got along famously.
13. When young, the opera had seemed too complicated.
14. Now, however, having matured, she enjoyed almost all performances.
15. Returning home in a taxi, the music of Verdi still seemed to sing in her ears.

29

§ 29. Emphasis in the Sentence

The relative importance of ideas in a sentence may be shown by various devices of structure. The principle is known as *emphasis*.

Emphasis is a word that may be understood in more than one sense. A speaker may emphasize words by shouting or screaming them; a writer may emphasize words by indicating that they be printed in italics or capitals. Some writers and speakers have used these methods. But that is not the sense in which the word is used here. Here *emphasis* means using rhetorical devices that show the relative importance or prominence of ideas and details in a sentence or paragraph. Some of these devices have been discussed elsewhere in connection with other qualities of good writing – clarity, directness, order, coherence, conciseness, directness. Two or three others will be pointed out here and in the following sections.

It may be useful to restate the various devices by which the relative importance of ideas can be shown:

1. By placing the important idea by itself in a short sentence. [Empire policies bred rebellion.]
2. By placing the idea in a main clause of a complex sentence. [The Empire depended too heavily on military force, which it could not generate after losing its weapons.]
3. By changing the normal order of a sentence. [Such unrest the rulers could not tolerate.]
4. By using parallel structure. [No one could have predicted the extent or the destructiveness of the rebellion. *See §31.*]
5. By using the order of climax. [The rebel leaders were intelligent, bold, and successful. Their tactics were simple, their weapons portable, and their victories stunning.]
6. By repeating key words. [Their spoils were money and influence: money to hire more mercenaries, influence to gain political advantage. *See §24a.*]
7. By using the active instead of the passive voice. [Darth Vader fired the laser gun; *not*, The laser gun was fired by Darth Vader. *See §29c.*]
8. By giving an important idea fuller treatment. [Without the help of warp thrust, a system that aided the ship in achieving star speed, the rebels could not have escaped.]
9. By placing important words in prominent positions. [*Firepower* was what gave the Empire a crucial advantage. No one could deny that one quality gave the rebels the final edge: *determination*. *See §29a.*]

29

10. By using periodic structure. [To continue to fight against all odds is of course impractical but brave; *not*, It is of course impractical but brave to continue to fight against all odds. *See §29b.*]

29a. Placing important words in key positions in the sentence will help to show the relative importance of ideas.

The most conspicuous positions in a sentence of some length are the beginning and the end. These are the positions that should be used for ideas that deserve attention and emphasis. The less important details, the modifiers, the qualifying comments, should be tucked away inside the sentence.

Weak
Students who cheat in an examination are cheating only themselves ultimately.

Better
Students who cheat in an examination are ultimately cheating only themselves.

Weak
Public speaking should be taught in first-year English, I think.

Better
Public speaking, I think, should be taught in first-year English.

29

No writer can consistently rearrange sentences to begin and end them with important ideas. Many sentences are so short that the reader's mind comprehends them as units. In many others the word order is determined by the nature of the English language. A writer may occasionally construct a sentence such as this – as Stephen Leacock once did – "Him they elected president," but in sentences such as the following no problems of emphasis can arise: "He is a good person." "Her son was killed at Dunkirk." "The day's work is done." "The captain saluted the flag."

29b. Occasionally you may express a thought more effectively by changing a sentence from the loose to the periodic form.

A *periodic sentence* is one in which the main idea is held until the end; *a loose sentence* is one in which the main idea is followed by details and modifiers. The effect of a periodic sentence is one of suspense – that is, the reader is asked to wait for the main idea until the details upon which the main idea is based or by which it is limited or changed are outlined. Not all sentences in English are periodic; many of them, in fact, are loose. It is precisely for this reason that an occasional periodic sentence is emphatic.

Loose

In recent years many factories were established in the city, especially plants engaged in the manufacture of rubber ducks.

Periodic

In recent years many factories, especially plants engaged in the manufacture of rubber ducks, were established in the city.

Loose

Stop writing if you have nothing more to say.

Periodic

If you have nothing more to say, stop writing.

Loose

It is of course impractical to legislate for those who will behave themselves while completely ignoring those who will not.

Periodic

To legislate for those who will behave themselves while completely ignoring those who will not is, of course, impractical.

29

Note the way a writer can create suspense by using a summarizing main clause.

Confusion where there has been clarity, mystification where there has been understanding, abstruseness where there has been simplicity – these are the results of your ''help.''

29c. Use the active instead of the passive voice where the active is more direct and natural.

The use of the passive voice is not in itself a grammatical or stylistic fault; it is the *overuse* of it that is a fault. The passive voice has several proper and necessary uses: (1) when the object or receiver of the action of the verb is more important than the doer; (2) when the doer of the action is not known; (3) when the writer wishes to place the emphasis on the receiver instead of on the doer.

> To the satisfaction of everyone, Grabowski was chosen best player of the tournament.
>
> Several priceless old manuscripts were destroyed.
>
> The wounded hostage was dragged into the building.

Then note the difference in the following sentences when the active voice replaces the passive:

Passive

A good time was had by everyone.

Then a driver's test was taken by me.

A feeling of nausea is experienced by the passengers.

Active

Everyone had a good time.

Then I took a driver's test.

The passengers experienced a feeling of nausea.

29

EXERCISES

EXERCISE 1, EMPHASIS. *Using the principle of emphasis by position, improve the following sentences.*

1. A fool can ask more questions than a wise man can answer, according to the Italian proverb.

2. Long sentences in a short essay are like large rooms in a small house, the professor explained.

3. Generally speaking it is well not to speak generally, as someone has said.

4. Generally speaking, one good teacher is worth a dozen good books.

5. When in danger or in doubt, run in circles, scream, and shout, the sergeant advised.

EXERCISE 2, LOOSE AND PERIODIC SENTENCES. *Change the following loose sentences to periodic sentences.*

1. Stress has a harmful effect on our ability to learn, it was discovered by these experiments.

2. For this experiment two control groups were selected who had the same ability to memorize.

3. One group was told that its scores were poor after they had completed about half the test.

4. Their performance at once deteriorated when the testing was resumed.

5. But their ability improved considerably after they had been praised for their improved performance.

EXERCISE 3, ACTIVE OR PASSIVE VERBS. *Improve the following sentences by changing the verb from the passive to the active.*

1. The skidding car was brought safely to a stop by the alert driver.

2. The police officer's warning was accepted by him with humility.

3. I thought that he would be nervous and frightened, but a very different reaction was observed by me.

4. As he informed me, a set of new tires had been bought by his wife a few days ago.

5. But the need for new tires, he said, was vetoed by him.

6. Instead, the new tires were returned to the dealer and a new guitar was purchased with the money by him.

7. "Do you think now that a new guitar is worth your life?" was asked by the officer.

29

8. The workings of a careless person's mind cannot be understood by more cautious people.

9. After a few minutes the trip to our destination was resumed by us.

10. Glancing up at the rear-view mirror, it was observed that the man's car was now following us.

§ 30. Shift in Point of View

Any unnecessary and illogical shift in point of view should be avoided.

Three common grammatical shifts in point of view are (1) from the active to the passive voice, (2) from the past to the present tense, and (3) from *one* to *you* and similar shifts of person. These and other shifts are described below. Writing is clearer and more pleasing if you maintain a consistent point of view.

30a.   Unnecessary shifts from the active to the passive voice are undesirable.

Shift

You wrap the gift carefully in paper; it is then tied securely.

We were acquainted with his brother, and his eighty-year-old father was also well known to us.

Paul drove the car into a ditch, but later it was pushed out by him.

Better

You wrap the gift carefully in paper and tie it securely.

We knew both his brother and his eighty-year-old father.

Paul drove the car into a ditch, but later he pushed it out.

30b.   Needless shifts in tense – from past to present or from present to past – are usually objectionable.

See also § 6.

30

Shift

I *go* right on into the room and then *looked* around me to see what he *would be doing* with all that furniture. [Such shifts in tense must be watched for, especially in narrative accounts.]

Better

I *went* right on into the room and then *looked* around me to see what he *might be doing* with all that furniture. [Or *might have done* with all that furniture]

Shift

After *planning* the trip I *had thought* I *deserved* a little credit for its success.

Better

After *having planned* the trip, I *thought* I *deserved* a little credit for its success. [All verbs in past tense]

Shift

MacLennan's character Athanase Tallard *worried* constantly while he *plans* to build a factory.

Better

MacLennan's character Athanase Tallard *worries* constantly while he *plans* to build a factory.

30c.   Needless shifts in number or person should be avoided.

Shift

If one really wishes to sample fine cooking, try that restaurant on the corner.

30

Correct in Formal Context

If one really wishes to sample superior cooking, one should try the restaurant on the corner.

Correct in Informal Style

If you really want to enjoy some good eating, try that restaurant on the corner.

See also § 26e for a discussion of number in pronouns.

30d. A writer should guard against mixing two distinctly separate constructions in a sentence.

A *mixed construction* is usually the result of hasty and careless writing. The writer begins one construction, and immediately, without troubling to look back on what has been written, continues with another construction.

Mixed

In our basement we found a small wood stove, which upon removing the front, made it resemble a fireplace. [*Which* refers to *stove*. The stove cannot remove its own front, nor can the stove make itself resemble anything.]

Clear

In our basement we found a small wood stove, which we made into a fireplace by removing its front.

In our basement we found a small wood stove. By removing its front, we made it resemble a fireplace.

Mixed

She did not say a word, but took me to the back yard in what seemed to me a bit hurriedly. [The writer has forgotten the original intention and could say either *took me in what seemed a hurried manner* or *took me a bit hurriedly*.]

Occasionally a writer will run an independent clause into a sentence in such a way that it appears to stand as the subject of a verb.

Mixed

We were tired of travelling is the main reason we came here.

I was all alone was what truly frightened me.

The loss of good pilots was what destroyed their strategic advantage.

Clear

We came here mainly because we were tired of travelling.

What truly frightened me was that I was all alone.

The loss of good pilots destroyed their strategic advantage.

**30e. Mixed figures of speech are inappropriate in serious
writing.**

In the teaching of writing, warnings against scrambled metaphors may have been given an undeserved and an unfortunate
prominence. A *mixed metaphor* is often a sign of mental vitality.
Even Shakespeare spoke of taking up arms against a sea of
troubles. The danger is that in scrambling two incongruous images your phrase or sentence may become unintentionally comic.
Speaking of Shakespeare, consider this blooper from a student
essay: "Shakespeare, not leaving a screw unturned, ties up the
first scene in a neat bundle."

Another danger is that in attempting to use metaphors students either misunderstand them or lapse into cliché. An example comes from a term paper in which the writer talked of the
college experience as "a tough road to hoe." The expression is
trite to begin with, but the city-dwelling student also did not
know that "rows," not "roads," are hoed.

The following samples illustrate more clearly what is meant
by "mixed imagery."

> Many high-school athletes think they can ride on their high-
> school laurels right into a position on the college team. [How
> can one ride on a laurel?]

> The future of jazz was at its lowest ebb. [Even were the future
> not transported to the past, a rare feat in itself, how could a future
> ebb?]

> A college education enables the graduate to meet the snares
> and pitfalls of life with a broader point of view.

30

EXERCISES

EXERCISE 1, ILLOGICAL SHIFTS. *In each of the following
sentences specify the type or types of illogical shift that you find – in tense,
voice, number, or person. Then make the necessary corrections.*

1. The submarine *Seashark* goes down in April of 1978, and many
   scientists participated in the investigation that followed.

2. They conducted research from several ships; also a survey of the ocean bottom was made.

3. One would suppose the task would have been easy, since all you have to do is find the hull on the ocean floor.

4. The scientific group had its hands full, however, for they could discover no trace of the missing craft.

5. The navy called off its search in September; they had done all they could.

6. New efforts have been undertaken by private scientific organizations and universities have continued research into the mishap.

7. Until late 1979, no one knows just where the ship is lying – you would have been amazed to learn how the discovery was finally made.

8. A bathysphere is ordered; it has been at work for some time on the scene.

9. No doubt many scientists on the project would prefer to return to shore as a laboratory researcher.

10. In the process, however, the ocean floor in the area has been fully investigated, which had been useful for future oceanographers.

EXERCISE 2, MIXED CONSTRUCTIONS. *Here are ten badly confused sentences. Rewrite them. Do not be afraid to break them up if they can be improved in that manner.*

1. You could view that painting as a complex pattern of colours or as an amateur who knows very little about art.

2. They had a big wedding which I regret to say they never asked me to come.

3. The table was made of inlaid wood and a source of admiration to all who saw it.

4. Everybody considered her a beauty that she was an asset to the community.

5. The principal said he believed in a straightforward, middle-of-the-road, thoroughly well-rounded plan of education which everyone ought to have the opportunity.

6. Hard work has always been a bad point with me due to my time has always been so preoccupied with fun.

30

7. He looked bravely into the eye of the future with a fast and unfaltering step.
8. The reason things are at such a low ebb is because of the inevitable swing of the economic pendulum.
9. Sometimes you see Harry reading comfortably in the library and looks as if he has fallen asleep as indeed he has.
10. Anyone who writes sentences like these that thinks he can write English ought to know better.

§ 31. Parallel Structure

31a. Parallel structure expresses similar ideas in the same grammatical and rhetorical patterns.

Parallel structure is primarily a rhetorical device that writers use to give their sentences force, clearness, grace, and rhythm. In its more elementary uses it gives sentences greater clarity and smoothness. For a more complete discussion of rhetorical uses of parallelism and balance, turn to chapter 3.

In its simpler and more elementary form, parallel structure is a balancing of noun with noun, an infinitive with another infinitive, a phrase with another phrase, and a clause with another clause. Used at this level, the device will cure many a deformed or wandering sentence:

Awkward
Adults can teach children to be a friend and courteous. (Noun paralleled with adjective)

Parallel
Adults can teach children to be friendly and courteous. (Adjective and adjective)

Awkward
Our English instructor asked us to close our books, to take pen and paper, and that we were to write a short paper. (Two infinitives and a clause)

31

Parallel

Our English instructor asked us to close our books, to take pen and paper, and to write a short paper. (Three infinitives)

Awkward

Few of the leaders anticipated the bitterness of the strike or how long it would last. (A noun and a clause)

Parallel

Few of the leaders anticipated the bitterness or the duration of the strike. (Noun and noun)

31b.   Avoid the *and who* and the *and which* constructions.

The "and who" or "and which" fault, as it is called, consists of using *and who* or *and which* in a sentence that does not have a preceding *who* or *which* clause.

Faulty

She is a woman of wide experience *and who* is also very popular with the farmers.

Parallel

She is a woman of wide experience and great popularity among the farmers.

Faulty

I am interested in computers, because it is a new field *and which* offers interesting opportunities to one who knows mathematics.

Parallel

I am interested in computers, which is a new field and which offers interesting opportunities. . .

31c.   Avoid the false parallel.

Straining for parallelism where it is not natural is a fault that occurs rarely in college writing. The false parallel, however, is not the result of too much care for form; it is purely accidental.

31

Illogical

I finally realized that my new personality was not making me happy, intelligent, or friends. [The three words seem to depend on *making me*, but two of them are adjectives and one is a noun. They are not logically parallel.]

Revised

I finally realized that my new personality was not making me happy and intelligent or bringing me friends.

Parallel forms may be used with the correlative conjunctions *both – and*, *either – or*, *neither – nor*, *not only – but also*. Care should be taken in placing these correlatives so that the intended meaning of the sentence is not obscured.

EXERCISES

EXERCISE 1, PARALLEL FORM. *In the following sentences underline the parts that should be expressed in parallel form. Then revise each sentence.*

1. Professor Macy is a middle-aged woman, short, stocky, blue eyes, and partly gray-haired.
2. Her lectures are witty, interesting and she outlines them carefully.
3. She told us that we should read our text and to write a short review of it.
4. The book is interesting and I can learn from it.
5. Ms. Macy said she would give us a quiz on the first chapter and for us to review it carefully.

EXERCISE 2, FALSE PARALLELS. *In the following sentences correct the faulty use of correlatives.*

1. My summer's work proved not only interesting but I also learned much from it.
2. I wondered whether I should continue with it or should I return to college.

31

3. My boss was not only pleasant but she was also generous.
4. A college education was both necessary and I could afford it.
5. Not only was I getting older fast, but I also planned to be married soon.

§ 32. Comparisons

32a.   In standard formal English, comparisons should be logical and complete.

Written English, especially formal written English, requires a logic and a precision in expressing comparisons that is often lacking in loose, informal speech. In informal speech certain illogical comparisons have become accepted as idioms. Some of these shortened comparisons, or illogical comparisons, are becoming more and more common in *both formal and informal* writing; as in other cases of divided usage, the choice made by the student should be based on an understanding of the facts of usage and a desire for clarity.

1. In informal writing do not omit than *or as* in *a double comparison.*

Inappropriate in Formal Usage

The bus is about as fast if not faster than the train.

Football coaches earn as much if not more than college presidents.

Quebec City is now as popular, if not more popular than Montreal.

Logical but Awkward

The bus is about as fast as, if not faster than, the train.

Football coaches earn as much as, if not more than, college presidents.

Quebec City is now as popular as, if not more popular than, Montreal.

32

The last three examples illustrate what is often called the *suspended construction*. Some writers use it; others object to it because of its awkwardness. It can easily be avoided.

Logical and Smooth

The bus is about as fast as the train, if not faster.

Football coaches earn as much as college presidents, if not more.

Quebec City is now as popular as Montreal, if not more so.

2. Avoid ambiguity in making comparisons.

Ambiguous

I saw more of him than Clark ["more than Clark did" or "more than I saw of Clark"?]

Clear

I saw more of him than I saw of Clark. [Or *more of him than Clark did*]

Ambiguous

Our country helped France more than England.

Clear

Our country helped France more than England did. [Or *more than our country helped England*]

3. Do not omit other *after* than *or as in comparing two members of the same group or class.*

Misleading

Ms. Jenkins is more literate than any woman in the class. [If Ms. Jenkins is not a member of the class, the sentence is clear. If she *is* in the class, she cannot be more literate than herself.]

32

Clear

Ms. Jenkins is more literate than any other woman in the class.

Better

Ms. Jenkins is the most literate woman in the class.

4. Finish your comparisons so that you will not seem to be comparing something that you do not intend to compare.

Misleading
The salary of an editor is lower than a teacher. [Are you comparing salaries, or are you comparing *salary* and *teacher*?]

Clear
The salary of an editor is lower than that of a teacher. [The *that* here completes the comparison and also avoids a needless repetition of *salary*.]

Misleading
The opening of *The Searchers* is more intriguing than *Final Entries*.

Clear
The opening of *The Searchers* is more intriguing than that of *Final Entries*.

Misleading
The duties and responsibilities of a traffic officer are more complex than a cabin attendant.

Clear
The duties and responsibilities of a traffic officer are more complex than those of a cabin attendant. [Name the second term of the comparison.]

32b.   In standard English, comparisons are completed except when the missing term of the comparison can be easily supplied by the reader.

32

Not Clear
It is easier to remain silent when attacks are made upon the people one loves. [Easier than what?]

Clear
It is easier to remain silent when attacks are made upon the people one loves than to risk criticism by defending them.

Not Clear

Students who live in a residence do better work. [Better than students who live where?]

Clear

Students who live in residences do better work than those who room in apartments. [Or *who live at home*].

There are, however, many idiomatic expressions in which an unfinished comparison is easily understood, such as "It is always better to tell the truth"; "we thought it wiser to agree." No misunderstanding is possible in statements like these. The uncompleted superlative is also used, especially in speech, and its sense is not that of a comparison but of an intensive, as in: "She is a *most* unselfish woman," "he is a *most* appealing man."

EXERCISE

EXERCISE, COMPARISONS. *Revise the comparisons in the following sentences. Use the forms appropriate in standard written English.*

1. The snails of South America known as apple snails are as interesting if not more interesting than the allied *Pila* of the Old World.
2. Their shells are like apples, greener and rounder than other snails.
3. They are one of, if not the most amphibious kind of snail known to science.
4. Equipped with both gills and lungs, they are better swimmers than any snails.
5. When one compares the two types, the apple snail is clearly the best adapted to its environment.
6. The English periwinkle is as common if not more common than most other snails.
7. The lungs of the periwinkle are more developed than most other such sea animals.

32

8. Here the development of the lungs has reached a point higher than any place on earth.
9. Some snails can live as long if not longer than six months out of water.
10. Snails are the most fascinating animals; they are so attractive and varied in appearance.

§ 33. Words Left Out

Words necessary for clearness should not be left out.

Two kinds of omissions need to be considered here. One is the result of carelessness. Its cure is careful proofreading. The second results from carrying speech habits into writing. We often speak in a more clipped or telegraphic manner than is acceptable in writing, especially in serious writing on serious subjects.

The following are some of the omissions that need to be guarded against.

33a. Do not omit *that*.

Misleading

I soon observed nearly all the women, especially the young and pretty ones, were carrying strange little baskets. [Did you "observe the women, especially the young and pretty ones," or did you observe *that* the women were carrying baskets?]

He told me his story in its original version had been rejected by thirteen publishers. [Supply *that*. "He told me *that* his story . . ." The confusion is undesirable even if it is momentary.]

33

(Be careful, however, about needless repetition of *that*, as in: "He told me that there were numerous obscene magazines in that store, and that that troubled him." A useful correction would be: "He told me that there were numerous obscene magazines in Redmond's Readery, a situation that troubled him.")

33b. Do not omit part of a verb or of a verb phrase.

Misleading

The patient was given an anaesthetic and the instruments made ready. [It is better to say *were made ready*, because *patient* is singular, and the verb *was*, which follows it, cannot be understood with *instruments made ready*. The sentence needs a plural verb.]

His ideas were progressive and adopted without debate. [Repeat *were*. The two verbs are not parallel. The first *were* is used as a main verb – *ideas were* – but the second *were* is an auxiliary verb – *were adopted*. *Progressive* is not part of the verb phrase.]

33c. Do not omit words required by the use of a noun or a verb in a double capacity.

Awkward

He never has and never will deceive a customer. [Supply *deceived* after *never has*. Although this sort of construction is common in speech, many people object to it in written English.]

This young man is one of the best, if not the best fullback I have ever watched. [Say *one of the best fullbacks*.]

33d. Do not omit necessary prepositions in idiomatic expressions.

Incomplete

Spring term the course will be repeated for all new students. [Say *During the spring term. . . .*]

We must show our faith and devotion to our cause. [Say *faith in. Faith to* is not idiomatic.]

Customers have neither respect nor faith in a merchant who cheats. [Say *respect for. Respect in* is not idiomatic.]

33e. Do not omit function words that indicate balanced and parallel constructions.

Weak

He said that communism had never had many adherents in

33

Canada and there were fewer party members today than at any time since the Depression.

Strengthened

He said *that* communism had never had many adherents in Canada and *that* there were fewer party members today than at any time since the Depression.

Weak

We thanked her for her kindness, which we had not always reciprocated, the stimulation we found in her classroom, and the long hours she had spent helping us with extracurricular activities.

Strengthened

We thanked her *for* her kindness, which we had not always reciprocated, *for* the stimulation we found in her classroom, and *for* the long hours she had spent helping us with extracurricular activities.

EXERCISE

EXERCISE, MISSING WORDS. *Supply the missing words in the following sentences. Rearrange the wording wherever necessary.*

1. This student, I feel sure, never has and never will write a passing essay.
2. We visited one of the oldest, if not the oldest church in Nova Scotia.
3. We noticed many churches were almost surrounded by graveyards.
4. He needed better evidence to prove his demands were justified.
5. Sundays more men studied their newspapers than women.
6. Critics noticed that Hope did not have funny material and the skits were too long.
7. Winter the economy will begin to slow again.
8. In order to behave in a humane way countries should show a sympathy and understanding of other countries' beliefs.

33

9. Her gifts were beautiful and accepted with favourable comments.
10. The team was given a rousing pep talk and their equipment repaired.

§ 34. Variety

Variety in the length and the structure of sentences usually makes writing more effective.

A writer may avoid monotony of sentence structure by avoiding the following:

1. Beginning a series of sentences with the same word or the same subject.
2. Beginning a series of sentences with participial phrases.
3. Using the same sentence pattern in a group of sentences.
4. Beginning each of a series of sentences with the same kind of subordinate clause.

Here are some elementary examples of monotony. Notice the consistent shortness of the sentences, the unvaried vocabulary, and the needless repetition of sentence structure.

Short Sentences, All Beginning with the Subject
Mrs. Helmer is a fine woman. She has always been kind to me. I have appreciated her efforts in my behalf. She helped me find a summer job. I met a number of interesting people through her. She has always been a good friend of mine.

Short Sentences Beginning with a Participial Phrase
Waking up in the morning, I dressed quickly. Hurrying into the kitchen, I saw my mother at the stove. Pouring me a cup of coffee, she advised me not to delay. Gulping my coffee quickly, I began to collect my thoughts for the day ahead.

34

Few students should be guilty of such monotonous writing; the examples cited make for monotonous reading. Some common techniques for introducing variety include the following:

1. Mixing simple sentences with complex or compound sentences.
2. Putting a short sentence in the midst of several long ones.
3. Occasionally beginning a sentence with modifiers instead of with the subject. ["Disappointed by this response, I . . . ;" "At other times, he . . ."]
4. Occasionally beginning with a conjunction instead of with the subject. ["But this decision was wrong;" "And no one accepted the plan."]

In the following excerpt, note how Ethel Wilson has made her narrative more vivid and interesting by varying her sentence structure.

> For seven days fog settled down upon Vancouver. It crept in from the ocean, advancing in its mysterious way in billowing banks which swallowed up the land. In the Bay, and the Inlet and False Creek, agitated voices spoke to one another. Small tugs that were waylaid in the blankets of fog cried shrilly and sharply 'Keep away! Keep away! I am here!' Fishing-boats lay inshore. Large freighters mooed continuously like monstrous cows. The foghorns at Point Atkinson and the Lions' Gate Bridge kept up their bellowings. Sometimes the fog quenched the sounds, sometimes the sounds were loud and near. If there had not been this continuous dense fog, all the piping and boo-hooing would have held a kind of beauty; but it signified danger and warning. People knew that when the fog lifted they would see great freighters looking disproportionately large riding at anchor in the Bay because passage through the Narrows into the harbour was not safe. Within the harbour, laden ships could not depart but remained lying fog-bound at great expense in the stream . . . booo . . . booo . . . they warned. 'I am here! Keep away!' All the ships listened. The CPR boat from Victoria crashed into the dock. Gulls collided in the pathless air. Water traffic ceased and there was no movement anywhere offshore.
> In the streets, cars crawled slowly. Drivers peered.

34

Pedestrians emerged and vanished like smoke. Up the draw of False Creek, fog packed thick on the bridges. Planes were grounded. People cancelled parties. Everyone arrived late for everything.

– Ethel Wilson, ''Fog''

§ 35. Awkwardness and Obscurity

Sentences that are confused, awkward, illogical, or obscure should be rewritten.

An awkward and confused sentence may occasionally be a sign of slovenly thinking, but it is probably more often a result of haste and carelessness in writing and revision. A confused sentence may have several faults:

1. The central thought may be lost in a tangle of modifiers.
2. The thoughts may not be arranged properly.
3. The words used may be inexact, ambiguous, or inappropriate.
4. Several constructions may be telescoped into one. See also § 30.

Confused
If more emphasis was stressed in college on extemporary speaking, the graduating student would be better prepared to face people of social prominence and college professors.

Revised
Colleges should stress courses in extemporary speaking in order to give their graduates more confidence and social ease.

Confused
The word *laureate* comes from the Greeks when they used laurels to crown certain people.

Revised
The word *laureate* comes from the language of the ancient Greeks, who used a laurel crown as a mark of special honour.

35

Confused
Hamlet wishes to act morally in the right way.

Revised
Hamlet wishes to act morally.

Confused
Iago is discovered at the end of the play, but that hardly makes things better.

Revised
Iago's villainy is discovered at the end of the play, but the discovery comes too late.

EXERCISE

EXERCISE, AWKWARD AND OBSCURE SENTENCES.
Revise the following sentences.

1. Some allergic people live in pollen-proof rooms created by air-conditioning, not including air-cooling, to escape paroxysms of sneezing caused by chilling.
2. The hay fever patient should be wary of spraying insecticides about the yard or house, for spraying pyrethrum, the ground-up flower of the chrysanthemum, which is a member of the composite family, also is contained in these.
3. A student spends two or three terms in college to become accustomed with the rules needed for comprehensive learning.
4. Proper use of the English language is very essential in any type of work, whether a business person or a profession.
5. Many people have sacrificed wonderful professions because of simple misconceptions of their judgement.
6. There are some students who really cannot afford to live in an apartment but who would rather have it known that they do and do without other things like food and clothes.
7. Having never attended college before gives me the opportunity to develop to the fullest extent my study habits and idle time.

35

8. Still half asleep and unconscious of what I was doing, I applied the makeup on the left-hand side of the table, which happened to be the kind used for formal occasions.

9. Privacy hindered my studying while in high school because living in a house where there are many children it is very hard to secure privacy.

10. The subject of classifying what I think is an ideal room-mate should be written to an unlimited length if one was to take every point in doing so.

§ 36. Coherence and Development in Paragraphs

36a. A skilful arrangement of details helps to produce an effective paragraph.

A discussion of coherence in an *opening* paragraph appears in chapter 4 under "Kinds of Introductory Paragraphs." In that section three common ways of beginning an essay with an effective paragraph are analysed:

1. A statement of the thesis to be argued.

2. Narration of an anecdote related to the argument to follow.

3. Definition of a key term important to the thesis.

Paragraphs in the body of a paper must maintain coherence too, and a few suggestions for their development are worth consideration.

1. Try presenting your material in "deductive order," that is, from the general to the particular. Most paragraphs of exposition follow this order. State your general idea first in a topic sentence, and then present the reasons, details, examples, illustrations, and so on, that make your general statement understandable and convincing.

36

2. Try the "order of enumeration." In your topic sentence state that your idea may be seen from two points of view, that it has three important aspects, that you are going to use four illustrations, that you have two excellent reasons for believing it, and so on. There are numerous uses for this method, and a declaration of an order contributes to a clear, compact, and well-organized paragraph.

The following topic sentences from the works of professional writers demonstrate how this method is used:

All social organization is of two forms.

There were also three less desirable results of the Peace Conference.

There are two uses of knowledge.

Among the leading purposes of law today we may list three.

Remember, however, that this sort of beginning gives a formal tone to your writing. Use the device occasionally, when the material of your paragraph is suited to classification and enumeration.

3. Try the "time order." If details can be arranged in the order of their occurrence, there is no particular advantage to be gained by trying any other arrangement. The order of time (often called the chronological order) or occurrence produces a clear and orderly paragraph. It is inherently simple, perhaps elementary – but it has the unquestioned virtue of being almost foolproof. It may be used with material that at first glance does not arrange itself in the order of time.

4. Try using the "inductive order." It may be that your paragraph idea should not be stated bluntly in the first sentence. The reader may not be ready for it. First use your details, your examples and instances, to guide the reader's thoughts, so that when you are ready to use your summarizing topic sentence the reader will be ready to accept it. This process is the reverse of "the general to the particular," for the generalization concludes the paragraph.

36

If the problem of coherence is in your concluding paragraph, especially in its relation to your beginning, review the section on "Beginnings and Endings" in chapter 6. In that section, eight possible beginning-and-ending combinations are listed, with examples.

36b. Paragraphs should be fully developed and of suitable length.

If your instructor writes "No ¶ " next to what you believe *is* a paragraph, your response will probably be one of surprise and confusion. The correction simply asks, however, that you *add details or examples* or *reveal the process of reasoning by which you reached the conclusion.* Often this problem is caused by a so-called paragraph that is in fact made up of one or two generalizations or abstractions: "Rome fell because of immoral behaviour"; "The war was caused by economic conditions." To develop and support such statements, start asking specific questions: What instances of immoral behaviour do I have in mind? Where did they occur? Who was involved? What led me to the conclusions that economic conditions caused the war? What specific conditions do I want the reader to notice? These questions will add more than just padding – i.e., needless repetition of words and phrases, circumlocution – to your underdressed paragraph.

If each page of your essay consists of four or more paragraphs, your instructor is likely to reach for his or her red-ink pen to write "No ¶ " or "Add details" or "Lacks dev."

36c. Paragraphs are made more effective by the skilful use of connectives and transitions.

Chapter 4 ("Problems of Internal Organization") lists four main ways of linking ideas – by using conjunctions and transitional words and phrases, by using pronouns, by repeating key words, and by expressing related ideas in parallel structure.

1. Transitional Expressions. The following is a brief list of transitional words and phrases. You must not think that this list is complete. The natural, spontaneous phrases of transition

36

that occur to you as you write are by no means necessarily incorrect or unliterary.

on the other hand	conversely	finally
in the second place	of course	after all
on the contrary	in conclusion	indeed
at the same time	to sum up	next
in particular	moreover	similarly
in spite of this	in addition	again
in like manner	for example	and truly
and so again	for instance	meanwhile
as I have said	furthermore	
in contrast to this	accordingly	

Examples of Transitions

Because of our proximity to the United States, Canadians never have to worry about protection; *on the other hand*, who protects us from the protector?

Violence in hockey should be banned. *At the same time*, let us remember that in a contact sport that is played at high speeds some violence will always be present.

Many people think that artists are a disreputable, shiftless lot, who do no real work, and who are supported by the glorified welfare agency we call the Canada Council. *In contrast to this*, I believe that artists are the jewel in the crown of any civilization. They should be encouraged, financially supported, and held in high regard by all citizens.

Louis Riel was hanged as a traitor in 1885. *In spite of this* he is today regarded by many people as a martyr and hero.

2. Pronouns Referring to Antecedents in the Preceding Sentences. The technique of using pronouns for transition is a standard practice, but often runs the risk of vagueness of reference. See § 26 for illustrations of vagueness.

36

Examples
In the summer, Jonas had his usual two or three weeks of

vacation. *These* were spent usually at our cabin in the mountains.

I know a woman who was a grade-school teacher for forty years. *She* had no children *herself*, and in fact didn't even like them. Nevertheless *she* enjoyed what is known as a "successful" career.

If the use of a pronoun in one sentence that refers to an antecedent in a preceding sentence is risky, the use of a pronoun in one paragraph with its antecedent in the preceding paragraph is even more likely to involve dangerous confusion. The wisest course is to rely on the use of pronouns from paragraph to paragraph only when the antecedent is emphatically central to both paragraphs – as in a discussion of the work of one author, who may be referred to as he or she after one identification.

3. Key Words Repeated. In the two following passages, the words *sin* and *human rights* are repeated to hold the arguments together.

Examples

There are two kinds of sin – sins of commission and sins of omission. Sins of commission occur when you do something wrong. Sins of omission occur when you don't do something right.

Governments talk about human rights the way they talk about building highways or lowering taxes. But human rights aren't something dispensed by politicians. Human rights are yours the same way that the English language is yours.

4. Parallel Structure. In the example, the repeated subject-verb phrasing relates each clause to all the others.

Life is made up of opposites. At this very moment a baby is born, an old woman is dying, a young couple have fallen in love, and someone is broken with grief.

36

§ 37. Glossary: A Guide to Usage

Correctness and incorrectness in English usage are relative terms. It is, perhaps, more helpful to speak of the appropriateness of an expression in a given context, rather than of its correctness. An expression is appropriate in a certain situation, on a certain occasion, in a certain locality, among certain people; it may be inappropriate in another situation, on another occasion, in another locality, among other people.

But saying this much hardly solves the difficulties in deciding what is or is not appropriate in various situations. You have a right to expect some firm assistance on such questions from an English handbook, in spite of the relativity in usage that we all recognize. Your questions will no doubt arise in a number of cases where the current status of an expression is debatable, and the list that follows is intended to help you respond intelligently to some of these cases, as well as to those many other cases of confusing or troublesome usage where no argument exists.

In considering this matter of status, important in perhaps half the items in our guide, it is useful to speak of three classifications of language even though these classifications are artificial constructions. First, there are all those words and expressions that are part of standard literary English, and as a matter of fact these account for most of the words in the language. Very many words in standard English are appropriate on any occasion, formal or informal, anywhere. Second, we label certain expressions colloquial or informal, which simply means that these expressions are perfectly natural in most conversations, and perhaps in some informal writing, but are usually not appropriate in formal expository writing. An example is the expression *I guess*: "I guess his analysis was correct." Most problems of usage arise from a failure to recognize and avoid the colloquial-informal in the writing of serious essays. (The fact remains, of course, that many fine writers of serious prose are able to modify their formality of style by the deliberate, occasional use of

37

informal language. Their skill depends, naturally, on a high sensitivity to the current status of words, so that just the right mixture can be concocted.) Finally, there is a small body of language that simply has to be called incorrect. For example, to use the phrase *could of* for *could have* ("I could of come if I'd wanted to") is acceptable in writing only if you are quoting someone who uses language of that sort.

There are some expressions whose current status is a matter of argument, and their number is probably increasing in our fast-changing society. For example, no one can tell just when it will become widely acceptable to use such words as *put-down* or *hassle* in formal prose – or if it ever will. Similar fluid and unpredictable conditions in words have reached a point where the editors of *Webster's Third New International Dictionary* (1971) have simply omitted such labels as *colloq.* in many of their dubious entries. This does not of course mean that these editors believe the status of all language is the same, but simply that the status of current English words has become so complicated and various that strict labels would be misleading.

You can learn much that is both useful and entertaining by following some of these controversies, or by examining the recent history of some fast-changing expressions. The books listed below, arranged in chronological order, will help you pursue a study of any doubtful expressions you choose. (The guide in this book contains only a small fraction of the words included in a full dictionary of usage.) It is important to recognize, however, that popular usage, in conversation or in informal writing, is *not* the same as usage in formal expository prose and that the differences between them matter. Although colloquial expressions may often be included in serious formal writing, they are usually effective only when the writer is clearly aware of the shifts in tone that he or she is introducing. The books below, and this book's guide to usage, should help you become aware of the available choices, so that you can be genuinely discriminating in your acts of composition. (For further examples, see § 20, "Similar Forms.")

37

BERGEN EVANS AND CORNELIA EVANS, *A Dictionary of Contemporary American Usage*. New York: Random House, 1957.

MARGARET M. BRYANT, *Current American Usage*. New York: Funk & Wagnalls, 1965.

H.W. FOWLER, *A Dictionary of Modern English Usage*. 2nd ed., revised by Sir Ernest Gowers. New York: Oxford University Press, 1965.

THEODORE M. BERNSTEIN, *The Careful Writer: A Modern Guide to English Usage*. New York: Atheneum, 1965.

WILSON FOLLETT et al., *Modern American Usage: A Guide*. New York: Hill and Wang, 1966.

ROY H. COPPERUD, *American Usage: The Consensus*. New York: Van Nostrand Reinhold, 1970.

EDWIN NEWMAN, *Strictly Speaking: Will America Be the Death of English?* Indianapolis: Bobbs-Merrill, 1974. Reprinted 1975.

CASEY MILLER AND KATE SWIFT, *The Handbook of Nonsexist Writing*. New York: Barnes and Nobles, 1980.

THE CHICAGO MANUAL OF STYLE, University of Chicago Press, 13th edition, 1982.

a, an.   Use *a* before a word beginning with any consonant sound except a silent *h*. EXAMPLES: *a book, a tree, a European, a union, a house*. Use *an* before a word beginning with a vowel sound. EXAMPLES: *an African, an onion, an hour, an honourable man*.

above.   Used awkwardly as a transition: "As we pointed out *above*. . . ." A better transition would be *Therefore* or *Consequently*.

accelerate, exhilarate.   Sometimes confused because of their resemblance in sound. To *accelerate* is to quicken or speed up. To *exhilarate* is to arouse joy, to give pleasure. EXAMPLE: *An exhilarating experience can accelerate the heartbeat.*

accept, except.   Often confused because of their resemblance in sound. *Accept* means to receive, to agree to; *except* means to exclude or make an exception. EXAMPLES: *He accepted the invitation. She was excepted from the list of guests.*

37   **acquiesce.**   Use *acquiesce in; to* and *with* are vague.

A.D., B.C. A.D. should be placed *before* the date: "A.D. 1540." B.C. *follows* the date: "85 B.C."

ad. This short form and others like it (such as *math*, *exam*, *bike*) are appropriate in informal speech, but in formal writing the words usually appear in full.

adapt, adept, adopt. To *adapt* is to modify something. *Adept* (adjective or noun) means skilful, or one skilled. To *adopt* is to take possession of. EXAMPLES: *He adapted the motor to another current. He was adept at fixing electric appliances. She was an adopted child.*

adverse, averse. *Adverse* means antagonistic or unfavourable; *averse* means disinclined. EXAMPLES: *He was a victim of adverse fortune. The company president was averse to his suggestion.*

advice, advise. *Advice* is a noun, *advise* is a verb. EXAMPLES: *She refused to heed his advice about swimming there. We asked Paul to advise us about home loans.*

affect, effect. To *affect* is to influence. To *effect* means to bring about. *Effect* as a noun means result, what has been brought about. EXAMPLES: *The strike will affect the industry. The effect of the strike will be severe. The labour board will try to effect a settlement.*

aggravate. *Aggravate* means to intensify, to increase. Colloquially it means to irritate, to annoy. COLLOQUIAL: *The speaker's mannerisms aggravated everyone.* FORMAL: *The speaker's mannerisms annoyed everyone.*

agree to, agree with. You *agree that* something is true. You *agree to* a proposal. You *agree with* a person. One thing *agrees with* (corresponds with) another.

aggression. Use the singular *aggression.* Avoid the plural as a general statement of your feelings: "I got rid of my *aggression* by kicking the chair." *Hostility* or *frustration* would be more precise in this context.

ain't. Colloquial. Avoid its use in your writing.

all right. See *alright.*

allude, refer. *Allude* means to refer to a person or thing indirectly or by suggestion. EXAMPLE: *When the teacher spoke of "budding Atwoods" every student wondered to whom he was alluding.* To *refer* to something means to mention it specifically. EXAMPLE: *I shall now take time to refer to the question of smoking on the campus.*

allusion, illusion. An *allusion* is an indirect reference. (See *allude.*) An *illusion* is a deceptive appearance or false notion. The two words have nothing in common except a resemblance in sound.

37

a lot.   Should not be written as "alot."

already, all ready.   *Already*, an adverb, means by this time, before this time. *All ready*, two words, means entirely ready or that everyone is ready. EXAMPLES: *The war had already started. The men were all ready to go.*

alright.   The correct spelling is *all right. Alright* is a colloquial expression.

alternately, alternatively.   *Alternately* means to follow one another by turns; *alternatively* means to choose between two or more things. EXAMPLES: *The contestants answered questions alternately. She did not have many alternatives.*

altogether, all together.   *Altogether* (one word) is an adverb meaning entirely, completely, on the whole. *All together* means in a group. EXAMPLES: *He was altogether too generous. They were all together again at last.*

alumnus, alumna, alumni, alumnae.   A male graduate is an *alumnus*, a female an *alumna*; male graduates are *alumni*, females *alumnae*.

A.M., P.M., a.m., p.m.   Should not be used for *in the morning, in the afternoon.* Correct only with the name of the hour.

among, between.   *Among* is used with three or more things or persons, as: "They divided the property *among* six relatives"; "talk this over *among* yourselves." *Between* usually refers to two things or persons, as: "Let nothing stand *between* you and me"; "much must be done *between* sunrise and breakfast." *Between* can sometimes refer to more than two things in such expressions as: "*between* the leaves of a book"; or "the agreement *between* France, West Germany, and England."

amoral, immoral.   *Amoral* describes acts not subject to moral or ethical judgements; *immoral* means consciously violating moral principles. EXAMPLES: *Because he lacks a sense of right and wrong, his actions must be considered amoral. The sadistic games of the camp guards were immoral.*

amount, number.   *Amount* refers to quantity; *number* refers to things that can be counted. EXAMPLES: *the number of pages, the amount of steel.*

analyzation.   No such word. The writer means *analysis.*

and etc.   *Etc.*, for *et cetera*, means "and so forth." *And etc.* is obviously redundant. In any case it is better for most purposes not to use the abbreviation.

angry at, angry with.   *Angry at* is used when a thing or situation is concerned; *angry with* when a person is involved.

ante-, anti-. Both are prefixes, but *ante-* means before, *anti-*, against.

any place, anyplace. These are colloquial forms for *anywhere*, like *no place* for *nowhere*, *every place* for *everywhere*, and *some place* for *somewhere*.

anyways, anywheres. Colloquial forms of *anyway* and *anywhere*. Avoid using them in formal prose.

a piece, apiece. *A piece* is a noun; *apiece* is an adverb. EXAMPLE: *All those present are to have a piece of pie apiece.*

apprehend, comprehend. To *apprehend* something is to perceive its *meaning*; to *comprehend* a system or a theory is to understand it completely. EXAMPLES: *I think I apprehend the sense of that word. I don't think I will ever comprehend the meaning of love.*

apt, likely, liable. *Apt* suggests a habitual or inherent tendency. *Likely* suggests a probability. *Liable* suggests a chance, a risk of some sort, or a danger. But all three are often used to mean a probability and nothing more. EXAMPLES: *She is apt to be irritable because she is not well. A cheerful boy is likely to succeed. You are liable to break your neck if you climb that rock.*

as. (1) Highly colloquial when used in place of *that* or *whether*. EXAMPLE: *I cannot say as I care much for that.* (2) *As* in the sense of *because* is frowned upon by some writers, but is widely current in speech and writing nevertheless, especially in clauses at the beginnings of sentences. EXAMPLE: *As I was free that day, I went along with him.*

as–as, so–as. In negative statements some careful writers prefer *so – as* to *as – as*. At present, *as – as* seems to be established in both speech and writing for both positive and negative statements. For negative statements in a very formal style, *so – as* is probably preferable. EXAMPLES: *Your promise is as good as your bond.* FORMAL: *A vast army is not so important as a well-equipped air force.* INFORMAL: *A vast army is not as important as a well-equipped air force.*

aspect. A clichéd word with no concrete basis for use as a synonym for *consideration*, as in: "There are many *aspects* of this problem." Use more precise words, such as *parts* or *sides*. (*Facet*, like *aspect*, has been overused without any hint of its literal meaning.)

assume, presume. *Assume* connotes taking something for granted, while *presume* implies a more forceful or defensive attitude. EXAMPLES: *Let us assume that the statement is true. You presume too much in your claim.*

37

at. Redundant, in both speech and writing, in such sentences as: ''Where are we *at* now?'' ''Where does he live *at?*''

at this point in time, at the present moment. The writer means *now*. Bureaucratic writing has engendered such silly redundancies as ''within this time frame'' and ''time bracket.'' Be sure that these redundancies do not creep into *your* prose.

avocation, vocation. A *vocation* is one's principal life work. An *avocation* is not. EXAMPLE: *His vocation was medicine; his avocation was collecting stamps.*

awake, wake, waken. For the most part these verbs are interchangeable. *Awake* is widely favoured for *becoming awake*: ''I *awoke* at noon.'' *Wake* is better suited for transitive constructions: ''I *waked* him at noon.'' For passive constructions, *waken* is probably best: ''I was *wakened* at noon.''

award, reward. You are given an *award* in a formal and specific sense, while *reward*, though it may be a specific amount of money or a gift, may also be used in an unofficial or general context. EXAMPLES: *Guy Vanderhaeghe won the 1982 Governor-General's Award for English-language fiction for* Man Descending. *Alice Munro didn't win the award, but her reward was the consolation of her friends.*

awful, awfully. Colloquially these words, and others like *frightful*, *terribly*, *shocking*, *disgusting*, are used as mild intensives. Often they mean little more than *very*. In formal writing, *awful* and *awfully* should be saved for their precise meaning, to describe something truly awe inspiring. EXAMPLE: *He accepted the awful responsibility of carrying on the war.*

bad, badly. In formal and informal writing *bad* should not be used as an adverb. *Bad* is an adjective and *badly* is an adverb. ''I feel bad'' refers to your health or conscience. ''I feel badly'' refers to your ability to feel.

balance. When used for the *remainder*, *the rest*, it is usually considered colloquial. COLLOQUIAL USES: *The balance of the crew will be released. We listened to records the balance of the evening.* FORMAL: *The rest of the crew will be released.*

basically, essential. These adverbs should be avoided in such sentences as: ''*Basically*, the government has a plan to end inflation.'' ''This is *essentially* what the president means.'' They add nothing to the meaning of the sentence.

because. Often used in informal speech, and sometimes in literary English, as a substitute for *that* in constructions like ''the reason

37

was *because. . . ." That* is still preferable in formal written prose.

being. This participle is frequently used redundantly in student writing: "The players were unhappy, with the better ones *being* ready to quit the team." Notice that *being* provides a too easy means of adding afterthoughts to the main clause. It can be dropped without any loss of coherence.

being as, being that. Dialectal for *since, because.* EXAMPLES: *Since* (not *being as*) *it is long past midnight, we should abandon the search.*

beside, besides. According to present usage, *beside* is used as a preposition meaning "at the side of," as in: "Please sit down *beside* me." *Besides* is ordinarily used as an adverb, meaning "in addition to," as in: "There were no casualties *besides* the one reported earlier."

between. See *among.*

between you and I. The writer means *between you and me. Between*, a preposition, requires the objective pronoun *me.*

broke. Colloquial when used as an adjective to mean poverty-stricken or short of cash.

bunch. Colloquial when used to mean several, a group. EXAMPLES: *We saw a group* (not *a bunch*) *of men near the gate. Several* (not *a bunch*) *of them belonged to another union.*

but however, but yet. These expressions are redundant. *However, yet, nevertheless, probably* should stand alone.

but what, but that. Formerly considered colloquial. *But that* now appears to be standard literary English in sentences like: "I don't doubt *but that* he is disappointed." *But what* should not be used to refer to persons. Most careful writers still prefer a simple *that* to both these expressions. EXAMPLE: *There is no doubt that* (not *but what* or *but that*) *the president wishes to provoke war.*

can, may. In formal usage, *may* implies permission or possibility, *can* implies ability. In informal usage, *can* is very often used in the sense of *may.* INFORMAL: *Mother, can I go now? Can't we stay up until midnight? No, you can't.* FORMAL: *Sir, may I go now? The delegate can speak three languages.*

cannot help but, can't help but. These forms are widely used in speech and by some writers in formal prose.

can't hardly. A double negative, objectionable in conversation, unacceptable in formal writing.

case, instance. *In the case, instance of* is a circumlocution. Note that *for* can be substituted for *in the case of* in the following sentence: "Who is to blame *in the case of* John's failure?"

37

cause and reason.   *Cause* is what produces an effect; *reason* is what humans produce to account for the effect, or to justify it. EXAMPLES: *His reasons for going were excellent. The cause of his departure remained a mystery.*

cause of.   To say that the *cause of* something was *on account of* is a muddled construction. EXAMPLES: *The cause of my late essay was my having* (not *on account of I had*) *too much work to do. The cause of my late essay was the fact that I had too much work to do.* Both of these sentences, however, are awkward. It may be better to avoid the *cause-of* construction entirely and simply say, ''My essay is late because I had too much to do.''

censor, censure.   A *censor* (who is censorious) is one who supervises public morals, expurgates literature, and so on. *Censure* is adverse judgement, condemnation.

centre around.   *Centre* means a point, not a circle. *Centre on* makes more sense, but even this expression is a circumlocution: ''The question *centres on* a failure of communication.'' (''The question *is*. . . .'')

climactic, climatic.   *Climactic* has to do with climax, as: ''The play had reached a *climactic* moment.'' *Climatic* has to do with climate, as: ''*Climatic* conditions in Bermuda are ideal.''

close proximity.   Redundant.

compare to, compare with, contrast.   *Compare to* means to represent as similar. *Compare with* means to examine the differences and similarities of two things. To *contrast* two things is to examine the differences between them. EXAMPLES: *One may compare some men to wolves. One may compare the novels of Dreiser with those of Zola. The novels of Dreiser can be contrasted to those of James.*

complementary, complimentary.   *Complementary* means completing or making up what is lacking; *complimentary* means paying a compliment or giving something as a courtesy. EXAMPLES: *His personality and hers are complementary. The note about John's performance was highly complimentary.*

comprise, compose.   *Comprise* means include; *compose* means make up. A whole *comprises* its parts, not the other way round. *Comprise* is used mistakenly in: ''The university is *comprised* of faculty, staff, and administrators.'' The sentence should read: ''The faculty, staff, and administrators *compose* (or *constitute*) the university.''

concept, idea.   *Concept* means a generalized or abstract notion that characterizes elements of a class. *Idea* is a broader term and generally more suitable than *concept* or *conception*. Note that *concept* would be too narrow a word in the following sentence: "My *idea* received little comment from the manager."

contact. Widely used in the sense of *communicate with*, *meet*, *interview*, but it should be used sparingly, if at all, in preference to more exact expressions.

contemptible, contemptuous. *Contemptible* is used to describe something or someone deserving contempt, while *contemptuous* means expressing contempt. EXAMPLES: *She told him his behaviour was contemptible. He was contemptuous of my argument.*

continual, continuous. Any event that recurs at intervals is *continual*; *continuous* means uninterrupted. EXAMPLES: *We were bothered by the continual dripping of the faucet. When I tried to repair the faucet, I was greeted by a continuous stream of water.*

contractions. Their use is less appropriate in formal writing, where they are occasionally found, than in speech and informal writing, where they are entirely at home. EXAMPLES: *I'd like to go, but I'm tired. Can't he explain it to you, or doesn't he care?*

convince, persuade. The following sentences illustrate the differing connotations of these two words: "I *convinced* her that she was wrong." "I *persuaded* her to join our group." *Convince* means winning agreement; *persuade* means moving to action.

could of. Incorrect for *could have*.

couple. Colloquial for *two*, *a few*, *several*. COLLOQUIAL: *A couple of men left the theatre.* FORMAL: *Two* (or *several*) *men left the theatre.* Standard for a man and woman married, betrothed, or otherwise appearing as partners.

credible, credulous. An event, fact, argument is *credible* when it is believable; you are said to be *credulous* if you are easily convinced, or gullible.

criteria. The plural form of *criterion*.

cute. A colloquialism to describe attractive children and small animals. Not to be used in formal writing.

data, strata, phenomena. These are the plurals of *datum*, *stratum*, and *phenomenon*. At present these words seem to be in a transitional stage, inasmuch as some good writers and speakers use them as singular forms while others believe strongly that only the correct Latin forms should be used. There is no doubt, however, that a mixture of forms is undesirable, as: "Although the *data* collected at the laboratory are vouched for by several scientists, much of it has to be restudied."

37

date.   Inappropriately colloquial when referring to an appointment with the dean, but perfectly acceptable when referring to Saturday night at the movies.

deal.   Used figuratively in phrases like "square *deal*," "new *deal*." Informal in the sense of a commercial transaction or political bargain. COLLOQUIAL: *Good deal!* But with the indefinite article it is literary English, as: "a good *deal* of trouble."

decimate.   To reduce by one tenth, not to destroy entirely.

deduce, deduct.   *Deduce* is used to mean infer; *deduct* means to take away. EXAMPLES: *We deduced a certain dislike in his actions. The company deducted ten dollars from her pay.*

denotation, connotation.   Use *denotation* when referring to a word's specific meaning; use *connotation* when speaking of a word's implications.

deprecate, depreciate.   *Deprecate* means to express regret over, or disapproval of, while *depreciate* means to lessen the value of.

device, devise.   A *device* is an instrument for performing some action. To *devise* something is to invent it, to contrive or plan it.

dichotomy.   A splitting into parts or pairs. The word is now overused, especially in contexts where *difference* or *split* is more appropriate.

differ from, differ with.   One thing *differs from* another. One person *differs with* another when they dispute or quarrel. A person may also *differ from* another person when they disagree.

different from, different than.   Both forms have been used by good writers. At present, *different from* seems to be preferred when a single word follows it, as in: "His suggestion is *different from* mine." When a clause follows, many speakers and writers use *than* to avoid a round-about construction, as in: "This group of engineers will use a very *different* method of extracting the ore *than* the old Quebec miners used."

discreet, discrete.   A *discreet* person is tactful or judicious; a *discrete* matter is distinct or separate from another.

dissociate, disassociate.   These words mean the same thing, but *dissociate* is more common in modern usage.

double negative.   An expression in which two or more negatives are used to make the negative more emphatic is of course wrong. EXAMPLES: *Nobody never tells me nothing. We ain't seen nobody.* Another type of concealed double negative appears in a very small number of expressions like *can't hardly, didn't hardly, wouldn't scarcely.* These expressions are not appropriate in writing, though

37

they are widely heard in speech. A third type of deliberate double negative is entirely correct, and common in formal writing. EXAMPLES: *The brief rest was not unwelcome. These people were not uneducated.* (Notice that these expressions are more cautious and moderate than the corollary affirmative statements: *The brief rest was welcome. The people were educated.*)

dove. The most generally used form is *dived*, though *dove* has been widely used in speech and occasionally in writing.

dubious, doubtful. The result of an action or the truth of a statement may be *dubious*, while the person who questions either is *doubtful*.

due to, owing to. *Due to* was originally an adjective, and no one questions its use in sentences like these: "His lameness was *due to* an accident." "The spring floods, *due to* prolonged rains, did much damage to the stockyards." The adverbial use of *due to* is also common, as: "*Due to* an accident, we arrived late." If a more formal tone is desired, the expression *owing to* may be substituted for *due to*. *Due to the fact that* is a common, and deplorable, substitute for a simple *because*.

each other, one another. The first refers to two people only, at least in formal discourse. The second refers to more than two. EXAMPLES: *The two officials started hitting each other. The whole council started hitting one another.*

effect. See *affect*.

e.g., i.e. Although these abbreviations are often used interchangeably, *e.g.* means "for example" and *i.e.* means "that is." They should be used only in parenthetical expressions and in footnotes.

elicit, illicit. You *elicit* a *reaction* or *response* from someone; a person may commit an *illicit act*. EXAMPLES: *His proposal elicited support. Society labels certain acts illicit.*

emigrate, immigrate. Use of these words depends on point of view. You *emigrate* when you leave Europe for Canada; from Canada's standpoint you have *immigrated* there, and are called an *immigrant*.

eminent, imminent, immanent. *Eminent* means outstanding, noteworthy; *imminent* means impending, threatening; *immanent* means inherent or operating within. EXAMPLES: *Stanley Knowles is an eminent statesman. Scientists have predicted the imminent eruption of Mount Vesuvius. God's power has been described as immanent.*

end up. Unacceptable colloquialism for *end* or *conclude*.

enthuse. Colloquial for "to be enthusiastic" or "to show enthusi-

37

asm." Many people dislike it thoroughly. FORMAL: *She never showed any enthusiasm* (not *enthused*) *about grand opera.*

equally as good. This may be wordy, but many educated people use the expression. It means "equally good," or "just as good." EXAMPLE: *My essay was just as good* (not *equally as good*) *as his.*

escalate. A currently attractive but inaccurate substitute for *increase. Escalate* means specifically to increase in intensity or size by calculated stages.

et al. Proper in footnotes and bibliographical lists, *et al.* means "and other people."

etc. See *and etc. Etc.* is to be avoided at the end of a series when the reader cannot grasp the reference. EXAMPLE: *All his friends – John, Al, Len, etc. – were invited.*

euphemism, euphuism. A *euphemism* is a mild or roundabout word that is substituted for another word thought to be too harsh or blunt ("passed away" for "died"). *Euphuism* is an artificially elegant style of writing that was popular in Renaissance England.

everyone, every one. EXAMPLES: *Everyone has arrived by now. Every one of those dishes must be washed thoroughly.*

exam. See *ad.*

except. See *accept.*

exception that proves the rule. A confusing cliché that should be avoided in formal and informal writing.

exhilarate. See *accelerate.*

expect. Colloquial in the sense of *suppose.*

facet. See *aspect.*

fact that. This expression can be easily deleted, thereby achieving economy and directness. "I was shocked by *the fact that* you behaved so childishly" should be rewritten: "I was shocked by your childish behaviour."

fallacy. The word has a specific meaning in logic: a formal mistake in reasoning or in the conclusion of an argument. It should not be used when *mistake* or *error* is meant in the general sense.

farther, further. The fine distinction between these two words, and between the superlative forms, *farthest, furthest,* is that both can be used to speak of distance, but that *further* and *furthest* have an additional meaning of "additional." STANDARD USAGE: *They could go no farther. The Johansen party penetrated furthest into the jungle. The newspaper promised further revelations soon.*

faze. Slang or colloquial for *disconcert, worry, disturb, bother, daunt.*

It has no connection with *phase.* COLLOQUIAL: *He wasn't fazed by the amount of work he had to do.*

feel.   A spineless substitute for *think* or *believe,* in such examples as "I *feel* that the United Nations is doing more harm than good." Don't feel it – just say it.

fewer, less.   Use *fewer* when referring to numbers. Use *less* when referring to quantity or degree. (See also *amount, number.*) EXAMPLES: *There will be fewer* (not *less*) *men on the team next year. Most women are earning less than they did last year.*

finalize.   Many are irritated by this and other recent coinages from business and officialese: *optionalize, prioritize, privatize.* Avoid these verbs in your writing. Also see *contact.*

fine.   See *nice.* A vague word of approval, entirely proper in conversation, but in exact writing a more precise word should be used.

first and foremost.   A cliché – avoid it like the plague (another cliché).

fix.   Colloquial in the sense of *predicament,* as: "The headmaster was in a predicament (not *fix*)." Also colloquial in the sense of *arrange* or *prepare.* COLLOQUIAL: *Give me a few minutes more to fix my hair.*

flaunt, flout.   You may *flaunt* your intelligence or your sexual prowess, but you *flout* rules and conventions when you *ignore* them.

flunk.   Colloquial for *fail.*

folks.   Colloquial for *relatives, family.*

former, latter.   Use only when referring to two items that your reader will clearly recognize. To avoid needless confusion, simply repeat the items. EXAMPLE: *Doctors and lawyers are fighting vigorously over malpractice insurance rates; lawyers* (not *the latter*) *have an advantage because of their expert knowledge.*

formulate.   Use only when you mean *state systematically.* EXAMPLE: *She formulated a new approach to teaching preschool children.* Otherwise, use *form.*

fun.   Not to be used as an adjective: "a *fun* thing to do." This is a transitory colloquialism.

funny.   Colloquial for *strange, queer, odd.*

gap.   Such expressions as *generation gap* or *credibility gap* are clichés – avoid them.

get.   *Get* has a large number of uses, both formal and informal. In formal or literary contexts, it means obtain, receive, procure, acquire. In informal and conversational usage, it has a large number of meanings, figurative, idiomatic, and otherwise. In speech *have got* in the sense of *have* is very common. The form *have got* in the sense

37

of *must* or *have to* is felt to be more emphatic. *Got* and *gotten* are both past participles found in speech and in writing.

graduate.   The passive *was graduated* is no longer required in formal usage. "She *graduated* from McGill" is proper in formal and informal writing.

guess.   The expression *I guess* is too colloquial for most formal prose. Write *I suppose*, or *I presume*, or *I assume*.

guys.   Colloquial for *friends* or *companions*.

had better, had best, had rather.   Correct idiomatic forms, as are *would better, would best, would rather.*

had ought, hadn't ought.   Colloquial. It is easy to substitute *ought, should, should have, shouldn't have*, all forms appropriate in both speech and writing.

hanged, hung.   People are *hanged*; objects are *hung*. EXAMPLES: *The murderer was hanged. The clothes were hung on the line.*

hangup.   Colloquial for *problem, inhibition, perversion*. Precisely because it is too often used to mean any one or all of these states, *hangup* should be avoided in your writing.

hardly, scarcely.   See *double negative.*

hassle.   Colloquial for *problem, conflict, annoyance, fuss*. Do not use it in formal writing.

have got.   See *get.*

healthy, healthful.   Strictly speaking, *healthy* means being in a state of health; *healthful* means serving to promote health. People are healthy, but good food is healthful.

hear, listen.   *Hear* means auditing any sound; *listen* means focussing your hearing. EXAMPLE: *She listened for his voice but heard only the birds' song.*

hopefully.   When used in the sense of *it is hoped* (i.e., "*Hopefully* we can agree on a price"), the word is inappropriate.

humaneness, humanity.   Both words may be used to mean possessing compassion or sympathy, but *humanity* is also used to describe human kind. There is no such word as *humanness*.

identify, relate.   These words should not be used without the reflexive pronoun. EXAMPLES: *I identify myself with Othello's fate. He cannot relate himself to any institution.* In most cases other constructions are more exact: "I feel a strong identity with Othello's fate."

if, whether.   Both *if* and *whether* are used to introduce a noun clause in indirect questions after verbs like *doubt, ask, wonder. Whether* is more likely to be used if an alternative introduced by *or* is stated.

37

There is still some feeling among teachers and writers that *whether* is more formal, but both words are used and have been used for many years to introduce noun clauses. EXAMPLES: *I doubt if they can come. He wondered whether or not he should warn the settlers. Ask him if he has any food left.*

ignorant, stupid. *Ignorant* means lacking knowledge of, while *stupid* means unable to comprehend. EXAMPLES: *She was ignorant of the facts in the case. Running into other cars is a stupid habit.*

illusion. See *allusion.*

imply, infer. *Imply* means to indicate or suggest without stating; *infer* means to derive or conclude a meaning. EXAMPLES: *The professor implied that her answer was wrong. She inferred a different meaning from his words.*

important. *More important*, not *importantly*, is the correct adverbial usage of the word.

in, into. In theory, the distinction between these words is that *in* denotes location inside something, whereas *into* denotes motion from outside to inside something. In practice, however, *in* is also used in the sense of *into.* EXAMPLES: *Throw that in the waste basket. Go jump in the lake.* "Are you *into* painting?" is a colloquialism.

in back of, back of. Both forms, still considered by many to belong to informal speech, have been used in writing for some time. The more formal word is *behind.*

in conclusion, in summary. To use such expressions as introductions to the final paragraph of an essay is awkward and mechanical. Simply state your conclusion (your reader can *see* that you have reached your last paragraph) without this rhetorical throat-clearing.

in terms of, in connection with. Officialese. These phrases should be avoided, as they add nothing to the import of sentences. EXAMPLE: *(In terms of sheer power,) Guy Lafleur is the best shooter in hockey.*

in this day and age. Cliché. Use *now.*

ingenious, ingenuous. An *ingenious* person is inventive, or clever; an *ingenuous* person is unaffected, or artless. EXAMPLES: *The general's plan showed ingenious thinking. Tom is so ingenuous he didn't realize that he was being tricked.*

insightful. A recently invented adjective, which has quickly become overworked: "an *insightful* person," "an *insightful* comment." It is probably better to declare that "She *showed insight*" or that hers was "a *perceptive* remark."

37

irony, ironic.   Use *irony* or *ironic* only when there is a *dramatic* discrepancy between what is said and what is meant, or between what is supposed to happen and what does happen. It is a *coincidence* if two people with the same car models have an accident. It is *ironic* if both are members of the Canadian Automobile Association.

irregardless.   The writer means *regardless*.

is when, is where.   These expressions when used in definitions appear awkward and juvenile.

its, it's.   *Its* is the possessive form of *it*. *It's* is the contraction of *it is*. The two forms should not be confused.

kind, sort.   In colloquial usage, these words are often felt to be plural in constructions like this: "These *kind* of dogs are usually hard to train." In more formal situations, both in speech and in writing, most people prefer the singular, as: "I do not like this *sort* of entertainment." "That *kind* of man is not to be trusted."

kind of, sort of.   Colloquial when used to modify a verb or an adjective. Use *somewhat, somehow, a little, in some degree, rather, for some reason* in formal contexts.

lay, lie.   The principal parts of *lay* are as follows: "Now I *lay* it down"; "I *laid* it down"; "I have *laid* it down." The principal parts of *lie* are these: "I *lie* down"; "I *lay* down yesterday morning"; "the dog *had lain* in the shade all day." The participles of *lie* and *lay* are *lying* and *laying*. STANDARD: *He had laid* (not *lain*) *his bundle on the table. It had lain* (not *laid*) *there all morning. The dog was lying* (not *laying*) *in the road.*

lead, led.   The past tense of *lead* (pronounced *leed*) is *led* (pronounced like the metal *lead*).

leave, let.   It is just as correct to say *leave him alone* as *let him alone*. But *leave* cannot be used for *allow* in such a sentence as "I begged my mother to *leave* me do it."

lend, loan.   Generally speaking, *lend* should be used as a verb, *loan* as a noun. EXAMPLES: *I lent him ten dollars. We signed many forms to get the loan.*

less.   Often used in place of *fewer* with collective nouns: "*less* clothes, *less* people." But say *fewer hats, fewer persons.*

liable, likely.   See *apt*.

lie.   See *lay*.

like, as, as if.   In written English, *as* and *as if* introduce clauses; *like* generally governs a noun or pronoun. In speech the substitution of *like* for *as* is widespread. It is probable that the use of *like* as a conjunction will eventually gain acceptance in formal writing. It has not done so yet. INFORMAL: *I wish you would do it like I said you should.* FORMAL: *The war, just as he had predicted, lasted more than five years. Few men could sway an audience as he did.*

line.   Often vague and redundant, as: "Have you anything interesting in the *line* of fiction?" "He wrote epics and other works along that *line.*" BETTER: *Have you any interesting novels? He wrote epics and other narrative poems.*

locate.   In the sense of *settle*, it is appropriate only in informal use.

lose, loose.   These two words are often confused. Careless writers sometimes write *loose* when they mean *lose*. You may *lose* a game or your keys. When screws are *loose* they should be tightened.

lots, lots of.   Widely used colloquially for *many, much, a large number, a large amount, a great deal.* COLLOQUIAL: *He has a lot to learn. There are lots of exceptions to this rule.*

mad.   Colloquially *mad* is used in the sense of *angry.* In formal usage it means insane.

majority.   Inaccurate when used with measures of quantity, time, distance. The appropriate word is *most.* EXAMPLE: *Most of the day* (not *the majority of the day*) *we stood in line and waited.* Most people (not *the vast majority*) support some form of gun control.

material, materiel.   *Material* means any kind of substance, while *materiel* refers specifically to arms or other military equipment.

may be, maybe.   Don't confuse the two. EXAMPLES: *The plane may be late. Maybe the pilot had trouble with the weather.*

media.   The plural of *medium.* This word is now overworked as a shorthand label for newspapers, radio, and television. Be specific; write "the newspaper reporter," not "the *media* representative."

might of.   Incorrect for *might have.*

mighty.   Colloquial for *very.* Unacceptable in most writing.

militate, mitigate.   *Militate* means to have influence (used with *against*); *mitigate* means to make less severe. EXAMPLES: *Conditions militate against a peaceful solution. The extra pay mitigates the tedium of the work.*

most, almost.   *Most*, in formal written English, is the superlative form of *much* or *many.* EXAMPLES: *Much food, more food, most food, many men, more men, most men. Almost* is an adverb meaning nearly. In colloquial use *most* is often substituted for *almost.* FORMAL: *Almost* (not *Most*) *all of our friends have returned from college.* In conversational usage, *most* is frequently used to qualify *all, everyone, everybody, anyone, anybody, always.*

much, many.   *Much* should not be used in place of *many* with most plural nouns. EXAMPLES: *There was too much food. There were too many courses.*

nauseous, nauseated. Something that causes nausea is *nauseous*; a person experiencing nausea is *nauseated*. EXAMPLES: *The fish had a nauseous odour. He became nauseated after eating it.*

neat. When used as a general honorific ("That's *neat!*"), it is another overused and transitory colloquialism, like *the greatest*, or *fun* (adjective). To be avoided in writing.

neither, nor; either or. *Neither* should be followed by *nor* and *either* by *or*. Both *neither* and *either* may be used with more than two alternatives, as: "*Either* past, present, *or* future. . . ."

nice. Strictly used, *nice* means discriminating. When used as a vague word of mild approval, it is to be avoided in serious writing.

no good, no-good. Colloquial when used for *worthless*, *useless*, *of no value*.

no one. Not *noone.*

now. An adverb, not an adjective, as in "This is the *now* generation." Be on guard against letting such jargon creep into your writing.

nowhere near, nowheres near. The first is common in both speech and writing; the second is common in colloquial speech. In formal writing it is better to use *not nearly.* EXAMPLE: *That was not nearly* (not *nowhere near*) *as much as he had expected.*

O, oh. *O* is used with another word, a substantive, usually in direct address, often in poetry. It is always capitalized and is not followed by any mark of punctuation. *Oh* is an exclamation, not capitalized except when it begins a sentence, and is followed by either a comma or an exclamation point.

obviate. *Obviate* means to dispose of or provide for, as in "The arms agreement *obviated* the risk of war." It does not mean to make obvious.

occur, take place. *Occur* is a broader term than *take place*, which is properly used to refer to planned activities. EXAMPLES: *The accident occurred on the corner. The trial will take place on June 10th.*

of, have. Never use "would *of*" or "should *of*" for "would *have*" or "should *have*."

off of. The *of* is unnecessary. EXAMPLE: *He took the book off* (not *off of*) *the shelf.*

O.K. Colloquial.

on account of. The writer means *because of.*

one another. See *each other.*

37

oral, verbal. *Oral* refers to spoken language; *verbal* refers to all words, spoken or written.

orient, orientate. Modern usage generally prefers *orient* to *orientate*, as in: "We waited until we became *oriented* to the campus rules."

out loud. Somewhat less formal than *aloud, loudly, audibly.*

outside of. Colloquial for *except, besides.* EXAMPLE: *There was no witness to the robbery except* (not *outside of*) *the teacher.*

over with. Colloquial in the sense of *finished, ended.*

party. Except in legal and telephone usage, *party* is colloquial and semihumorous when it means a person.

past history. *Past* is redundant here.

percent. Used after numbers. The sign % is not used except after figures in tabulations or in technical writing. *Percent* is not an exact synonym for *percentage.*

persecute, prosecute. To *persecute* is to harass or treat oppressively; to *prosecute* is to bring suit against, with a legal connotation.

personal, personally. Students are understandably disposed to hedge their bets, with expressions like *in my personal opinion, personally I believe, my view is,* and so on. In essays on literary interpretation, expressions such as *I get the feeling that . . .* are common. In many cases such qualification weakens the force of what is being said. If you are wrong in what you say, then you are wrong, whether you say it's your personal opinion or not.

plenty. Colloquial when used as an adverb in such expressions as *plenty good, plenty good enough, plenty rich,* and so on, or as an adjective before a noun. COLLOQUIAL: *He was plenty rich. The room is plenty large. There is plenty wood for another fire.* FORMAL: *He was very rich. The room is large enough. There is plenty of wood for another fire. Ten dollars is plenty.*

plus. *Plus* should not be used in place of *moreover* or *in addition.* "I worked overtime; moreover (not *plus*), I had to wait weeks for my paycheck."

P.M. See *A.M., a.m.*

poorly. Colloquial for *in poor health, not well, unwell.*

practicable, practical. *Practicable* means something possible, feasible, usable. *Practical* means useful, not theoretical, experienced. *Practical* may apply to persons, things, ideas; *practicable* may not apply to persons.

predominate, predominant. *Predominate* is a verb, *predominant* an adjective. Be sure to keep these words distinct in your writing.

37

EXAMPLES: *Threatening weather conditions predominate today. He has the predominant army on his side.*

prescribe, proscribe.   *Prescribe* means to set down or give directions; *proscribe* means to prohibit.

principal, principle.   *Principal* is an adjective or noun meaning chief or first in rank. *Principle* is a noun meaning fundamental law or truth. EXAMPLES: *The principal reason we failed was poor organization. His belief in the principle of fair play guides his behaviour.*

proceed, precede.   *Proceed* means to go on with; *precede* means to go before. EXAMPLES: *After a short interruption, she proceeded with her analysis. His wife preceded him to the stage.*

prophecy, prophesy.   Don't confuse these words. *Prophecy* is a noun ("The *prophecy* came true"), *prophesy* a verb ("He claimed he could *prophesy* the outcome").

proposition, proposal.   *Proposal* implies a direct and explicit act of proposing; *proposition* implies a statement or principle for discussion. The loose use of *proposition* to mean an idea, a thing, a task, a business enterprise, a problem is disliked by many people. EXAMPLES: *It is a poor practice* (not *proposition*) *to study until three in the morning. Moving the settlers out of the district was an impractical plan* (not *proposition*).

quiet, quite.   These two words are carelessly confused. *Quiet* has to do with stillness or calmness. In formal standard usage, *quite* means entirely, completely. "You are *quite* right." In informal usage it may also be used to mean very, to a considerable degree. "The dog seems *quite* friendly."

quite a few, quite a bit.   Overused in student writing.

raise, rise.   Two verbs often confused. The principal parts of *raise*: "I *raise* my hand"; "he *raised* the window"; "they *have raised* the flag." The principal parts of *rise*: "I *rise* in the morning"; "they *rose* before I did"; "they *had risen* at sunset."

rap.   Colloquial for *sentence* or *judgement*, as in "a bum *rap*." The word has also been used as a verb and noun to mean discuss or debate: "We *rapped* about drug abuse." It is colloquial in this use too.

ravage, ravish.   These words are often confused but they mean different things. EXAMPLES: *The city was ravaged (destroyed) by fire. She was ravished (raped) by her abductor. Ravish* also means to carry away or transport with joy or pleasure.

37   **real.**   *Real* as an adverb, in the sense of *very* ("It was a *real* exciting game") is colloquial. Its formal equivalent is *really.* Both, however,

are vague and weak intensifiers, of little use in promoting meaning. See *awful, so, such.*

reason is because. See *because.*

refer. See *allude.*

relation, relationship. These words are used synonymously, though *relationship* means specifically the state of being related. EXAMPLE: *Something has changed in the relationship* (not *relation* or *relations*) *between John and his father.*

relevant. This word should be used with *to,* then a noun: "*relevant to* her beliefs"; "*relevant to* the funds available." Such sentences as "This book is not *relevant*" are vague and misleading. The book is *certainly* relevant to someone's interests, if only to the author's.

same, such. Appropriate in legal documents. In ordinary speech and writing it is better to use *it, this, that.* EXAMPLE: *When you have repaired the watch, please ship it* (not *same*) *to me.*

scene. Colloquial when used in such sentences as "This is a bad *scene.*"

see where. For *see that,* as: "I *see where* the team lost another game." Permissible only in colloquial speech.

sensibility, sensitivity. *Sensibility* means the ability to perceive or feel; *sensitivity* means ready susceptibility to outside influences. EXAMPLES: *The music critic possesses a mature sensibility. The plant's reaction revealed its sensitivity to light.*

sensual, sensuous. *Sensual* usually means lewd or unchaste; *sensuous* means pertaining to the senses. A *sensuous* person is one who puts value in experiences of the senses, but he or she need not be *sensual* in the process.

set, sit. Two verbs often confused. Learn the principal parts: "I *set* it down"; "I *have* set it down"; "now he *sits* down"; "I *sat* down"; "they *have* sat down." But of course one may speak of "a *setting* hen," and the sun *sets,* not *sits.* "You may *set* the cup on the shelf and then *sit* down." "I *sat* on the stool after I had *set* the cup down."

shape. Colloquial for *condition.* COLLOQUIAL: *The athlete was in excellent shape.* FORMAL: *The equipment was in very good condition* (not *shape*).

situation, position. Both words are abused in officialese: "Regarding the present *situation* . . ."; "With respect to the premier's *position on.* . . ." If you must use these words, try to restrict their connotations as much as possible. EXAMPLE: *Her position on the team was right field.*

so. As a conjunction between main clauses, *so* is much overused in

37

student writing. Usually the primary fault is too little subordination instead of too much use of *so*. EXAMPLES: *The bridge was blown up during the night, and so the attack was delayed. The attack was delayed because the bridge had been blown up during the night. The Russians were not ready, so they waited until August to declare war on Japan. Since the Russians were not ready, they waited until August to declare war on Japan.*

In clauses of purpose, the standard subordinating conjunction is *so that*, as in: ''They flew low *so that* they could observe the results of the bombing.'' But *so* is also used, especially in spoken English.

So as an intensive can be easily overworked in speech and it often is. EXAMPLES: *She is so kind and so charming. The work is so hard.*

social, societal.   *Social* describes society or its organization, persons living in it, or the public. *Societal* should be reserved for describing large social groups, their customs and activities. EXAMPLES: *Excessive drinking is a major social problem. Doctors and lawyers hold opposing societal views.*

sort of.   See *kind of.*

state.   Used frequently when *say* is more precise. *State* is appropriate when you mean an official declaration.

strata.   See *data.*

such.   As an intensive, it is used like *awful* or *so*. Also see *real*. *Such* introducing a clause of result is followed by *that*. EXAMPLE: *There was such an explosion that it could be felt for miles.* When introducing a relative clause, *such* is followed by *as*. EXAMPLE: *Such improvements as are necessary will be made immediately.*

sure.   Colloquial for *certainly, surely, indeed.*

tactics, strategy.   *Tactics* means specific actions, while *strategy* means an overall plan. EXAMPLES: *Her tactics included holding long meetings and evading questions. Her strategy was to avoid confrontation.*

temerity, timorousness.   *Temerity* means rashness; *timorousness* means fearfulness. Be sure not to confuse these two words.

that there, this here.   Unsuitable forms.

their, they're.   *Their* is a possessive pronoun. *They're* means ''they are.'' EXAMPLE: *They're happy because their team won.*

theirself, theirselves.   Nonstandard for *themselves.*

thorough, through.   An elementary spelling problem.

to, too, two.   Another elementary spelling problem. EXAMPLE: *He too should make two trips to the dictionary to learn how to spell. It's not too hard.* Do not use *too* as a substitute for *very.*

try and. The writer means *try to.*

type of. The phrase is excess baggage and should be avoided. EXAMPLES: *He is a moody type of person (a moody person). It is a racing-type bicycle (a racing bicycle).*

use, utilize. In most cases *utilize* is officialese for *use. Utilize* means specifically to put to use. Note the awkwardness in the following sentence: "To these people the *utilization* of knives and forks is foreign."

verbal. See *oral.*

very, very much. Many educated people object to *very* instead of *very much* or *very greatly* as a modifier of a verb or a participle in a verb phrase. Others point out examples of its use in the works of reputable writers. See the note under *very* in *Webster's Third New International.* EXAMPLES: *They were very pleased. They were very much pleased. They seemed very disturbed. They seemed very greatly disturbed.*

viable. Now overworked in officialese: "a *viable* alternative." Use *workable* or *practicable* in its place.

vocation. See *avocation.*

wait on. Sometimes used to mean "wait for," "stay for." Standard in the sense of attend, perform services for, as: "It was the other girl who waited on me."

want in, want out, want off, etc. Dialectal forms of *want to come in, want to go out, want to get off,* and so forth.

way, ways. *Way* is colloquial for *condition. Ways* is dialectal for *distance, way.* FORMAL: *When we saw him, he was in bad health* (not *in a bad way*). *We walked a long distance* (not *ways*) *before we rested.*

where at. The *at* is unnecessary. EXAMPLE: *Where is he now?* (not *Where is he at now?*) A sentence such as "I don't know *where* you're *at* intellectually" is both colloquial and redundant. You may get away with it in speaking but not in writing.

which and that, who and that. *Which* refers to things; *who* refers to people. *That* can refer to either things or people, usually in restrictive clauses. EXAMPLES: *The pictures, which were gaudy and overdecorated, made me wince. The pictures that I bought yesterday were genuine; the others were fake. Who* can also be used in a restrictive clause, as: "I want to see all the people *who* care to see me." With *that,* the same clause is still restrictive: "I want to see all the people *that* care to see me."

37

while. This word is frequently overused as a conjunction. Usually *but*, *and*, or *whereas* would be more precise. It is standard in the sense of *at the same time as* or *although*. It is colloquial in the sense of *whereas*.

who, whom. *Who* should be used for subjects, *whom* for objects of prepositions, direct or indirect objects, subjects and objects of infinitives.

-wise. This suffix has been so absurdly overused that it has become largely a joke. "He is a competent administrator *economy-wise*, but *politics-wise* he is a failure." Avoid.

THE LETTER

The Formal Letter and its Parts

Every letter is a composition. Each is in some degree governed by the considerations that govern other kinds of writing. But when you dash off a note to a close friend you need not worry very much about your grammar and punctuation. Your first draft is probably adequate. On the other hand, a letter to a prospective employer may be the most important document you ever write, one in which every detail may count. The variety of letters is enormous. In every letter you write, however, even the one to your friend, you are expressing yourself to one other individual. *A letter is not an essay intended for general interest; it is, usually, a private communication between you and another person.* In no other writing, therefore, is the emphasis so heavily on the character of your reader, and what you know and expect of that person.

Your letter to your friend probably needs no improvement. Furthermore no one, not even an English teacher, should presume to tell you how to write your most personal correspondence. You know best what ought to go into it. (The history of literature, however, provides many a love letter composed with grace and style, even if true love never did run smoothly.)

What a teacher *can* help you to write, and what this chapter is concerned with, are all those relatively formal letters, letters addressed to individuals you don't know intimately, or composed under circumstances inappropriate to a casual style. These include not only letters of application and business letters, but all those letters you have to write to people with whom you are not on familiar terms.

Formal letters, then, are governed by considerations similar to those you must have in mind for all compositions. They should be clear, well organized, coherent. You should be careful about spelling, grammar, and punctuation. But in addition to these familiar injunctions, there are certain other conventions of usage that the letter writer cannot ignore.

These are the parts of a letter:

1. The heading
2. The inside address.
3. The salutation or greeting.
4. The body of the letter.
5. The complimentary close.
6. The signature.

For each of these parts usage has prescribed certain set forms. These forms should not be ignored or altered, especially in business letters. Conformity, not originality, is a virtue here.

THE HEADING

The parts of a heading, written in the following order, are *the street address, the name of city or town, the name of the province, the postal code, the date.* A printed letterhead takes the place of a typed address. On paper with letterheads, the writer types the date either directly under the letterhead or flush with the left-hand margin of the letter.

[Letterhead]

September 23, 1984 [or] September 23, 1984

A growing number of letter writers, possibly influenced by European practice or by the military services, are writing dates with the number of the day first, the month next, then the year

– all without punctuation; for example, 23 September 1984. There is a logic and simplicity to this form that may in time win universal acceptance.

On paper that does not have a letterhead, the writer types the heading at the right according to one of the following forms:

Block form with open punctuation – that is, end punctuation is omitted. This form is rapidly becoming almost universal.

> 327 Walnut Street
> Estevan, Saskatchewan
> S4A 1W4
> November 14, 1985

Indented form, with closed punctuation. Final punctuation is usually omitted.

> 76 Belmont Street,
> Flin Flon, Manitoba,
> R8A 1J6,
> Aug. 11, 1984

Whichever form is used, the writer should be consistent throughout the letter – in the heading, in the inside address, and in the address on the envelope.

THE INSIDE ADDRESS

In a business letter *the inside address is the address of the person written to.* The envelope of a business letter is often discarded before the letter reaches the intended recipient. Repeating the address inside ensures that the addressee's identity is not accidentally lost and that it remains on any copy of the letter kept in the sender's files.

In a personal letter the inside address is usually omitted, though it may be added at the bottom of a fairly formal personal letter, in the lower left-hand corner. The first line of the inside address should be flush with the left-hand margin of the letter.

Either the block form or the indented form may be used.

> Mr. C.P. Bell
> Bell & Stacey, Builders
> 132 First Avenue
> Vancouver, B.C. V5M 2A9
>
> Dear Mr. Bell:

or

> Parr Oil Company,
>   20 Main Street,
>   Petawawa, Ontario
>   K8H 3A7
>
> Dear Sir or Madam:

The block form, illustrated first, is preferred by a majority of business letter writers.

Use a title, such as *Miss*, *Mr.*, or *Ms.*, only when you are sure it is accurate. If you are not sure, use the person's first name or initials: Pat Green, L.P. Rao. A business title designating the office or function of an individual should not precede the person's name but should either follow the name immediately if the title is short or, if it is long, appear on the line below.

> Mr. T.C. Howard
> Secretary
> Pueblo Rose Society
>
> Dr. James L. Pendleton
> Director of Admissions

> Mr. William R. Jones
> Personnel Manager
>
> Ms. Laura Jackson
> Treasurer
> City Action Club

The inclusion of a business title usually implies that the writer is addressing the reader in his or her capacity as holder of a particular office or authority. In such cases, answers may properly be made by an assistant who speaks for his or her superior, or by a successor, should the original addressee have left office for some reason.

THE SALUTATION OR GREETING

The following forms are correct for business and professional letters:

Dear Sir or Madam:	Dear Sirs:
Dear Sir:	Dear Madam:
Dear Mr. Jackson:	Dear Miss (or Ms.) White:

In personal letters the range of greetings is unlimited, but choose something somewhere between the inappropriately formal *Sir* or *Madam* at one extreme, and the inappropriately affable *Hi Swinger* at the other. The following are usually appropriate:

Dear Jack,
Dear Mr. Howard,
Dear Miss (or Ms.) Brown,

You also ought to be aware that a great deal of modern business is transacted on a first-name basis, even when the relations between the parties are entirely professional.

Correct usage in addressing government officials and other dignitaries will be found in a good desk dictionary or books like the *Canadian Secretary's Handbook* (Collier Macmillan 1983). Local newspapers will also provide titles and addresses of government officials.

A colon is used after the salutation in a business letter; either a colon or a comma may be used in a personal letter. A comma is considered less formal. A dash – appropriate enough for a letter to an intimate friend – should be avoided in formal letters.

THE BODY OF THE LETTER

The composition of business letters is a subject much too complex to be discussed here except in a very introductory way. A good letter, again, obeys the principles of any good writing. It should be clear, direct, coherent, and courteous. A student who can write a good class paper ought to be able to write a good business letter. But there are whole college courses devoted to the subject, and the interested student should either enroll in such a course or consult one of the numerous special guidebooks available.

At its best, the efficient and graceful composition of a business letter is a genuine art. Much more flexibility is required than is generally understood. There are times when a letter must speak very formally, as if in the abstract voice of its letterhead, a large and impersonal corporation. There are other times when warmth and genial good fellowship are appropriate. The executive who can say no without hurting a reader's feelings is a valuable person to the company. But these skills, however interesting and important, are beyond the range of this handbook.

THE COMPLIMENTARY CLOSE

Correct forms for the complimentary close of business letters are as follows:

Yours truly,	Sincerely,
Yours very truly,	Yours sincerely,
Respectfully yours,	Cordially,

It is now considered bad taste to use a participial phrase in closing a letter, such as *Hoping you are well.* A comma is the usual punctuation after the complimentary close; only the first letter is capitalized. In ordinary formal business letters, *Yours truly* or *Yours very truly* is the accepted form. In business letters between persons who know each other well, *Yours sincerely* and *Cordially*, are used, or even, more informally, *Sincerely* and simply *Yours*.

THE SIGNATURE

For the ordinary person it is correct to sign a business letter as he or she would sign a cheque. If possible, you should write your name legibly. But just to make sure, it is desirable to type the name under the signature.

Some of the conventions that govern the form of a signature are the following:

1. Neither professional titles, such as *Professor*, *Dr.*, *Rev.*, nor academic degrees, such as *Ph.D.*, *LL.D.*, *M.A.*, should be used with a signature.

2. Titles such as *Miss*, *Mrs.*, or *Ms.* may be written in parentheses before the signature or the typewritten name.
3. A married woman or a widow who elects to adopt her husband's last name signs her own name, not her married name. For example, *Diana Holoday Brown* is her own name; *Mrs. George Brown* is her married name. She may place *Mrs.* in parentheses before her signature, or her married name in parentheses under it.
4. Secretaries who sign their employer's name to a letter should add their own initials below the signature.

The following is an example of a business letter that might be written to a business organization from a private individual:

37 Oka Av.
Lachine, P.Q. H8R 3M6
June 22, 1984

Acme Camera Shop
4699 Joly Av.
Montreal, P.Q. H2J 1S6

Dear Sir or Madam:

I am returning to you a lens that you sent me, on my order, on June 16. The lens is a 35-mm F 2.5 (wide angle) P. Angenieux Retrofocus, with a bayonet mount to fit the Exacta camera. The number of the lens is 463513.

You will notice by holding the lens against a bright light that there is a distinct scratch on the front element. As the lens is guaranteed to be free from imperfections, I am returning it to you for a replacement.

Will you kindly send me a new lens as soon as you can? I must have it by June 30, as I am leaving then on a camera trip to B.C.

You have my cheque for $120, dated June 12, in payment.

Yours very truly,

Martin H. Hanson

Martin H. Hanson

Letters of Application

One of the most difficult and probably most important letters that you will have to write is the letter of application for a job. Of course it is impossible to say what will appeal to every employer, but there are certain general guides. In applying for work you usually have to fill out a printed application form. So will five hundred others applying for the same job. The letter you write will help you stand apart from that crowd.

A letter of application should be direct, sincere, and informative. It must not be vague; it must not grovel with undue modesty or boastfully promise what cannot be delivered. It should not include irrelevant personal information. Something is to be gained, as it often is in other types of writing, by putting yourself in the place of the person you are addressing. Suppose *you* were a busy personnel manager, shuffling through dozens of letters of application. What would attract you favourably?

An effective letter of application contains the following components:

1. An introductory statement in which the writer indicates that he or she has heard of a possible vacancy.

2. Personal data.

3. Record of education.

4. Personal experience in the job area.

5. References.

6. Request for an interview.

Probably the most important section is the one in which you outline how your experience or education has a vital bearing on the job for which you are applying. This is difficult to write, but it can also be decisive.

2727 Aberdeen St.
Yarmouth, N.S., B5A 1L7
April 10, 1985

Mr. F.C. McVey
Personnel Officer
Department of Parks and Recreation
1 Queen St.
Halifax, N.S. B3P 2C6

Dear Mr. McVey:

Ms. Jane Ryan, one of the counsellors on your staff, has informed me that you will need several guides for your residence camps this summer. I wish to apply for a job as a camp guide.

I am twenty years old and in excellent health.

Two years ago, when I was eighteen, I graduated from Central High School, where I took the college preparatory course with emphasis on botany and geology. With this background, I am trained to point out many interesting natural phenomena to the children.

When I was in high school, I spent my weekends and vacations working for Bert's Camping Equipment, where I learned a great deal about the operation and maintenance of various types of outdoor equipment. Mr. Bert Jenkins will write you about my work there.

Since then I have worked at various jobs to earn money for my college education. I am now finishing my first year in the division of arts and sciences at St Francis Xavier University. After graduation from high school I spent a year working for the Ochoco Ranch, near Hairy Hill, Alberta, where I taught hiking and horseback riding to beginners. Then last summer I entered the Banff Mountainclimbing Club, an experience that taught me a good deal about organizing outings of various kinds. Here I also learned to conduct nature trips. I believe that my experience should qualify me for this job.

The following employers have given me permission to use their names as references:

Mr. H.D. Winslow
Ochoco Ranch
Hairy Hill, TOB 1SO
Alberta

Mr. Karl Swensen
Banff Mountainclimbing Club
Banff National Park, Alberta TOL OCO

I would appreciate the opportunity to come to your office for an interview at any time that you designate. My telephone number is 749/753-5948.

Yours very truly,

Jane Williamson

Jane Williamson

Sometimes a shorter letter of application, though for a more permanent position, may be used as a supplement to other records – college grades, statements of recommendation – that are forwarded to an employer by a placement service. Here is an example of such a letter, in which it is wise not to repeat much of the information that the employer already possesses in the official dossier.

1401 Ridge Avenue
Kakabeka Falls
Ontario POT 1WO
May 10, 1986

Dr. Leroy Faust
Superintendent of Schools
Toronto, Ont. M9J 3K3

I understand from our local placement office that a position as third grade teacher is open for next fall in your school system. I believe I am qualified for that position. My record of training at the University of Toronto is being forwarded to you, and as you will see, I maintained a "B" average and completed all necessary requirements in teacher training. I hold a temporary teacher's certificate for the province of Ontario. This letter is meant to convey, in addition, my great enthusiasm for teaching and my personal interest in becoming a part of your system.

Though I have done no classroom teaching beyond that provided by my university courses, I believe my devotion to young people may in part compensate for inexperience. My enthusiasm for teaching those younger than I began early in my life, and was increased by my years as a leader in Boy Scout work. Summer jobs as a camp counsellor, involving instruction in outdoor activities for young children, improved my confidence in handling the eight-to-ten age group. Considerable testimony from parents and from the children themselves convinced me that I have been successful in reaching these young people.

Naturally I am eager to become a part of a school system so well thought of as yours. I am available on short notice for interview, at your convenience.

Sincerely yours,

James A. Clark

James A. Clark

Some Familiar Faults to Avoid

Do not omit pronouns, prepositions, and articles where they are grammatically necessary. If your letter should begin with *I* or *we*, begin with *I* or *we*.

Old Fashioned

Received your letter yesterday.

Am writing to you in reply. . . .

Have not heard from you. . . .

Better

I received your letter yesterday.

I am writing to you. . . .

I have not heard from you. . . .

Do not close a letter with a sentence or a phrase introduced by a participle.

Indirect

Hoping to hear from you soon. . . .

Hoping for an early answer. . . .

Thanking you again for your past favours. . . .

Trusting to hear from you by return mail. . . .

Do not write *yours, your, your favour*, or *your esteemed favour* for *letter*.

Affected

In reply to yours of the 20th. . . .

Your esteemed favour at hand, and in reply. . . .

And avoid certain other trite and stilted expressions frequently used in business letters.

In reply would say. . . .

And contents thereof noted. . . .

Your valued favour. . . .

And oblige, Yours truly. . . .

Enclosed please find. . . .

Public Letters

Letters are usually private communications from one individual to another. The exception is the public letter in which the writer, while ostensibly addressing a single person, is in fact addressing a larger audience. An obvious example is the letter to the editor, in which the greeting might more accurately read *Dear Everybody* or *Dear World.* Many business letters, without being directed to the world, are intended for more than one reader – a committee, a sales force, a staff of officers. Modern duplicating methods are so cheap and efficient that any member of an organization may expect to find a semipublic report to a superior photocopied and spread all over the office. When this happens, of course, errors of expression, misspellings, and vague logic are photocopied too.

The composition of a public, or semipublic, letter requires a special kind of skill. When addressing a group of individuals – a committee, for example – one must often be aware of the likes and dislikes of particular individuals among one's readers. Sometimes these likes and dislikes conflict. How can one persuade some of one's readers without offending others? What modified expression of one's own view might win a majority approval, or at least acquiescence? Astute corporate and bureaucratic officials often report that every word they write is chosen for its suitability to a variety of possible responses from readers whose prejudices may be, or are known to be, in conflict. If there is any excuse for the astounding circumlocutions of *officialese* (see § 24g.), it is the need to perform verbal high-wire acts to the detriment of precise, vigorous prose.

EXERCISES

EXERCISE 1, A LETTER OFFERING SUGGESTIONS. *Write a letter to the principal of your high school in which you suggest two or three specific ways students might be better prepared for college.*

EXERCISE 2, A LETTER OF CORRECTION. *Write a letter to your college newspaper in which you correct a wrong impression produced by a news story that has just appeared in the paper. Make your letter courteous, dignified, and logical.*

EXERCISE 3, A LETTER REQUESTING A SPECIAL PRIVILEGE. *Write a letter to your instructor in which you request permission to take your final examinations several days before the scheduled period. Give your reason clearly and convincingly.*

EXERCISE 4, A LETTER URGING ACTION. *As secretary of a student organization, write a letter to the members urging them to pay their dues.*

EXERCISE 5, A LETTER OF PROTEST. *As a member of the same organization, write a letter to its secretary protesting the undue anxiety about the members' dues.*

EXERCISE 6, A LETTER OF APPLICATION. *You plan to work at one of the provincial parks during the summer. Write a letter of application. Apply for some position that you could fill. Give adequate information about yourself and your qualifications.*

EXERCISE 7, A LETTER TO YOUR M.P. *Write to your member of parliament requesting an interview when you visit Ottawa in a month's time.*

EXERCISE 8, A LETTER REQUESTING PAYMENT. *A man for whom you worked last summer owes you ninety dollars. Write him a letter that will induce him to pay you what he owes you.*

EXERCISE 9, A LETTER TO THE EDITOR. *Write to your local newspaper complaining about the ear-splitting noise made by motorcycles zooming past your house late at night. Use humour to address the problem and in such a way as to make even motorcyclists want to support you.*

The Résumé

Anyone applying for a job should know how to compose an effective résumé or detailing of information sought by an employer. Although the format for such listings may vary, most résumés contain personal data, education and work experience, and names and addresses of references. This formal introduction to a prospective employer works best if it is short and readable. It is probably wise therefore to boil down your experience to essentials that can be listed on a single typed page.

FORM

The following order is suggested for listing information on the résumé.

1. *Personal data.* Name, address, and telephone number. Details about age, health, and marital status may also be added here.

2. *Education.* Use a separate heading as shown in the sample below. Starting with the most recent degree, list your educational experience back through high school. Information about scholastic honours should be included here.

3. *Experience.* Begin with the most recent jobs and work backward. Try to include details about the nature of your work, in addition to any title given the job. Even if you were unemployed for a period of time, be sure to cite that interlude.

4. *References.* Give the names, addresses, and telephone numbers of at least three people who have agreed to write strong supporting letters. College instructors and professors are usually willing to write such letters, but do not forget the names of people who have supervised you in job situations. Whenever possible, let these references know the kind of position for which you are applying.

The following is a sample résumé that might be used as a model.

Paul E. Green, Jr.
730 West Garden Street
Toronto
Ontario M4C 3K1
Telephone: 416/555-8766

Age: 22
Marital Status: Married, no children
Health: Excellent

Education

Sept. 1981 – May 1985	University of Toronto Toronto Will receive B.A. in English, May 1985
Sept. 1975 – June 1980	Centre High School, Cochrane Graduated with distinction
Honours	Francis P. Frachon Prize for Religious Studies University of Toronto May 1982 Ontario Scholarship June 1980

Experience

Sept. 1981 – present	The Varsity, University of Toronto Write sports and movie reviews
May – Sept. 1981	Pizza O Restaurant, Toronto Full-time waiter and cashier
May – Sept. 1980/ May – Sept. 1979	Radio Station WDAF, St. Catharines Full-time mail clerk; some work in radio sales

References

Mr. Paul Taylor, Manager
Pizza O Restaurant
5422 Small Ave.
Toronto M4A 2K2
Telephone: 416/555-2092

Dr. Charles Ruggles
Professor of English
University of Toronto
Toronto M4B 1X2
Telephone: 416/555-4000

Ms. Toni Smith
Business Manager
WDAF Radio
1800 Signal Hill St.
St Catharines L2N 1G4
Telephone: 416/555-8800

ACKNOWLEDGEMENTS

Page 18, copyright © by Earle Birney 1966, from *The Creative Writer* published by CBC Enterprises.

p. 22, excerpt from "The New Barbarians" by Geoffrey Durrant, from *In the Name of Language!* edited by Joseph Gold. Reprinted by permission of Macmillan of Canada, a Division of Gage Publishing Limited.

p. 23, from *Two Solitudes* by Hugh MacLennan.

p.25, copyright © by C.B. Macpherson 1965, from *The Real World of Democracy* published by CBC Enterprises.

p. 26, from *Looking for Philosophy*, F.E. Sparshott (Montreal: McGill-Queen's University Press, 1972), p. 87.

p. 29, © Michael Gregory and Susanne Carroll 1978. Used by permission of the publishers, Routledge and Kegan Paul Plc.

p. 30, from *The Tuning of the World* by R. Murray Schafer. Used by permission of The Canadian Publishers, McClelland and Stewart Limited, Toronto.

p. 31, from *The Foundations of Belief* by Leslie Dewart, published by Herder and Herder, 1969.

p. 32, from *A Painter's Country* by A.Y. Jackson. © 1958 by Clarke Irwin (1983) Inc. Used by permission.

p. 33, from *The Prophet's Camel Bell* by Margaret Laurence. Used by permission of The Canadian Publishers, McClelland and Stewart Limited, Toronto.

p. 34, reprinted with permission from *Photography for the Joy of It* by Freeman Patterson, published by Key Porter Books, Toronto.

p. 37, "The Writer and the University," by Northrop Frye.

p. 48, from *Wolf Willow* by Wallace Stegner, copyright © 1955, 1957, 1958, 1959, 1962, by Wallace Stegner. Reprinted by permission of Brandt and Brandt Literary Agents, Inc.

p. 49, from *Progress and Perspectives* by Gregory Baum, published by Sheed and Ward, 1962.

p. 49, from *And Now . . . Here's Max* by Max Ferguson. Reprinted by permission from McGraw-Hill Ryerson Limited, Toronto.

p. 50, reprinted from *The Canadian Worker in the Twentieth Century* edited by Irving Abella and David Millar. © Oxford University Press Canada.

p. 51, from "The Lamp at Noon" in *The Lamp at Noon and Other Stories* by Sinclair Ross. Used by permission of The Canadian Publishers, McClelland and Stewart Limited, Toronto.

p. 70, from *The Honeyman Festival* by Marian Engel (Toronto: House of Anansi Press, 1970).

p. 70, from *John A. Macdonald* by Donald Creighton, reprinted by permission of Macmillan of Canada, a division of Gage Publishing Limited.

p. 71, from *Immigrants: A Portrait of the Urban Experience, 1890–1930* by Robert F. Harney and Harold Troper. (Toronto, 1975).

p. 76, letter reprinted by permission of *Now* magazine.

p. 77, letter reprinted courtesy of Dr. A.J. Abraham.

p. 83, from *The Suicide Murders*, by Howard Engel.

p. 83, from "You Better Not Pout" in *Everybody Gets Something Here* by Ken Mitchell. Reprinted by permission of Macmillan of Canada, a Division of Gage Publishing Limited.

p. 85, this selection from *The New Ancestors* by Dave Godfrey, published by McClelland and Stewart Limited in the New Canadian Library edition.

p. 89, from *None is Too Many: Canada and the Jews of Europe 1933–1948* © 1982, 1983 by Irving Abella and Harold Troper. Published in Canada by Lester and Orpen Dennys Limited.

p. 90, from *My Grandfather's Cape Breton* by Clive Doucet. Reprinted by permission of McGraw-Hill Ryerson Limited.

p. 125, from "Need for Laughter" by Warren Tallman, printed in *Canadian Literature*, number 56, spring 1973.

p. 126, from "The Drummer of All the World" in *The Tomorrow Tamer* by Margaret Laurence. Used by permission of The Canadian Publishers, McClelland and Stewart Limited, Toronto.

p. 127, © 1982 Miriam Waddington. *Summer at Lonely Beach and other stories*. Mosaic Valley editions, 1982.

p. 128, from "Danger in the Chains of Freedom" by Barbara Amiel, *Maclean's*, April 26, 1982.

p. 129, from *Understanding Media: The Extensions of Man* by Marshall McLuhan, 1964, published by the McGraw-Hill Book Company.

p. 132, from *Dance of the Dialectic* by Larry Zolf, published by James Lorimer and Company, 1973.

p. 133, Northrop Frye, "Conclusion" to a *Literary History of Canada*, edited by Carl F. Klinck (Toronto: University of Toronto Press, 1976). Reprinted by permission of the author.

p. 135, from *At the Mermaid Inn*, published by the University of Toronto Press.

p. 136, from *One Half of Robertson Davies* by Robertson Davies, reprinted by permission of Macmillan of Canada, a division of Gage Publishing Limited.

p. 146, "Taste," from *Good Neighbourhood and Other Addresses in the United States* by Vincent Massey.

p. 147, from "Three Score and Ten" by Stephen Leacock. Used by permission of The Canadian Publishers, McClelland and Stewart Limited, Toronto.

p. 149, from *If You Can't Beat 'Em in the Alley* by Conn Smythe and Scott Young. Used by permission of The Canadian Publishers, McClelland and Stewart Limited, Toronto.

p. 151, from Margaret Laurence, "Ivory Tower or Grassroots: The Novelist as Socio-Political Being" in *A Political Art: Essays and Images in Honour of George Woodcock*, William H. New (ed.). Copyright © 1978 by the University of British Columbia Press.

p. 152, reprinted by permission of New York University Press from *Canadian Cultural Nationalism: The Fourth Lester B. Pearson Conference on the Canada–U.S. Relationship*, edited by Janice L. Murray. Copyright © 1977 by New York University.

p. 153, reprinted from *The Modern Century* by Northrop Frye. © Oxford University Press Canada.

p. 155, excerpt from "Is Your English Destroying Your Image?" by Michael Hornyansky from *In the Name of Language!* edited by Joseph Gold. Reprinted by permission of Macmillan of Canada, a Division of Gage Publishing Limited.

p. 161, from "The Tyranny of the Clock" in *The Rejection of Politics* by George Woodcock, published by New Press, 1972. Reprinted by permission of the author.

p. 162, from *The Trail of '98: A Northland Romance* by Robert Service. Used by permission of the estate of Robert Service.

p. 163, from "Writing for the Movies" in *Hunting Tigers Under Glass* by Mordecai Richler. Used by permission of The Canadian Publishers, McClelland and Stewart Limited, Toronto.

p. 164, from "Where Will You Go Sam Lee Wong" in *Garden in the Wind* by Gabrielle Roy, translated by Alan Brown. Used by permission of The Canadian Publishers, McClelland and Stewart Limited, Toronto.

p. 166, Claude Ryan, *Le Devoir*, September 18, 1964.

p. 168, René Levésque, Toronto *Star*, January 20, 1968.

p. 181, from *Klee Wyck* by Emily Carr. © 1941 by Clarke Irwin (1983) Inc. Used by permission.

p. 182, from *Ox Bells and Fireflies* by Ernest Buckler. Used by permission of The Canadian Publishers, McClelland and Stewart Limited, Toronto.

p. 183, reprinted by permission of Joy Kogawa and Lester and Orpen Dennys Publishers, from *Obasan* by Joy Kogawa, copyright © 1981 Joy Kogawa.

p. 186, the excerpt from *The Governor's Bridge is Closed* by Hugh Hood is reprinted by permission of Oberon Press.

p. 187, from *The Backwoods of Canada* by Catharine Parr Traill.

p. 188, from *Over Prairie Trails* by Frederick Philip Grove. Used by permission of The Canadian Publishers, McClelland and Stewart Limited, Toronto.

p.189, from *The Northern Magus* by Richard Gwyn. Used by permission of The Canadian Publishers, McClelland and Stewart Limited, Toronto.

p. 190, from *Stephen Leacock* by Robertson Davies. Used by permission of The Canadian Publishers, McClelland and Stewart Limited, Toronto.

p. 192, from *International Film Guide*, published by A.S. Barnes and Co.

p. 192, book review by Jan Marriott, from *Quill & Quire*, May 1983.

p. 195, from *Goaltending* by Jacques Plante, published by Collier Macmillan Canada, Inc.

p. 197, from *Roughing It in the Bush* by Susanna Moodie.

p. 199, from *Why We Act Like Canadians* by Pierre Berton. Used by permission of The Canadian Publishers, McClelland and Stewart Limited, Toronto.

p. 200, from *Short Circuits* by Stephen Leacock. Used by permission of The Canadian Publishers, McClelland and Stewart Limited, Toronto.

p. 200, from *Literary Lapses* by Stephen Leacock. Used by permission of The Canadian Publishers, McClelland and Stewart Limited, Toronto.

p. 204, from "The Religion of Work and the Dirtiest Job in the World" in *The Smug Minority* by Pierre Berton. Used by permission of The Canadian Publishers, McClelland and Stewart Limited, Toronto.

p. 205, from "Prize and Prejudice" by Eleanor Wachtel, from *Books in Canada*, March 1982.

p. 206, from *Fisherman's Fall* by Roderick Haig-Brown by permission of Collins Publishers, Toronto.

p. 207, from *Federalism and the French Canadians* by Pierre Elliott Trudeau. Reprinted by permission of Macmillan of Canada, a Division of Gage Publishing Limited.

p. 208, from *Lament for a Nation* by George Grant. Reprinted by permission of Carleton University Press.

p. 209, from Allan Fotheringham "Second Digression: The Bachelor Party" from *Malice in Blunderland* © 1982 by Key Porter Books, Toronto.

p. 210, from "Canadian Heroes" by Kildare Dobbs, in *Saturday Night*, February 1968.

p. 211, from *Fragile Freedoms* by Thomas R. Berger. © 1981 by Clarke Irwin (1983) Inc. Used by permission.

p. 221, "Choice for Canadians: Security or Freedom" in *Writings and Reflections* by Roderick Haig-Brown. Used by permission of The Canadian Publishers, McClelland and Stewart Limited, Toronto.

p. 237, from "The Androgynous Classroom: Liberation or Tyranny?" by Kathryn Morgan, in *Philosophy of Education: Canadian Perspectives*, edited by Donald Cochrane and Martin Schiralli. © 1982, Collier Macmillan Canada, Inc.

p. 237, from *Eruption to Hope* by Jean Vanier, Griffin House, Toronto, 1971.

p. 243, from *Power Politics* by Margaret Atwood.

p. 249, from *The Imperialist* by Sara Jeannette Duncan.

p. 251, from "The Blue Kimono" by Morley Callaghan, reprinted by permission of Macmillan of Canada, a Division of Gage Publishing Limited.

p. 252, copyright © 1974 by Alice Munro. All rights reserved. From the book *Something I've Been Meaning to Tell You* by Alice Munro. Reprinted by permission.

p. 254, from "City at the End of Things" by Archibald Lampman.

p. 254, from "The Bear on the Delhi Road" by Earle Birney. Used by permission of The Canadian Publishers, McClelland and Stewart Limited, Toronto.

p. 254, from the *Collected Poems of A.M. Klein*. Reprinted by permission of McGraw-Hill Ryerson Limited.

p. 254, from "Adolescence" by P.K. Page. Used by permission of the author.

p. 258, from "Saturday Sundae" and "Poetry" in *The Collected Poems of F.R. Scott* by F.R. Scott. Used by permission of The Canadian Publishers, McClelland and Stewart Limited, Toronto.

p. 262, from *The Classic Shade* by A.J.M. Smith. Used by permission of The Canadian Publishers, McClelland and Stewart Limited, Toronto.

p. 263, reprinted from *Memoirs of Montparnasse* by John Glassco, © Oxford University Press Canada (1970).

p. 279, from *Reader's Guide to Periodical Literature* copyright © 1983 by the H.W. Wilson Company. Material reproduced by permission of the publisher.

p. 396, from *The Mountain and the Valley* by Ernest Buckler. Used by permission of The Canadian Publishers, McClelland and Stewart Limited, Toronto.

p. 440, from "My Re-creation of the World" in *Lightning Struck My Dick* by Crad Kilodney, published by Virgo Press. Used by permission of the author.

p. 475, from "The Rejection of Politics" in *The Rejection of Politics* by George Woodcock. Used by permission of George Woodcock.

p. 483, the excerpt from *Shoeless Joe Jackson Comes to Iowa* by W.P. Kinsella is reprinted by permission of Oberon Press.

p. 483, from "A Deal's a Deal" by W.O. Mitchell. Used by permission of the author.

p. 483, from *I Once Knew an Indian Woman* © 1967, M. Ebbitt Cutler, published by Tundra Books Inc.

p. 524, from "Fog" by Ethel Wilson, reprinted by permission of Macmillan of Canada, a Division of Gage Publishing Limited.

INDEX

D

G

H

M

XYZ

Essay Correction Marks

Ab	Abbreviations, § 9
Adj	Adjectives, § 5
Adv	Adverbs, § 5
Agr	Agreement, §§ 3, 4, 26
Amb	Ambiguity, §§ 21, 35
Appr	Appropriateness, § 22
Arr	Arrangement, § 27
Awk	Awkward, § 35
C	Commas, § 13
Cap	Capitals, § 8
Case	Case Forms, § 4
Cl	Clearness, § 35
Coll	Colloquial, § 22
Cnst	Construction, §§ 30, 35
Coh	Coherence, §§ 27, 36
CF, CS	Comma Fault, § 2
Cmp	Comparisons, § 32
Dng	Danglers, § 28
D	Choice of Diction, §§ 21, 25
Dict	Consult Dictionary, § 21
Div	Division of Word, § 11
Emp	Emphasis, § 29
Ex	Exact Word, § 21
Fig	Figure of Speech, § 25
Frag	Sentence Fragment, § 1
GL	Glossary, § 37
Id	Idioms, § 23
Ital	Italics, § 10
lc	Lower Case (No Caps), § 8
Log	Logic
MS	Manuscript Form, § 7

Mix	Mixed Construction, § 30
Mean	Meaning Obscure, § 35
No ¶	No Paragraph, § 36
No pn	No Punctuation, §§ 12–18
Obs	Obscure, § 35
Om	Omission of Words, § 33
Org	Paragraph Organized Poorly
P	Period, § 12
¶	Paragraph, § 36
Pl	Plural Form, § 19
Pn	Punctuation, §§ 12–18
Par ‖	Parallel Structure, § 31
PF	Period Fault, § 1
Prep	Prepositions, § 23
Pron	Pronouns, §§ 4, 26
PV	Point of View, § 30
Ques	Question Mark, § 12
Quot	Quotation Marks, § 16
Ref	Reference, § 26
Rep	Repetition, § 24
RS	Run-on Sentence, § 2
Sp	Spelling, §§ 19–20
Sub	Subordination, § 27
T	Tenses, §§ 6, 30
Trans	Transitions, § 36
Tr	Transpose, § 27
Trite	Triteness, § 25
Un	Unity, §§ 24, 36
Var	Sentence Structure Lacks Variety, § 34
Vb	Verb Forms, § 6
Wdy	Wordy, § 24
WW	Wrong Word, § 21
X	Obvious Error
?	Do You Mean This?
∧	Omission